ON THE EDGE OF THE LAW

D1568274

CHAD RICHARDSON &
ROSALVA RESENDIZ

On the Edge
of the Law

CULTURE,

LABOR,

AND

DEVIANCE

ON THE

SOUTH TEXAS

BORDER

 University of Texas Press AUSTIN

Requests for permission to reproduce
material from this work should be sent to:
  Permissions
  University of Texas Press
  P.O. Box 7819
  Austin, TX 78713-7819
  www.utexas.edu/utpress/about/bpermission.html

⊗ The paper used in this book meets the minimum
requirements of ANSI/NISO z39.48-1992 (R1997)
(Permanence of Paper).

LIBRARY OF CONGRESS CATALOGING-IN-PUBLICATION DATA

Richardson, Chad, 1943–
  On the edge of the law : culture, labor, and deviance on the
south Texas border / Chad Richardson and Rosalva Resendiz. — 1st ed.
      p.   cm.
  Includes bibliographical references and index.
  ISBN-13: 978-0-292-71333-8 (cloth : alk. paper)
  ISBN-10: 0-292-71333-9 (cloth : alk. paper)
  ISBN-13: 978-0-292-71475-5 (pbk. : alk. paper)
  ISBN-10: 0-292-71475-0 (pbk. : alk. paper)
    1. Subculture—Texas.   2. Subculture—Mexican-American Border Region.
3. Mexicans—Texas—Social conditions.   4. Mexicans—Mexican-American
Border Region—Social conditions.   5. Labor—Texas.   6. Labor—Mexican-
American Border Region.   7. Crime—Texas.   8. Crime—Mexican-American
Border Region.   I. Resendiz, Rosalva.   II. Title.

HN79.T4R53   2006
306'.109721—dc22

2005037095

To the individuals along this great fault line of the South Texas/ Northern Mexico border who shared their lives with our student interviewers. They illuminated our lives and our understanding in the process.

Contents

Preface

In 1999 the University of Texas Press published our first book, *Batos, Bo-lillos, Pochos, and Pelados: Class and Culture on the South Texas Border.* That book was the culmination of eleven ethnographic research projects and ten surveys conducted almost entirely by students at the University of Texas–Pan American (UT-PA). It dealt with life on the South Texas border, particularly in relation to the impact of social class and race or ethnicity in this region. In it, we mentioned an intended follow-up book about deviance and other social issues on the border. The current volume is the result of that effort.

Both volumes have grown out of the Borderlife Research Project at the University of Texas–Pan American. The Borderlife Project, which was initiated in 1982, uses student interviews to investigate and describe cultural and social life situations of those living along the Northern Mexico–South Texas border. The project has accomplished more than 6,000 in-depth (ethnographic) interviews and over 4,000 survey interviews from a variety of populations on both sides of the border. Most research topics start out as in-depth (ethnographic) descriptions, followed by a survey research project. The patterns revealed in the anecdotal accounts suggest follow-up questions for survey interviews.

The basic purpose of the Borderlife Research Project is to empower students and the local community, and to support an appreciation for their culture and place. This is accomplished primarily by involving them in quality research about the life conditions of local cultural communities.

In 2004 the work of the Borderlife Project was recognized in a book published by Harvard University Press entitled *What the Best College Teachers Do.* The author, Ken Bain, describes the students who participated in the Borderlife Project as follows:

A few came from families that had prospered in the local agricultural economy that sprang up along the river. Most students, however, lived closer to the poverty line, and many came from the ranks of the one hundred thousand migrant farmworkers in Hidalgo County, people whose labor had created the wealth of the region but who enjoyed few of its benefits. But they were pioneers, often the first in their families to take a college course, and sometimes the first to read and write. The university, with its open admissions policy, cut across a wide swath of SAT scores and high school ranks, but generally didn't attract many students in higher registers.

In this border region, located on the fringes of two national civilizations and not quite comfortable with either, Hispanics valued tradition and culture, yet often found themselves the focus of mean-spirited caricatures that belittled their habits, language, and origins. The twenty percent of the local population that didn't come from Mexican roots—what locals called "Anglos"—sometimes felt isolated and alienated from the local cultures, even though, as a group, they had dominant economic and political power.

[The students] ... did original ethnographic research, collecting stories from friends, relatives, and others on both sides of the border: employers of undocumented Mexican workers, smugglers who helped these people enter the United States, immigration officials who apprehended "illegal aliens," Anglos who found themselves in a tiny minority in a Valley high school, Mexican Americans who didn't know Spanish, and others.[1]

The Borderlife Project involves student researchers at all levels. Most of those who contributed to this and to the preceding (*Batos*) volume did so in introductory classes in sociology and other disciplines of the social sciences. Others in advanced courses in social stratification, U.S. minorities, and the sociology of education also participated. A few graduate students, including most of the chapter coauthors, made the topics of their respective chapters the focus of their master's research projects.

Methodology

The research generated through this process is more exploratory than explanatory and more hypothesis-suggesting than hypothesis-testing. There are three major reasons for this. First, the ethnographic research techniques used are much better suited to exploratory and descriptive research than to hypothesis testing or theoretical research. Second, many of the topics described in this book lack a solid descriptive research base, at least in a South Texas environment. Much needs to be observed and documented by exploratory research before it can be conceptualized in a theoretical framework. In Chapters 1 and 2, for example, many of the cultural practices we describe have not been thoroughly documented by research that identifies the nature of such practices. Before research can address *why* certain cultural practices exist (by hypothesis-testing research), for instance, we must understand *what* these practices are, *who* practices them, *when,* and *under what circumstances* (exploratory and descriptive research). Finally the use of student researchers lends itself much more to in-depth ethnographic and exploratory research. Though we do utilize survey research to propose and preliminarily test select hypotheses, the project emphasizes in-depth understanding of life in this border environment.

Our sampling procedures are also strongly affected by the exploratory nature of the research and by our use of student interviewers. Since most of the research topics discussed in this volume involved highly sensitive topics, including deviant or underground activities, random sampling was neither possible nor advisable.[2] Rather, by directing student researchers to include individuals with certain characteristics among those they approached, and then using those first contacts to help them locate and secure the participating of others, we used a combination of purposive and snowball sampling.

This methodological approach allows us to paint a broad picture of life on the South Texas border, focusing on many populations and topics, as opposed to a single issue or phenomenon. In *Batos, Bolillos, Pochos, and Pelados,* for example, we were able to describe migrant farmworkers, colonia residents, undocumented domestic servants, maquila workers in Mexico, and Mexican street children. In addition, in that volume we looked at racial and ethnic relations among such diverse South Texas groups as Hispanics, Mexican immigrants, Anglo newcomers or tourists, and African Americans. In the current volume, we continue that multidimensional approach, focusing on a set of issues related to major forces of change operating, often underground, in the Rio Grande/Rio Bravo Valley of South Texas and Northeastern Mexico.

The Rio Grande / Rio Bravo Valley

Many areas of the United States look for distinctiveness in ways that will portray them as "number one." South Texas, especially in the McAllen area (and surrounding Hidalgo County), frequently is number one in a variety of areas, but not in ways that customarily convey bragging rights. Despite a booming economy, for example, this region frequently leads the nation in unemployment. Similarly, though it has one of the three highest population growth rates in the U.S., it ranks near the bottom nationally in per capita income. This border area also has the highest rate of drug seizures in the nation. Finally, it is number one in the number of low-income housing enclaves (*colonias*), in large part because it also hosts the largest number of migrant farmworkers in the U.S. during the winter months.

Perhaps more than any other area along the U.S.-Mexico border, the extreme South Texas border area is characterized by several puzzling contradictions. Demographic statistics for the region, for example, show a pattern of substantial growth, but without the top-to-bottom prosperity that usually characterizes high-growth areas. Similarly, though it has the highest rate of drug seizures in the nation, its violent crime rate is below the state and national averages. Its colonias are home to the poorest residents in the nation, but their rate of home ownership and of intact two-parent families is among the highest in the nation for low-income residential areas.

Growth in the McAllen area (and the contiguous Reynosa area in Mexico) has been phenomenal, particularly over the last decade. This growth is especially evident in business activity, population increases, and the labor force. Indeed, the McAllen metropolitan statistical area (MSA) recently recorded the third-highest population growth in the U.S., following only Las Vegas and Laredo (another South Texas border city). While much of this growth can be traced to increasing trade with Mexico, other less obvious factors have had a powerful impact, sometimes in unexpected ways. One major factor is migration. People are drawn to this border region from the interior of each country.

Health care is another area of seeming irrationality. Though South Texas has some of the fastest-growing hospitals in the nation, it experiences many of the health problems associated with Third World nations. Nevertheless, some health risks are lower here than in other parts of the state. The rates of sexually transmitted diseases, for example, are lower in Hidalgo County than the average for Texas and the United States as a whole.[3] In addition, despite the county's many health problems, the infant mortality rate for

Hidalgo County (6.3) is slightly lower than that of the entire state (6.5). The same is true of the death rate for heart disease (151.9 in Hidalgo County vs. 223.5 for Texas as a whole).[4]

There are a number of factors that help produce these irrationalities. One is a thriving underground economy. Another is migration and its increasing strain on the infrastructure, including transportation and communication systems, schools, housing, and health and social services. Finally, the region's location—so far away from political and economic centers of power in the U.S. and Mexico—is also an important factor.

Free trade and the creation of the maquiladora industry in Mexico were supposed to help Mexico industrialize. Though they have mainly provided low-skilled jobs, they have also produced a migration to the Northern Mexico border. This, in turn, puts enormous stress on the local infrastructure of schools, transportation systems, and law enforcement agencies.

At the political centers of each nation, governments tend to respond to the pressures described above with solutions that often compound the problems. The Immigration Reform and Control Act (IRCA) of 1986, for example, made it illegal to hire undocumented workers, though it appears to have actually increased the flow of undocumented immigrants into the Valley. Many undocumented workers become trapped between the official border (the river) and the Border Patrol checkpoints sixty miles to the north. This not only contributes to the growth of colonias but puts enormous pressure on the local economy to provide jobs for people at the bottom who have little formal education and limited English proficiency but a great desire to work and sustain a family.

These factors, in turn, contribute to an underground employment economy. Some people find occasional work in local agriculture or construction. Others are self-employed, selling used articles at local *pulgas* [flea markets] or finding odd jobs in the area. Some take articles across to Mexico for resale and others even have jobs or small businesses in Mexico, commuting daily or weekly using a *mica*, a border-crossing card issued by U.S. consulates in Mexico to Mexican border residents. More recently, they have begun issuing laser visa cards.

Thus, the frequent pattern here and elsewhere along the border is for the benefits of border economic development to flow toward the center of each nation, while the costs are absorbed primarily by border residents. In Mexico, for example, the federal government keeps most of the total corporate and income taxes collected along the border.[5] Similarly, on the U.S. side of the border, economists generally agree that the federal government reaps a net benefit from taxes paid by undocumented workers, though lo-cal governments must absorb most of the health, education, and welfare costs.[6] The same pattern is found in drug enforcement. When the federal government dramatically increased the number of federal agents interdict-ing drugs from Mexico in recent years, the expense of prosecuting the re-sulting drug cases was passed on to state and local jurisdictions.[7]

Though border areas are often regarded as a backward hinterlands, these areas may also be at the leading edge of important social changes. Undocumented Mexican immigration is having an impact throughout the entire United States, for example. Still, it is experienced first and felt most strongly along the border. Similarly, the impact of the drug trade, modern-ization, and high dropout rates are often experienced by border residents long before—and with much greater intensity—than they affect interior areas of the United States. Residents of border areas have often already found ways to deal with such problems by the time those living in the in-terior are just beginning to deal with them.

The Research Projects

In the *Batos* volume, we were able to present survey research findings to document the patterns identified for almost all of the in-depth ethno-graphic topics. Though we will also combine these two approaches in this volume, our focus on deviant activities suggested a reliance more on eth-nographic projects, which utilize in-depth interviews. These will be de-scribed in each chapter. Though we still conducted some survey research projects, the topics covered in the present volume made them more prob-lematic. One doesn't ask student interviewers to approach a random sam-ple of drug smugglers, auto thieves, or alien smugglers, for example, and ask them to answer survey questions. As a result, we utilized fewer survey research projects to answer questions about the frequency of certain prac-tices, or how such practices are perceived by the local population.

We did, however, conduct several survey research projects. One was our Cultural Practices Survey (which will be described in more detail in Chap-ters 1 and 2). To create it, we incorporated responses from approximately 250 in-depth ethnographic interviews on cultural practices among Mexi-can-origin residents of South Texas to identify forty-two specific practices associated with Mexico. Based on these findings, we designed a survey, ad-ministered to 433 Mexican-origin residents of the Rio Grande Valley, to assess how frequently respondents participated in these practices and how they felt about keeping them.

A second survey project was our Undocumented Workers Survey, which will be described primarily in Chapter 4. This survey, also developed from prior in-depth interviews, posed questions to 150 undocumented Mexicans regarding why they came and how they were treated.

The remaining chapters utilize responses to our Perceptions of Deviance Survey. This project asked 424 people to rate how good or how bad forty-eight specific forms of border-related behavior were. This allowed us not only to compare the relative perceptions of "deviancy" of these items with one another, but to show how specific population groups felt about each practice.

In the Conclusion, we briefly utilize still another survey research project, an earlier version of the Perceptions of Deviance Survey which we called the Perceptions of Culture and Deviance Survey. Though this survey was successfully administered to 303 respondents, its results were not subsequently utilized because of significant problems with item reliability. Nevertheless, we were able to salvage measures forming two indexes that allowed us to assess how the number of generations in the United States is related to acculturation.

These four surveys, as we indicated earlier, utilized purposive and snowball sampling procedures.[8] These surveys, together with the in-depth ethnographic projects, are summarized in Appendix A.

Acknowledgments

Many individuals have contributed to the publication of this work. First and foremost are students at the University of Texas–Pan American who have participated in the interview projects. Those whose stories were gleaned from ethnographic interviews, and who permitted us to use their names, are listed in Appendix B.

The chapters in this work, more than in *Batos, Bolillos, Pochos, and Pelados,* represent the work of many graduate students at UT-PA, ten of whom are listed as chapter coauthors. Countless others, however, contributed by reviewing the chapter drafts, making suggestions, and permitting portions of their seminar papers to be included. Ruth Lopez, Priti Verma, Sandra Rodriquez, Cristina De Juana, and Ana Leos all worked as graduate research assistants, helping to organize and archive all the interview materials in a way that made them accessible for this and other publications. Cynthia Garza, secretary for the Sociology Department, also provided valuable assistance in coordinating many of the administrative details involved in maintaining the Borderlife Project.

Several colleagues at UT Pan American have contributed greatly to this publication. Drs. José Pagán and Cynthia Brown, both directors of the Center for Border Economic Studies (CBEST), not only provided funding for three important research projects included in this volume, but gave invaluable comments on many portions of the manuscript. Much of the funding provided by CBEST, as well as additional academic support, was made possible by Roland Arriola, vice president for External Affairs at UT-PA. Dr. Miguel Nevarez, former president of UT-PA, also provided economic support at key times for the Borderlife Project. Countless other colleagues at this university and elsewhere have provided constructive criticism.

We are especially indebted to Theresa May, executive editor of the University of Texas Press, who gave valuable encouragement for the project from the early stages of writing through the reviewing and editing. Her suggestions were always timely and valuable.

ON THE EDGE OF THE LAW

Map of South Texas and Northeastern Mexico

TEXAS

☆ Austin

Amistad Reservoir

■ Del Rio

● San Antonio

■ Eagle Pass

Río Grande
Río Bravo

■ Laredo

Corpus Christi ■

MEXICO

Falcon Reservoir

Roma
■
Rio Grande City
■
Edinburg
■
McAllen ■
Hidalgo ■
Harlingen ■
Gulf of Mexico

Miguel Alemán
■

Brownsville ■
South Padre Island —

Reynosa

● Monterrey

Matamoros ■

Earthquakes and Volcanoes
along the South Texas Border

When Alicia was a young girl living in Mexico, her parents moved to the United States. Because she loved Mexico and wanted to finish her education there, she stayed behind with family members in Mexico City. After graduating from the National University of Mexico, her parents convinced her to come to the Rio Grande Valley to find work and live with them. They had become U.S. citizens and were able to help her become a legal resident. After obtaining her residency, she went back to Mexico City for six months, where she married a young man she had known for many years.

When she tried to establish legal residency for him also, an immigration lawyer told her that it would be difficult unless she were a U.S. citizen. When she tried to become one, the Immigration Service informed her that she had disrupted her eligibility by having left the U.S. for six months. In fact, they told her, she might lose her own residency as a result of this stay in Mexico, even if it was to get married.

When she tried to find a job, local employers would not recognize her degree in computer programming, though it was given by the largest university in Mexico. In addition, many of them felt that her limited English was an obstacle. She finally managed to land an assembly-line job with an electronics manufacturing firm in Edinburg, Texas, though it only paid $7 an hour. She and her husband built a small home in Edinburg next to her parents. Because her husband was unable to gain legal residency, he had to commute every day to and from his work in Reynosa, Mexico, using a *mica*, or border-crossing card intended for shopping.

After five years, her employers threatened to move the plant to Mexico in order to pressure workers at the plant to accept a 10 percent cut in pay. Then, in 2003, the plant managers abruptly closed the plant anyway and moved operations to Reynosa, Mexico. None of the assembly workers were offered a chance to keep their jobs if they moved to Mexico, though it is doubtful that any could have survived on the dollar an hour salary the company was paying assembly workers there. When Alicia sought help from the employment office, she was told they could help her only if she enrolled in a GED class. She was angry that they were treating her as a high school dropout when she had a college degree. She knew she needed to learn English, but they resisted helping her with that. After four frustrating weeks of making frequent trips to the employment office, she was finally able to enroll in an English class at the University of Texas–Pan American. At the time of her interview in 2003, she and her husband were falling seriously into debt because they could not survive on his meager salary.

Alicia has experienced, up close and personally, many of the promises and problems related to a major change sweeping the world: the process of globalization. Globalization entices people like Alicia with the promise of better jobs if they will move to countries where their skills are needed. Sometimes, however—as in her case—movement is hampered by regulations that prohibit the movement of workers across international borders. In addition, though globalization is supposed to promote uniform standards, so that a degree from an accredited university in one country will be recognized in others, nationalistic obstacles often keep such recognition from happening. In the end, Alicia experienced another problem of globalization—the exodus of low-skilled assembly-line jobs from postindustrial countries like the U.S. to Mexico and other developing nations.

People like Alicia not only experience personally the pain of globalization but get caught in its battle with another worldwide phenomenon: nationalism. Nationalism gives people a strong attachment to their home countries, such as the feelings that kept Alicia in Mexico for many years. In addition, it promotes regulations that discourage the immigration of "foreigners," so that her husband was unable to live and work legally in the United States.

Ellwyn Stoddard, a pioneering borderlands scholar, observed recently that U.S. officials at the U.S.-Mexico border are beset by these competing forces. Congress, he notes, makes laws to cut down on the flow of people and goods across U.S. binational borders. At the same time, other federal agencies that regulate international trade are trying to increase U.S. trade and tourism with other countries. Thus there is a constant fight within the government as to whether U.S. borders with Canada and Mexico should be open or closed.[1]

This conflict within the government over regulating the U.S.-Mexico border sometimes results in erratic regulations for the people who live there, especially noncitizens. As a consequence, illicit activities often spring up along and across the border. Alicia's husband, for example, does not use his temporary border card, or *mica*, for its legally defined function of shopping but to live surreptitiously with his wife in the United States and to commute daily to a job in Mexico.

A useful frame of analysis, one introduced in our earlier book (*Batos, Bolillos, Pochos, and Pelados*), is related to the distinction between culture and structure. Both of these terms can refer to major social forces, or ways that society affects human behavior. Culture, as we explained it, consists of the patterned ways that a society collectively interprets or understands things. This includes their shared understandings of right and wrong, truth and error, and appropriate ways of behaving. The structure of a society, in contrast, consists of the patterns of established relationships among its recognized components, or parts. Thus, structure is all the accepted ways that these parts fit together, or their relation to one another. Culture is a collective mentality, while structure is a web of relationships.

Variations in culture and structure are powerful social forces that sometimes compete with each other in accelerating or holding back change. Throughout the world, for example, shared *cultural* beliefs among religious fundamentalists have fomented revolutions, blocked globalization, and promoted terrorism. Similarly, the emergence of new trade relations and the resulting struggles over power and wealth are *structural* factors that have led to wars, colonization, and revolution throughout history.

These two social forces often pull in opposite directions. For example, since the economic structure of U.S. business is based on using the cheapest labor possible, the business community encourages the flow of undocumented immigrants northward from Mexico. This force is countered by strong cultural feelings among U.S. nationalists who want to keep the ethnic balance in this country the way it is now. They demand that federal troops be stationed on the border to repel the "alien invaders." In their actions, nationalists are motivated by a strong sense of "cultural superiority" and a desire to protect their own countrymen against "foreign" workers. Thus, the structural drive to expand markets is countered by a cultural drive toward protectionism and ethnocentric thinking. Similarly, though our me-first culture of individualism[2] has been linked to drug abuse, we set in place an enormous law-enforcement structure to block the flow of drugs across the border—and then blame Mexico for most of our drug problems.

Several scholars have noted the conflict between nationalism and globalization and its impact on people in borderland communities. David Keeling, for example, notes that many governments are increasingly resistant to both legal and illegal migration, even while they promote globalization by saying that they believe in the free movement of "people, goods, capital, and information" associated with free trade. Keeling states that the U.S.-Mexico border is probably the most heavily militarized border in the Western Hemisphere and is "symbolic of the sharp divide in economic opportunity, quality of life, and migration policy" between the two countries, which is the basis of significant political and cultural conflict.[3]

As a result of these conflicts between cultural and structural forces, social problems in each nation seem to be more pronounced in the borderlands. Drug use and drug trafficking, for example, are problems found throughout both countries. Nevertheless, these problems are found in a much exaggerated fashion at the border. In Mexican border towns, rival drug cartels battle for turf and public officials are pressured to turn a blind eye. And on both sides of the Rio Grande/Río Bravo, corruption among law enforcement officers and public officials is often highly pronounced. In addition, pollution and other environmental issues are frequently worse along the border. So are the problems of broken infrastructure and overcrowding.

The same pattern is found with many other social issues. Auto theft is also more common in Texas border cities than elsewhere in the United States. Although there are pockets of poverty in several areas of the U.S., poverty and its attendant problems are most pronounced in the South Texas borderlands. Dropout rates among Hispanics are highest in this border location. So are the problems of undocumented workers, broken infrastructure, and cultural divisions.

Why? Some observers attribute such problems to the fact that the border is the juncture between two countries with very different cultures, laws, and political systems. Others state that the borderlands have more pronounced problems because the periphery of a nation usually has less political and economic power than its center.

Though such explanations are certainly important, there is something deeper going on. The South Texas–Northern Mexico border is not only a place where the periphery of each nation battles for resources with its respective center and where there are great cultural differences, but the location where monumental forces of social change collide.

In his 1996 book *The Future of Capitalism*, economist Lester Thurow borrows the concept of plate tectonic theory from geology to create a useful metaphor. He states:

> In geology, visible earthquakes and volcanoes are caused by the invisible movement of the continental plates floating on the earth's molten inner core ... The geophysicist must probe deeper to look at forces generated below the surface of the earth by the continental plates. So too, no one can understand what happened to Mexico [in its economic crises] by looking at the clumsy mistakes made by policy makers in Mexico City. Those suddenly in the middle of an economic earthquake cannot tell you why it is happening any more than those in the middle of a real earthquake can.[4]

Thurow makes the point that, just as real earthquakes and volcanoes occur most frequently where the earth's tectonic plates come in contact, social earthquakes and volcanoes occur most often where major social forces come together. Applying this analogy to the borderlands, many of the social problems encountered in this location can similarly be viewed as part of long-term shifts in the cultural and structural forces shaping our world today. The immediate social problems are surface manifestations of long-term shifts in these plates. In the location where these plates collide, the social landscape is profoundly altered by social and cultural earthquakes and volcanoes, or sudden, negative upheavals visited most profoundly on societies where these pressures are strongest.

For some, these tectonic social plates at the U.S.-Mexico border might be the cultural and sociopolitical systems of Mexico and the United States. Other major social forces, however, are exerting even greater pressure at the border. Chief among these opposing social tectonic plates are globalization and nationalism. Globalization tries to erase borders, while nationalism tries to erect and reinforce them. Both of these forces, incidentally, are often pushed onto the weaker borderlands by the powerful centers of each nation.

Arthur Schlesinger Jr. sees globalization and the counterforces of nationalism (and the corresponding ethnocentrism associated with natural culture) as powerful competing forces.

> The world is torn today in opposite directions. Globalization is in the saddle and rides mankind, but at the same time, drives people to seek refuge from its powerful forces beyond their control and comprehension. They retreat into familiar intelligible protective units. They crave the politics of identity [nationalism]. The faster the world integrates, the more people will huddle in their religious or ethnic or tribal enclaves ... Nor is the fundamentalist revival confined to the Third World. Many people living lives of quiet desperation in modern societies hunger for transcendent meaning and turn to inerrant faith for solace and support.[5]

A brief description of each of these two forces will illuminate their conflictive nature for the U.S.-Mexico borderlands.

Globalization

Globalization is a process by which money, information, labor, goods, and services move with increasing ease across international boundaries. It is closely related to market capitalism, which proposes that goods and services be produced where production costs are the lowest, and then sold wherever the greatest profit can be made. In a truly free market, capitalists and workers alike are free to produce a product (or increase the value of their labor) wherever they can, and at the lowest possible cost. They should then be free to sell this product (or their labor) where it can bring them the greatest profit. Obviously, both the creation of a product and taking it to where it can be sold for the greatest profit require free movement across international boundaries. Such international movement also requires the nations of the world to lower trade barriers and to create networks regulating transportation and money transfers while encouraging information sharing and standardized trade processes. Globalization has been accelerating rapidly in the past twenty years, as market capitalism has become the dominant economic force among the nations of the world.[6] As barriers to free trade have fallen, transportation and communication networks have grown exponentially.

This phenomenon is aptly described by geographer David J. Keeling, who says:

> For the first time in human history, multinational corporations can produce anything anywhere on the planet and can sell anything anywhere on the planet ... Time-space compression has "stretched" capital and information activities across the traditional boundaries constructed by political and geographical structures. This theoretically borderless world now presents few impediments to the rapid and efficient movement of people, capital, goods, services, and information, thus facilitating the emergence of a truly global marketplace.[7]

The giant expansion in trade around the world has produced greater interdependence among the nations of the world. Nations that originally resisted it found themselves left out of the economic development promised by such trade. Thus, even nations of the former Second World—the Soviet Union and Communist China—have rushed to embrace market capitalism, rather than remain isolated from its globalizing influences.

Largely, they have done so based on their desire for the outcomes predicted by the theory of globalization. The *theory* of globalization proposes that free market capitalism, unfettered by trade barriers, will have four outcomes: it will (1) produce greater political stability, (2) promote democracy, (3) establish worldwide economic and political cooperation, and (4) raise the standard of living for all who actively participate.

That so many nations have bought into the theory of globalization requires, of course, more than just faith in an abstract theory. The nations of the former Soviet Union and China, for example, did not convert to free market capitalism without some fairly substantial evidence. Though these nations have experienced major dislocations as they have embraced globalization, it seems to be working to increase the overall standard of living for many of them.

Latin America has also embraced globalization and free market capitalism, though most Latin American countries have not experienced the economic benefits that have come to Asian nations. The number of people living in poverty in Latin America has grown from 120 million in 1970 to over 220 million in 2000.[8] In 2000 over 40 percent of the population in Latin America was considered poor.[9] Also as a consequence of globalization, many national firms throughout Latin America have been forced out of business by multinational corporations with much better financing, technology, and market connections.[10]

Mexico, as a member of NAFTA, has experienced globalization in particularly negative ways. When Mexico became a member of NAFTA, government price supports for many commodities were abandoned, rural-urban migration increased, and falling agricultural prices depressed an already fragile rural economy.[11] In addition, Mexico changed its constitution to allow the free sale of once-sacred *ejido* [cooperative farm] lands and reduced barriers to external trade, capital, and goods. Because people at the bottom were drastically affected by these changes, highly nationalistic reactions soon erupted, including the Zapatista rebellion in Chiapas.

Throughout other emerging regions of the world, vast segments of society have become further impoverished by globalization. These nations also find themselves losing the power to regulate themselves, because they are often in debt to international financial institutions (such as the International Monetary Fund and the World Bank) and have to follow the regulations set by these lenders. As those at the bottom fall farther and farther behind, many countries experience nationalistic rebellions by ethnic, religious, and political groups who feel threatened by these global forces. Indeed, as Brecher and Costello suggest, the experience of many of these impoverished populations has been closer to "global pillage" than to "global village."[12]

Nationalism is also aroused when globalization begins to weaken national cultures and national identity.[13] Many observers contend, for example, that globalization leads to a worldwide homogenization of culture—often culture associated with U.S. products and popular culture. According to this view, U.S. corporations have spread U.S. goods and media productions across the globe, especially to developing countries like Mexico and the nations of Latin America. Proponents of this view propose that other countries are becoming Americanized by our advertisements, movies, and TV, and by our "fizzy drinks, faded pants, and fatty foods."[14]

Nationalism / National Culture

Nationalism, the force that often rises to oppose globalization, is hard to define. It means so many different things to so many different people, and these meanings seem to change over time. Many definitions that one hears are negative. Pfaff, for example, jokingly states that "a nation is a people united by a common dislike of its neighbors and a common mistake about its origins."[15] Sigmund Freud saw similar negative features of nationalism when he said, "It is always possible to bind together a considerable number of people in love, so long as there are other people left over to receive the manifestations of their aggressiveness."[16]

Anthony Smith defines nationalism as an ideology which

> holds that the world is divided into nations, each of which has its own character and destiny; that an individual's first loyalty is to his or her nation; that the nation is the source of all political power; that to be free and fulfilled, the individual must belong to a nation; that each nation must express its authentic nature by being autonomous; and that a world of peace and justice can only be built on autonomous nations.[17]

Smith points out that a fundamental aspect of nationalism is a strong sense of identity based upon shared national cultural values and symbols. This national culture, he says, inspires men and women to sacrifice their personal well-being for the higher well-being of the nation. It inspires dedicated effort and comforts individuals when they experience loss and grief. It provides shared national memories, glorifying myths and symbols, core values, and a common identity. In short, it is the glue that holds people together and inspires individuals to act out of something besides economic self-interest.

Nationalism, then, is a strong social bond, a form of social solidarity. It is somewhat related to Emile Durkheim's idea of "mechanical solidarity," which is based more on feelings of attachment than on "what's in it for me." As members of a crowd watch the flag being raised, for example, their attention is focused on an object—the flag—and its shared meaning. They feel that they are part of something greater than themselves, the nation. With this sense of belonging comes a feeling of moral obligation to live up to the demands of membership.

Even in the early part of the twentieth century, Durkheim saw the emergence of a competing form of solidarity, which he called "organic solidarity." This social bond was more structural than cultural, since it was created by an increasingly specialized division of labor. People were becoming dependent upon one another, not because of shared feelings, but because they had become so specialized in their work that each could not produce all the things needed for his or her well-being. That is, the basis of their dependency on each other was not shared feelings but economic interdependence.[18]

Durkheim could see that mechanical solidarity was being replaced, to a degree, by organic solidarity in industrialized nations. Today, we can see a similar pattern, in which nationalism seems to be threatened by globalization. The question for us today, as it was for Durkheim, is whether a structural bond (globalization) will replace a cultural bond (nationalism).

Eric Hobsbawm is a leading advocate of the idea that globalization will eventually replace nationalism. He proposes that as global interdependence grows, multinational mechanisms, such as the Internet, the World Bank, and the United Nations will become increasingly important, and that individual nations will be able to provide fewer and fewer of the needs of their people. Indeed, he sees the nation state as becoming increasingly bound by international laws, treaties, and organizations and consequently losing its autonomy.[19]

Many other observers of globalization have argued that it will eventually destroy nationalism. Shin, who disagrees with this proposition, summarizes their arguments:

> [T]o the extent that globalism is a fact of social life, there is no place for a sense of national identity, based on one land, one language, or one race. The nation state, guided by nationalism as ideology or as emotion, has outlived its usefulness in maintaining world order. Just as modernization theorists and Marxists predicted the demise of nationalism in the 1960s and 1970s . . . proponents of globalization expect transnational forces of late modernity gradually to supersede nations and nationalism . . . Both proponents and critics support the premise that the nation state, nationalism, or national identity is antithetical to globalization. The proponents believe globalization will weaken the functional power of the nation state and the critics worry that it will disrupt ethnic or national identity. Despite their opposing views, they arrive at the same conclusion—globalization cannot coexist with nationalism.[20]

But many observers argue that nationalism is not giving way to globalization. Indeed, many see feelings of nationalism as increasing in reaction to the pressures of globalization. Anthony Smith proposes several reasons why advocates of globalization fail to recognize this resurgence of nationalism and ethnic conflict. Their first error—their main one, he says—is to confuse the *state* with the *nation*, assuming that if the functions of the state decline, then the nation (and nationalism) will also decline. Smith points out that the state is limited to national government structures, while the nation includes both national government structures and the national culture. He indicates that the main failure of advocates of globalization is

> their refusal to link the consequences of modernity with an understanding of the continuing role played by cultural ties and ethnic identities which originated in pre-modern epochs. These ties and identities are found among local and regional communities, that is, among the lower strata—the peasants, tribesmen, artisans, labourers ... This failure has meant a systematic neglect of the popular base and cultural framework of nationalism.[21]

Thus, the cultural changes produced by globalization, Smith argues, are really superficial ones that do not fundamentally change national cultures. Accordingly, the idea that globalization will destroy nationalism is wrong in at least two very important ways. First, recent history shows that nationalism, especially of an ethnic nature, is on the rise. While everyone is talking about market integration, multiculturalism, and religious tolerance, the reality is that ethnic and religious wars and rebellions are erupting all around the globe. We see these, not only among countries of the former Soviet Union and in the Third World, but also in many Western nations (Quebec wanting to separate from Canada, the Basques and Cataluña seeking independence in Spain, etc.). We also see a rising nationalism in the United States and Mexico. Smith, for example, states:

> In the United States of America, itself, the most dynamic arena of modernization, a powerful continental providential nationalism is not hard to mobilize. Every time United States soldiers are killed or captured in a UN mission, every time the President agonizes over a foreign-policy issue involving an American military presence, every time trade negotiations threaten to favour America's competitors, the sense of a separate and unique American history and destiny looms in the background, encouraging Americans to feel their common historical mission as bearers of freedom and democracy ... The belief in an American Creed, Constitution, and way of life, overarching the many cultures of its constituent [ethnic groups], has remained a resilient force, despite the

many setbacks and disappointments of Americans at home and abroad.[22]

The second error of those who predict the death of nationalism, according to Smith, is that many nations today are using globalization to further their nationalistic aims. Certainly, the foreign policy of the United States in recent years has been both pro-globalization and nationalistic. Shin proposes that many nations—especially, in his study, Korea—are using globalization for nationalistic purposes. He states that in many of the nations that have used globalization for nationalistic aims, there has been an increase in ethnic identity and nationalism.[23]

One writer who sees a rise in both globalization and a subset of nationalism is Benjamin Barber. In an article entitled "Jihad vs. McWorld," he identifies the recent rise in religious and ethnic strife as Jihad. For Barber, Jihad is a level below nationalism, involving cultures within a nation rather than entire countries. Also, Jihad involves sects, rather than entire religions. Jihad, he contends, battles not only against globalization but against the jihadists' respective nation states. The second force, McWorld, is essentially the spread of globalization. He sees both forces as antidemocratic and each feeding the antagonism of the other.[24]

Samuel Huntington also recognizes an increase in the pressures of globalization on subnational cultures. American identity and culture, he argues, are being threatened by the competing pressures of globalization and increasing multiculturalism. He is especially concerned about Mexican immigrants because he believes that even when they want to stay in the United States, they remain strongly tied to Mexican national culture and refuse to assimilate.[25]

Huntington is right that many Mexicans who come to the United States, either legally or illegally, are strongly influenced by Mexican national culture and bring with them strong feelings of nationalism. Many are keenly aware that much of the territory of the United States was taken by force from Mexico in a nationalistic war of aggression. As we will show in the chapters to come, however, he is wrong in assuming that these immigrants and their children refuse to assimilate. While globalization pulls them to the United States, the pull of U.S. nationalism, especially in Texas schools, rather quickly diminishes their patriotic ties to Mexico and the continuation of many of the cultural practices brought from Mexico.

As we indicated earlier, globalization and nationalism are like tectonic plates that, when they collide, cause volcanoes and earthquakes to erupt along their main point of contact—the U.S.-Mexico border. Though all parts of the U.S. and Mexico are affected by these forces, their greatest impact is felt at the border.

Each of the topics selected for this volume is directly related to this dialectic between globalization and nationalism. The first two chapters, for example, examine the intergenerational process by which Mexican-origin people in the borderlands are "Americanized." At issue is how long—how many succeeding generations—Mexican cultural practices can be maintained among those who are pulled here by the process of globalization. We examine which aspects of Mexican culture are retained, which are dropped, and which are merged into Mexican American culture. Overall, we look at the conflicts that are created when people from Mexico, which has its own powerful form of nationalism, become part of a global flow of people into the United States, and become exposed to the powerful nationalism experienced in U.S. culture and education.

In Chapter 1, we look specifically at the extent to which traditional Mexican health-related practices are maintained by Mexican-origin people in South Texas. We focus on the negative stigma attached to many of these practices in the dominant Anglo[26] culture. In addition, we examine the extent to which these practices are accepted, and whether cultural preferences or the high cost of conventional medicine best explains their prevalence. This look at traditional medicine also includes an examination of traditional practitioners, including *curanderos* [folk healers], and why Mexican-origin people in South Texas sometimes prefer them to conventional medical practitioners. Finally, we examine why many border residents of Mexican ancestry regularly cross back into Mexico to receive health care.

Chapter 2 extends the analysis of specific Mexican-origin cultural practices to those practices associated with gender, with interpersonal and family relations, and with special occasions and food. We again examine the extent to which pressures toward assimilation make these practices disappear after several generations in the United States. We also examine which practices seem to be more resistant to change and how the proximity of Mexico might prolong their use.

The remaining chapters also reflect major "earthquakes and volcanoes" arising on the border as globalization and nationalism collide. In Chapter 3, we examine the case of people like Alicia (mentioned in the beginning of this introduction) who, after being drawn by globalization to the United States, become displaced workers as assembly operations move to Mexico and beyond. This chapter also examines the issue of labor flight as a response either to global competition or to an effort by management to exploit workers. We deal primarily in this chapter, however, with how the problems of displaced workers in border cities differ from those experienced by displaced workers elsewhere.

Chapters 4 and 5 examine issues related to undocumented workers in South Texas. Their case is particularly important, because they help us to understand what happens when labor is not free to cross international boundaries but capital is. We also examine how the policy of the United States, which is driven in large part by strong nationalistic sentiments, responds to a labor flow that is increasingly driven by the forces of globalization. The occasional presence of vigilante groups on the border highlights this conflict. U.S. employers seeking the free movement of labor from Mexico and elsewhere run into strong nationalistic sentiments among those who are striving to preserve the culture and "integrity" of the United States. We also observe how the U.S. has pushed globalization onto Mexico through the North American Free Trade Agreement (NAFTA) but reacts with horror when we get some of the unwanted effects of this agreement.

Chapter 4 briefly examines such issues as whether undocumented workers are an economic cost or a net benefit, whether they use more tax-supported services than they contribute in taxes, and whether they threaten U.S. culture by refusing to assimilate. Our primary focus, however, is on the way undocumented workers are treated. We examine how the type of treatment they receive is related to the structural conditions of their employment situation.

In Chapter 5, we examine the law enforcement aspects of undocumented immigration. First, we look at how Mexicans who come legally to South Texas to shop or to visit are treated and whether our laws and our enforcement mechanisms are biased against them. The rest of the chapter discusses how our immigration-control apparatus deals with undocumented immigration. Is immigration enforcement working, or does it simply make the undocumented more easily exploited and abused? Do harsher measures keep the undocumented out, or do they simply increase the rate of injury, abuse, and death? Should U.S. immigration officers seek cooperation with Mexican police, or would this contribute to the exploitation and abuse of the undocumented?

In Chapter 6, we look at another negative effect of globalization, the flow of illegal drugs into the United States in response to the strong undercurrents of free market capitalism. In addition, we examine how U.S. national culture, with its emphasis on individualism, consumption, and maximization of individual pleasure, promotes the flow of drugs. We also examine how our nationalism causes us to overlook our insatiable demand for drugs and to shift to Mexico much of the blame for our drug problems. We also discuss how NAFTA has made it more difficult to stop the flow of illegal drugs. This chapter considers whether drug enforcement policies have done more to slow down the flow of drugs or have added to the burden of lawlessness and deviance, especially in the borderlands. In addition, we examine how cultural and structural factors influence the involvement of local border residents in the drug trade. Finally, we examine a consequence of the flow of drugs through South Texas: how this flow has affected rates of drug dependency in this region.

In Chapter 7, we look at cross-border juvenile and property crime. This is especially important in light of the nationalistic policies of each nation. This nationalism frequently promotes an environment, not of cooperation, but of opportunities for thieves to take property across the border and to involve juveniles in this illicit cross-border "trade." We discuss ways that young shoplifters and auto thieves are able to operate with relative impunity along the border. We further examine whether their involvement in such crimes is due to economic hardships, to lax enforcement, or to the ease with which they can escape prosecution in a border environment. We examine the failure of each nation (and corresponding state governments) to adopt cooperative law-enforcement networks and standardized laws, as would be suggested by globalization. We also observe how nationalistic restrictions on free trade create markets on both sides of the border (making stolen automobiles and firearms more valuable in Mexico, for example, while causing Freon and prescriptions drugs that can be purchased without a prescription to become more desirable in the U.S.). This chapter also addresses the pattern by which an underground economy is created when border people who are excluded from the formal economy become involved in prohibited economic activities.

Chapter 8 describes another underground activity among underage teens in U.S. border cities: going to the Mexican side of the border for alcoholic beverages in clubs and bars. We also look at how the Mexican criminal justice system, especially its jails and prisons, has failed to conform to the pressures of globalization for uniform international standards. We further consider how this lack of cooperation by police agencies on both sides of the border contributes to border crimes. Further, we discuss the issue of Mexican police corruption, asking what cultural and structural factors promote it, even when many Mexicans find it distasteful and unethical.

Finally, we look at the conditions in Mexican jails and prisons, examining whether they serve more to curtail crime or to facilitate exploitation and abuse by public officials.

In our final chapter, Chapter 9, we examine what happens when one segment of the U.S. population fails to get the educational preparation needed for full participation in a postindustrial (and supposedly meritocratic) society. Hispanic dropouts become increasingly polarized as globalization leaves behind those without significant education. Schools are not only the major force for participation in a global society, but the main means by which nationalistic culture is promoted. In many U.S. schools, nationalism relegates the contributions of Mexico and Mexicans to a very peripheral role. Nationalism also prevents cooperation across borders that could foster better educational systems to the benefit of both countries. Nationalistic tendencies in the U.S. also push against true bilingual education on the border, where it is needed for globalization. We examine how the proximity of Mexico to the United States affects the dropout rate, especially in a border environment. We examine the relative importance of cultural and structural factors in explaining this high dropout rate, and examine why Mexican immigrant children are so much more likely to drop out of school than children of later generations. Finally, we examine whether bilingual education classes really help native Spanish speakers complete school, or whether they contribute more to a negative stigma and to lower expectations.

Traditional Health Care Practices

WITH CRISTINA DE JUANA

Don Antonio[1] and his daughter Lisa live in a colonia. A doctor diagnosed Lisa as having cancer. He suggested they get a second opinion, but the family has been unable to do so because of severe economic limitations. Instead, they visit a doctor in Mexico who is providing some type of chemotherapy. Don Antonio does not trust this physician, but his services are the best care the family can afford. Lisa's father is thinking of taking her to a *curandero* [folk healer], because he trusts them more than regular doctors.

As this story illustrates, South Texas people of Mexican origin who use traditional folk healing practices do so not just for economic reasons but for cultural considerations as well. In South Texas communities, folk medicine often coexists with Western biomedicine because standard health care is beyond the reach of many residents.[2] More than one-quarter of the Texas border population currently lives below the poverty line. Roughly one in three Texas border residents has no health insurance. In South Texas colonias (where Don Antonio and his daughter live), 64 percent of residents are not covered by health insurance.[3] Hispanic women, like Lisa, especially those who are foreign born or who are fifty to sixty-four, have the lowest percentage of health coverage and lowest contact with health care facilities in the country.[4] To make matters worse, physicians may be scarce even when people can afford them. In the year 2000, all but one of Texas' thirty-two border counties were designated as medically underserved.[5]

Even if doctors and insurance were more readily available, the health crisis that exists in the Rio Grande Valley would not go away. This area suffers from higher rates of some diseases than are experienced elsewhere in the United States. The mortality rate for diabetes in the McAllen area, for example, is 26.4, compared to a state average of 17.8. Women in the Rio Grande Valley are dying of cervical cancer at twice the national rate.

Tuberculosis and liver disease are also twice as common on the border as in other parts of the state.[6] The U.S.-Mexico border has been defined as an area of "epidemiological transition," a condition in which areas of developed nations begin to acquire some of the health problems of developing countries.[7]

Many of the poor in South Texas with roots in Mexico have a long history of using traditional forms of medicine, including folk healers, folk medicines, and a variety of cultural practices believed to ward off or cure illnesses. Often, these practices are at odds with conventional medical interventions. As a result, some observers fault Mexican culture for maintaining traditional medicine, claiming it reduces the utilization of doctors and leads to poor health among the Mexican-origin population of the United States. This charge is related to several key issues that we will address in this chapter, including the following questions:

—Should traditional health-related practices be seen as a viable option for Mexican-origin people in South Texas, or do such practices put their health and well being at risk?

—Do people of Mexican origin in South Texas use alternative (and traditional) forms of medicine because they can't afford conventional medical interventions or because they prefer traditional practices?

—Do doctors in Mexico provide a more economical and personal form of health care than do physicians in Texas, or do they constitute a severe threat to the well being of those who utilize their services?

—Should the use of curanderos be severely discouraged for individuals of Mexican origin so they will use conventional medical practitioners?

—Do health-related cultural practices of Mexican-origin people diminish with each generation in the U.S., or do they become part of Mexican American culture?

Methodology

The Texas-Mexico border is an excellent location for examining Mexican culture and the changes that take place as Mexican immigrants become

Mexican Americans. There are large numbers of people of Mexican origin (almost 90 percent of the Hidalgo County population). This situation allows us to examine what happens to traditional cultural practices, especially those related to health care, when Mexican-origin people live near their homeland, surrounded by *paisanos* [compatriots]. In such an environment, will these immigrants maintain their cultural practices from one generation to the next, or will they assimilate into the dominant Anglo culture?

By means of approximately 250 in-depth ethnographic interviews on cultural practices with Mexican-origin residents of South Texas, we identified forty-two specific practices associated with Mexico. Based on these findings, we designed a survey, administered to 433 Mexican-origin residents of the Rio Grande Valley, to assess how frequently respondents participated in each of these practices. This is our Cultural Practices Survey (N = 433). In it, we asked respondents to indicate whether they felt each cultural practice should be kept or forgotten, or whether they felt it really did not matter. We then compared the responses of participants to their generational status (how many generations each participant's family had been in the U.S.). Survey results specifically related to health care are reported in this chapter. The responses related to other, nonhealth cultural practices are discussed in Chapter 2.

CULTURAL PRACTICES AS MEASURES OF ACCULTURATION

Though extensive research has documented the processes by which ethnic cultures change over several generations, few studies have examined specific cultural practices as indices of acculturation.[8] Those few that have often asked respondents only to indicate awareness of a custom, not the frequency with which it was practiced. Even one of the most comprehensive measures of acculturation, one by Keefe and Padilla, inquired concerning only a few cultural practices, and these were mostly related to food preparation.[9]

Each student participating in our study was instructed to interview at least four respondents, including a person born in Mexico who had lived at least five years in the United States; a Mexican American born and raised in the Valley but with at least one parent born and raised in Mexico; a Mexican American with U.S.-born parents but at least one grandparent born and raised in Mexico; and a Mexican American whose parents and grandparents were all born in the United States.[10] As previously indicated, this resulted in a total survey sample of 433 respondents.

MEASURING GENERATIONAL STATUS

Many scholars who write about acculturation (some prefer the term "cultural assimilation") commonly describe the phenomenon as a change that takes place by "generation," with each successive generation more assimilated than its predecessor. It is commonly assumed in relevant literature that by the third generation, most cultural practices brought by the immigrant generation will have largely disappeared.[11]

Testing this assumption is made more difficult by the complexity of measuring generational status. In it simplest terms, the first generation is thought to include the immigrants; the second consists of their American-born children; and the third consists of native-born children of native-born parents. Despite the appealing simplicity of such theoretical constructs, one does not have to consider very many cases to appreciate the actual complexity involved in measuring generational status. For example, most Mexican Americans living on the South Texas border could claim a combination of generations. One's father may have been born in the U.S. but her or his mother may have been born in Mexico. In addition, any of the four grandparents could have been born in either country.

Some attempts to address such complexity have been made.[12] Cuellar, for example, establishes Generation 1 as a person born in Mexico but living in the U.S.; Generation 2 as an individual born in the U.S., with at least one parent born in Mexico; Generation 3 as a respondent born in the U.S., with both parents born in the U.S. but all grandparents born in Mexico; Generation 4 as a respondent born in the U.S., with both parents and at least one grandparent born in the U.S.; and Generation 5 as a respondent born in the U.S., with both parents and all grandparents also born in the U.S.[13]

Granados, by comparison, defines the generational groups into three categories. The UU group includes a U.S.-born child and a U.S.-born parent. The UI group includes a U.S.-born child and an immigrant parent and the II group is composed of an immigrant child and an immigrant parent.[14]

As one sees the many different ways of measuring generational status, it becomes obvious that a simpler means of measuring this variable is needed. A more useful measure would recognize the multiple possibilities for the birthplace of each respondent, and his or her parents and grandparents, while representing a continuum of increasing U.S.-born ancestry. To accomplish this, we developed a measure that treats generational status as an ordinal/ratio variable, thus dispensing with the need to name each generation.

This variable, which we called the generation score, was calculated by allotting a total of 4 points to each generation born in the United States. If a respondent was born in the U.S., for example, he/she would be given 4 points. Two points were then given for each parent born in the United States, and 1 point for each grandparent born here.[15] This produced a range of generation scores from 0 (all foreign born) to 12 (all U.S. born).

Economic Conditions and Health Care in South Texas

Regardless of the generation to which an individual belongs, those who live below the poverty line often find access to conventional health care extremely limited. This is particularly so on the South Texas border. According to a report by the Texas Comptroller of Public Accounts, "Health conditions on the Texas-Mexico border are among the worst in the United States.[16] The relationship between economic status and utilization of conventional health care was demonstrated in a study that found that Mexican Americans with health insurance were 1.5 times more likely to consult a physician than those without.[17]

This situation was clearly demonstrated by many of our study's 250 ethnographic interviews on health care practices. One of these respondents, a young woman we'll call Eva, relates a not uncommon but difficult situation she faced a few years ago:

> One day, I went to my parents' house to visit and found my father in great pain. He had a molar that needed to come out, but he didn't have any money to go to the dentist. He had been suffering the whole week, waiting for some money to get it taken care of. My father is a strong man, so to see him nearly reduced to tears was very difficult for me. My husband and I took him to a dentist where he had the molar taken out. The power of money is amazing. A few dollars meant the difference between excruciating pain and feeling great.

Workers in the medical industry on the Texas-Mexico border regularly witness the pain of inadequate health care. An ambulance driver recalls one morning when he and his partner had to handle a transfer out of a local hospital's ICU ward.

> It was a thirteen-year-old boy diagnosed with a brain tumor. When we arrived at the ward, we found his mother and aunt with him. His mother was waiting for a phone call from Reynosa [Mexico] to acknowledge that a Cruz Roja [Mexican Red Cross] ambulance would be at the bridge. She was taking him home because she didn't have the money to keep him alive.
>
> My partner and a respiratory technician were to keep him alive long enough to get across the border. Once they reached their house, his mother was going to allow him to die because his condition was said to be terminal. When we arrived at the bridge, the mother's control over her emotions began to fade.
>
> I couldn't even begin to imagine what she was going through. While waiting for the Mexican ambulance, my partner became angry. She wondered if their lack of money or knowledge of their legal options was behind what they were doing.
>
> Finally, the boy was placed in the other ambulance and they drove away. We stood there watching, knowing that in less than an hour it would be over. My partner and I have never talked about this since.[18]

The difficulties that many of the poor suffer from inadequate health care are not limited to issues of affordability. Many suffer humiliation as well. One student who interviewed his mother found exactly this to be the case. She told him:

> I remember we lived about two miles from the doctor's office and your brother Mario was about a year old. Your father was working in the fields and the baby was real sick. So I wrapped him up and walked to the doctor's office.
>
> I only had $5 and your father wasn't getting paid until the end of the week. Still, the doctor saw him and gave me a prescription. The nurse at the front office then told me to give the baby the medication and bring him back in two days. I tried to tell her that I didn't have any money to buy the medicine and that I hoped the doctor was going to give him a shot.

I still remember how she yelled at me in front of all those people at the doctor's office. She told me that I had better find the money unless I wanted my son to die. She told me to do anything I had to—steal, cheat, or rob a bank. It didn't matter as long as I got the money.

I was so humiliated. I walked home carrying my baby and crying all the way. Thank God for my neighbor. She loaned me the money and her husband took me to get the medicine.[19]

Many of the poor cannot afford visits to a doctor's office. They instead visit clinics established to assist low-income residents. One woman who was seven months pregnant at the time of her interview described a recent visit to a clinic:

I had to wait many long hours. I am usually the first to arrive at the clinic but often have to wait until after lunch to see a doctor. The clinic staff doesn't even inform us if the doctor is not in or has gone to lunch. It really upsets me to finally get to see the doctor and find out that he was not there all morning.

Though low-income patients are expected to put up with long waits for a doctor, they often receive little patience in return. Berta describes getting to a clinic one cold Monday morning.

We arrived at the clinic after a three-and-a-half-mile walk. My three daughters and I walked in thinking, "At last, the warmth of a heater." As I walked up to the counter, being only ten minutes late for my appointment, the receptionist told me, "Your appointment will be one month from today. Next time, be on time." As tears rolled down my eyes I tried to explain that I had absolutely no transportation. She just shut the window. I felt devastated. I just wanted to die. I had to tell my little girls, "Let's go home." As we prepared for the long walk home, a patient who overheard what happened offered to give us a ride home.

Of course, not everyone in these clinics is rude. Many people who work in such facilities are sincerely motivated to help the poor. One nurse describes how she decided to work in a clinic, rather than in private practice, because she felt that the needy are always more thankful.

One day, an old man came into the clinic asking to consult with the doctor. The receptionist told him he couldn't be seen without an appointment. He became very fearful and frustrated, exclaiming, "But I'm in pain." The receptionist just dismissed him, calling out, "Next."

I couldn't help myself. I had to step in. I said "Come on in, sir." The doctor found that he was having early signs of a heart attack. He was immediately rushed to the hospital, where there was proper equipment to help him.

I never really thought much of what happened until one day I walked in a restaurant where I immediately felt as if everyone was watching me. Then I heard a loud applause and the people invited me over. I saw the old man, his wife, five daughters, three sons, twenty-eight grandchildren, and three great grandchildren, who were there celebrating his ninety-fifth birthday. It was a wonderful feeling.

Often, health care workers who behave rudely are simply responding to stereotypes of the indigent. And, as is unfortunately the case with many stereotypes, a few individuals seem to justify these negative perceptions. There are among the poor, just as there are in the larger population, those who abuse the system.

One student talked to Victor, an emergency medical driver. He described a fifty-year-old woman who used to call them daily, even if just to have her blood pressure checked.

One day she called three times complaining of chest pains. The third time we went we finally transported her to the hospital. They refused to take her seriously. She comes in practically every day with the same complaint and nothing is wrong with her. They just give her an EKG and send her home. Since her Medicare was revoked, however, we have not heard much from her.

In an effort to screen such cases, however, hospitals may shut out those truly in need. Victor continues, describing what he saw in one hospital.

After one busy day, we were waiting for some information. The emergency room clerk was registering a patient to be seen by the doctor. I noticed he reached into a drawer and pulled out a white name tag. I also noticed there were other, different-colored name tags there.

When I asked him about it, he stated that each color was to let the hospital or the doctor know the patient's pay status. Green tag means one type of insurance. Blue tag means another type. Orange means self-pay, and white means welfare. From then on, I noticed that every person given a white tag waited for the longest time. Some even went home without being seen.

Victor's observations depict an ongoing process that is taking place throughout the United States. It is common to have to wait six to eight hours in a hospital emergency room. Since the 1990s, over a thousand hospitals and eleven hundred emergency rooms have closed due to increasing costs and a lack of health care providers. The situation is compounded by increasing numbers of uninsured people who visit emergency rooms instead of going first to primary care physicians.[20]

Crossing the Border for Health Care

While the South Texas border area is a region characterized by poverty and limited health options for many residents, this area also provides alternative forms of health care. Many border residents, such as the woman whose story follows, have learned to use the Mexican medical system when their own community's care is out of reach.

One day my seven-year-old son got sick and I took him to a doctor here. He examined my son in less than five minutes and wrote a prescription. For these few minutes he charged me $45. For a person that earns what I earn, $45 is a lot of money. When my son continued to be sick, I took him to Mexico to see a doctor there. He also examined him and prescribed medication. The two doctors did the same thing, but the difference was that the U.S. doctor charged me $45 and the doctor in Mexico only charged me $15. That is why I always go across the border now to consult doctors.

Migrant farmworkers sometimes find that the health care they receive in Mexico and in the northern states where they work is superior to that which they receive in South Texas. Francisco Perez is a fifty-five-year-old migrant worker who has been going to the same farm in Michigan for ten years. He reports that things are very good for them in Michigan.

> There are nice clinics for me and my family that provide inexpensive health care. Things are different for us here in the Valley, though. During the off-season, I work at odd jobs as a self-employed carpenter. Sometimes there is not much work, so we have little money for health care. So we go to a doctor in Mexico. There have been times that I couldn't afford to pay even him. When I can't, he lets me do odd jobs in exchange for his services for me and my family.

Other Mexican-origin respondents report greater difficulties accessing medical facilities when working as migrant farmers, mainly because they are not familiar with the services in the regions they go to and they have limited knowledge of English. These factors greatly limit their use of preventive medical services. If doctors refuse to see them unless they are insured, many wait until a situation becomes an emergency and hospital emergency rooms have to take them. Hispanics in the U.S. make use of emergency rooms twice as frequently as do non-Hispanics,[21] in large part, we propose, because of their difficulty in accessing other services.

Even families in which both parents are employed may find medical services in Texas out of reach. Thelma and her husband are both employed. However, they still find it difficult to ever have any money available to pay medical bills.

Thelma reports that her place of employment finally got a group health insurance plan for her and the family. It came about four months too late. Thelma was working one day and received a phone call from her mother saying that the youngest daughter was extremely ill. After Thelma's child had been diagnosed, the doctor suggested that she immediately be taken to the hospital.

Lacking money and knowing their insurance would not cover the child's condition, Thelma and her husband decided to have their daughter admitted to a hospital in Reynosa, Mexico. Thelma could only hope that the care her daughter would receive in the Mexican hospital would be as good as the care that she would have received here in Texas.

Arturo Heredia is also employed full-time. He earns $900 a month. Although his company provides health care insurance for him, it would cost

Arturo $120 per month to add his wife and child to the plan. They simply cannot afford this expense. Arturo's wife, Ester, works as a record keeper in a nearby auto parts store. She works for a few cents over minimum wage and receives no health care benefits. During the winter, their son stays sick with chronic bronchitis. Ester takes him over to Mexico for shots every week and pays about $5 a visit. Ester is not satisfied with the health care her son receives in Mexico, but she knows of no alternative to her family's dilemma.

In some cases, the decision to seek medical attention in Mexico is not based entirely upon finding cheaper care there. Vilma recently had an experience with Mexican medical care that was quite positive.

> Our parents are not rich, but we're not that poor. We can afford health care in the Valley, but doctors from a hospital here in McAllen suggested we go to Monterrey [Mexico] when I needed heart surgery. I was scared. I knew this was going to be a very delicate operation.
>
> I always thought medicine anywhere in the United States was more advanced. The doctors from the McAllen hospital told my parents, though, that doctors in Monterrey were more experienced, the operation was going to be cheaper, and that I had a better chance to survive. They said that in Monterrey heart surgeries are performed almost every day, while they do them only occasionally here in the Valley. I was treated very well there and the operation was successful.

Unfortunately, some people don't have such positive experiences with hospitals in Mexico. Raquel is the mother of one daughter and says that she would die rather than trust medical care in Mexico again.

> One afternoon, my aunt was extremely ill. Having no money and no insurance, she had no alternative but to go to the hospital in Mexico. After being admitted, she was told she needed to go into surgery. While in surgery, she was given a blood transfusion. The blood, it turned out, was contaminated. After a few hours, she died. The hospital told my family that the cause of death was "complications." There was nothing we could do.

As these accounts show, the quality of the health care system in Mexico varies enormously from place to place. Horn describes it as "two contrasting pictures of health status and two contrasting patterns of healthcare. On the one hand is an urban-industrial society affected by chronic and degenerative diseases cared for by hospital-based, technological, curative services, and on the other is a rural and slum society where nutritional and infectious diseases predominate."[22]

Even though the system varies greatly in Mexico, health care there is considered a fundamental human right. Forty percent of Mexicans have access to their Social Security system [Seguro Social] or to clinics of the Health Ministry. Health care in the U.S., in contrast, is seen as a privilege. Some areas of the U.S., like South Texas, lack facilities for the uninsured indigent population.[23] This deficiency is compounded by the fact that 40 percent of the children of immigrants in Texas have no health insurance and 50 percent of these children are in families that report difficulty in affording food.[24] This prompts many Mexican-origin people (and even some non-Hispanics) to seek health care in Mexico. At least 15 percent of Mexican Americans seek the care of Mexican doctors and dentists.[25]

Traditional Health Care Practices and Practitioners

One day I saw my mother massaging my little niece's abdomen with olive oil. I asked her what she was doing and she responded that my little niece was complaining of abdominal pain, that she had eaten something that made her sick. She said that my little niece was *empachada* [bloated]. When I asked her where she had learned this remedy, she said she had learned it from her mother. My mother said that this remedy was very old. She explained to me that back in those days people lived out in the country and it was very hard to travel a long distance to consult a doctor and sometimes people did not have money to pay for medical services. This is the reason why sometimes people would learn home remedies. My grandmother also taught my mother to make herbal tea for a cough. This tea is made with orange tree leaves and honey. Many home remedies that my mother makes for us when we are sick were learned from her mother, and her mother learned them from her mother. These remedies were passed on from generation to generation.

Those unable to afford health care in Mexico or in Texas often rely on various forms of folk healing. The term "folk healing" refers to the use of culturally known herbs and remedies that are either self-administered or obtained from a folk healer.[26] Folk healing consists of a variety of *remedios caseros* [home remedies], folk health care practitioners, and cultural beliefs about the causes of various ailments. Many households in South Texas use these home remedies to deal with minor aches and pains. They include mint for an upset stomach, chamomile baths to calm the nerves, and aloe vera for burns.[27] Most of these remedies were brought from Mexico and have endured for generations.

When families themselves are insufficiently familiar with the application of culturally based cures, some turn to traditional health care practitioners, such as *curanderos* [folk healers], *parteras* [midwives], and hierberos [those who sell herbs]. They do so despite the opposition of many doctors to such practices and practitioners. However, a few physicians admit these unconventional cures may provide some limited benefits.

For example, one local doctor, Dr. Cantú, said, "I personally don't see anything wrong with most teas or herbs, as long as my patients also take what I prescribe. In fact, I used to take the teas before I became a doctor. I was delivered by a *partera* [midwife]. I still occasionally drink tea made from *manzanilla* [chamomile] leaves. It is good on the stomach."

We will begin this section by describing a range of health care practices brought from Mexico. This includes the use of curanderos, traditional herbs (especially those sold in *hierberías*, or folk pharmacies), and folk illnesses (such as *mal de ojo* and *susto*).

Curanderos

Curanderos are folk healers, generally regarded as having a special, magical gift of healing. They treat individuals with physical as well as traditional and spiritual illnesses.[28] *Curanderismo* is a system of folk medicine that includes rituals, herbal remedies, prayers, and spiritual states of consciousness practiced within communities with long-established Native American, Mexican, and Catholic traditions.[29] Curanderismo is based on the belief that good health results from a positive equilibrium with forces for good and healing ceremonies designed to promote physical, spiritual, and mental healing.[30]

Don Julio is a sixty-one-year-old curandero who immigrated to the United States from Mexico. He tells the following story:

> Several years ago, when I lived in Mexico, an elderly man from the village came to me in the middle of the night with bad pain from arthritis. I woke up to the sound of him knocking at my door. His wife, who accompanied him, explained that her husband could not sleep because of the incredible pain in his bones. I gave him a *barrida* [sweeping] with a lemon from head to toe. This calmed some of his pain, and I asked him to come back for some more *barridas* in the days that followed. After he left, I could not go back to sleep, so I lit up some candles and began to pray for my patients.

The term "curandero"—literally, "one who cures"—has special significance among many people of Mexican origin. Though folk healers date back to pre-Columbian times, they may still be found in most rural societies.[31] Even in some parts of the United States, certain individuals are regarded as having a gift of healing.[32] Indeed, the National Institute of Health, Office of Alternative Medicine, estimates that anywhere from 70 to 90 percent of human health care worldwide is based on traditional health practices, rather than interventions administered by practitioners with a Western biomedical orientation.[33]

> Immigrants from Mexico may bring these beliefs with them. Many still believe, for example, in El Niño Fidencio, a famous curandero who lived in the small town of Espinazo, Nuevo Leon (about one hundred miles from the South Texas border). He began practicing his gifts of healing in the early twentieth century, shortly after the Mexican Revolution, and soon became famous throughout Mexico. Thousands of people came to him for cures, including President Calles of Mexico. Fidencio often performed surgeries with a piece of glass and a sewing needle, though most of his healing utilized other methods, including having people sit in a swing and take a mud bath. His fame became so great that demand for his services sometimes necessitated his going days without sleep. Fidencio literally died of exhaustion in 1938 at the age of forty.[34]

Many current folk healers continue to invoke the name and powers of El Niño Fidencio. One such healer has even erected a shrine in Edinburg,

Texas, to this healer. Additionally, many hierberías sell Niño Fidencio candles to carry on his powers.

While some people of Mexican ancestry cross the border to visit curanderos in Mexico, there have also been curanderos of some renown on the Texas side. One of the most famous was Don Pedro Jaramillo, who was deeply respected and loved during his lifetime. Although he died at the age of seventy-seven in 1907, his name and reputation are widely recognized and respected in South Texas and elsewhere in the United States. That he never charged for his work and even donated much of the money he received to help the local community is partly responsible for his veneration. A shrine to his memory can be found just outside of Falfurrias, seventy miles north of the border. Some curanderos still claim to draw on his powers.[35]

One local curandero, Don Juan, claims that his power was given to him by the Lord himself:

> This power came to me through a beautiful dream. He [Jesus] stretched out his arms and touched me and said, "Juan, the time has come for you to fulfill why you are in this earth. You are here to help those who are in need of cures, and with this I want you to help them." As soon as he touched me, I woke up from my dream, determined to help those who are in need.

Though often repudiated by the Catholic Church, many curanderos incorporate a host of religious beliefs and practices into their cures. Sr. Hernandez, another local curandero, has a certificate hanging on the wall that reads, "Dr. Ignacio Hernandez," though it is definitely not a medical degree. People of all ages come to him for advice on health, marriage, family, crime—whatever their problem happens to be.

Like many curanderos, Mr. Hernandez has no set schedule of fees but instead accepts donations (including goods) for his services. His number one recommendation is always faith in God. In front of his desk is a stack of cards and small bottles of lotions and herbs, surrounded by several religious statues of varying size. Mr. Hernandez professes a lot of faith in these items. He explains:

> Sure, we sometimes need doctors to obtain a prescription, but my faith in God is my cure. What I do for treatments for myself for the stroke I suffered is to make a tea of arnica and give myself some

> heating pad treatments. When people come in with a problem, I listen to them or I recommend a particular tea. Praying is what will make them feel better.

People have many reasons for visiting curanderos. Some simply cannot afford a doctor. Others use a curandero as a last resort, after medical treatments have failed to bring relief. Others are motivated by a sense of hopelessness and alienation regarding modern medicine. They may prefer the more personal and religious treatment they believe curanderos provide. High degrees of familism are also linked to the use of folk medicine.[36] Probably the main reason many South Texas Hispanics consult a curandero, however, is cost. Most of these healers do not charge a set fee, allowing patents to pay whatever they can.

Their work, however, generates considerable suspicion. Don Temo, for example, frequently runs into opposition from some people in his community.

> I used to attend mass every Sunday. One Sunday, shortly after I was married, I attended a mass. As it ended, on our way out, we shook the priest's hand as usual. He whispered in my ear that he had heard that I was a curandero. I told him, "Yes, yes I am. Why?" "Well, curanderos work for evil," he said. I explained that I help the less fortunate people, giving help to those who can't afford doctors. But he was stubborn in believing that my work was evil.

People commonly seek out curanderos ostensibly to help with physical ailments. The assistance, however, is often as much spiritual as physical. Various physical complaints are attributed to *sustos*, or fright, for example. Many people of Mexican origin believe that intense fright can lead to the soul's escape from the body. Hence, a spiritual cure seems to be required.

Curanderos are also consulted for help with other problems. Paula, an elementary school teacher in her mid-thirties, got married when she was only seventeen years old. Her husband was notorious for his womanizing. One day he ran off with a woman to another state.

Paula was devastated and wanted him back—no matter what. She consulted a curandero who recommended she use a breakup candle. It was to be lit and have the names of her husband and the other woman on the bottom.

"When the candle was all burned up," she says, "my husband and his mistress were supposed to break up. The curandero also told me to put the names of my husband and the other lady on a piece of paper and stick it in an ant hole. I did these things, plus many others, to get my husband back. He was gone for about ten years. Then all of a sudden he showed up. As a result, I believe very strongly in curanderos and still go to see one often."

Roberta also places great confidence in curanderos. Her husband was nearly incarcerated for several years after getting caught with drugs. When she went to a curandero, he told her to put three peppers on a piece of paper in her purse during her husband's court hearing. "Ever since that day," she says, "he has never been in trouble with the law again."

Others, like Roberta, have very positive stories regarding curanderos to relate. Celina recalls her experience when she was twenty-five and was very lonely.

I had failed many times at relationships and employment. I had just about given up on everything when my cousin told me about this old lady curandera in Mexico. When we got there I was so surprised to see a lot of people there. There were at least ten or fifteen waiting to see her.

When my turn came to enter the curandera's room, it was all dark with a lot of candles and religious pictures. She told me to write my name on a piece of paper. Then she asked how she could help me. I told her that I wanted a steady job and boyfriend. She recommended that I go out and buy some powders and perfumes sold in hierberías. I did so, and within two months I was so happy because I had a good job and had met a very nice guy.

Positive impressions of curanderos may result from the apparent success of their interventions when doctors and other help systems have failed. Tina describes her family's experience when they were living in Corpus Christi in the late 1960s.

My mother was pregnant and we knew that something was terribly wrong. She had given birth to six children before, but this time it was different. She had a very high fever and was shaking and shivering uncontrollably. Finally, late that night she gave birth.

Afterward, she didn't get any better. She was taken to doctors several times, but they could find nothing wrong. Finally, my aunt came over and got her out of bed, dressed her, and took her to a curandera.

The lady told my mother that her illness was *mal puesto*, a hex put on her by an envious neighbor. The curandera placed my mom on the floor, made a cross out of palm tree branches, swept her with a broom, and recited many prayers. Then she gave my aunt some teas to brew.

Four days later my mom was well. She began to eat, got her strength back, and her eyesight cleared up. My mom had never been to a curandera before and she hasn't gone to one since, but she has always been more accepting of them since then.

Not everyone has such positive stories to tell. Carlos Almaguer describes his situation about five months prior to his interview.

I became very ill and had to go to the family doctor. He did some tests on me but found nothing wrong. I told him that I had stomach pains and threw up almost every day, so he gave me some pills to take and I went home.

The medication didn't seem to help with the pain, so I consulted another doctor. Like the previous doctor, he didn't find anything wrong with me and just gave me Tylenol. Again, I didn't seem to have any change and the pains kept getting worse.

Finally, my mother suggested that I go to a curandero to see if he could help. I went to see him and he gave me some type of herbs for my stomach. Those made me feel even worse, and I finally went to a doctor who was a stomach specialist. He found amoebas in my stomach and told me that the herbs had caused more harm to my body. From that day on, visiting a curandero for an illness is out of the question for me.

Interestingly, such negative results do not always cause people to abandon their belief in curanderos. Another student interviewed his father, who told him, "You know Mama and how she believes in that stuff. One time she almost killed you."

Remembering the incident, the student says, "I had hepatitis when I was eleven. My mother took me to a curandero and he gave me some kind of tea. He prayed over me and did some kind of ritual. This went on for two weeks. My father finally got tired of the curandero and took me to Dr. Garza. He was the one who told me I had hepatitis and put me in the hospital. I could have died. I probably would have if my mother had continued to take me to the curandero. To this day, though, she still believes in them. She'll never stop."

Changing Beliefs

People of Mexican origin in South Texas seem deeply divided over the efficacy of curanderos. Most trust conventional medicine, though a significant number still hold to beliefs that illnesses and health are strongly influenced by spiritual and otherworldly factors.[37] Josefa, a fifty-nine-year-old curandera, has seen the demand for her services decline as the old beliefs fade.

> Money is not important to me, but service to my community is. In the past several years, the number of patients I see has gone down from around twenty-five to ten a day. I recently lost one of my favorite patients to modern medicine. I don't blame her. She had cancer and only modern treatment could ease her pain.

We asked our respondents who favored curanderos if they hid this belief from people who did not know them well. Men tended to say they would not volunteer such information but would not deny it if asked. On the other hand, many of the women admitted that they would hide this part of their lives from people they did not know well. One woman, Rosa, answered, "Yes, I would hide it because people think you're crazy. They don't believe and they laugh at you."

Sometimes even a positive experience with a curandero is not enough to make people believe. Marina is twenty-one years old. Several years ago, her little brother fell in a pool and almost drowned. "After that occasion," she says, "he was very afraid of the water. He wouldn't take baths or go swimming. My mother took him to see a curandera, who gave my brother some kind of tea and performed a ritual to help him get over his fear of water. I look back on it now and I really don't think it mattered. It still took him a long time to get over his fear. It's just another custom that my parents believe very strongly in and I don't."

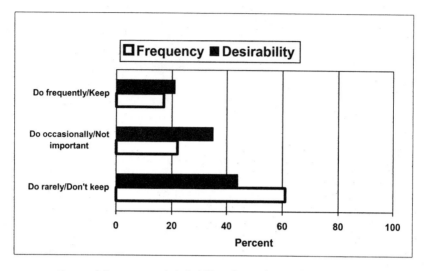

FIG. 1.1. Reported frequency and desirability of use of curanderos among South Texas Hispanics

Roberto Guzman's faith in curanderos, if he ever had any, disappeared when he was young. "When I was in high school," he explains, "I tore a ligament in my knee, and my dad took me to a curandero. I was so mad. I needed surgery, not a curandero!"

In our Cultural Practices Survey (of 433 Hispanic individuals), we included questions about how frequently respondents visited a curandero when doctors did not seem to help. We also asked them whether they felt this practice should be kept. With respect to the frequency of their participation in this practice, people could answer that they (and their family and neighbors) did it frequently, occasionally, or rarely/never. The question about how important it was to keep the custom gave them the choices of saying they would keep the custom, believed that it really did not matter, or did not want to keep the custom. Responses to both of these questions are shown in Figure 1.1.

As Figure 1.1 indicates, a rather small percentage of respondents indicated either a practice of using curanderos or a desire to keep the custom (17 and 21 percent, respectively). Over 60 percent said they rarely or never practiced this custom, and 44 percent said the custom should not be kept. So, while the use of curanderos is a custom often associated with Mexican culture in South Texas, the percentage of people who practice it or want to keep it appears to be quite small.[38]

Ceremonies to Cure *Susto*

One of the afflictions that curanderos most often cure is *susto*, or fright. It is a condition believed to arise from some traumatic experience that causes one's spirit to leave the body.[39] Symptoms are thought to include anorexia, insomnia, hallucinations, weakness, and pain.[40] When someone is afflicted with susto, folk healers generally have them lie down on the floor with arms outstretched in the form of a cross. The body is then swept with leafy branches. Herbs are administered and prayers may be recited to coax the lost spirit to reenter the person's body.[41]

While curanderos are often called upon to cure susto, other individuals often perform the curing ceremony. Alicia, for example, grew up seeing neighbors and family members cure susto. "I recall an old lady in our neighborhood," she says, "who would 'sweep' our bodies with wild flowers of some sort while reciting prayers as she went through a bunch of motions whenever we had been scared and had jittery feelings." Nora describes an experience that she had with susto and its cure when she was only seven years old.

> I had a little pet bunny, Adelita, that was getting old and sick. My neighbor said she was going to die sooner or later. One day, while playing outside, I saw my neighbor grab my bunny and take her to the tool shed, where he killed her.
>
> I got so scared that I ran to my room and started to cry. Later that night I was called to dinner. I was told that what we were going to eat was chicken with *mole* [a spicy sauce]. When we were through eating, my family admitted that it wasn't really chicken but my pet, Adelita.
>
> On top of seeing Adelita get killed, I found out I had eaten her too. I got sick for several days, and my parents brought someone to help me. She rubbed my body with a stone they call *piedra de alumbre*. I was cured, but I never trusted my neighbor again.

The Cultural Practices Survey described earlier included one item about healing susto, again asking respondents to describe how frequently they engaged in this practice and how they felt about keeping the practice. The results to both questions are reported in Figure 1.2. The results shown in this figure reveal a pattern similar to that described in relation to the use of curanderos. The percentages of respondents who frequently practiced

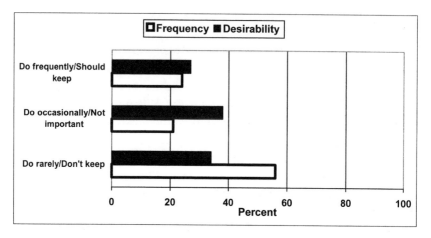

FIG. 1.2. Reported frequency and desirability of use of certain ceremonies to cure susto among South Texas Hispanics

it and/or wanted to keep it is smaller than the percentages who said they rarely or never practiced it and who thought it should not be kept.

Touching Child to Prevent Ojo

We found a very different pattern of responses among Hispanics in South Texas regarding *ojo*, another folk ailment. *Ojo*,—also called *mal de ojo*, meaning illness caused by the eye—is believed to be caused by someone with a powerful gaze who casts an admiring glance at a child, or in some cases, an object. If the gaze is not followed by a touch, the person or thing admired will be negatively affected. The effects on a child might include insomnia, aches and pains, excessive crying, fever, severe headache, or restlessness.[42]

Children are seen as particularly susceptible to ojo. As a result, it is common for Hispanics of South Texas to touch any child they admire. Many Anglos moving to the area soon discover that they too may be expected to touch children they admire to avoid bringing harm to the little one. Babies are often gently touched, generally on the head, to prevent them from getting sick from ojo.

Mal de ojo is often translated as "evil eye," giving the impression of intentional harm. In reality, most of our respondents saw it, not as the result of evil intentions, but of strong powers transmitted through an admiring glance. In some cases, admiration may be equated with envy, thus creating the association with evil. People who are suspected of having caused ojo are often sought out to come touch the child so that the damage will be repaired. Some parents even expect admirers to make the sign of the cross in addition to touching the child.[43] Felipe, one of the people interviewed, explains his own experience with this practice.

> I was six years old and was at my sister's tenth birthday party. We were playing around when the lady came to my sister to give her a gift. She told my sister how pretty she looked in her birthday dress and left the house without touching her.
>
> My mom came up to us to tell us that it was time to cut the cake. She then asked what the lady had told my sister. We told my mother and she left in an instant trying to find the lady.
>
> That night my sister grew ill with a fever and a rash. My mom finally found the lady and told her that she had given my sister the evil eye. The lady came as soon as possible and touched my sister and apologized to my mother. After that, my sister's fever and rash disappeared.

Don Juanito, a curandero for twenty-five years, describes how to cure ojo in children.

> If the person who caused the ojo cannot be found to come and touch the child, then a cure must be administered. This is done by having the child lie down and sweeping him three times with an unbroken raw egg. While sweeping, the healer recites the Apostle's Creed three times, making sure he sweeps the front and back of the child.
>
> The egg is cracked and dropped into a glass of water to examine the yolk. Then the glass is placed under the head of the child's bed to draw out the evil force. The next morning, the egg must be buried.[44]

The admiring eyes of some individuals are regarded as being especially potent. Rachel recalls believing that her grandmother always had a powerful eye.

> I remember once when my grandmother admired one of my cousins who was playing around, laughing and smiling. Minutes

later, my cousin felt very sick, with a massive headache and fever. When my grandmother found out about her condition, she simply walked up to her and touched her face and hair. I couldn't believe what happened just minutes later. Her fever and headache immediately went away, and within minutes she was running and playing again.

Some people believe that ojo affects animals as well as children. Pablo remembers one day when he and his family were coming out of church. "There was this beautiful horse just across the street," he recalls. "I walked over to where it was and tried to touch him, but the horse moved away. We went home and about three hours later the owner of the horse called. He told us the horse was dying. We all went back and I rubbed him with some ointment. The horse was up and around the following day. This was the 'evil eye' I had given the horse."

Not everyone, of course, believes in ojo. Some believe in the condition but do not believe in the remedy described earlier by the curandero. One woman, for example, said, "Ojo is real, but I don't believe that the rebuking ceremony done with an egg is what takes ojo away. It's the prayer that's done in this ceremony that works to heal the sick person."

Among local Hispanics, there are many who do not believe in ojo and others who are not sure whether to believe or not. It is hard to find anyone, however, who has not had an experience with it. Patricia describes one event that happened about ten years ago.

My sister, Gloria, had a daughter who was seven years old. She suddenly came down with a fever and stomachache. Gloria had taken her to the doctor the day before. He had told her that it was some kind of virus and that the medication would take three days to have an effect.

My mother told Gloria that she would like to try to cure her granddaughter with an egg, to see if it was mal de ojo. My sister told my mom, "You know I don't believe in those things." My mother asked her granddaughter, Lori, if she minded if she tried. Lori said she did not.

My mother got a warm egg and proceeded with the ritual praying of Our Father and other Catholic prayers. Lori fell asleep and Gloria carried her to the car, then home. The next day she called

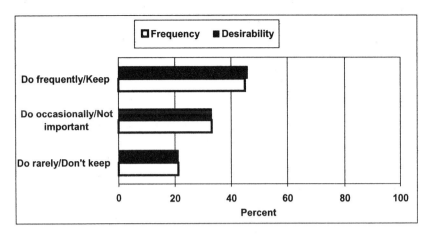

FIG. 1.3. Reported frequency and desirability of belief in ojo among South Texas Hispanics

my mom, astonished, saying that just a couple of hours after leaving my mother's, Lori had completely recovered. After this Gloria often brought her daughters to my mom whenever they had a sudden, unexplained fever.

Other South Texas Hispanics, however, remain skeptical of ojo. Anastacio, for example, says, "I grew up with my aunts and grandma being into all [those] superstitious beliefs. I was never into that kind of stuff. I would hear all about it, but that was it. I recall my grandma rubbing our bodies with a raw egg. She would then break the egg in a glass. If the yolk came out black, then it meant that someone had done ojo to us."

Using the Cultural Practices Survey, we sought to determine how frequently people practiced beliefs associated with ojo. We additionally measured how strongly they felt about the practice by asking them if they thought it should be kept, forgotten, or it really did not matter. The results of this analysis are presented in Figure 1.3.

Figure 1.3 demonstrates that a rather large percentage (45 percent) of people frequently practice beliefs related to ojo. In addition, the portion of respondents believing ojo ought to be preserved as part of their culture (46 percent) is also large. Indeed, nearly half of the 433 people who were surveyed said they frequently practiced it *and* thought it ought to be kept.

Traditional Herbs for Illnesses

Another practice that still enjoys widespread acceptance is that of using traditional herbs for illnesses or injuries. Josefa remembers these traditional remedies and the part they played in her life.

> Whenever we would get a cut, we'd run to an abandoned building and grab some spiderwebs to place on the cut to keep it from getting infected. My mother used a little bit of *ruda* [rue] and warm olive oil to cure earaches. It always felt so good when dropped into the ear. I still use *manzanilla* [chamomile] leaves to smooth a baby's colicky stomach. I have to admit I am a bit hesitant to use the ear remedy on my baby. I guess I'm hesitant because I can afford to go to a doctor.

Many of those who use traditional herbal remedies purchase these products in hierberías. One owner of a hierbería describes the type of products he sells.

> I work with herbs every day. For example, *mariquilla*, or goldenrod as it is known in English, helps cure diabetes. However, people with diabetes who drink this tea still need to seek medical help and follow proper diets. Some don't and then come back to me angry, claiming the tea doesn't work. People need to be careful using these products. Some herbs can poison you if you don't use them properly.[45] All the dried herbs I sell in my store, however, are safe for the general public. The ones that people pick out in the fields can be dangerous. One of my favorite plants is aloe vera. I call it my magic plant. It helps with burns, cuts, insect bites, and when brewed into a tea, it will clear up stomach troubles. Anyone can grow this plant at home, and it is very safe. Still, herbs are not a cure-all and my best advice is to combine herbs with common sense, sound medical advice, and a healthy lifestyle.

Some people fail to heed such advice. One hierbería owner, for example, remembers a case when he was blamed for overreliance on the *hierbas* [herbs] he sells. "One lady," he says, "had a bad ulcer. She asked what she could take for it. I told her of a tea that another lady had been using. She claimed that her doctor had found no trace of the ulcer after she had used the tea for a year. She quickly bought a monthlong supply of this tea. A few weeks later her son came by quite angry, claiming that his mother was in the hospital and that it was my fault. She apparently had given up any medical treatment other than the tea."

Because some hierbería owners themselves overly hype their products, the U.S. Food and Drug Administration occasionally checks on them. One student who conducted interviews with owners of hierberías found initial hesitation because some owners thought he looked like an FDA agent. "In fact," he says, "one shop in McAllen closed as soon as I walked in. The man said that he could not talk to me because he had to go out of town. Three hours later, I passed by his hierbería and he was open. Later, a lady who owned another hierbería explained to me why that had happened."

An overreliance on herbs to cure health problems may stem as much from poverty as from personal belief in the efficacy of traditional remedies. "A lot of times after I have closed the hierbería and have gone to bed," says one shop owner, "I have people who come to my home and get me out of bed because they need a certain herb for a baby or an elderly person who is sick. I will get up and give them what they need, even if they don't have any money to pay me for it."

Other people use hierberías because they are dissatisfied with doctors. "I really believe in taking herbs," said one woman. "I have been taking them for years. Even though I have Medicare, I don't like to go to doctors. They make you wait for hours, and when they see you it's only for two minutes. The doctor listens to your breathing, your heart, and then prescribes some medicine. They charge a lot of money and don't make you feel any better."

Some who are affluent and can afford conventional treatments simply prefer traditional remedies. "I sell to the rich the same as the poor," said one hierbería owner. "See that bank [across the street from his store]? A lot of my customers come from there. In fact, I get attorneys and bankers, as well as homeless people."

Some hierbería owners claim that in recent years they have been selling products to people other than those of Mexican origin. Mr. Zarate reports that about 80 percent of his clients are Mexican or Mexican American, 15 percent are Anglos, and 5 percent are Black. "It is mostly the older Whites that come in here," he says. "Many of them are retired Winter Texans who have heard of the herbs and want to try them." Another owner

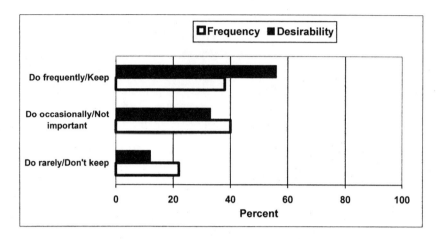

FIG. 1.4. Reported frequency and desirability of use of traditional herbs among South Texas Hispanics

said that the Winter Texans who come to her are looking for something for stomach problems and diabetes. "They are even starting to try the candles," she says.

Figure 1.4 depicts the frequency with which our 433 survey respondents claimed they used herbs for traditional cures. It also shows how these people felt about maintaining this practice as part of their culture. Figure 1.4 shows strong acceptance of traditional herbs, both in relation to the reported frequency of use and the desire to keep this aspect of culture. Indeed, 56 percent of those surveyed said they wanted to keep the practice.

Manzanilla Tea for Stomach Problems

One traditional herb that enjoys widespread acceptance among local Hispanics is *manzanilla* [chamomile] tea—recall Dr. Cantú's approval of manzanilla tea described a few pages back. Many Valley residents of Mexican origin swear by the medicinal properties of manzanilla tea. A mother explained, "My first baby used to have a lot of colic. I asked my mother for help, because nothing could stop him from crying. She boiled some manzanilla and gave it to him. It seemed to help calm him down, so I have used it with the rest of my babies. I thank my mother for showing me the benefits of manzanilla tea."

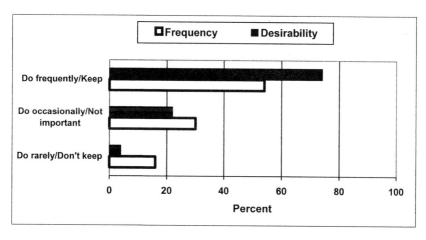

FIG. 1.5. Reported frequency and desirability of use of manzanilla tea among South Texas Hispanics

The results of our survey items dealing with manzanilla tea are presented in Figure 1.5. They show a very high level of practice and acceptance of this herb among our Mexican-origin respondents. Indeed, 54 percent said that it was frequently used in their family and neighborhood and 74 percent of respondents said it should be kept as part of Hispanic culture.

Comparing the Desirability and Durability of Mexican Health Care Practices

Up to this point, we have examined these health-related cultural practices individually. Now, let's look at them together, comparing the frequency with which they are practiced against the professed desire that a sample of the population of Mexican origin in South Texas manifested to either maintain the practices as part of their culture or to forget them. Figure 1.6 provides such a comparison, taking the first set of bars ("Do Frequently/Keep") from each of the preceding five figures.

This comparison reveals that some of the preceding health-related practices are much more popular than others. Apparently, the most popular is using manzanilla tea for stomach problems. Since we find that even an occasional doctor recommends it, this might appear to be a fairly safe practice for many respondents. There is little danger of disapproval from as-

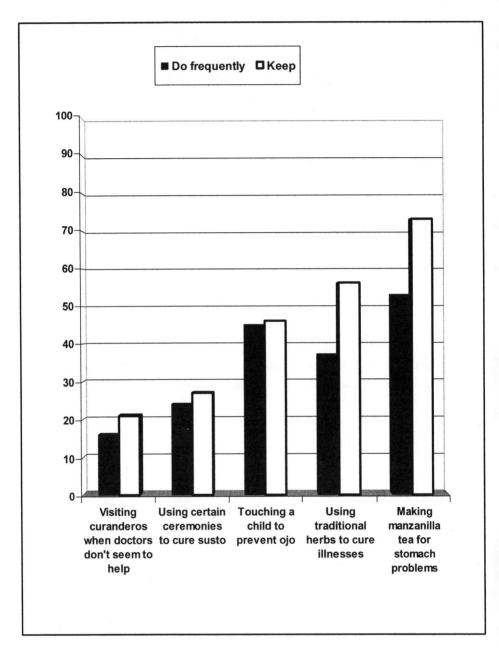

FIG. 1.6. Percent South Texas respondents who said they frequently practice, and desire to keep, certain health-related practices

sociates or being embarrassed if others find out the tea is being used. The same would appear to be true of the use of other traditional herbs. Thirty-eight percent of respondents reported that they frequently followed this practice, while 56 percent said it should be kept as part of their culture.

One custom that slightly less than half (45 percent) of respondents reported frequently practicing is touching a child one admires to prevent ojo. About the same percentage (46 percent) said it should be kept. The reported frequency of this practice is roughly similar to that of using manzanilla tea and other traditional herbs, yet the desire to keep it is somewhat lower. We could hypothesize that while many individuals believe in touching an admired child or animal and frequently do so, at least some of these people might feel some embarrassment about the practice, particularly since it is not a part of the dominant Anglo culture.

Indeed, as the distance of any practice from the dominant culture gets larger, the use and acceptance of it seems to diminish. June Macklin found, for example, that the acceptance of folk medicine practices varies from generation to generation and is related to the degree to which Anglo American culture has been assimilated.[46] Less than a quarter of participants in our survey reported frequently utilizing the services of curanderos or conducting ceremonies to cure susto. We also found that the percentage of those who said they wanted to keep these practices was about the same as the percentage who said they practiced them (see Fig. 1.6).

This by itself, of course, does not demonstrate a move toward the assimilation of contemporary medical practices. In order to determine whether these practices are being abandoned, we would need to see how their use changes over several generations in the United States. After calculating a mean generation score, we conducted an analysis of variance on each to see how much change each would undergo with increasing time in the United States. This analysis is presented in Figure 1.7.

This analysis yields some interesting findings. All but one of the health-related cultural practices shows a significant relation to the mean generation score. As the graph demonstrates, people who reported frequently using each practice have a lower mean generation score (which indicates the number of generations their family has been in the U.S.) than those who said they occasionally used them. Those who said they rarely or never used them have even higher generation scores, showing that the frequency of these practices seems to drop significantly with each generation in the United States.

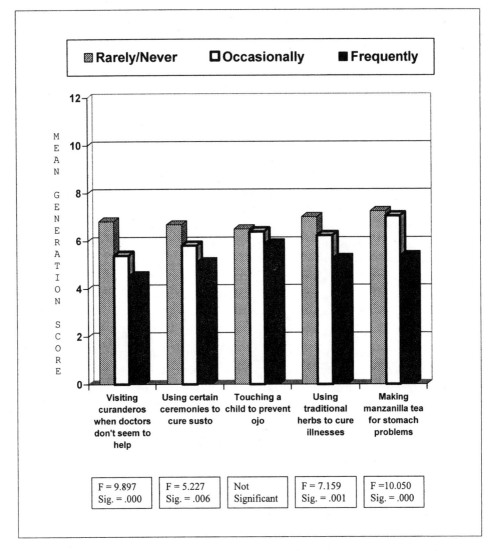

FIG. 1.7. Relation of mean generation score to frequency of practicing selected health-related practices among South Texas Hispanics

With each of these practices, the stronger this association (or the higher the F-score), the more likely the process of acculturation is working to reduce the frequency of utilization. The customs with the highest measure of association (or F-scores) are making manzanilla tea for stomach problems, visiting curanderos when doctors do not seem to help, and using traditional herbs to cure illnesses. Thus, we would predict that these practices tend to be lost more quickly than those with lower F-scores.

The one variable that did not demonstrate a significant association with the mean generation score was touching a child to prevent ojo. Apparently, this practice is much more resistant to acculturation. Significant numbers of people of Mexican origin in South Texas, even those who are several generations removed from Mexico, seem to maintain fairly strong belief in this practice. While there are many possible reasons for this, we propose that Mexican Americans on the border are more inclined to keep the custom because touching a child one admires is positive even if one does not believe in ojo. Like many Anglos who avoid using the number thirteen whether or not they truly believe it is unlucky, Mexican-origin people may simply be playing it safe (or being polite, like those who say "Bless you!" when someone sneezes).

In addition, touching a child to prevent ojo also does not conflict with standard health practices, as some of the other health-related cultural practices might. Going to a curandero, for example, may involve considerable risk if one chooses a curandero over a doctor. Many people of Mexican origin who choose traditional health care over contemporary medical practices, however, generally do so because conventional health care is too expensive.

Conclusion

Increasingly, medical science is recognizing the importance of belief systems in healing. Recent studies, for example, show that prayer and a commitment to a higher power can help sick people heal faster than not maintaining such beliefs.[47] Thus, even if traditional medical practices are found to have no scientific properties that would enable them to cure a particular disease, the belief that they can, together with the strong family and community bonds that support them, aids the healing process. This point is increasingly acknowledged in programs of psychiatry, holistic medicine, and public health.[48]

This is not to say that the reliance on traditional health care practices will produce greater gains than reliance on conventional medicine. The best results seem to be obtained when conventional medical practitioners try to understand and, where possible, accommodate the beliefs of traditional medical practices and integrate them into their practice. Indeed, most of the people we talked to who utilize traditional medicine do so in concert with their utilization of doctors when they are able to afford them.[49]

Politicians and the medical community also need to take a hard look at why people in South Texas rely on doctors in Mexico and on traditional practitioners. Many simply cannot afford to go to a doctor every time they are sick. Many use prescription drugs from a family member to treat what seems to be the same condition, because the costs of getting and filling a prescription are so prohibitive. When health insurance, doctors, and conventional medicine are outside the means of so many people, we should not be surprised that they turn to less expensive alternatives.

The medical community also needs to examine some of the cultural reasons people of Mexican origin may not utilize their services.[50] Paternalistic or rude treatment by doctors and their staffs, failure to really listen to them and take their concerns seriously, also plays a role in the decision to go outside the medical community in South Texas. One paramedic, for example, says, "Yesterday I took a nursing home patient to see a doctor. Without even putting her in an exam room, he just pulled back the covers, felt around the operation area and said, 'OK, take her back.' All this in about forty-five seconds, and all being paid for by the taxpayers."

Forcing people to use conventional medicine without providing the means and cultural reasons to do so only adds to the medical problems of South Texas. Unless people are treated with dignity and respect, they and their families will seek other alternatives. When the effort is made, however, practitioners find themselves rewarded. This is illustrated by the same paramedic mentioned in the preceding paragraph, who recounts a recent experience with rude, stereotype-laden behavior:

> One day my partner and I went to a run-down house on the south side of town for somebody having seizures. My partner mumbled something about Medicare people. As we entered the house, he did not want to say anything or even shake hands with anyone. He quickly put the patient on the stretcher and moved out to the unit. While I talked with the family to find what happened, I found them to be the nicest and kindest people I have ever met. They were cooperative and well-mannered. My partner, who was all too eager to get this patient off his hands, will never see these people as anything more than "welfare freeloaders."

Other Cultural Beliefs and Practices

WITH ANA LEOS AND MARÍA ISABEL AYALA

Introduction

> The Mexican people here don't have the same customs that we did in Mexico. I stopped celebrating the holidays we used to honor in Veracruz because it's hard to celebrate by yourself. After you've lived here for awhile, you tend to forget to celebrate those days. If you do celebrate, people give you funny looks. I remember celebrating one of our Mexican holidays and everybody was looking at me as if I was insane, even those who are from Mexico. Since then, I haven't celebrated that day anymore.

Ignacio, the Mexican immigrant making this statement, clearly feels he is losing something important. He is especially dismayed that other people with origins in Mexico seem to be forgetting their culture. He is not alone in his concern. Many Mexican immigrants are alarmed when they encounter people with Mexican roots who do not seem to follow practices long associated with Mexican identity.

Culture, of course, includes much more than traditional practices. Most social scientists include beliefs, values, and attitudes as important aspects of culture.[1] Nevertheless, the behavioral aspects are the easiest to observe. As a result, their disappearance will be much more noticeable to people like Ignacio because they can be directly observed.

This loss of traditional cultural practices seems to happen even more quickly north of South Texas, especially in communities with few people of Mexican origin. One young woman who was born in the Rio Grande Valley to Mexican parents was raised in an area of Houston where Anglos predominate. She was interviewed for our Cultural Practices Survey. Her interviewer reports, "Since she returned to the Valley two years ago, some people have teased her about how Anglo she has become. Some even call her a 'coconut,' meaning that she is brown on the outside but white on the inside. When I asked her about several cultural practices, she looked confused. When I asked her if she ate *buñuelos*[fried pastries] for New Year's, for example, she replied, "Buñuelos? What are those? They sound like something that grows on your foot."

Like every immigrant group, Mexicans experience pressures to drop or change many of the cultural practices they learned as children. In part, this is because they encounter strong nationalistic attitudes among some U.S. citizens who believe that immigrants should leave old ways behind and become "American." It is also because many cultural practices are harder to practice in the new environment. Thus, the rapidity or slowness with which immigrants and their descendents drop these traditional practices is a cause of considerable controversy. Often, these issues are debated in the political arena. Many, however, are also the focus of considerable academic debate. These issues, of both political and academic interest, include questions like the following:

—Do the pressures towards assimilation make Mexican culture largely disappear after two or three generations in the United States, or is this culture likely to endure for many generations with only minor changes?
—Does culture uniformly slip away with each generation in the United States, or are some aspects of it much more resistant to change than others?
—Is Mexican American culture just a combination of Mexican and U.S. cultures, or does a new culture emerge unlike either Mexican or U.S. culture?
—Does proximity to Mexico and a large Mexican-origin population ensure cultural survival, or do pressures to assimilate cause changes regardless of the proximity of an ethnic population to its homeland?

Virtually all scholars recognize that cultural change is inevitable. Most of the debate focuses on how this process takes place and how long it takes. Some researchers, for example, see the acculturation of immigrants (when they drop their culture in favor of the host culture) as the predominant process. Others argue that ethnogenesis (the creation of a new culture by combining parts of the new and old cultures, but also adding elements drawn from the new environment) is the dominant process taking place.[2]

The evidence related to cultural practices that we will present in this chapter seems to favor the ethnogenesis model. Let's illustrate. Though Thanksgiving is not an important holiday in Mexico (and certainly not celebrated on the same date as the U.S. celebration), many Mexican Americans in South Texas have adopted Thanksgiving Day as an important time for family celebrations. Many, however, such as Juan Gomez, focus the family gathering around making and eating tamales. He says, "I like these gatherings on Thanksgiving and Christmas because the family is together as one. We are all very close to each other. I think this is very important because I want to be able to share and talk to my children the way my father and mother shared their views with us. It would be nice if more and more families could be as close as our families are."

Thus, the Mexican cultural values on family unity can find expression in new forms, such as celebrating Thanksgiving. As this example illustrates, however, the celebration takes aspects of the culture of each society and combines them into a celebration unlike that found in either the U.S. or Mexico. In some cases, this takes place through the process of *substitution*, or replacing an element of the host culture with one of the immigrants' culture (like celebrating Thanksgiving with tamales instead of turkey). In other cases, the chosen form will be *biculturalism*, or combining both cultures (such as having turkey and tamales served together). In still others, acculturation will proceed along the lines of *integration*, or combining elements of the native culture with elements of the host culture (making turkey tamales, for example).[3]

It is easy to forget that every culture is the product of some degree of previous acculturation. Indeed, Mexican culture is an amalgam of Native American cultures combined with the culture of Spain, and constantly shaped by the Mexican nation that emerged. This is illustrated by the statement of a descendent of Native Americans who inhabited the Texas-Mexico borderlands long before the Spanish came. "To me," he says, "it is important to maintain our customs and traditions from our native land, regardless of the fact that we are in a different area. In my case, my ancestors are Coahuiltecan Indians who practiced several dances and rituals. I remember when I was growing up in Coahuila and my grandfather's brother would teach me his native tongue, as well as the different *danzas* [dances] they performed. Unfortunately, I have lost most of this, since it happened many years ago and the contact I had with *el tío abuelo* [my great-uncle] was scarce. Today, I know that my heritage was not left behind the day I crossed the boundary that separates the United States and Mexico — it's still in my heart, *akitahuali*.

The ethnogenesis approach helps us understand that some of what we call Mexican culture may have its origins on the northern side of the border. Flour tortillas, which are rare in many parts of Mexico, for example, seem to be more a part of Mexican American culture than Mexican. Thus, Mexican-origin people in South Texas may have a culture that is not entirely Mexican in origin. Wherever people have experiences that are unique, they adapt and modify their culture. Sometimes the experience is so unique that neither the old ways nor the ways of the host society are adequate. In such cases, new cultural forms emerge unlike those of either the sending country or the host society.

Cultural Practices as Measures of Acculturation

Many of the people we interviewed also recognize the importance of cultural practices as evidence of either acculturation or maintaining cultural identity. Irma, for example, is a twenty-year-old student who recognizes that she has lost many of the customs or traditions of Mexico. "Maybe it's because I've lived here [in the Valley] all my life," she says, "but I don't know much about the way of life in Mexico. I don't have any relatives in Mexico and I only go over there with my friends to hang out at the Mexican clubs. My parents never really taught us that it's important to know about how our ancestors lived. Maybe that's because both of them and even my grandparents were born and raised in the Valley. We have never believed in curanderos or susto. Also, we've never believed in making *promesas* [promises] to saints for something we really want. I believe that when one is in need of something one should turn to God."

In contrast, Juan is a forty-two-year-old man whose family has also been in the Valley for several generations. He feels that it is very important to hold on to many practices associated with Mexican culture. "I always try to teach my kids a little about our culture," he says. "Once, for example, my daughter in elementary school came home and told me that a little 'Mexican boy' had been picking on her. This really bothered me. Not so much that some boy was picking on her, but that she described him as a 'Mexican boy.' I have a lot to teach my children about who they are and where they come from. It is also very important to me that they keep speaking Spanish. No matter what they may speak with their friends, I always tell them that I prefer that they speak Spanish around the house so they won't forget it."

In this chapter, we will examine what has happened to a variety of specific Mexican cultural practices over succeeding generations as Mexican-origin people live in South Texas. We will show that some are not very widely practiced to begin with, that many disappear rather quickly, and that some are maintained in a form quite different from that brought over by the first generation.

MEASURING CULTURAL PRACTICES

Culture is hard to quantify and to measure. A "static view" of culture regards it as "the distinctive set of beliefs, values, morals, and institutions that people inherit."[4] While these aspects of culture are important, they are hard to measure. Cultural practices, on the other hand, are more directly observable. Measurement involves determining how frequently respondents practice certain behaviors, as well as using more attitudinal measures whose reliability and validity are frequently questionable.[5]

Items for the cultural practices scale used in this study were developed from in-depth ethnographic interviews that preceded the Cultural Practices Survey. From the in-depth interviews, we identified a total of forty-two separate behavioral customs and practices identified with Mexico. As indicated in the previous chapter, the respondents in the Cultural Practices Survey interviews were then asked to indicate the frequency with which they, their friends, and their family practiced each activity, and were offered the response choices of "frequently," "occasionally," and "rarely or never." In addition, respondents were asked to indicate for each item whether they thought the item "should be kept," "should be forgotten," or "it doesn't matter." By this means, we were able to establish a measure of desirability for each practice.[6]

Categories of Cultural Practices in South Texas

After we identified the forty-two specific cultural practices through ethnographic interviews, we broke them down into four separate categories. Those cultural practices concerned with health care and other health-related issues were examined in Chapter 1. In this chapter, we examine cultural practices related to gender roles, interpersonal and family relations, and cultural practices related to special occasions and food practices. The specific cultural practices that we examine for these three categories were identified through the Cultural Practices In-Depth Interviews.

A. GENDER-RELATED CULTURAL PRACTICES

One of the assertions often made regarding Mexican culture is that it over-emphasizes male dominance. This dominance is sometimes referred to as "machismo,"[7] though this term has taken on a lot of baggage in recent years. Mexican culture is also frequently described as giving strong emphasis to the role of women as caregivers. Related to both of these tendencies is the assertion that Mexican culture also promotes a double standard of sexuality, with much stronger prohibitions against sexual relations outside of marriage for women than for men.[8] One older immigrant woman, for example, is dismayed at the changes she sees taking place in her granddaughters. "When they visit," she says, "I hear them talking about boys and school. I don't speak English very well, but I can understand what they say. They are being exposed to many bad things. Nowadays they know all about sex. Society gives them too much freedom. Marriages don't last. And when the family starts to break up, so does everything else. In Mexico, the woman is not so free and I believe that works. Coming to the United States was better for us economically but not morally. Our children have become too much like the gringos. They have forgotten who they really are."[9]

There is, of course, considerable debate about the accuracy of portrayals of Mexican culture. Rather than joining the debate, in this chapter we propose to simply identify certain gender-related practices from the ethnographic research, determine the frequency with which they are accepted or practiced, and then explore how long they might be maintained by each succeeding generation in the United States.

One gender-related cultural practice that we found mentioned in the ethnographic interviews was the custom of brides wearing a white wedding gown as a sign of virginity. When one student asked her mother if only a virgin should wear a white dress to her wedding, for example, she said, "Yes, otherwise she would not only be insulting the brides who deserve the white dress, but most important, she would be disrespecting the house of God."

Another teen describes her family's experience with this custom. "My mother was asked by my cousin Claudia to make her wedding dress. My mom agreed. Claudia confessed to my mom that she was getting married because she was pregnant. So a few weeks after, Claudia brought the fabric for the dress. My mother left the white silk fabric in the plastic bag that my cousin had brought it in. When my mother opened the bag later that day, she discovered that the cat had defecated on it. My mom ran to the sink and washed it. A few days later the cat did it again. My mother told her aunt about what had happened twice to the fabric. Her elderly aunt said, "It's because she doesn't deserve to wear white and that cat knows it." My mom finished the dress as fast as she could and gave it to my cousin before the cat could do it again."

A young woman whose family has lived in the United States for several generations describes some of the change that is taking place in relation to this custom. "White is the color of purity in which you come before God to get married. But nowadays this has changed. Sexuality is more open and there is more premarital sex than before. But many people still have a strong belief about virgins."

Another item that came up frequently in the ethnographic interviews was the double standard regarding interaction with the opposite sex. We were frequently told, for example, that many Mexican-origin parents disapprove of girls calling boys or initiating a relationship. One of the interviewers, for example, found this practice mentioned when she interviewed one of her cousins. Her cousin recently wanted to call a friend from school, a boy, but her parents would not permit her to do so. "I met this guy at school in my math class," she said, "and he gave me his phone number so that we could talk more after school. Well, when I got home and tried to dial his number, my mother hung up the phone. I was so furious, but I couldn't argue with my mother. Anyway, when my dad found out he gave me this lecture about guys. All I said was that I just wanted to have a simple conversation with this guy, since I felt I was old enough. He said it was OK if the guy called me, but for me not to call any guy. I couldn't believe what my dad was saying. Why couldn't he see that times have changed and things are different these days? The next day I apologized to the guy at school. It was so embarrassing to tell him why I hadn't called him, but I wanted him to call me so I had to tell him the truth."

One celebration with great religious and cultural significance for Mexican-origin people is the *quinceañera*, or celebration of a girl's fifteenth birthday.[10] Nora says, "a quinceañera is a ceremony that shows when a girl enters womanhood.[11] At my quinceañera I had fourteen maids symbolizing the fourteen years that had gone by. I was the fifteenth girl because I was the one who was turning fifteen. My quinceañera started with a church ceremony that is similar to a wedding. My father walked me down the aisle, and then I took an oath and received a blessing from God through the priest. After the church ceremony I had a formal dance and my family and friends attended."

Ana describes an additional element. "I chose to use chamberlains because I liked the way boys looked in tuxedos. Some of the boys I chose were my cousins and the others were from school. Three weeks before my quinceañera we started getting together at my house after school to practice for the dance we were going to do. I chose the song "Quinceañera" by the Arroyo Band because it went perfectly with the whole meaning of a quinceañera. Well, the beginning of the dance started when, one by one, the chamberlains made a circle and sort of swayed back and forth until they had all completed the circle. After that, I danced in the middle with my dad until he gave me to one of the boys. I danced with him for a couple of seconds before I rotated to the next one. The dance went on for a couple of more minutes, until it concluded with me sitting and fourteen chamberlains bowed down handing me a rose and me holding the fifteenth one. I was so happy!"

Often, quinceañeras are major events that require large sums of money. Juan Garcia describes his sister's quinceañera. "You are not going to believe how many people were at my sister's quinceañera. When my family gets together, we get together! We rented a pavilion in Corpus Christi, and that thing was packed to the top. I never realized how many relatives I had. My dad was walking around with his head up high, full of pride. You see, this is La Raza [the Mexican race]. These people here will do anything for you if you ever need it and you should do the same for them. This is our *familia*. I began to feel the pride that my dad felt and I am proud to be a Garcia."

Not all young women, of course, are willing or able to have a quinceañera. "Quinceañeras are still very popular," says Nora, "and many girls wish to have one. I didn't have one—not because we couldn't afford it. Instead, I had a sweet sixteen party for my sixteenth birthday. It was a big party too, but it wasn't the same as a quinceañera. Not all of my family attended, and I didn't have the privilege of dancing with a group of people. Now I regret not having one, but my sister, who is almost fifteen, hopes to have one. My grandmother just died a year and a half ago, so she never experienced a granddaughter having a quinceañera. Maybe if I had chosen to have one I wouldn't be regretting it so much."

In many households of Mexican-origin people, we also found the practice of the husband acting as the sole provider to be quite strong.[12] One student found her interviewee, Mrs. Garcia, a bit shy and reluctant to answer some of the questions. But when asked if she expected to get a job, Mrs. Garcia quickly responded that her husband would never hear of her working. "That's part of our Mexican tradition," she said. "The women must stay home and her husband should be the sole provider. My job is to keep house, have meals ready for the family, and to bear as many children as possible." They have had eight children in their ten years of marriage.

Many young people have trouble accepting this tradition. Monica, a nineteen-year-old, for example, says, "My mother stays at home and works around the house while my father goes to work, but at one point in time she wanted to work and help provide for the family. She wanted to be at home and take care of us kids and my father, but she also thought it would help to bring in some additional income. She didn't tell my father that she wanted to work because she knew he would disapprove. But my mother got a job at a grocery store and worked there while we were at school. Eventually, after keeping her job a secret for several months, she finally told my father. He was more hurt than he was mad, because he didn't think that she respected his efforts to provide for the family. My mom quit her job and stayed home with us from then on.

Many respondents described the tradition in many Mexican-origin homes of the father being in charge of the home.[13] One young woman, for example, described her mother's teaching on the subject. "Mi hijita [My daughter]," she would tell me, "when you marry you should obey your husband without question. That way there will be less fighting between both of you and you will live in more harmony."

Young men often have to contend with this custom during courtship. One eighteen-year-old described his relationship with his girlfriend's father. "My girlfriend's father does not allow me to pick up her up at her home," he says. "Rather, I have to go pick her up at the home of a relative or a friend. Her father is aware of our relationship, but he still refuses to allow me at the house. This seems too 'Mexican' to me, and I think it's unfair because her father has not given me a chance to show that I can be trusted. My girlfriend says her father doesn't have anything against me but just doesn't want the neighbors to look down on his daughter. I don't like it, but I agree that the man should be the head of the house."

While many respondents agree with the custom, they sometimes work behind the back of a husband or father when they feel he is wrong. One fifty-two-year-old woman remembers when she was going to high school. "My gym teacher told us we needed to wear a white blouse and white shorts for PE," she recalls. "The problem wasn't wearing or getting the clothes. The real problem was my father, who was very strict and religious. He never let his daughters wear shorts around the house, much less at school. So my sister and I would have to keep them at the home of one of our aunts and go pick them up there before school every morning. This went on most of the time I was in high school, until he found out about it when he saw the shorts at his sister's home. He was furious at all of us for what we were doing behind his back."

Some men, of course, abuse their authority. Manolo describes his own father and the problems he had growing up under his domination. "My dad always had to act so macho," he says. "This kept me upset most of the time, especially how he used to treat my mom. El era el hombre, el que mandaba en la casa [He was the man, the one in charge in his home]. We had to do what he said because he was the king of the castle. The time that really upset me, though, and made me want to have nothing to do with him, was one of the times he beat up my mother. I was fifteen years old at the time. He came home really drunk that time, smelling of alcohol and perfume. My mom had been walking back and forth, waiting for my dad to get home. He never bothered to call, and when he got home he got upset with her because she didn't have his food cooked for him. My mom was mad because he was at the bars drinking and carousing. I tried to take care of my sisters so they would not see all the violence. I have never been able to forgive my father for what he put my mother through." [14]

Closely related to the authority of the man of the house are the traditional restrictions on young women, especially young women needing permission to go out. Dania, for example, describes her father's absolute authority and his rules for his daughters. "One time," she says, I wanted to go to the movies with some friends. My father wasn't home and my mother didn't feel she could let me go without my father's permission. This was a pretty common practice at our home." The young woman who interviewed Dania comments that she finds this odd, since Dania is twenty-one years old. She says, "I could understand her father being authoritative if Dania were fourteen or fifteen years old, but she's twenty-one and that's a bit of a stretch."

Often, however, these restrictions are upheld as much by mothers as they are by fathers. Sonia remembers a time in high school that caused her considerable embarrassment. "There was this guy that I was crazy about," she says. "One day he asked me if wanted to go with him to a football game. I was really excited about it. It would have been our first date. I couldn't give him an immediate answer, though, because I needed to get permission from my mother. I was nervous about asking, thinking for sure she would say no. But to my surprise, she said I could go. About fifteen minutes before my date showed up, my mother tells me to check on my two younger brothers and my younger sister and see if they were ready. I panicked, fighting tears and rage. I calmly asked my mother where they were going. She replied, 'Well, with you of course. You didn't think you were going on this date by yourself, did you?' There was nothing I could do except smile and pretend not to care."

Not all young women are so compliant. Gina, for example, who is nineteen years old, says, "if my mom and grandparents knew half the stuff I do, they'd freak out. I love to go out dancing and meet new people. If they knew this, they would take me out of school and lock me in the house. I'm not kidding. They think a girl shouldn't be allowed to go out and have fun. I just don't agree with their beliefs. I'm a grown woman and should be allowed to make choices for myself. I had to fight to come here to the university and live in the dorm. They wanted me to stay home and commute to school. If I don't go home some weekend, they think I'm doing bad stuff. After my first semester, they backed off a lot. Still, my mom insists on seeing me every weekend, so when I don't go home she comes here on Sundays. When I do go home, they say I don't take care of my grandpa like I'm supposed to. I think my family has given up trying to get me to mold to their traditions."

One tradition that particularly rankles some young women is the practice of the oldest son being in charge if father is gone. Some young women, as a result, have to put up with a brother having authority over them. Carlos Garza strongly believes in this tradition. He says, "I tell my sister what to do and she'd better listen. I am very strict with her and I don't allow her to go out or wear makeup. I feel she is still too young to accept the responsibilities of a young woman. At fifteen, she'll be allowed to do things like that gradually. It hurts me at times, but I only do it for her well being. Someday—not very soon—she may thank me."

Such authority, however, also may carry certain obligations. Antonio is the oldest son in one family. He says, "My dad became very ill and was put in the hospital for a month. While there, he wasn't getting paid because he worked part-time at a factory and didn't have sick leave. My mother didn't work, and I was the oldest of five kids. Since there was no steady income, I had to find a job to support the family. I became the man of the house while my father was sick. My family depended on me to pay the bills and put food on the table. Although I was only sixteen at the time, I still had to take on my father's role until he got better."

As the preceding examples illustrate, there is often considerable disagreement regarding many of these traditional gender-based practices. Figure 2.1 reports the results of our Cultural Practices Survey, through which we attempted to determine how widespread these practices are and how much support they still have.[15] This figure indicates the percentage of respondents that answered "frequently" when asked how often they, their family, or their friends practiced each custom. It also shows the percentage of respondents that indicated they believed that the custom should be kept. In addition, since these are gender-based items, we show how the responses of females in the survey differed from the responses of males.

This figure reveals several important findings. First, in all cases, the percentage indicating that an item should be kept was higher than the percentage reporting that respondents frequently practiced that item. One possibile explanation is that some items are not things that one would "practice" on a frequent basis. Another possibility is that these items enjoy rather widespread support, as indicated by the percentage reporting a desire to keep them.

The items with greatest support and reported practice are the practice of quinceañeras for girls, a husband or father being in charge in his home, and the idea that young single women should have permission to go out. On the first, the percentage of males and females reporting that this was frequently practiced in their home is quite similar (66 percent for males and 68 percent for females). The second of these three items, a husband/father being in charge in his home, showed 64 percent of males and 62 percent for females saying this happened frequently, though 10 percent more males wanted to keep it than did females. On the third item, girls needing permission to go out, slightly more females reported this being a frequent occurrence in their home than did males (62 percent vs. 58 percent). Sig-

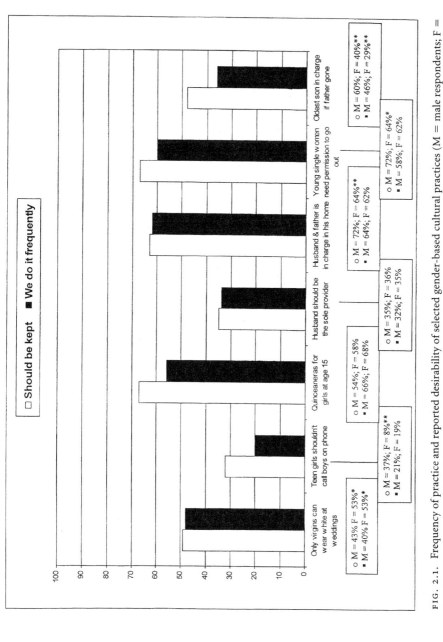

FIG. 2.1. Frequency of practice and reported desirability of selected gender-based cultural practices (M = male respondents; F = female respondents; asterisks indicate whether the responses of males were statistically different from those of females at the .05 level [*] or at the .005 level [**])

nificantly more males than females wanted to keep it, however (72 percent of males and 64 percent of females).

The item on which males and females varied most significantly, in both reported frequency and desire to maintain the practice, was whether the oldest son should be in charge when the father was gone. The frequency of females reporting this as a frequent occurrence in their home was only 29 percent, compared to 46 percent of males who reported it. Similarly, fully 20 percent more males wanted to maintain the practice than did females (60 percent vs. 40 percent).

The percentage of respondents who indicated a desire to keep each item might help us see whether each practice will be kept or not. A better measure of whether each item will survive the multigeneration process of Americanization, however, is an analysis of how those who have lived in the United States for several generations compare on each item with those who are recent arrivals from Mexico. We used the generation score to determine how long a respondent's family had been in the United States (with 12 being the highest score possible and the longest time here and a 0 the lowest). By running an analysis of variance on the preceding items, we can show how the average (mean) score varies among those who say they frequently practice an item, occasionally practice it, and rarely or never practice it. If assimilation is indeed taking place, individuals who say they frequently practice each item should have a lower generation score (less time in the United States) than those who say they rarely or never practice that item. Figure 2.2 shows the results of this comparison.

As we can see from these findings, there is a pronounced trend toward Americanization. That is, people who said they rarely or never practice these traditions have a much higher generation score, indicating that they and their families have been in the United States for a longer time than those who said they frequently practice each tradition. The results were statistically significant in the predicted direction on every single practice, not only with regard to frequency of practice, but also in relation to the expressed desire to keep each practice. In addition, the results were all statistically significant at rather high levels of association. Basically, this seems to support the hypothesis that the longer Mexican-origin people are in the United States, the less likely they are to practice and desire to keep these gender-related practices.[16]

This conclusion is further supported by data from another survey we conducted, the Perceptions of Deviance Survey. On this survey of 424 respondents, we also included items that allowed us to calculate each re-

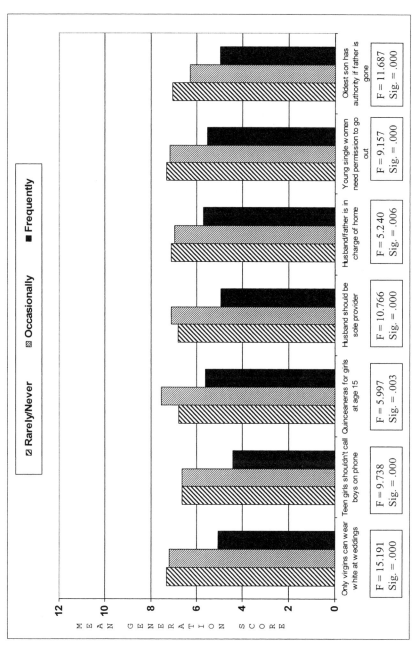

FIG. 2.2. Relation of mean generation scores to the frequency of practicing selected gender-related cultural practices among South Texas Hispanics

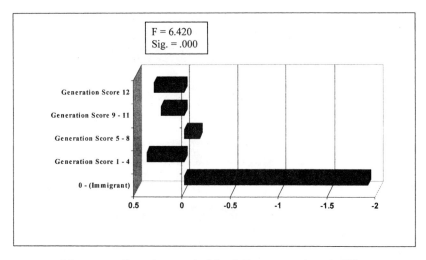

FIG. 2.3. Mean scores (from +5 to −5) of South Texas respondents in different generational categories selecting each level of how good or how bad it is for a married man to stay home and raise the children while his wife works

spondent's generation score. Then we asked a series of questions designed to measure respondents' perceptions of how good or how bad a variety of border-related practices are. One of these items was the question "How good or how bad is it for a married man to stay home and raise the children while his wife works?" The results of responses to this item are shown in relation to categories of generation scores in Figure 2.3.

In this figure, generation scores were grouped into five categories, so that we could look at the mean scores of how good or bad respondents regarded this item. Those in the lowest category (0) are immigrants whose parents, grandparents, and even themselves were born outside the United States. Those in the top category (12) are those who themselves, their parents, and their grandparents were all born in the United States. As the figure shows, the average response by immigrants was considerably negative to this role reversal, while the categories with higher average generation scores were either more positive (though only slightly so) or only slightly negative (those with a generation score of 5 to 8). The F-scores on these results (F = 6.420) showed they were statistically significant (Sig. = .000). Essentially, these findings from a separate survey support the conclusion that beliefs about gender-related practices change with increasing generations in the United States.

B. FAMILY-RELATED AND OTHER INTERPERSONAL CULTURAL PRACTICES

Another category of cultural practices identified in the in-depth interviews was beliefs and customs related to family and other interpersonal relations. In much of the literature about Mexican culture, family and interpersonal relations are frequently mentioned as important in Mexican culture. For many Mexican-origin people, this translates into loyalty to one's family and ranks high among the practices they consider important. Guillermina, a thirty-five-year-old woman, illustrates this perception. "When I was about nine years old," she says, "my brothers and sisters and I, and all our cousins, walked down to a nearby park to play while our parents prepared lunch. A little boy there started picking a fight with my sister, and my brother Roberto came to her rescue. A fight broke out, and by the time you knew it, everyone was involved, including the girls. When they arrived, our parents got upset. But later on, my cousins and I overheard my dad and uncles talking about how proud they were that we had stuck together. Today, that is what I still try to instill in my small children, to stand up together as a family. In the Mexican culture, it's all for one and one for all."

Though other interpersonal relations may not be as important in Mexican culture as are family relations, they are still given great importance. Obligations of friendship run deep and facilitate even business negotiations. In the following section we will illustrate the nature of specific interpersonal and family cultural practices among Mexican-origin people in South Texas. Then we will again show how widely practiced they are, how many people believe that each item should be kept. Finally, we will discuss how these beliefs change with each succeeding generation in the United States.

One important family-related custom is having *padrinos* [godparents] for children.[17] Guillermina has two small boys, both of whom she had baptized. She felt that it was her duty as a parent to seek out second parents, or padrinos, for her boys. "The padrinos baptize the child," she says, "promising to care for them in case the natural parents ever become unable to do so." Carmen adds, "After a baptism, it is customary for the family to get together outside the church. The family forms a circle around the padrinos. The padrinos then throw up in the air a handful of coins for all the children to get."

Often, a strong bond forms between a child's parents and the padrinos. They become *compadres*, or co-parents. Ana and her husband, who are migrant farmworkers, have been asked to be padrinos on several occasions. "We ended up being padrinos for one or more of the children in each family," she says. "We were all very close, and up north we still do everything together. We buy groceries together. We wash our clothes at the laundromat together, and we even go out and get drunk together."

Another practice that is fairly widespread among both family and friends is the custom of the *abrazo* [hug] as a greeting among men. Jorge, who grew up outside the Rio Grande Valley of South Texas, was surprised when his interviewer asked about the abrazo. "I hug no man," he said, "not even my father." His interviewer writes, "I told him that it was customary for me to hug and kiss my father and he could not believe it. He could never kiss his father, saying that if he were to attempt it his father would beat him up. But the most interesting thing that I was able to observe was that although he did follow many of the traditions that were listed in the questionnaire, he felt that they were not that important to carry on. That was something I was not able to understand."

Jorge's response helps explain not only why we asked whether respondents practiced an item, but whether or not they thought it should be kept or forgotten. Jorge does not practice the abrazo, but apparently thinks it is a custom that is worth keeping.

Another family-related custom is for married children to take elderly parents into their homes. Though men may be expected to open their homes to an elderly parent, either their own or their wife's parent, the actual care is frequently left to the women, as the following story by Erica illustrates. She takes care of her elderly (ninety-two-year-old) mother in her home. Her sisters help out by taking turns. The male siblings are not required to help out, but they are required to have their wives help. Her interviewer says, "I asked her if her father was still alive, would her brothers be expected to help? She replied no. I asked why. She simply said, 'Because they are men.'"

This respect for the elderly also influences another custom, that of grandparents disciplining their grandchildren, even if the parents are present. One man recalls an incident that illustrates the nature of this custom and the problems it sometimes causes. "My two nephews," he says, "live at my parents' house. This gives my parents full opportunity to help in raising their grandchildren. Whether my sister (the boys' mother) is around or not, my parents will spank the children for disciplinary purposes. Although my sister sometimes protests, she knows that my parents are doing it for the good of their grandchildren."

Diego completely agrees with this custom. "I remember a Thanksgiving Day in 1992," he says. "Everyone was having a good time until my two sons, who were ages twelve and eleven at that time, got into a fight in the kitchen. My wife was serving food at that time and ended up getting food thrown on her back. I was outside when my wife came out and told me that my dad had taken the two boys into our bedroom to talk about what had happened. To this day I thank my father a great deal for what he did, because they haven't fought at all since then. I still don't know what he told my boys, but whatever it was it opened up their eyes and mine."

Not everyone, of course, agrees with this custom. "When my older sister brings her little girl over," reports Jaime, "she is always getting into trouble. When my mother yells at Jessica, her granddaughter, it really makes my sister angry. The other day, when Jessica broke one of mom's favorite bowls, she told her, 'No!' and spanked her on the hand. Jessica started to cry and this made my sister very mad. They left the house right away." Jaime says that he thinks that this conflict between his mother and his sister is humorous. "My mother was raised to believe that you always respect your elders," he continues, "and the older the person in the family is, the more authority they have. I guess things change from one generation to the next."

Another cultural practice important to many Mexican immigrants is speaking Spanish in the home so that children will learn it. Many parents we interviewed were dismayed to see English overtaking Spanish as the primary language of their children. But because English is the preferred language in local schools, many children do not retain as much Spanish as their parents would like. Arturo reports, "When I first started school here, I was in a Spanish-speaking class. Most of my classmates spoke the language well. Unfortunately, I had trouble with it because we don't speak it much at home. My parents didn't consider it very important for us. In class, each of the students was asked to read aloud a sentence in Spanish. When my turn came to read, I had a hard time pronouncing some of the words. Since I am dark and have a Mexican name, one of the students thought that I was making up my difficulties with Spanish. He asked me, 'How can you not read or speak Spanish? You have *el nopal en la frente* [cactus on your forehead].' I later found out that was an expression used to make sure people remember they are Mexicans."

For many, however, retaining Spanish is difficult. Consuelo has lived in the United States for more than ten years, having come here as a young girl. "Even though I am a Mexican," she says, "I can express myself better in English than in Spanish. But for my parents it's very important for me to speak good Spanish, because they don't understand me when I speak English. And even though my name is Consuelo, I prefer Connie, the Anglo version of my name. The problem is that my parents want me to use the Spanish version rather than the Anglo version. They say Spanish is very important because it's our native language."

In spite of parental efforts to maintain Spanish among their children, many children and grandchildren of immigrants do lose it. Diana grew up around Spanish-speaking grandparents but could not speak Spanish well. "I was always scared to communicate with my grandmother," she says. "I remember a few incidents at my grandmother's house. She would start talking to me, and the only thing that I could do was to run to my mother and ask her to translate what she was telling me. I guess I had that habit of my mother rescuing me all the time, so I did not try to understand the language or try to speak it. My parents did not emphasize that we learn to speak Spanish. I now wish they had. I regret not trying harder to speak the language. I can speak Spanish, but not as much and as often as I want. Sometimes I get all tongue-tied in Spanish. That's why I don't speak the language very often."

Another practice closely related to family relationships is sending family representatives to propose marriage. Diana, a twenty-year-old young woman, describes how her father asked her mom to marry him. "My dad had to send someone to ask for my mother's hand," she says, "so my grandparents went. It was a scary feeling for him and a happy one for my mom to know that a young man was going to ask for her hand in marriage. It was scary for my dad because he didn't know whether the answer would be yes or no. If the answer was no, he couldn't do anything about it and would just have to accept it. My father was so anxious to know if the answer was yes that he stayed in the backseat of the car outside my mom's house, to know the news right away. He was real scared because he knew that my mom's dad was very strict. But he got his wish, because he married my mom."

Though some of our respondents did not like this tradition (or were even unaware of it), others were emphatic about its importance. Nelda is twenty years old and recalls how important it was for her. "My boyfriend and I had been going out since we were very young," she says. "When we finally decided to get married, we had a serious problem. My father was locked up for drug dealing. He still had a year and a half to go on his two-year sentence. I really wanted Hugo to ask for my hand, but how could he when my father was in jail? We finally went to the prison and Hugo asked my father for my hand. My dad said yes and we began making the wedding plans. This was really important because of our bond as a family. Two weeks before my wedding, my father was released and walked me down the aisle and gave me away to my fiancé. He now is in the clear and works for my husband as a truck driver."

With each of these relationship items, we again compared the responses from the survey to find out the frequency of practice that was reported for each item and the percentage of respondents who indicated they wanted to keep each item. Unlike our analysis in Table 2.2, we did not conduct an analysis by gender on these items, because they are not directly related to gender practices. The analysis is presented in Figure 2.4.

Again, we found a rather consistent pattern showing a greater percentage of respondents saying that an item should be kept than the percentage who said they actually practiced it. The item that had the greatest difference between the percentage saying they practiced an item and the percentage who thought it should be kept is the item "married children take in elderly parents." Roughly 70 percent of respondents said they practiced it frequently, compared to only 40 percent who said they thought this custom should be kept. It is obviously a tradition important to many people, but perhaps one that is difficult for many to practice, especially when several children are available to do so.

In order to determine how these practices are affected by Americanization, we again conducted an analysis of variance to assess the degree of association between each practice and generation scores. These results are shown in Figure 2.5.

Similar to our analysis of gender-based cultural practices, these practices related to family and other interpersonal relations follow the same pattern, whereby those who said they rarely or never practiced each item reported more time in the United States. In this case, however, only four of the items have differences great enough to be considered statistically significant. This would seem to suggest that the two items that are not (giving an abrazo and grandparents disciplining grandchildren) are not as likely to disappear as quickly as the gender-based items.

The item having the strongest relationship to generational status is the last item, "Speak Spanish so children will learn it," shown in Figure 2.5. Indeed, this item seems to reveal the greatest difference between those relatively new to the United States and those who are children or grandchildren of immigrants. The difference in the mean generation score for those who said they seldom or never practice this item is almost twice that of

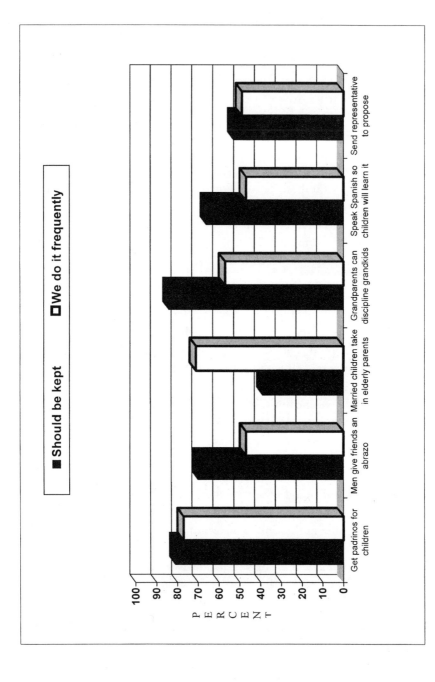

FIG. 2.4. Frequency of practice and reported desirability of selected interpersonal and family-related cultural practices

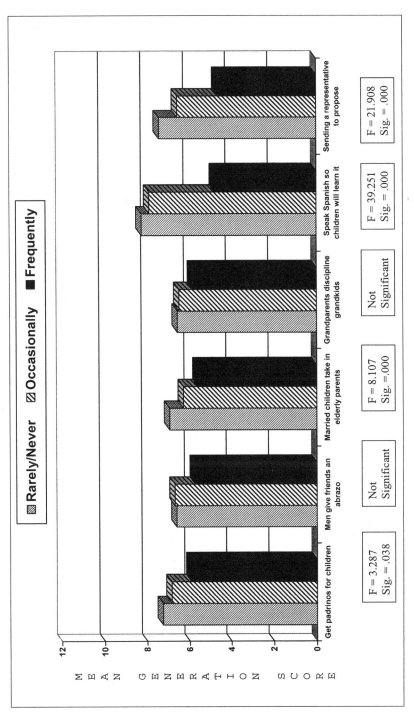

FIG. 2.5. Relation of mean generation score to frequency of practicing selected interpersonal and family-related practices among South Texas Hispanics

those who said they frequently practice it. This suggests, contrary to Samuel Huntington's predictions,[18] that teaching children Spanish is one of the first cultural practices to be lost in the process of Americanization, even in this area contiguous to Mexico where the population is overwhelmingly of Mexican origin.

C. CULTURAL PRACTICES RELATED TO SPECIAL OCCASIONS AND FOOD

A major form of the cultural practices that bind a people together are the particular ways they celebrate special occasions and the foods they eat. Often, proximity to the border facilitates both the ability to get together and the maintenance of these traditions. Ramón particularly appreciates this advantage of the border. "Because we live so close to the border, he says, my parents have always liked having family members come from Mexico, believing it helps hold our family together. Well it has. Unfortunately, when my parents passed away, our family stopped having the gatherings that my father so strongly believed in. Now it is very rare for our family to come together to celebrate these traditions. I try to keep the traditions alive within my family so that my two girls can have a sense of belonging to a culture. Even though our relatives don't come anymore for holidays, we invite others in our colonia to celebrate Christmas and other special occasions with us."

In Mexico, honoring the dead is an important tradition. Death is often regarded with awe, and the Angel of Death [La Santísima Muerte] is honored year-round, with many candles, statues, and even jewelry honoring death. This attention to death is especially important on November 1 of each year, the Day of the Dead, a day on which to honor deceased relatives and friends. In some parts of Mexico (like Monterrey in the north), the custom is dying out or being replaced by an imported version of Halloween. Mrs. Gutierrez believes it is a tradition that should be continued in Mexico and in the United States. "This is a day," she says, "when relatives go and clean up or decorate the grave of a loved one. You don't see many people doing that anymore. Some people have already forgotten their traditions."

Another special-occasion custom in many cultures is the celebration of New Year's. Many Mexican-origin families in our interviews described how making and eating of buñuelos on New Year's had special significance for them. Patricia explains that buñuelos are flour tortillas fried in oil and covered with sugar and cinnamon. "Instead of singing 'Auld Lang Syne,'" she says, "we get to eat these rarely seen pastries. We stuff ourselves. The buñuelos are never made fast enough to feed all of the people in the house. Still, between all the crunching of the crispy tortillas you can always hear and feel the love of the family and friends. There is closeness you can only feel on these special occasions. Even though I know the closeness we share would be there without the traditional buñuelos, it is a horrible thought having them absent from our New Year's celebration."

Many Mexican Americans in South Texas believe that having a pi-ñata for a child's birthday is an important custom. A piñata is a papier-mâché, cartoonlike container filled with candy and goodies that children take turns trying to break with a stick as it is raised and lowered. Some families, of course, may be unable to afford a piñata. Ricardo remembers going to such a party. "I got to the party," he explains, "and the family was just having a cookout. All they could really afford was to fill up little plastic bags with Mexican candies for the kids. Without realizing their circumstances, I had asked if they had already broken the piñata and discovered they had not bought one. So I offered to go buy ice at the store, not only to get the ice, but to go across town and buy the child a piñata too."

Seferino Rivas, who is ninety-one years old, explains another important custom related to birthdays—singing "Las Mañanitas" for someone's birthday. "When we celebrate my birthday every July," he says, "my children make sure that we have a large party. We invite family, friends, and neighbors to join us. We make a large meal consisting of everything from barbeque to *menudo* [tripe stew]. There's plenty of rice, beans, and tortillas, enough to last for a week as leftovers. They sing 'Las Mañanitas' to me and I still get a piñata filled with candy, also an old Mexican tradition. We usually have mariachis come and play. Also, a few of the local men who played in bands of the past come over and play a few songs. My children and grandchildren always ask me to bring out my guitar and play along with the musicians. Of course I can't resist. When they bring me my guitar, I run my fingers over the strings. Soon everyone joins in singing. Whether you're drunk or not, you still sing along whole-heartedly."

The mariachis Seferino mentions also play an important part in another holiday: many Mexican-origin people hire mariachis to sing to their mothers on Mother's Day. One of the interviewers says, "All of the people that I interviewed felt that this is a special day, especially for Mexican American mothers. They felt strongly that this is a day when husbands and children actually show how much they appreciate what their wives and mothers have done for them. What most people do is hire a group of mariachis and have them serenade their mothers. The song that is always sung is

'Las Mañanitas.' This song is not only sung on Mother's Day but also on birthdays."

One student recalls, "I will never forget the look on my mother's face. I had come down for one of my nieces' graduation and on Mother's Day decided to hire some mariachis to sing 'Las Mañanitas' to my mother. At midnight, all of us were at my mother's. When she heard the singing, at first she didn't get up, but then curiosity got the best of her so she investigated. And to her surprise they were singing to her! She was so happy that she cried."

Some of the celebrations and traditions mentioned above can be very expensive, well beyond the means of many low-income families. A popular way of reducing the financial difficulty, especially among low-income families, is to ask several individuals to be padrinos to help pay for the celebration. This custom extends the notion of padrinos, thus giving honorary family status to other individuals who help. Indeed, one of the first surprise experiences I (the *bolillo* author of this text) had after moving to the Rio Grande Valley was to be invited to be the *padrino del queque* [godfather of the cake] at the wedding reception for a student assistant.

Julieta describes the importance of this tradition for her family. She became teary-eyed as she related how difficult it was for her parents to feed her and her siblings three meals a day or to get new shoes at least once a year. "My parents could not feed our family of nine three proper meals a day," she says. "It was difficult to keep warm during the winter, and we wore hand-me-down shoes that had to be repaired by my brother-in-law, who sometimes used chicken wire to mend them. Still, we kept our family together—and family togetherness is very important to me. I remember preparing for our children's baptisms and later their weddings by asking close relatives to be padrinos."

Quinceañeras, as we indicated earlier, can be very expensive. Clarisa explains how her family handled the overwhelming expense of her daughter's celebration. "When my daughter had her quinceañera," she says, "the whole family pulled together and volunteered to be padrinos so that we could afford it. I remember when she got married we also had a lot of padrinos and were able to give her a special wedding. We even got padrinos to send them on their honeymoon, which we couldn't have afforded."

Food is an important part of many celebrations for Mexican-origin people, and certain foods seem to become identified with certain times of the year. For many Mexican-origin people, this means tamales at Christmastime. Felipe loves to eat the tamales that his mother and aunts make.

Though one can buy tamales anytime of the year, he loves Christmas because it is the only time his family makes tamales. "When I was little," he recalls, I remember waking up one morning around Christmas to a lot of talking and laughing. I found out that my family was making tamales that day. I remember getting scared when I saw my aunts because they weren't wearing any makeup. I saw my mom laughing with her sisters. I had not seen her enjoy herself like that in a long time.

Oralia, recently a grandmother, likes everything about making tamales for Christmas except having to wake up early. "My sister gets me up at 6:00 a.m.," she says "to go to my parents' house. We sit around the kitchen without makeup and hairnets and I catch up on news as we watch our soap operas. Making tamales with my sisters is a tradition that our mother started and I hope my daughters and nieces keep up."

Men also are involved in this tradition, though not usually in actually making the tamales. Melisa remembers how her grandfather, every Christmas, would go out and buy a pig to slaughter in order to make the tamales that everyone loved. "He would go out and talk to many farmers," she says, "until he found the perfect pig to kill for the tamales. But my grandmother always got mad at him because he would always kill the pig in front of all the grandchildren."

Arturo is a grandfather whose wife died a few years ago. Speaking of the most recent Christmastime, he explains why this tradition means so much to him. "When I arrived at home at eight thirty in the morning, I saw all my children and grandchildren in the kitchen. It gave me great joy to see the grandchildren old enough to help there in the kitchen making tamales. My wife started this tradition, and though she was not able to see it with her own eyes I know she was happy. My children were laughing and joking the whole time we were making tamales. I will always treasure my children and grandchildren for keeping a tradition that my wife started."

It would be hard to find anything that is more closely associated with Mexican culture than tortillas served with meals. They are important also because they truly represent Native American culture and culture of the poor. In Spain, the tortilla is more like an omelet, made of potatoes and eggs and served in slices. The corn tortilla was generally looked down on by the Spanish, who considered corn a food for animals and the corn tortilla a food used only by people too poor to afford utensils.

If the corn tortilla is a classic in Mexican culture, then the flour tortilla is symbolic of the culture of Mexican Americans. Until recent years, it was hard to find corn *masa* [dough] from which to make corn tortillas in the United States. So, Mexican-origin people improvised, using flour and creating a truly delicious innovation. Though one can find flour tortillas in some parts of Mexico, they are not common and do not match the quality found north of the Río Bravo.

Not all people with origins in Mexico still use tortillas as a regular part of meals, however. Melisa, a twenty-five-year-old woman born in Mexico, discovered that when she first came to the United States. "When I was about six or seven," she says, "we took a trip to the United States. I really couldn't understand why the Mexican Americans would eat everything with bread, because at home we ate everything with tortillas. I was very puzzled, so I asked my mother and she insisted that this was just the way that Mexican Americans have changed their heritage because of the fact that they live in the United States."

Obviously, not everyone has changed. Ignacio is fifty years old, divorced, and has lived in the United States for many years. Homemade tortillas are something he is not willing to give up. "If I marry again," he says, "she better know how to make tortillas. If she doesn't, I'll make her take some tortilla-making classes or something like that."

The tendency to associate tortillas with Mexican culture is so strong that many are not aware of the appeal they have among Anglos. Angela is a twenty-four-year-old Anglo woman who has lived in the Valley most of her life. "I remember when I was a junior in high school," she says. "I was dating a guy named George who was Hispanic. Though I was white, neither his parents nor mine seemed to mind that we were dating. One day, his parents invited me to dinner. I was thrilled because I thought they had accepted me. I noticed we were having chicken with rice and beans. Everything smelled delicious. When I sat down, George's mother came in from the kitchen and handed me a plate with white bread. I really wanted to eat the corn tortillas they were eating and not the bread, but I didn't want to be disrespectful to George's family. So, I had my meal with white bread. George later told me that his mother gave me bread because she thought I wouldn't eat corn tortillas."

Another Mexican custom related to foods is the use of the *molcajete* [a bowl-shaped stone for grinding spices]. Elena says, "The molcajete is used to grind spices until they are almost powdered. There are several uses for it. I use it to make *picante* [hot, spicy] sauce. It turns out hotter and spicier. It never turns out as good when you use the blender. I also grind pepper and garlic and add water to it. I then pour this mixture on pastas or I use it as a sauce or dip."

Molcajetes, however, are not always easy to find on the U.S. side of the border. One woman, a migrant farmworker, describes how they took their molcajete with them when they went up north. "Our family of eight had a very small car," she says, and it had very used tires. My husband never bought new ones, so we always had flat tires. We always took a molcajete with us on our trips. We used it to prepare our food, but we also found it useful to stop the car from rolling backward when we changed a tire. One time we accidentally left it behind in Marshall, Texas."

Again using the survey of 433 respondents, we compared the percentage of respondents who claimed to frequently engage in each of these practices related to food and special days with the percentage who believed each practice should be kept. These results are shown in Figure 2.6.

Figure 2.6 reveals that all but three of the items were reported to be frequently practiced by a majority of respondents. The three that fell below 50 percent reporting frequent practice of an item were hiring mariachis to sing on Mother's Day, having a *posada* at Christmastime, and celebrating Día de los Reyes in January.[19] Perhaps these are not more frequently practiced because they are difficult to do (especially hiring mariachis, as fewer are available on the Texas side of the border). Nevertheless, all of the items had a larger percentage saying they would like to keep the item than the percentage who claimed to practice each tradition.

The greatest difference between reported frequency and desirability of an item was the one on hiring mariachis for Mother's Day. Apparently this is a custom with wide appeal but greater difficulty to carry out. We also found considerable difference between the reported practice of having homemade tortillas for meals and respondents affirming the desirability of keeping the custom. Apparently, this item is also something people like but find more difficult to practice. Flour and corn tortillas can be easily and cheaply purchased at any local supermarket, and though their taste is clearly inferior to that of homemade tortillas, a lack of time—especially among mothers who work—may make this a difficult practice to keep.

We next looked at the relationship of these items to each respondent's generation score. The results of this comparison are presented in Figure 2.7.

The results shown in Figure 2.7 indicate that only one association (having a piñata for children for their birthday party) was not statistically significant. It would appear that this tradition has been widely accepted by Mexican Americans—almost as widely as among Mexican immigrants, perhaps because of the ease with which one can buy a piñata on the Texas

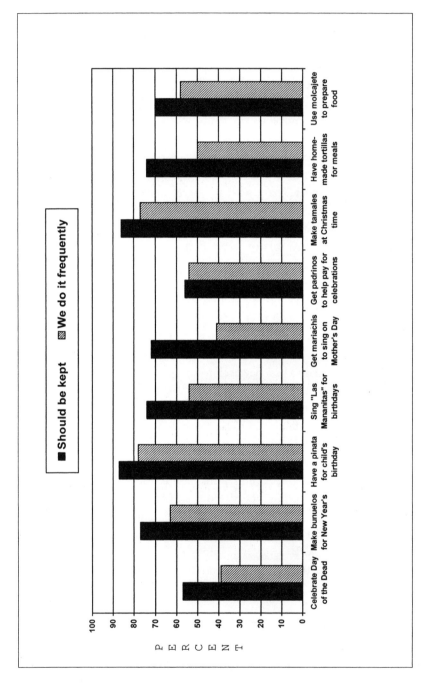

FIG. 2.6. Frequency of practice and reported desirability of practicing selected celebrations and special food practices among South Texas Hispanics

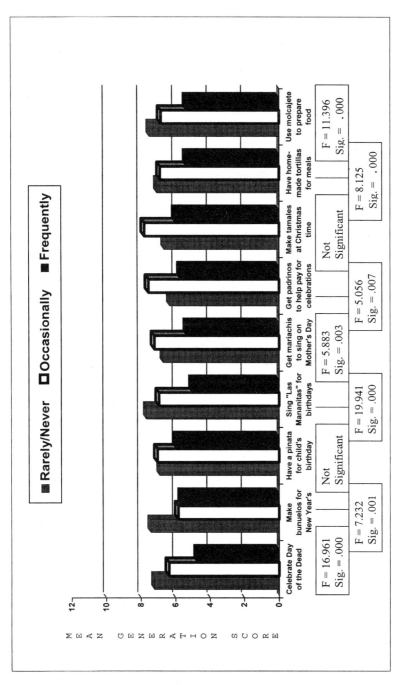

FIG. 2.7. Relationship of mean generation score to frequency of practicing selected celebrations and special food practices among South Texas Hispanics

side of the border. We even found evidence of some Anglos adopting this tradition, much to the delight of their children.

The remaining items, however, all showed a rather pronounced and statistically significant relation with acculturation, or Americanization. Two items, celebrating the Day of the Dead and singing "Las Mañanitas" for birthdays, both had F-scores above 76.0. On this basis, we could predict that these two customs associated with special celebrations would be the first to disappear with succeeding generations in the United States.

Conclusion

The process of interviewing people about their cultural practices proved enlightening for many student interviewers. One, for example, commented, "I truly enjoyed doing this project because it helped me understand the differences among Hispanics of different generations. The longer they seem to live here, the less they practice the traditions of Mexico. Many have forgotten about their ethnic background and mistreat others from Mexico who have just crossed the border seeking a better life. I too have many relatives in Mexico and I believe that we should continue to value our traditions and culture because it's who we are and a large part of the beauty we share."

As this student discovered, even in sections of the borderlands where Mexican-origin people make up the vast majority of the population, pressures toward assimilation are at work, making Mexican culture more likely to diminish after several generations in the United States. Still, though the culture of Mexican-origin people may be changed by this process, it will likely endure in some form for many generations.

Nevertheless, culture does not uniformly slip away with each generation in the United States. Some aspects of it, such as speaking Spanish in the home so that children will learn it, seem to fade away rather quickly. Other aspects, such as the use of piñatas for birthdays, are more resistant to change.

The end result is that Mexican American culture is a product of ethnogenesis, not just a combination of Mexican and U.S. culture. Like the language of the border (Tex-Mex), the culture that emerges on the border, where there is a strong concentration of Mexican-origin people, has its roots in both the Mexican and U.S. cultures but is at the same time somewhat different from both.

Thus, our findings run contrary to the hypothesis by Huntington and others who propose that Mexican-origin people will not assimilate, will increasingly reject U.S. culture, and will even become increasingly oriented toward forming a separate nation or community. The process of Americanization, though different on the border, clearly does not lead to such consequences.

Most Mexican-origin people will continue to struggle with identity. José Gonzalez, a twenty-eight-year-old man, illustrates some of the reasons many do not want to let go of their cultural traditions. "The Christmas after my grandfather died," he says, "I learned something about our culture. Right after we had Christmas lunch, my dad was sitting outside alone, smoking a cigarette. I walked out to throw away some trash, and he asked me to come and sit down. He told me numerous stories of when he was my age. He remembered all the time spent with his father at parties and family gatherings. My father told me, 'Don't ever forget the way you feel today, because that is the best feeling in the world. It is a beautiful day. We just had a great lunch and everyone in the family is together and doing fine. These are the kind of days that you live for and will never forget. Someday you'll have a son and you'll talk to him, just like I am talking with you and my father talked with me. You will tell your son stories just like I have told you of my experiences. You must not forget who you are and where you come from. It is important to keep these traditions alive.'"

3 Displaced Workers

WITH PRITI VERMA

Gloria is a forty-eight-year-old woman who worked eighteen years at a recently closed clothing manufacturing plant in Hidalgo County. Her husband died a short time before the plant closed.

"When I was laid off," she says, "I tried to get a job as an orderly in a hospital. I had many sewing and cooking skills and had previous experience of working in the fields. But they told me I didn't have enough experience and that I needed to speak English and have a GED. They wouldn't hire me because they could hire younger workers who know English.

"In order to get training and to collect unemployment, I had to enroll in an English class and take a GED course at a private technical institute. They were supposed to be preparing us for the GED, but they started out teaching us algebra. We really needed to learn English first. They didn't divide us up according to our abilities or our level in either English or our preparation for the GED. Every Friday they would give us an exam and told us that if we didn't pass it we would no longer receive unemployment. I would leave the classroom crying because of the pressure. Before, we were depressed because of the lack of work. Now we were depressed because of the bad education that we were getting. Our complaints to the employment office and to the director of the institute did no good. I finally quit because I wasn't learning anything and I needed more time to look for work.

"Since I quit the classes, I haven't been able to find work and I lost my unemployment benefits. I have a lot of credit card debt and have to rely on food stamps and help from the Salvation Army. I am paying a lot of money in interest. Before I lost my job, I had never even used a credit card. I know I won't get a job that pays as much as I was making at the plant, but right now I would be satisfied with anything. I think about going to work in another state, but I'm afraid I'll lose my rent assistance. It makes me angry that the company got rich and didn't share with us."

Gloria and thousands of other South Texas workers have lost their jobs due to plant closings.[1] Some of these manufacturers had previously closed plants in other parts of the United States in order to move to the cheaper labor environment of South Texas. NAFTA (North American Free Trade Agreement) contained provisions which largely eliminated quotas and tariffs in the textile and apparel industry, resulting in a flood of cheap imports. This forced many U.S.-based factories either to go out of business or move their operations abroad, often to Mexico. Between 1994 and 2004, employment in U.S. textile and apparel manufacturing fell by almost 60 percent, with the loss of over 780,000 jobs.[2] As these jobs went south to Mexico and Central America, as well as to Asia, millions of displaced workers like Gloria were left with shattered lives.

In some ways, the situation experienced by displaced workers in South Texas and elsewhere along the U.S.-Mexico border bears many similarities to the situation of displaced workers elsewhere in the United States. Roughly 1 million U.S. workers were displaced in the 1990s.[3] There are, however, many structural and cultural differences unique to the U.S.-Mexico border.[4] Many, like Gloria, lack a GED or don't know English. With these handicaps, finding a good job in an area that has some of the highest unemployment rates in the nation presents an almost insurmountable obstacle.[5]

Often this difficulty stems not only from workers having given their life to a particular sector (and therefore lacking experience to qualify for a job in another sector) but from a host of factors related to the border location. The South Texas border region follows the national pattern of displaced workers in that they come predominantly from industries that have done worse than average. Displaced workers here also follow the national pattern of being concentrated in occupations with below-average levels of education.[6]

The phenomenon of worker displacement along the U.S.-Mexico border is related to a number of important social issues. Among these are such questions as:

—Do workers experience displacement because of the pressures of
   manufacturing companies to compete in a global economy, or

are these multinationals guilty of exploiting workers and running away to escape their responsibilities to them?

—Do these companies have a responsibility to help their displaced workers become productively employed elsewhere, or should workers be expected to make it on their own?

—Are the problems of displaced workers on the border essentially the same as those experienced by displaced workers elsewhere, or does the border create special problems and special needs for displaced workers?

Displaced Workers in the United States

There has been an ongoing debate about who should be classified as displaced workers. The *most* restrictive definition of a displaced worker includes those workers who are trade-displaced and those long-tenured workers whose plants closed down. The *least* restrictive definition simply includes all workers that have been laid off.[7] Further, according to the Bureau of Labor Statistics, a displaced worker is someone at least twenty years old with at least three years of tenure on a job (excepting temporary and seasonal jobs), who lost that job (without being recalled) due to slack work, abolition of a position or shift, or plant closing or relocation.[8] As Bruce Fallick[9] points out, displaced workers are not workers who are fired for cause. Rather, they are workers who are "displaced" for structural reasons for which they are not responsible.

The Bureau of Labor Statistics in 2002 published a study of workers displaced over a three-year period. This study gives the numbers and percentages of displaced workers in select demographic and industry groups. The period covered in this study was from 1999 to 2001, during which time nearly 4 million workers were displaced. A summary of many of these figures is presented in Table 3.1.

Table 3.1 also shows that older workers (those aged fifty-five to sixty-four) were approximately 15 percent of all displaced workers. The data further show that displacement was more prevalent among men than women. Table 3.1 also shows that nearly one-third of the displaced workers in the United States have been displaced from the manufacturing industry. This proportion continues to be much larger than that of any other sector. Nevertheless, in the mid-1990s, the concentration of displaced workers had

TABLE 3.1. Characteristics of Displaced Workers in the United States, 1999–2001

Characteristic	No. Displaced Workers (in thousands)	% All Displaced Workers
AGE		
20–24	132	3.3
25–54	3,117	78.5
55–64	593	14.9
65+	127	3.2
GENDER		
Men	2,186	55.1
Women	1,783	44.9
RACE/ETHNICITY		
Blacks	474	11.9
Hispanics	335	8.4
Non-Hispanic Whites, other	3,160	79.7
INDUSTRY		
Durable manufacturing	862	21.7
Nondurable manufacturing	456	11.5
Transportation and public utilities	295	7.4
Wholesale and retail trade	723	18.2
Finance, insurance, real estate	284	7.2
Construction	256	6.4
Services	858	21.6
OCCUPATION		
Managerial and professional	1,200	30.2
Technical, sales, administrative	1,133	28.5
Service occupations	229	5.8
Precision production, craft, repair	571	14.4
Operators, fabricators, laborers	745	18.8
Farming, forestry, fishing	37	.9
REASONS FOR JOB LOSS		
Plant closed down	1,874	47.2
Insufficient work	1,010	25.4
Position shifted or abolished	1,085	27.3

Source: U.S. Department of Labor, Bureau of Labor Statistics.

begun to shift from the manufacturing, construction, and mining sectors to the retail and services sectors.[10]

In addition, managers and professionals were beginning to experience a much greater risk of displacement. Fully 30.2 percent of the displaced workers in Table 3.1 were from these categories. Still, they did not make up as large a proportion of displaced workers as blue-collar workers, who generally have below-average levels of education.[11] In Table 3.1, operators, fabricators, laborers, precision production, craft, and repair workers combined made up 33 percent of all displaced workers. Many studies find that high school graduates are more likely to be displaced than college graduates.[12]

Table 3.1 also shows that displacement results more from plant closings than from insufficient work or position shifts. Nearly half of the displaced workers mentioned plant closings as the reason for their displacement. This was true even in the 1980s, when displacement by plant closings was higher than other forms of job losses.[13]

Even when displaced workers again find work, it is often at jobs that pay less than their previous employment. Jacobson, LaLonde, and Sullivan found that the quarterly earnings of displaced workers were 25 percent less than those of nondisplaced workers five years after their displacement.[14] Fallick offers four reasons for this. First, the experience and training of displaced workers is often not applicable to their new job. Second, many must take a new job for which they have had little training. Third, many lose union wage premiums. Finally, most also lose the benefits of job seniority.[15]

Displaced Workers on the South Texas Border

In 1998 the Texas Comptroller of Public Accounts published a report on the economic and social situation of the Texas-Mexico border entitled *Bordering the Future: Challenge and Opportunity in the Texas Border Region*. This report pointed to a disturbing trend in the border region that defies conventional logic. Despite tremendous and rapid growth since the early 1980s, the region's economic standing was not only far below that of the rest of the state and the nation but was actually deteriorating. This pattern was summarized as "growth without prosperity."[16]

The authors of the report summarized economic and social conditions in three distinct areas of the Texas-Mexico border. In this comparison, they concluded that "Lower South Texas is the poorest and the most rapidly growing Border area . . . With nearly 15 percent of its labor force out of work in 1995, Lower South Texas had the highest jobless rate of any area in the State[17] . . . [Its] per-capita income of $13,200 was almost 20 percent less than the average for the Border region and nearly 40 percent less than the state average." In 2001 the data from this report were updated. This update showed per capita income at $18,390.[18] In 1999 the average annual pay in manufacturing was $28,802, which ranked at or near the bottom for any region in the United States. Still, with an unemployment rate in 1999 of 7.5 percent and 27 percent of the border population in poverty, those who held manufacturing jobs were fortunate.

As bad as this situation was for the border as a whole,[19] it was far worse in Hidalgo County. The unemployment rate in the McAllen/Mission/Edinburg metropolitan area was around 20 percent in 1995. Though it declined to around 13 percent in subsequent years, this decline was due primarily to higher-skilled jobs being attracted to the area. Taylor found that professional, technical, and teaching jobs in the Lower Rio Grande Valley paid *more* than equivalent jobs in other parts of the state.[20] Thus, South Texas experienced a situation of more jobs than workers among technical and professional technical positions, while jobs for less skilled workers were scarce.

Then, around 1995, lower-skilled manufacturing jobs began to disappear. Many of these job losses were deemed to be related to NAFTA. From 1994 through 2002, a total of 5,582 workers lost jobs in the cities of the Lower Rio Grande Valley and were certified as eligible for assistance under the NAFTA Trade Adjustment Assistance Program (TAA).[21] Many more workers who were not similarly certified lost their jobs. In the McAllen/Mission/Edinburg area alone, over 4,000 manufacturing jobs were lost between 1995 and 2004, as indicated by Figure 3.1. Under NAFTA and other forms of the globalization of trade, clothing and electronic manufacturing jobs that had been lured to South Texas because of an abundant supply of low-cost labor began to move across the border where labor costs were even lower. Workers in these plants experienced "displacement," though its consequences were far more devastating for many than for manufacturing workers in other parts of the United States.

In part, these devastating consequences were due to dramatic changes taking place in the labor market of the area. Low-skill jobs were being lost at a rapid rate, while NAFTA and other forces were creating higher-skilled jobs that often went begging for lack of qualified workers. As a result, dis-

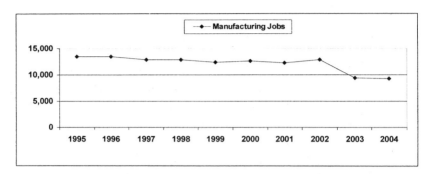

FIG. 3.1. Number of manufacturing jobs in the McAllen/Mission/Edinburg SMA, for years 1995 through 2004 (Data as of February of each of the years indicated. Source: Texas Workforce Commission)

placed manufacturing workers found a shrinking low-skilled job market. Though training was offered that might have made some eligible for the high-skilled jobs that were becoming available, most training programs left them totally unprepared to participate in the higher-skilled and professional labor market. As a result, many had to find work at the very bottom—as laborers, migrant farmworkers, or in other jobs that paid only a fraction of their previous wages.[22] Throughout this chapter, we'll examine the personal and social consequences of worker dislocation on the South Texas border.

Methodology

The research for this analysis was based on eighty-two interviews with displaced workers in Hidalgo County, the largest county (in both size and population) in the South Texas border region. We selected workers who had experienced dislocation at three separate plants: one electronics manufacturer and two separate clothing manufacturers. All three of these plants had closed within two years prior to the interviews. The interviews were conducted in the spring and summer of 2002. Though they contained a few fixed-response questions, they were designed to pose mainly open-ended questions about the experience of these workers leading up to their dislocation and the resulting effects as they attempted to put their lives back together. Because we were looking for ethnographic accounts, we encouraged those interviewed to share experiences and incidents that would illustrate what they had gone through. Many of their stories are included in this book, though we do not use their real names, in order to protect their identities.

Fifteen of the eighty-two interviews had to be conducted by telephone because the person selected for the interview could not be interviewed in person. All of the interviews were conducted in Spanish by one bilingual interviewer who spoke native Spanish.[23] The heavy concentration of Spanish-speaking interviews reflects the overwhelming Hispanic makeup of Hidalgo County (89 percent Hispanic) and the even higher concentration of Hispanic workers in these three plants before they closed.[24]

One of the most common problems in doing the interviews was the difficulty of establishing our identity as researchers. Many of the workers wondered if the interviewer was representing their previous employer. Others were reluctant to talk because they had become involved in a lawsuit against one of the companies and had been warned by their attorney not to speak to anyone. In some cases, the people being interviewed thought the interviewer was going to offer them some help in getting employment, or perhaps some help in getting some benefit from their previous employer. In such cases, we emphasized the strictly research nature of the interview. Still, it was difficult for the interviewer to maintain strict objectivity because of the pain that many of these people were experiencing.

Originally, we hoped to get about the same number of interviews with displaced workers from each of the three companies. We found that displaced workers from the first clothing plant (hereafter referred to as C-1) were not only easier to approach but anxious to talk about their experience. More than half of the former workers from this company that we approached consented to the interview. In addition, the size of the displaced workforce in this plant (718 employees) was much larger than the workforce in either of the other two plants. As a result of these factors, most of the interviews (fifty-eight) were with former employees of this plant.

By contrast, we were only able to interview twelve former employees of the second clothing manufacturer (hereafter called C-2) and fourteen from the electronics company (which we'll call E-1). C-2 had displaced 180 employees, while E-1 displaced only sixty employees. Many of the workers from the electronics company (E-1) whom we approached for an interview turned down the offer because they were still angry at the company for still owing them money and for the way they had been treated. As a result of the smaller size of these last two plants and their greater reluctance to allow interviews, we were able to obtain much less information about displaced workers in them than we did with the first clothing manufacturer (C-1). We will say more about this presently.

A Brief Description of Each of the Plants

C-1

Prior to detailing the experiences of other displaced workers, it is important to point out some of the important characteristics of the three plants where those interviewed had been employed.[25] The first clothing manufacturing plant (C-1) opened in 1974 and closed down in 1999, laying off 718 employees. Ana's husband, Leo, was one of the first workers employed there. Most of the workers that we interviewed felt that this plant had been a good place to work. Many, for example, commented on the efforts of the company to provide benefits and the opportunities extended to workers to get insurance, training, or extra pay after they were dismissed.

Still, there were complaints among the workers about the working conditions in the plant. Some, for example, complained of the asbestos removal, which many of the workers felt had damaged their lungs. Indeed, a fear of cancer seems to have spread among many of the workers, as many talked with some fear about the number of workers who were sick with or had died from cancer.

By far, the most common complaint, however, was injuries related to working conditions. A fifty-year-old woman who had worked for fifteen years at this company, for example, complained of problems with her hands and the loud noises that she had put up with over the years. She claims to have severe hearing loss and very restricted movement in her hands. She believes this is partly because the plant did not give adequate protection to the workers until just a few years before the plant closed. Fully 45 percent of the former workers that we interviewed who had worked at C-1 (twenty-six of the fifty-eight former C-1 workers) mentioned a serious work-related injury from which they were still suffering (mostly in joints—wrists, shoulders, and knees). In addition, three workers were suffering from severe depression, and one was undergoing treatment for breast and bone cancer.

Many workers appreciated the fact that during most of the years the plant was open they were able to work at an accelerated rate and be adequately compensated for doing so. Although this may have worked well for many of the younger workers, older workers often felt that the push for faster work and longer working hours left its toll in work injuries. One fifty-eight-year-old woman described how this situation affected her and her coworkers.

> They pushed us hard to work at higher levels, but within a short time many of us were having problems for which we needed medical attention. They would give you money if you developed an injury, but the money would run out and the injury would not. My wrists and hands hurt a lot. I would rub them and at first it helped. A doctor told me I needed to have rehabilitation and an operation, but some of my fellow workers had had the operation and they had not improved. So I kept working, even though I would sometimes be crying because of the pain while I was sewing. One day, another woman saw me crying and asked what was wrong. When I showed her my swollen wrists, she told me about a traditional Mexican cure—to put a hot onion on the swollen part, along with saliva. I tried it and it helped a lot. I am glad I did not have the operation. Many of those who did get it cannot move their fingers today.

One complaint mentioned by many former C-1 workers was an incentive they had been offered which, because of the plant closing, was not awarded. Apparently, three years before the plant closed, workers were promised that if they would maintain a particular level of productivity over a five-year period, they would receive a very substantial pay bonus. Though they maintained a sufficient level of productivity to meet this goal for three years, the plant closed and no one received any part of this bonus. Miguel, a forty-nine-year-old worker at C-1, relates, "During this time, our plant had become number four in productivity in the entire company. They were supposed to give us this reward in the year 2001, but they closed in 1999. They did not give us anything of what was promised. They deliberately planned it that way, and that's not fair."

In general, however, most of the former C-1 workers had positive things to say about the company. Several expressed gratitude for the efforts the company had made to get them maximum benefits. Others felt pleased that the company had given them some of the sewing machines and other equipment. Many remembered their work with fondness. Of the three plants examined, workers from C-1 seemed to feel best about the treatment they had been given, both during their years of work there and relative to the efforts made by the company to minimize the damage resulting from the plant closing.

It is noteworthy that many of the former workers at C-1 had minimal education, English skills, or prior manufacturing experience.[26] Indeed, many of the workers were former migrant farmworkers for whom a job at this plant represented a major increase in pay. For some, it was the first time they had worked indoors. The benefits provided by the company were often far beyond what many workers had previously experienced.

C-2

In contrast to the first clothing manufacturer, many displaced workers at the second clothing manufacturer, C-2, were still attempting to get promised benefits. In addition, the benefits they received were far less generous than those granted to workers at C-1. None of the 12 displaced workers from this company mentioned having received any assistance in starting their own business. There was an offer made of a week's pay for each year worked, but many expressed frustration in getting these funds. Likewise, some workers mentioned getting health insurance, but for very limited periods of time (in all cases, less than a year).

One couple from C-2 expressed a great deal of frustration at the benefits offered. The husband is fifty-eight years old and his wife is fifty-six. He worked eighteen years at C-2 and she worked there for twenty years. They do not have medical insurance and were not offered any funds to start a business. They hope to get a job until they qualify for Social Security. They had only been out of work for four months at the time of the interview, so they had not really begun to feel the pressures as yet, though they did say that right now they only buy those things that are necessary.

Carlos, another former worker from C-2, felt betrayed by his former employer. He had worked for the company for twenty years. Two years prior to the interview, he had experienced a plant closing by the same company in another location. He requested a move to the plant in Hidalgo County and was granted the transfer, but he found his pay reduced by $1.16 an hour. "Since the work did not require much mental capacity," he says, "I had to accept it because I had a lot of debts and many other workers wanted the job." He is currently receiving unemployment but has called the Texas Employment Commission to report that he has not received the amount TEC promised him. They had told him they would fix the problem, but he had received no further word.

Elena, who worked for eight years at C-2, also felt frustrated by the lack of information about her situation. She hoped her interviewer could help her find out what benefits were available for former workers from C-2. "We did not receive much information," she says. "We had heard about the possibility of funds from NAFTA, but never got any further information." She likewise has had difficulty gaining unemployment benefits and was still waiting to get them seven months after the plant closed.

Unlike workers at C-1, who were skillfully counseled about unemployment, insurance, NAFTA funds, and other benefits, workers at C-2 seem to have been given much less information or assistance. One worker reported he was offered the chance to relocate to another plant in a city five hundred miles to the north but turned down the offer because of the expense involved in making such a move. This worker was the only one from C-2 who reported such an offer.

E-1

This electronics plant manufactured components for computers. The company opened in 1989 and finally closed in May 2001.[27] The official notice that the plant would close was given in February 2001. There had been rumors that it would close, since the company had opened a second plant in Reynosa, Mexico, about fifteen miles away. Still, the company would not confirm them. Finally, several workers went to the Texas Employment Commission to complain that they were losing their job because the plant was moving to Mexico. When the TEC investigated, company officials confirmed that they indeed were planning to close the plant. Some engineers and supervisors were offered the opportunity to transfer to the new plant in Reynosa, Mexico, but at greatly reduced salaries.

Diego is one of the workers who did go to Reynosa. Because he didn't want to lose his supervisory position, he felt it would be better to transfer. He only stayed a few months, however, as the lower pay and the daily hassle of crossing the border became unacceptable. Like many other workers, he is resentful. "It serves the company right to have gone to Reynosa," he says. "Recently, I heard that they were going to close that plant too."

The only other displaced worker that we interviewed who had been offered a transfer to Reynosa was Rebeca. "I could have gone to Reynosa," she says, "but I would have been very afraid of traveling in Mexico and I really don't know anything or anyone over there."

Several of the workers said that they were promised more money than they have actually received. Company officials had told them that they would receive one week's pay for each year that they had worked at the plant. When they received their money, however, some workers found that they had been cut short. Alfredo, one of these workers, is sixty-four years old and suffers from poor eyesight that he blames on the poor lighting in the plant and not having opportunities to rest his eyes. He worked for thirteen years at the plant but was only given two weeks' salary when the plant closed. He comments, "When we found out that they had not paid us what they promised, we went to the employment commission. We are still waiting to see if they can help us get the money that we were promised. I think it's especially unfair since I was one of the workers who stayed until the end to help them close the plant. It wouldn't be so bad, but my wife is sick and I have no health insurance now and Medicaid says I'm not eligible."

Rebeca (mentioned above) also has medical needs and no insurance. She suffers from arthritis and the medicine she needs is so expensive that she had to quit taking it. She is still waiting to see if she qualifies for some training that she would like to take in Houston. She received unemployment but is worried because she will lose it if she is not able to get into a training program.

Sonia, who only worked for E-1 for two years, says someone did try to explain some of the benefits they could apply for. She also is still waiting to find out if she will be accepted in the pharmacy program she selected. She says that many workers have been turned down for training programs because the agency they have gone to claims to be out of funds. Her husband, who is undocumented, works part-time as a janitor. Even though his wife, Sonia, is a U.S. citizen, he cannot apply for residency until they can show that her income is 125 percent of the official poverty line. They are staying with her mother in a small mobile home and living off her unemployment and his part-time wages.

Jose is one worker from E-1 who has been able to get into a training program. "It is a NAFTA-related program," he says, "that pays for our training for a specified period of time. If we require more time than that, we have to pay for it ourselves." He says that people from the employment commission came to the plant shortly after the notices were handed out. "They helped get a lot of people over their fear," he said, "because they told us that we would be able to get training for a different job. It helped calm us down for a time, but many have not been able to learn much English in their classes and many have not been able to find any work."

As the preceding accounts illustrate, plant closings on the South Texas border present some special problems for displaced workers. We can illustrate many of these problems by looking with a bit more detail at one family's experience.

Ana's Family—A Case Study

Ana is a fifty-four-year-old woman who worked fourteen years at C-1. Her husband, Leonardo (Leo), is fifty-three years old and worked at the same plant for twenty years. Their youngest son, Manuel, is twenty-three years old. He also worked at C-1, but only for six years. Ana says that there were many workers who, like themselves, had a spouse or another family member working at the plant. After Leo got a job at C-1, and after he had worked there for a few years, they decided they needed to own their own home, so she applied for and got a job there also.

> The first day was really hard, and I came home crying because I thought I would never be able to learn how to use the machines. My husband helped me get through it, though, and I came to really enjoy the work. For the whole time I worked there, if anyone needed a day off the company would let them work some other day. There was good teamwork and we worked in cells, earning according to how much we produced.
>
> Several years ago, the company decided to change the covering on the plant floor because it contained asbestos. They moved me and the other workers to a different part of the building, but we could still see featherlike dust in the air. They didn't give us much protection, and those who complained were sent to a doctor. He told us that he could find no effects. We found out later that the effects sometimes take ten years to show up. The company had us sign a paper saying that we would not bring any lawsuits against them.
>
> One day, not long after the plant closed, I talked to a man at the grocery store who told me I should be happy for being able

to rest. I thought to myself, "He doesn't know what he's talking about. When we have work we always want to rest. But when the work runs out, no one wants to be resting."

After being laid off, Ana went to an English class for a while but found English very difficult. "I understand a few words," she says, "but I have a difficult time speaking it. Years before, when my children were growing up, I would sometimes practice with them. I would try, for example, to call them to dinner using English. They would laugh themselves to death at the table, so I never had the courage to speak English."

Ana also tried to get her GED but found that neither she nor any of her former workmates were learning much.

The teacher would give us a lot of tests. Just as I'd think I was learning something, she would give us another exam and assign me to another group. I didn't understand anything. Many students complained, but the supervisor didn't pay any attention. I really tried hard, but at my age it's really difficult.

My husband was out of work for three months. He had looked everywhere but could find nothing. He turned down the training and the unemployment that went with it because, he said, someone in the family had to be earning a living. When they offered us $6,000 to start a business, he decided to buy equipment to start a roofing business. Not long after he purchased his tools and equipment, he went to work one Monday morning and found that someone had stolen everything. Finally, my husband got a job in construction, where he earns $8 an hour. It's hard when I see him come home covered with dust and extremely tired. I tell him that I wish he could have done that work when he was younger.

One day, a friend from the plant called to say that a company that packs clothing for Wal-Mart might be hiring. My husband laughed when I told him that I was going with a neighbor who had also worked at the plant. He had been trying every day for three months and no one would hire him because he, like us, didn't know enough English and didn't have a GED. It took us two hours to fill out the application. They hired us on the spot and wanted us to start immediately. They put us to work stacking bundles of clothing. When I got home, my husband was cooking a meal for me. I lasted there for six months, but when I saw how little I was making and when my sister let me take over cleaning a dentist's office, I quit. I was able to do that in the afternoons and be at home with my grandchildren during the time my daughter had to work.

Many of my former workmates talk a lot about being sick. Many of the workers from the plant have died of cancer. A lot of [former workers] believe that the real reason the plant [C-1] closed was so they wouldn't have to pay us damages. I don't know. But they were good to us. They gave us money to start a business and gave us health insurance when we left. While we were working, they also helped pay some of my son's tuition at the community college. They even sponsored a soccer team for one of my sons.

Lately, I have been trying to get my husband to ask for permission at his work for us to go to Mexico for a few days to visit my parents. He tells me that his boss will not let him do that. They also won't pay him for working on holidays. The last time we went back to our hometown in Mexico, we could see that they were building some American factories over there. I don't resent the Mexicans for that. They need the work more than we do. It's sad, though, that they pay so little over there and that we have lost those good jobs on this side.

Factors Affecting Plant Closings in South Texas

Ana's case exemplifies the difficulty that dislocated workers in a border environment experience. Like Ana and her husband, the majority of the workers we interviewed from the two clothing manufacturers had not graduated from high school or completed a GED. Many had not learned English prior to losing their jobs. Ana and her husband each had less than the sixth-grade education that is mandatory in Mexico.[28] "The company offered classes," Ana told us, "but I was so tired after work that I never took advantage of their offer." Their son, Manuel, dropped out of school prior to completing his senior year to go to work at C-1. Like many other young displaced workers, he was close enough to having finished high school that he was able to get a GED without much difficulty.

A number of factors that might help explain worker displacement at the national level may not be valid in this border setting. At each of the three plants, for example, most workers had very limited English-speaking ability.[29] At the two clothing plants, most had not completed high school (at least not in the United States) and did not have a GED. Because of the overall lack of even low-tech jobs in the area,[30] many are faced with long-term unemployment, or employment at or below minimum wage.

GIVING NOTICE

Though the amount of notice given to workers when their plants closed varied considerably from plant to plant, none of the workers had adequate time to prepare themselves economically or psychologically. Some observers might argue, of course, that there is never enough time to adjust to the notice that your work will disappear. Some limited research suggests that at the national level in the United States, increasing the amount of advance notice is not related to more positive employment results. Written notice of more than two months before displacement—the sort of notice mandated by the WARN Act—appears to decrease joblessness by only a small amount, on the average.[31] The primary effect is to increase the likelihood that those who would otherwise experience short spells of nonemployment will avoid it altogether. Lengthy written notice is often associated with higher postdisplacement earnings.[32]

Another factor related to advance notice is the problem of rumors and misinformation. We interviewed two workers at the C-1 plant who technically were not displaced, since they took retirement just weeks before the plant closed. One is a sixty-five-year-old female who worked for twenty years at the C-1 plant. She quit work shortly before the plant closed because of rumors that the plant was closing and might go bankrupt. Several people told her she might lose her retirement if she waited. Because she took retirement shortly before the plant closed, she lost the opportunity to get training and/or unemployment. She says that with better information she would have stayed longer in order to get these benefits. She and her husband both work part-time. She does sewing in her home, even though her hands and wrists are very swollen and she has a hard time using the machine.

As happens throughout the United States, workers along the border react with shock and dismay when plants close. As the reader may recall from her story, Ana said, "When it became certain that the plant would close, many people began to cry and to hold on to one another." For many workers, especially those who have given a good portion of their life to a plant that is closing, losing their job is similar to losing a loved one. Many go through a similar grieving process. Numerous workers at C-1, for example, described extreme emotional turmoil for days and weeks following the announcement. Three of the workers were being treated for severe depression. Several others would have sought treatment but had no insurance or other way to pay for it.

One of these workers, Tomasa, describes her experience with depression. "When I found out the plant was closing, I became very depressed. Even though I began receiving unemployment, I didn't have the desire to do anything. I wanted to be away from everyone and everything. I couldn't sleep at night and I actually longed for the routine of the work and the social opportunities I always had to visit with other workers. During one week, I lost twelve pounds. The doctor told me I was very sick. I'd never thought I would feel so bad about being able to rest and stay home."

GETTING TRAINING AND/OR A NEW JOB

As frustrating and emotional as the shock of having been displaced by a plant closure might have been, most of the people interviewed expressed even greater frustration with the process of trying to find another job. Juanita, a fifty-six-year-old woman with twelve years of experience at C-1, illustrates this frustration. After being laid off, she received unemployment compensation by opting to receive training. Like many former workers at C-1, she was attracted to a course in flower design. She also needed to enroll in a GED class, but was unable to accomplish much there without first taking an English class. She studied hard for both of these classes but completed neither. "They didn't teach us what they told us they would," she says.

Shortly before quitting the courses, she began searching for a job. "I am very shy," she says, "and it has been hard for me to go ask for work. I would get very nervous in the interviews. One employer asked me what I hoped to gain from working for them, and I told him I hoped to gain medical insurance and a roof over my head. I could tell immediately that was the wrong thing to say, but no one had ever told me what to say in an interview. He immediately ended the interview and told me he might call me."

After that, she tried to get a job at Head Start. "I passed out fliers to get a local politician elected, so one of the teachers at Head Start would help me get a job there," she said. "That teacher was supporting him and gave me a lot of fliers and promised to help me with my application if I would hand them out. The politician won the election, but the teacher left the agency. The politician didn't even know me, so I never got any help from him."

Next, Juanita enrolled in a course to become a nurse's assistant. "I couldn't finish it," she says, "because I don't feel qualified to be connecting hoses to people." She says that she heard about another company on Military Highway that was hiring other former workers from C-1. She applied, but they never called her back. She went to another place that makes auto parts and they said they would give her work, but from four till midnight. "I couldn't take the job," she says, "because I would be getting home at one o'clock in the morning. The train goes by at the same time and I was very afraid."

She doesn't have to make house payments, but she does have to pay for the light and other house expenses. "I will have to work till I'm much older to get social security," she observed. "I finally found a job taking care of older people in their homes, but it's only for thirty hours a week. The only thing I don't like is having to work on Saturdays and Sundays and making only $5.35 an hour. They tell me to go and visit a particular person and see if that person likes me. Sometimes the elderly people want me to stay past my assigned hours and they don't understand that I won't get paid for it. Sometimes I do stay, but only as a favor to them. Some of the people have even asked me to cut their lawn and do other work that is not part of my responsibility. Our job is to take care of their physical needs but not to be their servants. It doesn't provide insurance for myself or my son, but at least they let me add my parents, who live across the street, to the list of people I get paid to visit."

Among the eighty-two displaced workers we interviewed, only 17 percent were employed full-time when we interviewed them. Twenty-one percent were employed part-time or in seasonal work (often farmwork), and 4 percent were self-employed. This is consistent with the pattern found in other research, and indicates that displaced workers experience more nonemployment than do nondisplaced workers.[33] It is also consistent with the pattern of older workers having greater difficulty finding work and/ or having to take substantial wage cuts when they do find work.[34] Though the situation for displaced workers in South Texas follows these national patterns, they seem to offer a much more extreme version of each pattern.

Sadly, many of the older workers that we interviewed reported that their job-related injuries often kept them from working. Juanita, mentioned two paragraphs above, is one of these. "I've had problems with an allergy," she says, "but the doctor told me it was because of depression. I can't do much about it, though, because I was not quite fifty years old when the plant closed, so I didn't get health insurance. I have problems moving my hands. I also have problems with my hearing. I can't be sure, but I believe it's partly because the plant did not give us protection for our ears until a short time before it closed."

Other workers choose to turn down potential jobs because of the tremendous cut in pay, coupled with the feeling that they can be of greater benefit in helping care for young, disabled, or elderly family members. This is an option selected by Ana (also mentioned above), who combined caring for her grandchildren (thus freeing up her daughter to work) with a part-time job cleaning a dentist's office.

In spite of the serious depression suffered by many of the workers following their displacement, most made great efforts to obtain employment. Many went to local establishments seeking employment, including a few clothing manufacturers still remaining in the area. Because of the tremendous layoffs, however, hardly anyone got a job at these companies. Others tried to do something in a related industry. Some, for example, were able to get employment in local businesses that sort used clothing for resale. These businesses are increasingly common along the South Texas border, collecting used clothing from around the U.S. for resale in Mexico and elsewhere. Those who obtained employment in these businesses, however, often had to settle for minimum wage on a temporary basis, with no benefits provided.

The length of time that displaced workers remain unemployed is generally greater than that of the general working population, especially during times of economic recession.[35] As we pointed out, many displaced workers in our study suffered reduced employment rather than nonemployment. They also experienced lower rates of pay. For some, these economic problems are the result of a scarcity of jobs in their community. Maria, a worker laid off from the C-2 plant, for example, lives in a small town fifteen miles from the plant where she used to work. The only job possibilities she has been able to locate within fifteen miles are jobs that would require her to work at night. Her husband doesn't want her to take such jobs because of the negative effect it would have on their children. She is bilingual but needs a GED. Though she really wants to study, she feels desperate because bills are piling up and she is afraid they will lose their home.

In all ways that we could identify, displaced workers in this South Texas border community are harder hit by the plant closings than are workers in other parts of the United States. Fallick[36] for example, found that displaced workers who become re-employed in a different industry experience wage cuts on the order of 16 to 20 percent. Most of the workers in our study have not been able to gain *any* subsequent reemployment, and most of those who have are earning at or near minimum wage. For most, this represents a pay cut of over 50 percent. In addition, their inability to keep a job in the same sectors (clothing or electronics manufacturing) represents a substantial loss of human capital. Workers who were deemed very productive in their previous employment now find their skills of virtually no economic value.

As several of the people we interviewed mentioned, one strategy that many workers consider is moving to a different location. Tomás, a worker displaced by the closing of E-1, for example, has been unable to find any work opportunities in the electronics assembly industry in South Texas. He has been told of opportunities elsewhere, but he says he will resist moving as long as possible. "My wife and I both have parents and other family members living in Mexico," he says. It would be hard to leave them. If I can pass the TOEFL exam, I am hoping to get admitted to a program at the university [UT-PA]."

Another problem common in the border is what to do with displaced workers who have educational credentials from Mexican educational centers. Some of the workers we interviewed had a college-level education in Mexico, only to find their credentials disregarded on this side of the border. José, an E-1 worker mentioned above, is one of these. He graduated with a degree in accounting in Mexico but has been unable to use it here, not only because his degree is not recognized, but because he has limited English. Lorenzo is another worker who fits this category. He has an engineering degree from a reputable Mexican university. He has applied for work in several places, but they tell him he needs to complete his GED first, essentially invalidating not only his engineering degree but his high school education in Mexico as well.

Many displaced workers were faced with a dilemma. They recognize the need for better education and training, but their need for income is often severe and immediate.[37] As a result, some turned down courses that could have better prepared them for a different job simply because economic pressures were overwhelming. In such cases, they lose not only the opportunity for training but unemployment compensation as well. Some of these workers have taken jobs as migrant farmworkers or construction workers because they had family members to feed and other very pressing financial situations.

Joaquín, for example, is a fifty-three-year-old man with a wife and four children. He worked fourteen years at the C-1 plant. Upon losing his job, he received unemployment and enrolled in an English class. The unemployment was insufficient to meet the bills, however, so he left the English class and the unemployment benefits to take a job that a friend told him about, working in Iowa as a migrant farmworker. Joaquín and his wife had been purchasing a home in Mexico but lost it after being unable to make two payments. His wife, whom we interviewed in his absence, is unable to work because they have four children in school. Joaquín has only been able to come home for two weeks in the past year. His wife and children miss him greatly, but Joaquín and his wife do not want to leave the Valley because the children are doing so well in school and they hang on to the hope that they will be able to get scholarships and go to college. Throughout the interview, Joaquín's wife had great difficulty speaking because of the hardships they are having, especially having her husband gone for so much of the year.

It became clear during the interviews that many of the displaced workers from all three plants had been poorly advised or poorly served in relation to training classes. Eleven workers in our sample, for example, had been enrolled in a flower design class to help them get a job in garden or flower shops. Only one of these women, however, was able to eventually get a job in this field, and that was only part-time. Another woman from the same plant also got a part-time job in this field, but she did so without enrolling in the course. Several of the workers who took the class are quite angry because, they said, the nine-month course has produced few tangible benefits. When they went to look for jobs, they found no openings and little interest by shop owners. Three of the women were also quite upset because they found that the cost of this course (and an English course some of the others took) was deducted from their $6,000 NAFTA grant, while other participants in the class received these courses as a benefit coupled with their unemployment.

Perhaps worse, many displaced workers were encouraged to enroll in classes for which they were clearly unprepared. Many workers, for example, were enrolled in GED classes—most often taught in English—before they learned to speak English. One woman complained about a GED teacher who spoke no Spanish and virtually ignored the displaced workers in her class who spoke limited or no English. Gloria's problems in a GED course (discussed in the chapter opening) illustrate the frustration of displaced workers in such situations.

Some of the displaced workers we interviewed have become quite innovative in their efforts to find work. One former C-1 worker, for example, began doing volunteer work at her son's school. Eventually, she was able to get occasional work as a substitute teacher, though she gets paid only by the day and receives no benefits. She hopes to get a teaching certificate so that she can become a full-time teacher. Another has gone to a supermarket near her home and occasionally helps straighten up items on the shelves in hopes of being offered a job there.

A handful of workers saw their displacement as a blessing in disguise. Two younger workers from C-2, for example, had been wanting to go back to school to become more employable. The opportunity to have some of the costs paid while receiving unemployment compensation was seen as a positive development.

Getting Benefits

The most important government program to assist displaced workers is undoubtedly the unemployment insurance program. A high percentage of displaced workers nationally are eligible for benefits. Several programs, like the start-up program available through the NAFTA agreement, are more tailored to displaced workers in a border environment.[38]

The role of governmental agencies is obvious in the lives of these workers at every level. Often this presence is more of an obstruction than a benefit. Displaced workers who were productive for many years, for example, were denied benefits because they owned their own homes. Some were denied food stamps for the same reason. Others attempted to open small businesses in their homes but were stopped by city regulations prohibiting such activities. Some of the workers who lived outside the city limits in colonias were able to open shops in their homes, but were located so far from established communities that it was difficult for them to obtain a clientele.

Governmental programs were also notable by their absence. Many workers were unable to get any medical assistance, either because of their residency status or because of severely restricted funds for health clinics in a geographical area where there is much more demand than supply. In such a situation, many workers and their families resorted to alternatives. Elva, for example is a fifty-six-year-old woman, a former migrant farmworker who worked ten years at the C-1 plant. She qualified for medical insurance on the basis of her age but did not have enough years working there to get it. She has rather severe back pains and went for a while to a doctor. He charged her $100 for each visit, so she quit going. When the pain got very intense she went back, but his office staff refused to set up an appointment because she had quit earlier. Then she went to the county health clinic, but they told her she did not qualify. Most recently, she has been going across the border to a Mexican doctor because he charges much less.

STARTING A BUSINESS

While some moderately successful businesses were started from the $6,000 many of the C-1 workers received, the majority of respondents invested their money in ventures that either failed or were discontinued. Often, these failures resulted from an inability to manage the complex governmental regulations that apply to starting a business. In other cases, the failures resulted from a lack of business knowledge. Some resulted because the $6,000 was inadequate to provide the needs—rent, materials, equipment, etc.—of a particular business. Usually these ventures were limited to enterprises commonly found in this minority community in the Valley. Table 3.2 presents a brief analysis of the 23 ventures started by workers we interviewed who had been displaced from the C-1 plant, including the types of business attempted and the results described in the interviews. The final column presents our own analysis of how successful the venture was.

An examination of the data in this table reveals that 11 of the ventures had failed by the time of the interviews, 7 were struggling but still trying to make it, and 5 could be judged to be moderately successful. Three significant difficulties stand out among the failures. The first is a lack of information and/or preparation for running a business. The second is insufficient capital. The third involves problems with family members. Some examples will illustrate these obstacles.

Veronica, a sixty-one-year-old worker at the C-1 plant, was pleased by the offer of $6,000 to start a business. She used the money to buy merchandise to sell in the local flea market. The business failed because, Veronica observes, she wasn't prepared to handle all that a business entails. "It was a waste of money," she says.

Another former C-1 worker wanted to open a Mexican restaurant, but she eventually turned down the offer of $6,000 because she knew it would

TABLE 3.2. Individual Results of NAFTA-Financed Start-up Ventures among 23 Former C-1 Workers

Gender	Type of Business	Outcomes and Reasons Given	Evaluation*
F	Selling used clothing at flea market	Failed. Too many unfamiliar details.	x
F	Selling gold	Few sales. Sold to niece who owes money.	x
F	Sewing intimate clothing	Struggling. Needs more money and training.	?
F	Flower/garden/other shop	Moderate success. Needs new location.	+
F	Flower design course and shop	Insufficient funds to start. Still trying.	?
F	Renting mobile home	Daughter lives there and can't pay rent.	x
F	Restaurant	Invested in with others. No profit for two years. Sold at a loss.	x
F	Investment in land for apartments	Son-in-law is waiting for loan to build.	?
F	Renting tables and chairs for parties	Small income shared among relatives.	+
F	Selling children's clothing	Virtually no sales. Closed in two months.	x
F	Renting tables and chairs for parties	Virtually no customers. Still trying.	?
F	Beauty salon	No profit yet. Seeking new location.	?
F	Band	Equipment bought for son, who plays occasionally. No profit.	x
F	Selling plants at flea market	Some profit. Needs money for own shop.	?
F	Beauty salon	Equipment purchased. Can't start because of cancer treatments.	?
M/F	Renting small house	Fixed up. Small monthly income.	+
F	Unclear	Unclear how money was spent. No business established.	x
M/F	Roofing	Roofing equipment and tools stolen. Business failed.	x
F	Renting small house	Fixed up. No income. Relative stays rent-free.	x
F	Building own home	Finished building. No profit. Only family members.	x
F	Taking English course/Selling jewelry	Counselor paid for English course. Jewelry purchased for resale and making modest profit.	+
M	Selling used clothing at flea market	Making modest profit.	+
M/F	Selling clothing (pants)	Lost money last year. Owe IRS.	x

*Evaluation: + = success; x = failure; ? = too early to determine whether success or failure.

be impossible to open a restaurant with such limited funds. A group of ten women from the same plant had a similar desire, so they decided to pool their funds. They opened a restaurant in McAllen. Lucinda, a forty-five-year-old displaced worker from C-1 that we interviewed, was one of these women. "We came up with the idea of a restaurant while we were still working at [C-1]," she says. Though it looked for a while like we might be successful, we eventually had to close it. I am sorry, but at least we gained some good experience. It was hard to make the restaurant work because we didn't know anything about a lot of the requirements. We got some help from an attorney who explained some things to us, but because we didn't have enough experience we sold the food too cheaply. It was also hard to pay the rent and the taxes. At the same time, many of us were trying to take classes so it was even harder. The restaurant lasted for two years, but we closed it because we were having to pay salaries out of our own pocket. I learned to cook by asking the cooks to show me each thing they did. At the end, we felt like some of us were doing more than others and none of us were receiving any salary. I got back $1,900 of my $6,000 investment, but we never received any profit. Everyone we hired to work for us got a salary, but we didn't. Later, a friend and I thought we could start a tortilla factory, but there are just too many requirements."

Among the moderately successful ventures were two that used the $6,000 to fix up homes they already owned for rental income. Felipe is a fifty-nine-year-old man who worked twelve years at the C-1 plant. He was happy to receive the $6,000, even though the company did not give him medical insurance. He used the money to fix up a rental home, and it brings in a modest monthly return. He also gets some money by working as a security guard for a brother-in-law who has a restaurant. He has studied English but doesn't feel he has learned much. In Mexico he only went through the eighth grade. At the time of the interview, he and his wife were living in an apartment because their home had problems with mold, but the insurance company gave them money to rent an apartment while the home was being fixed. Before he was laid off, his wife was taking medicine that she was supposed to take for the rest of her life. Now they don't have insurance, so she's taking medicinal herbs. He has not gone to look for other jobs because he has problems with his hands and at times he can't control their shaking.

Not all unsuccessful workers, of course, gave up after their apparent failures. This determination is exemplified by Juana, a forty-seven-year-old worker from C-1 who invested her $6,000 in a flower shop. She chose this venture because of the course she was offered when the plant failed. The business failed, however, because there were just too many details. Her son also became sick during this time and she was not able to finish the course. She finally decided to abandon the flower shop and, with the little money she had left, opened a business to supply a variety of services for traditional Mexican celebrations (quinceañeras, weddings, etc.). Her children leave fliers on car windows as advertising. Her business currently brings in a very moderate income.

Findings and Conclusions

The most difficult aspect of this research was seeing the pain of these displaced workers and having to dash what few hopes our contact had raised by telling them we were only there to interview and could do little to help. We were deeply impressed with these workers. Many had formed an extremely deep attachment to their work. It became clear that their jobs were not just their source of income but part of their persona, their self-image, and a big part of their social world. Many workers mentioned having had to struggle with deep depression after their plant closed. Nevertheless, only a few with medical insurance were being treated for it.

When seeing such pain, one wonders if it could have been prevented. We are not in a position, of course, to determine whether the plants really had to close for their corporations to remain profitable. Many manufacturing firms are leaving the United States to take advantage of cheaper labor in other countries. Some, we suspect, simply want to increase their profit margin, even if loyal workers are hurt in the process. Others likely leave because they find it hard to compete with those now paying greatly reduced labor costs in other countries.

But there is more to corporate responsibility than the search for cheaper labor. As we became aware of many of the injuries and health problems apparently caused by working at the plants, for example, we wondered, along with the workers, whether the decision to relocate to Mexico was calculated to avoid lawsuits or obligations to compensate those who had been injured. There was an extremely high number of work-related injuries at the C-1 plant. If the other two companies had similarly elevated rates of injuries, we were unable to detect it from the limited number of interviews we did with their workers. Certainly, relocating plants in Mexico presents a much lower risk of having to compensate work-related injuries.

Though many of the workers at the C-1 plant liked their company, they also suspected it of exploiting them by not paying any portion of the bonus they had been promised for greatly increased production. The pressures to achieve this production level had undoubtedly led to some of the stress-related injuries reported. Skipping out on this responsibility because the plant closed before the end of the designated period certainly created suspicions of exploitation.

We found it interesting that the C-1 plant management seems to have done the most to help their displaced workers become productively employed elsewhere. Unlike the other two plants, they continued to provide health insurance for older workers who had significant seniority in their jobs. In addition, they also helped workers receive the $6,000 from NAFTA funds to start up businesses. Finally, they seem to have provided better counseling for getting workers into training programs, though many of these training programs were poorly designed and implemented.

The training programs provided, however, rarely resulted in any lasting economic or occupational benefit to displaced workers. Unless workers could establish that their displacement resulted from the NAFTA agreement, they could only receive six months of unemployment benefits. If they did qualify under NAFTA, the longest unemployment time they were given was two years. Even this, however, was not enough time to learn English, much less take Adult Basic Education classes, obtain their GED certificate, and finish a training program that would truly prepare them for a good job.

Even when NAFTA funds were made available to start microenterprises, most displaced workers were largely unable to establish a successful business. Some system of counseling in basic business decisions could have helped many. One of the most common causes of failure, for example, was business locations that were costly or poorly located.

Perhaps the most important finding of the research was that the South Texas border environment greatly magnifies the problems that displaced workers elsewhere suffer. The high unemployment rate of the area, coupled with the very minimal educational background of the workers, seems to result in many workers being unable to get even lower-paying jobs. Many felt fortunate to find even a minimum-wage job, because many of their former workmates were still unemployed and no longer able to receive unemployment compensation.

This largely Mexican-origin population coped by falling back on traditional cultural responses. Those with no health insurance, for example, had to rely on traditional herbal remedies or visits to doctors across the border in Mexico (as described in Chapter 1). These responses were almost always selected, however, because they could not afford more conventional forms of medical treatment.

The family was also an important coping resource, though in some cases it also created an additional burden. For instance, the demands of some family members on displaced workers made it difficult for them to use their resources to their maximum benefit. Their strong attachment to the area and to family in Mexico, for example, kept many workers from relocating to regions where jobs were more plentiful. In some cases, family members wanted to use a part or all of the $6,000 grant for their own purposes (e.g., a son using the money for a band that never got off the ground; a husband letting his brother live rent-free in his wife's rental home; and a son-in-law borrowing the money to build a small apartment complex that he has not yet started). Though most of the workers we talked to found family members more a help than a hindrance, they were an additional burden for some workers. The married children of one woman, for example, suggested that she was a bad mother because she was not able to help them like she used to.

There were far more examples of the positive influence of the family, however. Many displaced workers were able to call on family members for housing, employment, child care, moral support, and financial assistance. We saw a lot of family resource pooling, for example, and shifting jobs and duties to maximize income-generating possibilities. Some displaced workers, for example, took care of grandchildren so the mother or father, who was often more employable (better education and English-speaking ability), could work full-time.

We also found evidence that considerable social capital had developed among the displaced workers at the C-1 plant. Many called each other on a regular basis, either to provide emotional and moral support or to pass on information about job opportunities or government programs that might be of assistance. In several cases, they worked together to form businesses or even long-term moral support groups. When one would find a job, he or she would frequently try to help others get a job there also. This is a resource that we believe is greatly underutilized and underexamined.

South Texas is a land of resilient people. Many of these workers had migrated from Mexico and started their lives here as migrant farmworkers. The jobs they obtained in these manufacturing plants represented a clear step up. Though great hardships resulted from the plant closings, many rallied together to overcome this setback. Others fell back on family. Though they somehow managed to cope, the losses they suffered translate into a great loss for the region. Good, loyal workers, especially those who have dedicated a major portion of their lives to these industries, should not be so easily cast aside.

4 Undocumented Workers

WITH ALBERTO RODRIGUEZ

Miguel is from the interior of Mexico. Many years ago, he came to the border searching for work.

"I came with just the clothes on my back," he says. "I've worked in restaurants on both sides of the border. People think that because we are poor and hungry, we will take any kind of abuse. In Reynosa, they tried to tell me that I should be grateful I had a place to eat and to sleep.

"So I decided to cross into the United States. I nearly drowned crossing the river. I went to the restaurants here and got a job really fast. After the first week, I asked the boss when I was going to get paid. He told me he would hold the money for me and put it in a bank. I was grateful that I had a place to eat and to sleep, but I needed to send money home. After the first six months, I went to the boss and told him I needed my money. He got really angry. I didn't know what to do. I begged him. Finally, he gave me $80, which I sent home right away. After that I knew to ask for my money right away, but it didn't help. He simply called La Migra [Border Patrol], and they sent me back across the river.

"So I tried again, this time with my family, and we made it all the way to Indiana. A farmer hired us, but many Americans there were angry at him for hiring us. He told us not to worry because none of them even wanted to pick tomatoes, so we weren't really taking anything away from them. They should have seen where we lived.

"Finally, we decided to come back to the border. I got part-time work in Rio Grande City, taking care of a car lot. It wasn't enough to live on. Finally, when my children hadn't eaten all day, we decided to go to the food stamp office. They gave us an appointment, but when my wife and I got there the lady said we were late and had missed our appointment. I explained that I couldn't read, but she made us wait all day. That day I wanted the earth to swallow me up. It's because I am stupid that my children have gone hungry. As soon as I get back on my feet, I'm going to tell those people at the food stamp office what they can do with their food stamps."

As Miguel points out, many U.S. citizens are angry, believing that "illegal aliens" are "invading" their country, trying to steal jobs and cheat on welfare. Many Americans see this migration in simplistic terms, as a crime that should be prevented or punished. Politicians often inflame the public, playing on fears of a loss of "the American way of life," U.S. jobs, and the swamping of our health, educational, and welfare systems.[1]

In this chapter, we will focus on the migration and work experiences of undocumented workers, paying special attention to the following:

—Do undocumented workers take away jobs from U.S. workers and hurt our economy, or does their cheap labor create jobs, provide us with cheaper goods and services, and help the U.S. economy?
—Do undocumented workers use more tax-supported services than citizens, or do they contribute more in taxes than they take out in services?
—Do undocumented workers threaten the U.S. culture by refusing to assimilate, or do they assimilate rapidly and even add positively to our culture?
—Are undocumented workers exploited and abused by U.S. employers, or should they be grateful for their pay and treatment in the U.S.?
—Should undocumented workers be given additional protections to prevent exploitation and abuse, or is such treatment an effective deterrent to continued undocumented immigration?
—Do most undocumented workers come to the United States seeking permanent residence, or are they simply trying to earn enough to live better in Mexico?

As Miguel pointed out in our opening story, one of the major complaints by U.S. citizens is that undocumented workers take jobs from U.S. citizens. A rather extensive body of research shows that while they do take some jobs desired by some U.S. workers, they also create many jobs. According to the Inter-American Commission on Human Rights, undocumented workers compete more with each other for wages than with U.S. workers.[2] A study by the University of Illinois at Chicago found that undocumented workers spend almost $3 billion a year in the Chicago region as consumers, which provides jobs to those who provide these goods or services.[3] The contribution of all Latino immigrants, of course, is much greater. In 2004 the Inter-American Development Bank, based on survey and census data, reported that Latin American immigrants (legal and undocumented) in 2004 contributed an estimated $450 billion to the U.S. economy, often doing jobs spurned by others.[4]

In addition, the low pay and hard work of undocumented immigrants also holds down the costs of goods and services for all the rest of us. Thomas Espenshade, after thoroughly reviewing the research on this question, concludes, "There is little evidence that undocumented migrants have negative labor market consequences, despite what the general public thinks . . . U.S. immigration may not be far from what society might view as socially optimal."[5]

Another frequently voiced complaint by U.S. citizens and politicians is that undocumented immigrants burden us with demands for tax-supported social services. Erasmo Ramirez, who has been living in McAllen, Texas, for the past four years without legal documents, is puzzled by this complaint because he pays taxes.[6] "Taxes have always been deducted from my paycheck," he says. Much of the research on this subject backs him up, showing that undocumented workers pay more in taxes than they get in benefits. Francisco Rivera-Batiz, for example, used survey research to show that the majority of undocumented workers do not come here seeking welfare payments, health care, or other government handouts. They come to work for short periods of time to earn quick money that they can then use to supplement their meager incomes in Mexico.[7]

Similarly, the study by the University of Illinois at Chicago that polled 1,653 documented and undocumented immigrants in metro Chicago found that only a very small number of them were receiving any government benefits. They concluded that undocumented immigrants support thousands of other workers in the local economy, pay taxes, and demonstrate little reliance on government benefits.[8]

At the national level, there is almost no evidence to indicate that immigrants impose net burdens on other taxpayers[9] at the federal level. In fact,

Espenshade shows that immigrants provide a fiscal surplus.[10] Sidney Weintraub and Gilberto Cardenas[11] also found that undocumented immigrants provide large fiscal benefits to the State of Texas because they don't use many public services and they make relatively high tax payments.

In reality, most of the costs to our social service systems that are created by undocumented immigrants are probably borne more by local governments than by the federal government. Still, Espenshade warns us against concluding that states and localities would be better off without undocumented immigrants. "Immigrants' participation in the economy is often ignored in these calculations," he states, "yet immigrants increase corporate profits and help generate employment for others through their work and consumption activities."[12]

Many Americans, however, are convinced that undocumented immigrants come to the United States to receive welfare. According to a study by the Urban Institute, U.S. citizens have a higher percentage of people on welfare than do noncitizens (17.9 percent for citizens versus 14.5 percent for noncitizens).[13] One official at a local Texas Department of Human Resources office agreed, especially in relation to food stamps. "Illegal aliens are not allowed to participate in the food stamp program," he said. "There are some exceptions and some illegal aliens [such as those with U.S. citizen children] do have rights to food stamps. But on the whole, most do not qualify. We get very few cases of illegal aliens coming in to apply for food stamps."

Another fear of undocumented Mexican immigrants is that they are coming in massive waves, threatening to overrun our country and our institutions.[14] Some alarmists use data on apprehensions by the Immigration and Naturalization Service (which show roughly 1 million apprehensions per year) to promote the idea that roughly that number manage to get into the U.S. each year. Actually, the INS estimates that only 350,000 aliens manage to enter the U.S. illegally each year. Probably the best guesses have been made by the Urban Institute Immigration Studies Program, which estimates that there are 9.3 million undocumented immigrants in the United States.[15] According to these figures, the largest concentrations are in California (2.4 million), Texas (1.1 million), Florida (0.9 million), New York (0.7 million), Illinois (0.4 million), and New Jersey (0.4 million); all others combined constitute 3.5 million.[16]

In recent years, undocumented immigrants have been accused of being major contributors to high crime rates in the United States. Peter

Brimelow, for example, reports that "criminal aliens—noncitizens who commit crimes—accounted for over 25 percent of the federal prison population in 1993."[17] Such figures are used to portray illegal aliens as more crime-prone that the rest of the population. These data distort reality in several ways. First, as Rebecca Clark and Scott Anderson[18] point out, almost half (47 percent) of illegal alien federal prisoners are in prison for unlawfully entering the United States, an offense that only applies to them and is generally seen as an administrative, not a criminal, violation. In addition, Clark and Anderson point out that "a tremendous share of the illegal aliens . . . are not resident illegal aliens; they are recent border crossers."[19] This would include many of the individuals who cross drugs illegally into the United States—hardly undocumented workers.

Though immigrants who cross the border without documentation have broken a law, most are rarely intent on preying on U.S. citizens. Most are more concerned with feeding a family than breaking our laws. George Friedman points out that the United States was founded by immigrants, many of whom entered without official permission. He points to two types of immigrants: "those who came to the United States and those to whom the United States came."[20] Native Americans, for example, did not come to the United States. The United States came to them and conquered them. Mexicans, he points out, are in a similar category. When the United States conquered half of Mexico's territory, the United States came to Mexicans. As a result, many Mexicans do not see the border between Mexico and the United States in a rigid political sense.[21] Friedman states, "The borderlands—and they run hundreds of miles deep into the United States at some points—have extremely close cultural and economic links with Mexico. Where there are economic links, there always are movements of population. It is inherent."[22]

The impact of undocumented immigrants on U.S. culture is similarly misunderstood. As we pointed out in the opening chapters, many Mexican immigrants tend to lose much of their Mexican culture within few generations (especially those who settle outside the borderlands). In addition, they contribute to a strong work ethic and are very supportive of family values. Nevertheless, writers such as Samuel Huntington promote the idea that Mexican-origin people do not assimilate. He says, without much evidence or justification, "Mexican Americans no longer think of themselves as members of a small minority who must accommodate the dominant group and adopt its culture. As their numbers increase, they become more committed to their own ethnic identity and culture."[23] He goes on to fret that this large immigration (especially by undocumented immigrants) will divide the United States into two countries.

Unlike Huntington, most scholars on this topic conclude, as we did in Chapters 1 and 2, that Mexican immigrants are assimilating rather quickly. Linda Chavez,[24] for example, points out that in California 40 percent of Mexican American voters supported Proposition 187, an anti-immigration initiative. Likewise, as she points out, people of Mexican descent were also partially responsible for passing other fairly conservative propositions, such as Proposition 209 (against affirmative action in 1996) and Proposition 227 (doing away with bilingual education in California). Finally, she shows that females of Mexican descent are intermarrying at faster rates than many members of other immigrant ethnic groups traditionally have in the past.[25]

Rodolfo Acuña looks at other measures of assimilation, including home ownership. Mexican immigrants who arrived in the 1990s, for example, had a 31.9 percent home ownership rate. In comparison, 51.6 percent of those who arrived in the 1980s now own homes and 70.5 percent of those who came before 1980 now own their own homes.[26] This is significant in light of a study by Douglas Massey and Kristin Espinosa that found that home ownership promotes greater stability and is associated with lower rates of repeat migration among undocumented migrants.[27] Thus, it would seem that Mexican immigrants are not only becoming assimilated but are also buying into Huntington's American Creed.

In the remainder of this chapter, we will examine undocumented Mexican immigration in relation to the issues raised above. We will also address such questions as why they come, how they are treated, and how they adjust to life in the United States.

Methodology

The research presented in this chapter relies on two major interview projects. The first is an in-depth interview project that spans the years 1982 to 2005 and involved more than 200 interviews with undocumented workers. Students who chose to participate in this aspect of the project usually identified the individuals to be interviewed by means of family members or friends. One young student, for example, did her project on undocumented workers during the 2005 spring semester. She describes her experience in finding people to interview as follows:

> My first attempt was to approach some undocumented workers who were working at a construction site near my home. They politely refused my request for an interview, saying, "Si hablo contigo, me corre el patrón!" [If I talk to you, the boss will fire me.] I felt dreadful for putting them in that sort of situation, so I left. Then I told my grandfather about the situation. He did what grandfathers do best and helped me find three undocumented workers willing to talk to me. The other four interviews came with great ease by using the snowball method. Each of these individuals had ties to many other undocumented workers who were willing to help me with my project.

The second project was a survey of 150 undocumented workers, conducted in 1994, that contained fixed-response questions. Many of the questions in this survey were designed to be comparable to questions asked in an earlier study of undocumented domestic servants (see *Batos Bolillos, Pochos, and Pelados*, chap. 3). In 1997, when the Undocumented Workers Survey was conducted, 30 percent of respondents reported that they had come to the U.S. since 1990. Another 37 percent reported having come in the 1980s, 20 percent during the 1970s, 9 percent during the 1960s, and 4 percent during the 1950s. More than 96 percent of the respondents were from Mexico. Forty-three percent of respondents in this Undocumented Worker Survey were from Northern Mexico, and 74 percent were males.

About a third of the student interviewers who conducted this survey project identified their subjects through a friend or neighbor.[28] Twenty-one percent interviewed someone whom they knew was here illegally. Eight percent found their respondent through the employer of the undocumented persons they interviewed. Thirty-four percent of student interviewers found their subjects with the help of family members. A few even interviewed family members who were undocumented. One student who interviewed her mother said, "I didn't expect to hear such sadness and remorse. My mother grew up in Mier, Tamaulipas, Mexico. When I asked her what they usually ate, she responded with a disgusted look on her face, 'No más puros frijoles' [Nothing but beans]. She asked me if I would eat beans for breakfast, lunch, and dinner every day. Of course, my answer was no. I was grossed out that she'd had nothing but beans every day. She told me that once in a while they would get a few eggs to eat from their neighbors' chickens."

Why They Leave Mexico

It is difficult for many immigrants to report a single reason for leaving their home in Mexico. This is illustrated by one immigrant who tells the following story: "My father was a drunk and my mother died when I was sixteen years old. I was the oldest of four children, so I had to find a way to support us. I came as an illegal and had no place to stay. I hid in a cemetery for many days, afraid of La Migra; it all seems like a bad dream now. I felt so lonely and missed my family. When I finally found work, I didn't like it because the work was so hard and they paid me so little."

In our Undocumented Workers Survey, we asked respondents to state the main reason why they had come to work in the United States. The vast majority of respondents reported economic reasons for coming, including 28 percent who said their main reason was to support their own family. Though economic factors are reported as the primary factor in their decision, economic considerations do not fully explain migration decisions. Douglas Massey, for example, found that other factors, such as number of friends or family already established in the United States, the number of times the person has come, and many other family and community-related factors are all important considerations. He says, for example, "In a narrow sense, of course, migration between the two countries is strictly economic . . . But these basic economic motivations are defined within a social context . . . Migration has a way of feeding back upon itself through a complex social process that is very poorly understood."[29]

Mr. Gonzalez is one of the migrants who claimed that economic factors were his main consideration. In 1983 he was a laborer in Mexico, earning the equivalent of $4.10 a day in U.S. money. Often, this was not enough to feed his family. Some days, they would go without eating because he could not afford food. Then he lost his job. Before coming to the United States, he spent months searching for another job. He says, "I would have taken any job, even if it paid $1 a day, but I couldn't find any work. So I decided to come to the United States to support my family." At the time of the interview, he was an undocumented farmworker, earning $15 and three meals a day working for a local farmer. He is happy to have a job, but he sees the abuse of undocumented farmworkers as a serious and unrecognized problem.

Twenty-seven percent of our respondents reported that lack of work in Mexico was their primary reason for coming. Isidro is one of these. "Most people are just like me," he says. "We were having a hard time getting by. Because I had relatives living in the U.S., I had a dream of going to *el otro lado* [the other side]. I just wanted to get enough money to return to Mexico, buy myself a house and a car, get married, and raise a family."

Isidro reports that in spite of the problems in Mexico, many people will not even consider leaving. "My friends and other people that I spoke to," he says, "don't even think of coming to the United States. First, most don't know anyone here. Second, they feel they could not leave their families behind. Some family members, they say, would feel betrayed or think everyone would believe that they were doing something illegal, like drug smuggling."

Twenty-four percent of the respondents in the Undocumented Workers Survey expressed the need to help their parents support the family as their main reason for coming. Many, of course, are sending money to their wives and children. We found, however, that fewer of the undocumented workers in this survey were sending money than we previously found in our Undocumented Maids Survey, as reported in *Batos, Bolillos, Pochos, and Pelados.* Over 35 percent of those in the Undocumented Workers Survey (three-fourths of whom were males) indicated that they were not sending money home to anyone. In contrast, 93 percent of those in the Undocumented Maids Survey (all of whom were female) reported that they were sending money home. This seems to reflect a greater independence of family obligations on the part of males who come as undocumented workers.

According to the survey by the Inter-American Development Bank mentioned above, Mexican and other Latin American immigrants who lived in the United States sent $30 billion a year back to their native countries in 2003.[30] This estimate was based on U.S. Census data and the findings of an unprecedented survey among Latin American immigrants in thirty-seven states and the District of Columbia. According to this survey, approximately 10 million of the 16.7 million Latin American–born adults in the United States send money regularly to their families abroad. The Bank of Mexico, using World Bank data, calculated that Mexicans and Mexican-origin people in the United States sent a total of $13.3 billion back home as remittances in 2003.[31]

Clearly, undocumented workers come not only for their own economic well-being but to aid their families in the home country as well. Most have left a very bleak economic situation. One of the male undocumented workers contacted in the in-depth interview project, for example, said, "When I left Monterrey, times were very hard. My father had lost his little store.

My mother, who had seven kids, could not work. So there were days when all we had to eat was tortillas. My leaving left one less mouth to feed in the house and it helped to bring in some outside money to the family."

Another man reported similar conditions as his reason for leaving Mexico. "There was no work in my town at all," he says, "so I contacted an aunt living here in Texas. She and her husband told me how to get across and somehow I made it. This is better. You can buy things besides food here." Then, pausing to reflect, he adds, "Well, not a lot but you can buy some."

One immigrant remembers the difficulty of life in Mexico. "I lived in a house that our family of four shared with two other families. My father would leave early in the morning to go and work as a laborer with the two other men. He would return home late in the evening with what little money he made. Some days, he would be paid with food and other days he would be paid with money. My mother would mend clothing for extra money. One day, my brother went to a nearby village and stole a chicken so we could eat that day. He was careful not to let our parents know how he had obtained our dinner."

Of the approximately one-fourth of our survey respondents who were women, economic issues were also of great importance. Many, however, also described personal aspects of the life they left behind. Mrs. Medina, for example, remembers times when her family in Mexico had no soap for a bath. "We would have to go to the neighbors to ask for a piece of soap," she says. "They would give us the pieces that were almost all used up." The female student who interviewed her says, "It boggles my mind to think of all the basic personal needs as a young lady she had to do without. She did mention other personal ordeals that she had to endure, but I felt they were too personal to include."

Family reunification is another important reason many immigrants cross the border illegally. Miguel, for example, is sixty-two and was born in Nuevo Leon, Mexico. "When I was a little boy of eight or nine," he says, "my mother remarried a man from the United States and moved over here. She left us behind with my grandmother. When our grandmother died, my older brother and I decided to come over and look for her. We had to swim the river because we had no papers. I was just fifteen and very scared. La Migra got us the first time, but we tried again and made it without any further problems. It was a good feeling. I have been here ever since and today I am a citizen of the United States."

Being close to family also influences where these migrants settle. Massey and Espinosa, for example, found that the web of social relations both at home and in the new country have a lot to do with where they eventually end up.[32] They report:

> Migration is very strongly encouraged by having social connections to U.S. migrants. During the initial stage of migration, ties to parents, siblings, and community members with U.S. experience are most important in raising the odds of taking a first U.S. trip, with or without documents ... The migration of wives and children and the birth of children in the United States strongly raise the odds of taking additional U.S. trips, documented or undocumented, and strongly lower the odds of returning to Mexico, especially among those with documents.[33]

Finding Work

For those who manage to enter the country without inspection and evade immigration officers, finding work is often the greatest hurdle. As many discover, however, finding work where they are not abused or exploited is an even greater obstacle. One undocumented man illustrates this sentiment. "Getting a job is easy if you are a Mexican citizen," reports Mario Cantú. "Most people who realize you don't have papers want to hire you because they know that you will take less money than someone who has papers. Jobs are easy to find. It is the pay that is hard to take."

Networks are often used by new immigrants to find a job. Aguilera and Massey found that the social capital created by networks is closely related to the migrant experience. They state that "having friends and relatives with migratory experience improves the efficiency and effectiveness of the job search to yield higher wages."[34]

Because of the difficulties in finding work, most undocumented immigrants stick close to well-established networks. This has led to the growth in recent years of immigrant enclaves. These enclaves help make the transition easier, as members can rely on the experience and assistance of other immigrants. In these communities, members are able to work and live around people who know and understand their culture and background. Nevertheless, these enclaves may also serve to make recent undocumented immigrants easy prey for unscrupulous con artists and employers who only offer exploitation wages.[35]

Undocumented Farmworkers

A report by the Pew Hispanic Center estimated the undocumented agricultural worker population to be around 1.2 million workers in 2001.[36] Other studies have found a pattern of undocumented workers with a rural background being drawn much more into agricultural work than those who grew up in urban areas. In an in-depth analysis of migrant employment, for example, Massey found that 91 percent of undocumented migrants from rural areas who were in their first year in the United States became migrant farmworkers. Among those from urban areas, 40 percent found jobs in the United States in agriculture. Even those individuals who had never worked in agriculture in Mexico often started out in agricultural jobs. After fifteen years, however, the figure for all undocumented agricultural workers, both urban and rural, fell to only 38 percent. Over time, then, undocumented Mexican workers tend to leave predominantly agricultural jobs and move into industrial and service occupations.[37]

There is evidence that one of the reasons Mexican migrants leave agricultural work is because of poor working conditions and exploitation. Among those we interviewed, accounts describing the most work-related abuse tended to come from undocumented workers employed in seasonal agricultural work. "The first day that I immigrated to the United States," says one, "I was offered work on a farm. I accepted the job because I needed money to buy food. I had to work the entire week without breaks. My job was to irrigate the fields. I was given shelter at night in a barn. That didn't bother me too much, because I only wanted to work. I really needed the money because I had promised my family that I would send money as soon as I started working. At the end of the week, I asked the employer for my paycheck and he replied, 'What paycheck? You didn't do as much work as I was expecting.' I felt really angry because I had worked the whole week in the hot sun for nothing. I wanted to quit, but he told me that I had to work the following week or else he would report me to the Border Patrol. I didn't have much choice, though the next week I left the farm at three in the morning without telling him. When I got to another town, I stopped by a store. The owner asked me where I was from. When I told him I needed work, he offered me a job in the store. This man was different because he paid me a fair wage and gave me a nice place to stay. Years later, I applied for amnesty, which gave me the opportunity to work legally, with rights." [38]

Though conditions have generally improved for documented farmworkers over the years, many farmworkers who are undocumented still

report occasional harsh treatment. One student interviewed two brothers and their sister who came to the United States four years ago seeking
work. They made it to Wisconsin, where they found work outside a small
town. "We had a bad experience the first day we started working there,"
says Beto. "It was a very hot day and our sister, María, got a really bad
headache. The farmer wasn't around, so we told her to go lie down under a big tree next to the field where we were working. When *el patrón* [the
boss] came back and saw her underneath the tree, he started yelling at her.
She tried to explain that she didn't feel well, but it was useless because she
couldn't speak English. Soon a friend of ours went over to explain that
María was ill and that was why she was resting. The boss said he was sorry
but that she needed to get back to work the second she felt better. María
felt so humiliated from being yelled at that she immediately went back to
work. Two hours later, she was sweating a lot and almost fainted. We took
her back to the camp and gave her two aspirins and put her to bed. It took
María nearly a week to recover from that incident and go back to work. We
all felt like going back to Mexico, but we just couldn't."

Though some social scientists claim that undocumented workers are
not really exploited,[39] there is clear evidence they are. Using data from the
Census Bureau and from the U.S. Department of Labor (Legalized Population Survey), Rivera-Batiz found that legal male Mexican immigrants in
the United States earned 38 percent more than undocumented workers in
the late 1980s. Legal female immigrants earned 37 percent more. Even when
such characteristics as knowledge of English, amount of time in the United
States, and educational attainment are taken into account, these characteristics explain only 15 percent of the wage gap between legal and undocumented male workers and only 32 percent of the difference between legal
and undocumented female workers.[40] In addition, Rivera-Batiz found that
undocumented workers who became legalized after the 1986 amnesty program showed significant gains in their wages in the four years following
legalization.[41]

In part, the exploitation of undocumented workers is affected by the
culture and attitudes of the U.S. public toward "illegal aliens." This term,
of course, reflects a strong negative bias against those who enter the U.S.
without authorization to work. Many residents of the Valley reject this
characterization, believing that undocumented people are only doing what
is necessary to survive. Others, however, believe it accurately reflects their
status as unwanted outsiders who are breaking the law. This ambiguity is

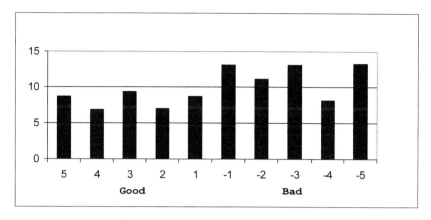

FIG. 4.1. Percent South Texas respondents selecting each level of how good or how bad it is for people from Mexico to cross illegally into the U.S. to work if they can't find work in Mexico

reflected by data collected in our Perceptions of Deviance Survey, shown in Figure 4.1. This figure summarizes how 424 respondents from the Rio Grande Valley responded to the question about how right or how wrong it is for people from Mexico to cross into the U.S. to find work, if no work is available in Mexico.

As Figure 4.1 illustrates, the combined percentages who considered it bad for illegal immigrants to come for work when no work is available in Mexico was somewhat higher (59 percent) than the categories who viewed it as something good (41 percent). Nevertheless, certain groups of people responded very differently to this question. When we calculated the average (mean) score for different ethnic/racial/national categories, for example, we found significant differences between Mexicans, Mexican Americans, Anglos, "Others," and "Americans." These differences are illustrated in Figure 4.2.

As Figure 4.2 indicates, those who call themselves Mexicans, on the average have a somewhat positive evaluation of undocumented workers coming to the U.S. All Mexican Americans combined, in comparison, have a slightly negative view[42] but significantly less so than those who classify themselves as Anglos, Whites, or Americans.[43] These results seem to confirm the strong pressures towards assimilation. They also appear to contradict the views of Huntington, Brimelow, and others who claim that Mexican immigrant families do not assimilate.

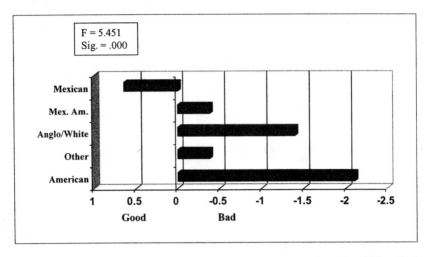

FIG. 4.2. Mean scores (from +5 to −5) of South Texas respondents in self-described racial/ethnic/national categories selecting each level of how good or how bad it is for Mexicans to come illegally to the U.S. to work

The Powerlessness of Undocumented Workers

In order to get some idea about how much undocumented workers in South Texas earn, we asked respondents in the survey to indicate which hourly amount was closest to their earnings. Over 80 percent of our respondents reported earning $4 an hour or less. By comparison, the earlier mentioned case study conducted by the University of Illinois at Chicago found that the median hourly wage of undocumented immigrants in the Chicago area was $7. Though this is a great improvement over the situation we found on the border, immigrants in the Chicago study who were legal had a median hourly wage of $9.00. Still, the Chicago study also found that 10 percent of undocumented immigrants in the study were paid less than the $5.15 minimum hourly wage.[44]

Arturo is one who feels cheated in his pay. "My employers pay me less than other employees who do the same job," he says. "I understand that they are taking a risk because I don't have papers. But they are greedy. Many of them are Mexicans themselves, but that doesn't matter. Just because we are undocumented, they think they don't have to pay us American wages. They want to keep all of their profit. If a worker is undocumented, he won't get paid by the hour. He'll get a weekly salary. I can't live on what they pay. To make extra money I sell herbs on the side. I study to be able to tell clients about how they can control high blood pressure and diabetes with herbs. I make more money through selling these herbs."

The most blatant form of cheating undocumented workers on their pay, however, is experienced by those who work for a period of time only to be fired with no pay. Domingo, for example, came to the U.S. in 1984 when a friend told him that a local farmer was hiring people at a great salary. "At the time," he says, "I was in a very difficult economic situation. I decided to leave my family in Jalisco and come here to work. I had to pay $500 to a smuggler to get me across the river. When I got to the farm, they gave me a very small trailer house to live in. It had no toilet and they only fed me one meal a day. At the end of three weeks, I decided to move, so I asked the farmer for my pay. He said that I was a *mojado* [wetback] and that I had not worked for him at all. I felt so angry that I yelled many bad words at him. He got really mad and called the police. I ended up in jail with no money and was finally deported."

More commonly, undocumented workers are not only underpaid but find they are expected to do more than other workers. Alberto, for example, got a construction job and was given $200 in advance. He spent long hours preparing to pour concrete foundations. "After working for several weeks," he says, "another worker told me that workers doing the same job made $65 to $75 a day. That made me angry. When I brought it to my employer's attention and insisted that he pay me more, he said that I was here illegally and that I was getting paid more than all the rest of his undocumented employees. My employer also reminded me that I was getting my room and board for free and that there were no deductions—that I was able to keep all the money I made without having taxes deducted. The next day, he told me that if I continued to do a good job, he would recommend me to some friends that had a bigger project and that they would be willing to pay me $30 a day. This made me happy because I knew that, although I wasn't getting paid at the regular rate, my wages were mine to keep and my employers supplied everything."

Pay, as Alberto's story illustrates, is only part of the compensation issue. Undocumented workers often fail to get many of the other benefits U.S. workers take for granted. Undocumented aliens who have fraudulent documents that permit them to work do have the Social Security tax, along with other taxes, deducted from their wages. Nevertheless, many of them will never receive any of the corresponding federal benefits, such as Social Security benefits.[45] Most also fail to receive unemployment or health-related benefits. Eliseo, for example, reported that his boss failed to make sure he received proper medical treatment for a work-related injury. "In the late sixties," he says, "I was working for a construction company in Weslaco when I injured myself. I fell off the top of a house and the foreman took me to the border instead of to the doctor. He gave me that day's pay and nothing more and told me to find a doctor in Mexico to get medical attention. I had broken my wrist on the job, and he didn't even give me enough money to cover the doctor bill!"

Some employers, however, also feel that undocumented workers have taken advantage of them. One student, for example, interviewed his own grandfather and four of his grandfather's friends, each of whom owns ranches or farms around the mid-Valley area. His grandfather told him, "I picked up a couple of men, two Mexican brothers, who were hitchhiking down the road near my ranch and asked them if they wanted to work. They both agreed, and I took them back to the ranch and explained what they had to do. They had been working for me for two months and were good hard workers. They respected me and we really got along. I paid them both $100 a week to feed and bathe some of the animals I raised. For the first couple of weeks, they did their jobs and they started earning my respect. But it wasn't too long before I started missing some chickens around the ranch. At first, I really didn't think anything of it because sometimes they were killed by dogs or some other animal. Then I actually saw one of the men carrying a chicken into a car by the side of the road. The men were selling chickens from my ranch! I fired them both then and there."

Kind Treatment by Employers

Though many employers are suspicious of undocumented workers, some establish a family-type relationship with them. Horacio, for example, is a twenty-eight-year-old mechanic employed in Edinburg. "At my first job here in the Valley," he says, "my boss let me stay at his house until I raised enough money to find a place of my own. He understood that I swam over here to make more money for myself and my family back home. It didn't seem to bother him, because he treated me like everybody else at work. While I stayed at his home, he treated me like part of the family by including me in their meals and family gatherings, such as birthdays and weddings. I consider him a second father to me because he welcomed me into his family like an extra child. He also gave me the opportunity to work as a mechanic without treating me like an outsider because of who I was and where I came from. If it wasn't for his guidance and support, I don't think I would be where I am today."

Though many of the undocumented workers we talked to had some complaints about their employers, most generally had positive impressions. Often, this was tempered by their work experience in Mexico. Raul, for example, is a forty-two-year-old Mexican worker who likes the United States. One of the things he likes most is being able to speak out when something is not right. "I remember once," he says, "when our boss had said we were lazy. I commented to another worker that if he wanted to see a lazy worker, he should start looking at himself. He overheard me and gave me an ugly look and told me to shut up, but that was all. In Mexico, the boss would have beat me up and then he would have fired me."

Treatment by Others

Sometimes an employer is not the greatest concern undocumented workers have. Rather, they may be more preoccupied by their relationship with neighbors, landlords, and other workers. Alejandro for example, is twenty-seven years old and does not worry about fellow workers. "Usually," he says, "if you don't have papers, you find yourself working with others who also don't have papers. So your situation is pretty safe. But you have to watch out for apartment managers and neighbors. They will all report you. I've told them I am here studying English and that my parents are sending me money, so some of them think I'm rich. I can't risk having them find out I'm working. Once you get deported you lose everything, like furniture, cars, and clothes. That's very scary."

Undocumented Mexicans who work in northern states often worry most about fellow workers. Alejandro Cantú, for example, is a twenty-nine year old who met a coyote while working in the Valley four years ago. The man offered to take him up north for $1,000. Alejandro wound up in a small city in Wisconsin where he found a job at a factory. "About 75 percent of the workers," he says, "were Anglos and the rest of us were undocumented. One day, one of the undocumented workers was picked up by the Border Patrol. He was married to an Anglo woman, and they had gotten into a big fight when she found out that he was going out with other women. She got upset and turned him in to the immigration officers. Everyone knew it was her, because officers came into the factory with a piece of paper with his name on it and he was the only one they arrested. None of the rest of us were even questioned."

Many undocumented workers feel highly vulnerable to threats from fellow workers, as the case of Melisa Nuñez illustrates. Using her *mica* to cross the border from Reynosa, Mexico, each day, she found work as a secretary in a packing plant in South Texas. Even though she had limited English, she was able to do the bookkeeping and answer the phone because most of the callers were from Mexico. She was also responsible for checking workers in each morning. One day, one of the workers came in fifty minutes late and told Melisa to mark her down as being on time. When Melisa refused to let her cheat, the woman became angry. Minutes later, some fellow workers told Melisa that the woman had reported her, and that La Migra would be coming to take her back to Mexico.

For many undocumented workers, fellow workers are their major worry. Pedro Palacios had to watch out for fellow workers in a produce shed where he worked in another state. "During lunch breaks," he says, "the Americans would try to intimidate us and would make racist remarks. Four of us were Mexicans and we learned to just keep quiet. They would call us 'wetbacks' and say things about us in English. What bothered me most, however, was that one of them was a Chicano. When our boss wasn't there, he would give us the hardest time. He threatened to tell the boss that we weren't doing our job. I couldn't believe that a person from our own race would not try to help his people. It made me angry that he turned his back on our culture, which places such strong value on helping out fellow Mexicans."

For many undocumented workers, the bigotry comes not from fellow workers but from other people with whom they must interact at work. Patricio, for example, described a job he had two years ago working in construction for an Anglo man. "I got along fine with him," he says, "but he had a brother who didn't like me because I am Mexican. I didn't worry about it and just minded my own business. One day I was using a shovel to fill up a small ditch in the driveway. My boss's brother drove up and started beating me with the shovel. Nobody was home and I couldn't make him stop. He dumped me in the back of his pickup truck and drove to the police station. He turned me in, claiming that I had stolen his shovel, so he had chased me and I had fallen down and hit my face on some rocks. They turned me over to the Border Patrol who returned me to Mexico. I came back a week later and have since brought my wife and children here to live with me."

Anselmo Treviño also had problems with his employer's family members. "Our boss, an Anglo, treated us very well," he says. "We lived on his property in some outbuildings. One of his grandsons, a young boy, used to come back to our little home. He liked to eat my wife's homemade tortillas, even though we knew his family probably did not approve of it. One day the boy came over and my wife gave him a tortilla, just like always. His father was looking for him and caught him eating one of my wife's tortillas on his way home. He yelled at the boy, telling him never to eat anything from our home because Mexicans were dirty people and that he could catch a disease. I don't understand why he said we were dirty. They're the ones who would eat from the same dishes they used to feed their dogs."

Some undocumented workers reported treatment that was worse than name calling or threats to call the INS. Alma is a forty-two-year-old mother of five children who has worked with her family for many years as undocumented farmworkers. She remembers with great sadness an event that happened two years prior to the interview. "In order to work," she says, "we had to leave our fifteen-year-old daughter at the camp babysitting our three year old. One day, another worker and his crew leader took advantage of her while the three year old watched. There was nothing we could do about it and my husband still can't talk about it. Our daughter now is a mother and she says she can't return to school."

The children of undocumented workers are frequent targets of harsh treatment in other contexts. Lydia Cerda is a twenty-two-year-old woman who went to school in a Valley school district that has few Anglo students. "I never had any problems with the teachers," she says, "but I did with the students. I remember them calling me King Kong. When I began school there after coming with my parents from Mexico, I was set back two grades. As a result, I was much older and larger than most of the other kids in my grade. They made me ashamed of where I came from, so I always lied about my place of birth. I felt that they would burst out laughing the minute I said that I was born in Mexico. I was even afraid to have my friends call me at home, because I was afraid they would find out that my mother couldn't speak English. Now I'm ashamed that I ever felt that way."

The Choice—To Stay and Fit in, or to Return to Mexico

As Lydia's story indicates, the difficulty of living in the United States involves more than just the risk of being deported. Many also feel they risk losing their culture and their family. Inevitably, undocumented workers must decide whether to try to remain in the United States or to return to Mexico. Ramón Infante, a forty-two-year-old former undocumented worker now living in Mexico, faced this choice. He had struggled for several years trying to earn enough in the United States to support his family in Mexico. "It was difficult for me to get my bosses to give me days off to visit my family in Mexico," he says. "Whenever I did, I only had enough time to give them the money I had made and to check in on them. On the last job, I had another problem. I was staying with my friend and his family. At first, things were great. His wife treated me like a visitor—but only for a few weeks. Then I think she got tired of feeding me for free. I had no right to invade their home. But that wasn't the real reason why I decided to come back. I missed my family and that really bothered me. I thought about bringing them with me, but where would we live? We didn't have any papers, and what if someone told on us? They would throw us back immediately. So, one night, after thinking it over, I told my friend how thankful I was he was letting me stay there, but that I just had to go back. He understood and that same night he took me home. At first, the situation was like I thought it would be—really tight economically. But that was just for a short time. My older kids started working and now they help out with the expenses."

Having one's family in the United States is an important factor in the decision of whether to stay. Jorge Morales, for example, married a Mexican American woman who is a citizen of the United States. "My wife is very understanding," he says. "She didn't care that I was a *mojado*. She has helped me become someone important in life. She has taught me to speak, read, and write English. We have two wonderful children who have encouraged me to become someone better in life. Now I own my business, a used auto parts store, and I am planning to organize my own dance academy and do something I love to do—teach dance. My wife is so proud of me that she has decided to help me organize my dance academy so that my life will be fulfilled."

Many undocumented workers, however, plan to return to Mexico. Cecilia Castillo, for example, goes back to Mexico as often as she can. "I don't live in the U.S. full-time," she says. "I work for four months in the U.S. and then go home to Monterrey for two months. When I have earned enough money to stop working, I will return full-time to Monterrey and live there permanently. As a Mexican, you miss out on so much living in the U.S. I miss my family most of all. Americans always complain that we want to live here, but actually we just want to make enough money to live at home."

In our Undocumented Workers Survey, we asked three of the same questions related to the decision of whether to stay in the U.S. or return to Mexico that we had previously asked in our Undocumented Maids Survey (see *Batos, Bolillos, Pochos, and Pelados*, chap. 3). For the first question we asked, "Has it been difficult to adapt to life in the United States?" The second question asked, "Do you plan to live in your own country some day?" On the third question we asked, "Do you prefer life in your own country to life in the United States?" In Figure 4.3, we compare the answers from each of these two groups of undocumented workers by reporting the percentage whose answers favored life in the United States.

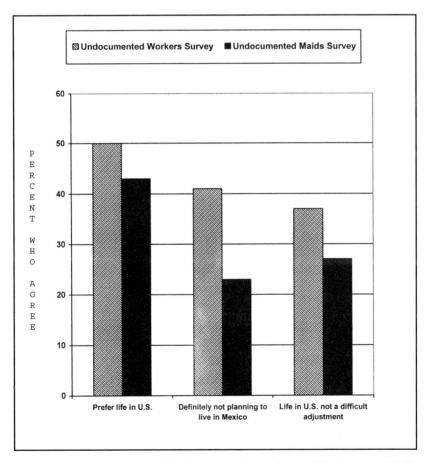

FIG. 4.3. Percent Undocumented Workers Survey respondents and Undocumented Maids Survey respondents who agree that they prefer life in the U.S., that they definitely do not plan to live in Mexico, and that life in the U.S. is not a difficult adjustment

The most immediate pattern revealed by this comparison is that those in the Undocumented Maids Survey seem less committed to remaining in the United States than the mostly male sample in the Undocumented Workers Survey. On each of the three questions, a lower percentage of undocumented maids favored life in the United States. This difference may be due in part to family-related factors, since all of those in the Undocumented Maids Survey were female and most of those in the Undocumented Workers Survey were male. We can also speculate that these results may have a structural cause. Because undocumented maids tend to live in the home of their employers, with limited outside contacts, they may have felt more cut off and alone than those in the Undocumented Workers Survey. This possibility is somewhat substantiated by the answers to another question, "What has been most difficult for you?" Although the largest percentage of each group chose the response "Being away from family and friends," 40 percent of those in the Undocumented Maids Survey chose this response, compared to only 32 percent of those in the Undocumented Workers Survey.

Many have other reasons for wanting to return to Mexico. Juan Perález, for example, moved back to Mexico because he found the controlled environment of the United States stifling. "I used to buy and resell cars. In Mexico, I didn't have to worry about whether the cars were stolen. I also had a bar where I could sell beer to anyone who could afford it. Here in the United States, you cannot be self-employed. I opened up a bar but can only sell beer or alcohol to people over twenty-one. I can't sell clothes at my house anymore. They fined me for not having a permit. There is no way you can make money your own way here. That is why I moved back. Now I can do whatever I want to make money and come over here once in a while. The United States is OK for people who like to be controlled."

Many undocumented workers who chose to stay in the United States have second thoughts later about their decision. Gilberto Pérez brought his family to the United States and now regrets it. "In the United States," he says, "children are lazy, disrespectful, and have no sense of morals. Their weekends are spent half the day in bed, talking back to parents, and getting into trouble. My oldest son, a sophomore in high school, was expelled because he and some friends were caught with marijuana in their school locker. Never before has anyone in my family or my wife's family ever been in any trouble with the law. These kids don't bother to think about the consequences. I have always worked hard to provide my kids with the material things they need, and this is the way they pay me back. We had no education and school was considered a luxury. Now, they take it for granted because it is handed to them without much of a fuss."

Conclusion

The concern over what to do about undocumented immigration to the United States is one of the most controversial issues facing our nation. Indeed, the issue has become so politicized that much of the information on the subject available to the general public is either biased or unreliable. It seems to become a major issue in each presidential election. Indeed, it frequently becomes attached to other issues, such as concerns about terrorism and drug smuggling, making it difficult to find a workable solution.

Our findings reveal significant abuse of undocumented immigrants in the United States. Our economy continues to demand their labor, though we have done little to protect or empower them by giving them minimal protections of the law. It seems clear that a variety of structural conditions affect the treatment they receive. Even though undocumented women workers, for example, are potentially more exploitable than undocumented men, the tendency of many of these women to reside in the homes of their employers seems to promote a closer relationship, which often leads to somewhat better treatment. Nevertheless, the way our legal system has been established to control them (the subject of our next chapter) makes them especially vulnerable.

It seems likely that we will continue to live in a situation in which large numbers of undocumented workers are enticed to enter the United States illegally, only to face exploitation and abuse when they do. Unfortunately, the status quo seems to work for all but cultural conservatives, who feel the undocumented are a threat to our way of life. We would urge them to consider how comfortable that way of life has become because of the exploitability of undocumented workers in the United States.

5 Immigration Enforcement Issues

WITH CRISTINA DE JUANA

The first time I came to the United States, some *bandidos* [bandits] robbed me just after I crossed the river. They threatened to kill me if I didn't give them everything. I even had to give them my shoes.

Later, I started looking for work, but no one would hire me. They said they could be fined $10,000 if they did.

Frustrated, without work and without money, I stopped a Border Patrolman and asked him to deport me back to Mexico. He laughed and asked me why. I told him my story.

I was very unfortunate that time. Now I'm in McAllen with friends. In the future, I hope that I can apply for residency.

Manuel, like many undocumented workers, is very determined. It is not uncommon to find Mexican workers in South Texas who have been caught and returned to Mexico many times, only to keep coming back. Their dogged determination makes sense in light of the great hardships in Mexico that they flee.

Many Americans simply dismiss them as "illegal aliens." The actual situation, of course, is not so simple. Though entering the country "without inspection" is against the law, it is generally not regarded as a crime but simply a violation of administrative law. For this reason, those apprehended are not accorded most of the rights granted to someone accused of a crime. Undocumented immigrants who cannot afford an attorney, for example, will not have one provided at government expense.

Indeed, if most of the immigrants detained for "entering without inspection" were to assert their right not to give evidence against themselves, the whole enforcement apparatus would virtually grind to a halt. Over 85 percent of those detained in 2001 were removed from the country by means of a "voluntary departure."[1] This procedure relies on getting an alien to admit her or his unauthorized status in exchange for a quick trip across the border. Most accept the offer because it is easier simply to admit guilt and try again. According to Audrey Singer and Douglas Massey, "Most immigrants learn one thing about their arrests—it carries relatively few consequences if one goes quietly and does not resist. One will be deported—and can try again later."[2] In some sectors of the Border Patrol, undocumented aliens can be caught and returned to Mexico ten times before being charged with an offense.[3]

The way the U.S. government enforces immigration laws is a source of considerable controversy. Some of the issues we will address are the following:

—Is there a bias in our immigration laws (and in the enforcement of those laws) against Mexico and people from other Latin American countries?

—Does the United States really want to keep undocumented workers out of the country? Even if there is a sincere national desire to do so, can the wave of undocumented workers be stopped when economic pressures for them to come are so great?

—Are the methods we employ in our effort to control immigration effective, or do these methods simply play into the hands of smugglers and unscrupulous employers who exploit undocumented workers?

—Should undocumented workers who have lived in the United States for many years be able to legalize their status, or does this simply reward them for illegal behavior?

—Do Hispanic officers of the Border Patrol experience discrimination? What pressures do Mexican-origin officers experience as they enforce the laws against people from Mexico?

In this chapter, we examine the experiences of legal Mexican visitors and undocumented immigrants as they come to the United States. We will describe how they are treated by smugglers, police, and immigration agents. We will also review the process that many of them utilize in their attempts to legalize their status here.

Methodology

Much of the anecdotal information in this chapter was obtained from the same in-depth interview projects described in the preceding chapter. In addition, the Undocumented Workers Survey described in the preceding chapter was again used to gain information about how undocumented immigrants are treated by immigration officers, smugglers, employers, and others with whom they must deal. An additional data source used in this chapter, one not previously described, was a convenience sample of 115 in-depth interviews of Mexican nationals visiting the U.S. for shopping, business, or tourism, which we called the Laser-Visa Opinion Survey. Though it was designed specifically to determine how these Mexican visitors felt about the effects of a new screening program (US-VISIT), it gave us the opportunity to ask them about how they had been treated by immigration officers. It was conducted during December 2003 and January 2004 by a single interviewer who talked to the 115 Mexican visitors at bridges and commercial establishments throughout the Valley.[4]

Legal Entries

On a typical day, approximately 205,000 vehicles and 100,000 pedestrians cross from Mexico into Texas.[5] During the year 2004, there were 17,444,684 private vehicle crossings in the Rio Grande Valley and 6,705,335 pedestrian crossings over bridges in the Valley.[6] The vast majority of these border crossers do so legally, with most using a border-crossing card called the "laser visa."[7] The laser visa replaced the *mica*, the previous border-crossing card. On January 1, 2004, the United States Citizenship and Immigration Services (USCIS, formerly the Immigration Service) introduced a new system of entry for Mexican visa holders, the US-VISIT program. This automated entry/exit system was designed to scan a foreign national's travel documents, take a digital photo and inkless fingerprints, and compare his or her name against those in the government databases. This system had worked relatively well at airports, where each passenger was required to place two fingers on a scanner and have an officer take a digital photograph. Though these procedures added only seconds to the overall processing time at airports, it was expected to cause major problems at border crossing points where major traffic congestion and long delays were already the norm. As originally proposed, visitors who had already waited in long lines of trucks and automobiles would have to find a place to park (with no facilities available), get in another line, and submit to the processing. In addition, they would have to repeat the process upon leaving the country, though leaving the country previously required no process at all.[8]

With laser visas, the U.S. government is able to use optical scanning to track visa holders as they enter and exit the country. Though the infrastructure was not initially in place to implement the system, the prospect of its implementation caused considerable alarm along both sides of the South Texas border. Mexicans expressed dismay at even more complicated crossings and U.S. merchants were worried that the visitors would quit coming, thus denying them a major source of income.

Perhaps the greatest alarm, however, was created by the resulting ability of the U.S. government to enforce the seventy-two-hour limit for each visit. Previously, laser visa holders were technically limited to three days in the U.S. for each entry, but the lack of entry and exit scanning had made it virtually impossible to enforce this limit. Those who had become used to staying much longer for tourism, business, or family visits began to think about not making these visits at all (and thus not spending their money in Texas). Since the economy of the Rio Grande Valley (and other portions of the border) had become dependent upon Mexicans spending their money here, opposition to the proposed changes arose from both sides of the border.[9]

The magnitude of the problem can be understood only in light of the number of crossings into Texas. Legal vehicle crossings from Mexico into Texas increased from 23 million vehicles in 1990 to 41 million in 2000. After the September 11 attacks (and increased security at the bridges), however, the number of crossings began to decrease slightly. These crossings were further reduced when Mexicans who applied for a laser visa were required to pay a new $65 fee and undergo extensive interviews with immigration officials.[10]

Because of strong opposition to the new procedures, the Department of Homeland Security in August 2004 announced that the length of time for Mexican laser visa holders to spend on each visit would be extended to thirty days. Though this action helped ease a great deal of anxiety, Mexicans were still aware that Canadians were not limited to seventy-two hours—or even to thirty days.

Much of the apprehension and the opposition to the proposed changes were caused by previous experiences with U.S. officials at the bridges. Mexicans who came to shop, to conduct business, engage in tourism, purchase real estate, visit family, or to utilize specialized services (such as medical care) almost always had personal stories about difficulties they had had upon entering the United States. From these experiences, almost all anticipated that these negatives would be greatly magnified under the proposed changes.

Almost everyone we interviewed believed that the new requirements would drastically worsen an already difficult crossing experience. They complained that U.S. officials seem to pay little attention to how long the lines back up in Mexico before opening additional lanes. One man from Zacatecas, for example, comes once or twice a month to buy clothing for resale in Mexico. "In December," he says, "I had to wait in line for more than an hour and a half. That tells me that with the new system it might take me even longer getting across and then I would have to worry about spending just as much time getting back into Mexico. Even if they only run the card through a scanner, I would have to get out of my car, especially if there are several of us traveling together."

Another woman states, "I've never had any really bad experiences while crossing, but the time we have to wait for them to check our papers is always frustrating. I would think that such a technologically advanced country could find ways to improve its inspection process and make it a lot faster." A young couple agreed. "With this program," says the wife, "I don't even want to imagine how long it will take to cross. If we're in a van with eight persons, for example, how long will it take to take everyone's fingerprints? I think most of us would rather not even try to cross."

The fear of what would happen when several people come in the same car was a major concern. One couple who own a business in Mexico live in a nice residential area in Mission. "A lot of people that come from Mexico," explains the wife, "travel in only one car in order to save gas. Sometimes, there are four or five friends in the same car. If they change the requirements, we will not be able to travel together, because if they did not let one of us cross we would all have to go back. This happened one time with one of my friends. We needed to get to the airport in McAllen to catch a flight to Miami. They wouldn't let one of us cross. We all had to go back because she had no other way to get back home."

One woman from Reynosa explained a problem for those who cross the bridge on foot. "When we cross," she says, "we are out in the open, waiting in long lines. When it is sunny and very hot, there is no way to protect ourselves. Imagine what it will be like if they take even longer to inspect us. Someone could get really sick waiting in lines like that."

This same woman described other difficulties of the inspection process. "Sometimes they say, 'You crossed yesterday. Why do you need to cross again today?' I recently had to explain that my husband had pawned a bracelet and I needed to get it back. It's embarrassing and frightening. I try to cross with my sons so they can help me with all the explaining. The officers sometimes check every little detail. I understand what the Americans have gone through with the terrorists and that they have a right to be strict, but I come just for shopping and they make me afraid they will take away my visa."

Perhaps an even greater frustration among the 115 people we interviewed was the constant atmosphere of suspicion. One Reynosa resident, for example, said, "It was very difficult to get our laser visa. My sister still has not been able to get hers. She has a good job in Mexico and that is what they said she needed. She and her son have a retail business. She has spent a lot of money on applications and they have denied her three times." Another man agreed. "It was very difficult for me to get my laser visa," he said. "They made me show a lot of papers and then they turned me down. I lost everything I had paid and then I had to start all over again. I have it now, but every time I cross, I'm really afraid they'll take it away. Sometimes, when I come to shop, they make me show how much money I have."

Many of our subjects dislike the inconsistency they experience with U.S. immigration officers. One resident of a very upscale neighborhood in the Valley, for example, said, "One day we went to get a permit for a relative to go north of the Border Patrol checkpoint at Falfurrias. They asked him if he had more than five hundred in cash. He told them he didn't carry that much cash but that he had credit cards. They were not going to give him a permit until he finally showed all his electric bills and every other receipt he had. Sometimes it is humiliating to even ask for a permit. Most officers ask for nothing and treat you very well. Others demand all kinds of paperwork—things that are not on any list of what is required. We never know what to expect."

Several of the people we interviewed were frustrated at having to constantly show proof that they intend to return to Mexico. "We had to bring all kinds of papers and documents to get the visa," says one. "Why should we have to keep bringing those same documents when we present our laser visa at the border?"

The resentment at this suspicious attitude was expressed by another woman, one from Veracruz. "Sometimes they think our cards are fake," she says. "We know people who have had their cards taken away just because the officer doesn't believe them. Some of the officers do not seem well trained. They seem to have a very narrow view of Mexicans. They think we are coming to see what we can get from them. Most of us come here to buy things. Many of us even pay taxes in the U.S. Why can't they treat us more like the Canadians who can come for six months? They only give us three days!"

This fear is not without basis. Several of the people we interviewed know someone whose visa was taken away, with no chance to appeal the officer's decision. One man from Reynosa says, "They took my brother's visa away when he was crossing. They told him he would not be able to get another laser visa for five years. They said he had been crossing too often, mostly in the mornings, so he must be coming to a job in the United States. He didn't have a job here. He was coming over on a frequent basis to buy things to resell in Mexico. That makes all of us afraid of what will happen when they start taking fingerprints and knowing with their computers how often we come. Some people have been banned from having a laser visa for ten years or even an indefinite time."

Sometimes the resentment arises from cultural misunderstandings. One older woman from Reynosa, for example, complained about the rude treatment she gets from immigration officers. "They talk to me impolitely," she says. "When I drive up in my car, they talk to me using the familiar [tú] form saying, '¿Cómo estás?' [How are you?] or '¿De dónde vienes?' [Where are you from?]. That is very rude when talking to a person of my age. They need more training." [11]

The apparent insensitivity of some officers was reflected in other interviews. One woman from Reynosa described the experience of her daughter who applied for a visa to go to Louisiana. "She was going to visit her boyfriend who is in jail there," she says. "The immigration officer asked her why she would want to see a man who is not good for her. They have no right to interfere in something that is none of their business."

Many border residents are fearful about what the long lines and tougher inspections will do to their visits to the interior of the United States. Most drive to the McAllen airport for flights to other parts of the U.S. "Three years ago," says one, "I was going to New York. They stopped me at the border for a more detailed inspection. I told them I would miss my plane, and there was someone waiting for me in the airport in New York. It made no difference to the officer. I missed my flight. Everything depends on which officer inspects you."

Antonio, a Mexican who has a business in McAllen, describes a probable effect of the new regulations. "Many people from Monterrey," he said, "will start flying into San Antonio. The officials at the airports there treat them much better,[12] so they will spend their money up there and we will lose their business here on the border."

Though wealthy people from Mexico do contribute substantially to the economy of South Texas, a great deal of the cross-border commerce is from shoppers with more modest incomes. One fifty-three-year-old woman from Reynosa, for example, comes about once a week to buy groceries for herself and for friends who do not have laser visas. "If they implement this program," she says, "I will come much less often because it took me too long to get the visa and I can't risk having them take it away from me. It was a great sacrifice for me to get the visa and no one else in my family could get one. I come to buy groceries because everything is cheaper here. But every time I come and make large purchases, I also run the risk that the Mexican officials will take away everything I bought when I cross back into Mexico."[13]

Many moderate-income Mexicans with laser visas like to come to the U.S. to buy used items at flea markets and other outlets for discontinued or used items. Many of them fear what will happen to them when U.S.C.I.S. is able to see that they cross frequently. One man crosses at least twenty times a month to take items to Mexico. "One time I was crossing every day for more than a week," he says, "and the immigration officers asked me why I was crossing so often, thinking maybe I was working in the U.S. illegally. I explained I was from Zacatecas and I liked to come to the flea market and to other places to buy many things. After I have made many trips back and forth across the border, I take the merchandise to Zacatecas."

One couple who have laser visas discovered another problem. "One time they stopped us," says the husband, "because my wife was pregnant. They did not let us cross because they thought we were bringing her over here to have her baby, even though she was only six months pregnant. I had to leave her at the border because I had some urgent things to take care of. She had to walk back to Mexico. I hurried and managed to get back to pick her up in forty-five minutes. They told us if she wanted to cross again while she was pregnant, she would have to have a letter from her doctor in Mexico. We couldn't do that, though, because everything in Mexico is handled by the hospital."

Many of the people we interviewed indicated that they had experienced poor treatment by U.S. border officials on at least one occasion. Many resented the inconsistency and the occasionally rude treatment. Perhaps the greatest objection, however, was the perception that even though they came to spend money that would help the local economy,[14] they were sometimes treated with the same disdain and inconsistency as that accorded illegal aliens. Though there is a distinct difference in the treatment of these two groups, it is clear that the suspicion and treatment of undocumented Mexican workers spills over into the way legal Mexican visitors are treated. This will become clear in the following section.

Becoming Legal

Most undocumented immigrants live with the hope that one day they can be legalized and lead normal lives, even if in poverty. This is reflected in many of their stories. Artemio, for example, describes how his life changed when he was finally able to legalize his status. "I came to the U.S. to work and to find a better way of living for my children," he says. "I am the father of seven children. I wanted them to get a better education in the U.S. and learn English. Here in the Valley, it is very difficult to make a living because field work doesn't last year round. This is the reason I have to migrate up north. We do the work that nobody wants to do. We do all the dirty and most dangerous work in the U.S.[15] Nobody appreciates what we do. Instead, society treats us like we're from another planet. People in the Valley tend to report undocumented workers for no reason. They don't realize that we work more than eight hours a day in the sun, wind, and rain. We also have to put up with the dangerous pesticides that farmers use in their fields to get more production from their plants.[16] I was finally able to get amnesty. Now I can demand better wages and better working conditions. I want to live in the U.S. for the rest of my life. I also want my children to find better jobs and get out of the fields."[17]

Rodolfo also describes how legalization changed his life. "I lived in fear for six years," he says. "Fear of being caught by La Migra haunted me day and night. Seeing a police officer would increase my heart rate. In 1987, I heard of the Amnesty program and decided to apply. By November 1988, I received my card. I had no trouble obtaining the documents required by the INS. In August 1989, I received my *tarjeta de residencia* [resident alien visa]. Ever since I got it, life has been so much better. Before I had it, I could never go to Mexico to visit my family, but I am now able to go when-ever I want. Now my life is *tranquila*."

Methods of Legalization

Some of the preceding stories may be somewhat misleading if they make it appear that becoming legal is simply a matter of applying at the local U.S.C.I.S. agency. Legalization, in reality, is a task that is very difficult, and, for many, impossible.[18] Indeed, the vast majority of undocumented work-ers will most likely never qualify. Most hope that a new amnesty program, like that carried out in 1987, will be enacted again. Even if it is, applying for amnesty will not be easy. There will be many papers and applications to fill out. Those who apply must be able to demonstrate continuous residence in the U.S. over a specified number of years. It might also require, as it did in 1987, that they demonstrate having worked in agriculture or some other specified occupation for a given number of years. Not all, of course, will succeed. One of those we interviewed, Alfredo, tried to use the amnesty provisions for agricultural workers in 1988. He put down on his application that he had worked picking cucumbers. When he was called for his inter-view, however, he was asked where they grow. Because he had never been a farmworker, he answered that they grow on trees. As a result, his appli-cation was denied.

There are other ways to become legal than waiting for a new amnesty program. Ramón, a forty-two-year-old undocumented worker from Tam-aulipas, Mexico, has decided to marry a U.S. citizen. He was brought over to the United States several years ago by a smuggler who promised to get him work. The coyote also agreed to help Ramón get his wife and children here after he was settled. He has had several jobs at construction sites. He and his wife have an agreement that he will hide the fact that he is married so that he can marry an American woman and eventually bring his family here. He has heard from several sources that there are women in the Valley who marry illegal aliens for a fee. "The fee is usually $800," he says. "These women marry for money, but not for a commitment."

Though what Ramón is attempting is referred to as a "sham marriage," many marriages to U.S. citizens or resident aliens are legitimate and can lead to legalization. But it is not automatic. Those attempting to use this route to legalize their status must first demonstrate that their marriage is not fraudulent. They must do this by being able to answer highly personal questions in separate interviews that cannot be rehearsed and allow immigration officers to determine if they are really living together. In addition, they must be able to prove that they will have enough income to not become a public charge. Many people who have married a U.S. citizen are still waiting because their income does not reach this level.[19]

Another route toward "legalization" is to get fraudulent documents to claim birth in the United States.[20] One notary public in Brownsville, Texas became somewhat adept at issuing fraudulent birth certificates, telling clients they were now "legal." He charged them about $500 to $1,000 each for each fraudulent birth certificate. Because his clients lacked education, many assumed they had become legal. In many cases, the individuals who purchased these certificates were arrested, interrogated, and deported.

Even those who surmount such difficulties find that the U.S. Government has some pretty difficult requirements, including the payment of some very high fees. Juan explained that he went to take an exam and was told he would need to pay a $90 fee. "I did not have the money at the time," he says, "because I couldn't find a job. I borrowed the money from a friend and then discovered that I would have to pay an application fee of $185 each for my wife and myself, and $50 for each of our children. Then I found out I had to pay for physical exams also. I had a hard time getting all this money." Juan told his interviewer that he finally got the money by doing something illegal, but he did not specify what it was.

The preceding stories show that undocumented immigrants have much more to fear than being apprehended by the Border Patrol. Many other individuals seek to take advantage of their plight, knowing that their illegal status makes them highly vulnerable. This exploitation and vulnerability starts even before they cross the river, where they must watch out for unscrupulous smugglers, corrupt Mexican police, and border bandits. Some of these same groups add to their problem of hiding from the Border Patrol once they get to this side of the river. We will present stories to illustrate the risks of these various groups, starting first with border bandits.

Border Bandits

As the story of Manuel at the beginning of the chapter illustrates, border bandits are one of the greatest risks faced by those who swim the river.

These are individuals, often from Mexico, who rape and rob immigrants at the point of highest vulnerability, crossing the Rio Grande. One of our interviewees, Rodolfo, related what happened to him and his pregnant wife, Rosario, just moments after crossing the river: "It was around seven in the evening," he says, "and we had just crossed the river. We had not even finished getting dressed, when out of nowhere came three guys. Two of them had knives and the other said he had a gun. They threatened us and demanded money. When we explained to them that we had almost no money, they got mad and began verbally harassing my wife. Since she was five months pregnant, I started defending her. This made matters worse because they started to beat me up. My wife was screaming hysterically and I was afraid to fight back because they were armed. The only thing that mattered to me was her and the baby's well-being. When they were finally satisfied that we had given them all we had, they left, taking all of our belongings, including some of the clothing we were wearing. I was badly beaten and Rosario was shaking and crying. To top it all, we were half naked. We finally had the strength to make it up to the nearest street, where, because of our appearance, we were picked up by immigration. Since we did not have any documents, they returned us to Reynosa. Fortunately, they provided us with food, clothing, and medical attention. I was grateful for that."

In recent years, both the Border Patrol and Mexican officials (both police and military) have been trying to do something against these bandits. Most appear to be Mexican residents who prey on undocumented immigrants, knowing that most will not complain. Frequently, their abuse is detected only if the Border Patrol picks up their victims, as the preceding case of Rodolfo and Rosario illustrates.

Another of our interviewees, Hector Garcia, paid the price of an inexpensive smuggler on his first trip. "We had just finished crossing the river," he says, "and the coyote went off and left us alone. He said that he wasn't taking us any farther than the bank of the river. There were twelve of us that he had crossed at the rate of $100 per person. After he left us, we started walking. Suddenly, four men came out nowhere and demanded our money. Within seconds everybody started to run. They grabbed a woman next to me and stabbed her with an ice pick. I could hear her scream as I started to run. I wanted to stop and help her, but I feared for my life. I can remember praying that I would get out of there alive. Just the thought of never seeing my children again was horrifying. I don't know if she survived the attack. I never saw or heard of her again. After that experience, I learned very fast who to deal with. Now I use a coyote who crosses me over the bridge for $400. He has some arrangement with an officer at the bridge. The coyote pays him part of what he gets and as we come up to him, he just says, 'Pásele' [Go ahead]. Although I don't have to worry about bandidos anymore, it is pretty expensive."

According to some Border Patrol agents, some of these coyotes are bandits themselves. One agent described a time when he was on routine patrol. "I sighted five aliens in some brush," he says. "All of them were dehydrated and in very bad condition. As we processed them, we learned that they had been in the brush for three days without a guide, food, or water. The coyote who had brought them across the river had led them to an isolated area where he took the rest of their money and their few possessions. He left them there, with nothing but the clothes on their backs. They stood there, looking at each other and wondering what they should do in the strange surroundings without food or water. It was a very isolated area, so it was as if he left them to die."

Smugglers (Coyotes)

Given their fear of police and immigration agents, many undocumented aliens seeking to enter the U.S. hire coyotes (smugglers) for protection. As we have seen, however, this is a risky choice. While some of the more "professional" smugglers do offer considerable protection, there are many would-be coyotes who have little experience. Often, they charge less than the more experienced smugglers. The risk in using them is greater, however, because some abandon their "clients," or, or in a few cases, engage in the abuse themselves.

Alien smugglers are disliked by just about everyone. Immigrants, especially those from the interior of Mexico, find them a necessary evil as the stepped-up presence of Border Patrol agents along the border makes old routes of immigration difficult or impossible. Virtually all veteran Border Patrol agents in South Texas can recount experiences of coming upon groups of aliens, dead or dying, who have been robbed, raped, or abandoned by smugglers. The reputation for cruelty of smugglers is verified when one hears them refer to those they smuggle as *pollos*, or chickens. Though their reputation for making a profit by endangering human lives is generally well deserved, there are many exceptions and some qualifications.

Generally speaking, Mexicans smuggled into the Rio Grande Valley do not use professional smugglers. The major smugglers are much too expensive and generally take people into cities in the interior of the United States. In addition, the "cargo" of professional smugglers often includes people of other nationalities (Chinese and Central Americans, for example) who pay several thousand dollars to make it across other borders, into Mexico, over the U.S. border, past the checkpoints farther north, and on to major U.S. cities. Often, these professional smugglers are hired by relatives seeking to bring a family member, or by employers wanting cheap labor, and sometimes by debt bondage, for sweatshops.

Many small-time smugglers are people who have crossed the river several times themselves and believe they can make a living by crossing other people. Patricio is one of these. "I was working at an iron works shop in the Valley," he says, "but I wasn't making enough money to support my family. Then, one afternoon, a co-worker told me that he was making a little extra money by crossing people over the river. I decided to join him. At first, I would bring them on tubes. After some time, I managed to buy a small row boat so I could cross people without anyone getting wet. I was crossing people almost every night. I started crossing some drugs along with the people. I was doing great. My only problem was I used the same place over and over and the Border Patrol noticed the worn areas in the grass. One night, I was caught unexpectedly with six people and some drugs. I was taken to jail and booked with smuggling illegal aliens and illegal drugs. I was sentenced for five years in prison."

One of our respondents one day was near the river and witnessed a smuggler from Reynosa bringing two girls from Mexico. "I found out," he says, "that he was not experienced at all. I watched him cross the two girls on a tube. He was just swimming in front by himself and not paying attention to the two girls on the tube. One of the girls got her foot stuck under water and was drowning. He didn't even notice. I jumped into the water and saved her. After they were safe, the coyote didn't say anything. He just smiled and said he was not experienced as a coyote and left. He didn't give them any directions whatsoever. He left the two girls in the middle of nowhere. I felt I had to help them, so I took them to the nearest church in town and left them, hoping the priest would help."

Some smugglers with a little more experience and connections don't use the river. They cross the bridge and go through the immigration checkpoints, using fraudulent documents to cross people in full view of immigration agents, rather than stuffing them in the trunk of a car or making them swim the river. Also, though professional smugglers are quite expensive, they generally pose less risk to immigrants than the small-time amateurs who may be nothing more than border bandits. Some of the stories obtained by students will illustrate some of these differences. "I met the coyote through my cousin," says one immigrant. "Our first meeting was in downtown Reynosa. He arranged to get me and two other teenagers across the border in a passenger car, just like legal people. It was scary, so I was relieved when we got to Hidalgo. I paid him and he dropped me off at a supermarket in McAllen."

Several interviews were conducted with alien smugglers themselves. Invariably, they reported the high degree of risk they run as they bring people to the United States. One of them started the interview by stating that he didn't feel sorry for the illegals that he smuggles who end up getting caught. "They know the consequences when they come," he explained. "We have to watch out for other smugglers [who he called "runners"]. I have a certain zone which I cover, looking for anyone willing to come over for a price. Smuggling is a big business and me and my people let other runners know that we'll protect our business. We also have to watch out for the Border Patrol. They'll do anything to stop us. They hate us, treating us like rapists and robbers. When the Border Patrol catches one of my runners, they sometimes try to bang him up real good. They have a lot of leeway and freedom to do anything they choose along the border. They beat me up pretty severely once and that's why I carry weapons every time I cross the border. Still, that was only a temporary setback and afterwards I was allowed to go back to Mexico. The legal system in the United States has enough loopholes for runners like myself to make a healthy profit."

Smugglers not only have to watch out for the U.S. Border Patrol, but must also guard against Mexican police. One smuggler stated, "As long as you only cross people about once a week, you can keep from attracting the attention of the *judiciales* [judicial police]. But if you get carried away and start crossing people every day, you'll leave a trail that sooner or later gives you away."

Mexican police and soldiers are a danger not only along the border, but throughout Mexico. This danger is particularly acute for Central Americans and those from other parts of Latin America who travel into and through Mexico. One Guatemalan man says, "I got caught on my first two attempts to come to the U.S." The first time was in Tapachula, just across from Guatemala. The Mexican police took all my money and beat me because I wouldn't give them the name of the coyote. I still remember the face of the *federal* [federal police officer] who beat me with the *chicote* [whip or braided leather club]. The second time they just took my money and deported me back to my country."

Border Patrol officers often come across "OTMs" ("other than Mexicans") who have been abused by Mexican police. One officer described an experience when he was processing a Guatemalan woman he had just caught. "She told me that while she was waiting for the coyote to get her across the river," he says, "she was picked up by a Mexican police officer. He told her he was arresting her for smuggling. He put her into his car and drove her to an isolated area where he repeatedly raped and beat her. She told me he had left her there, half-conscious, and she had made it the rest of the way by herself, before we picked her up."

The consequences of being caught are often worse for those who are smuggled than for the smuggler. Frequently, when smugglers are caught with a load of aliens, the aliens are held in detention centers as "material witnesses." The smuggler, in contrast, is generally able to bond himself out while awaiting a trial. These witnesses can be held for months without ever being called to testify because the smuggler's attorney arranges a plea bargain shortly before the trial. According to U.S.C.I.S. data, a total of 332 smuggling cases were "closed" during FY2002. A case is closed when "an adverse action has been taken against the target of the case, such as cessation of activity, conviction, removal, denial, disbarment, injunction, restitution/forfeiture, or other objectives that were identified." [21] In other words, coyotes are seldom imprisoned or put out of business even when they are caught.

This was recently illustrated by the death of seventeen people who suffocated in an abandoned truck near Victoria, Texas, allegedly at the hands of a smuggler from Brownsville, Texas. According to a *Brownsville Herald* report on May 20, 2003, the suspected smuggler used homes in McAllen and Brownsville to temporarily house the people being smuggled before loading them into the ill-fated tractor trailer that crossed the checkpoint at Sarita. The report indicated that Rodriguez had been previously arrested for smuggling on five previous occasions. According to this report, he

faced two counts of immigrant smuggling charges in 1980, for which he was sentenced to probation. Three years later, he faced one count of the same charge, although court logs do not reveal his sentence for that case. Then in October 1984, federal officials

> hit the Rodriguezes with conspiracy and alien smuggling charges, but both cases were dismissed. Victor Rodriguez answered to smuggling charges again in August 1985, although the outcome of that case was also not available.[22]

One smuggler we interviewed commented as follows on the danger of federal prosecution for smuggling. "I have been caught by the Border Patrol over ten times," he says, "and I have yet to spend a night in jail. When I am caught with a load of 'cargo' they throw my 'shipment' in detention and they have to wait for an undetermined amount of time. You see, I know there is a backlog of cases in the legal system and I know that they use these illegals as witnesses to get to us, but it never happens. I'm usually out on bond within minutes and never see a jail cell. I also know that a judge can give me a five-year sentence and a $2,000 fine for each person, but I know he will not punish me severely. He always gives me a $3,000 fine which I pay out of my pocket and I leave smiling."

Like many criminals, alien smugglers feel little remorse about the danger they create for their human cargo. One smuggler, Beto Hinojosa, for example, said he never felt guilty about leaving them behind in detention centers because many come back later asking him to bring them over again. He further justified his activity by saying, "The only reason I do this is because there is a demand for it. Mexico is in economic turmoil and when people are willing to pay me their last peso or dollar to come across to a place where they believe there is economic freedom, who am I to deny them. I have the means and capabilities to get them anywhere they want to go, for the right price. I can spot an illegal by the way he dresses, walks, and talks. I have three different ways I charge illegals. If they are Mexicans I charge anywhere from $100 to $350 per individual. If they are 'OTMs' I charge them anywhere from $500 to $1,500 because they usually have more money than the Mexicans. These people come from Guatemala, Nicaragua, and El Salvador. If they are from Europe, Asia, or even China I charge anywhere from $1,500 to $10,000 because they have the most money."[23]

Not all coyotes are cruel, of course. Approximately 20 percent of respondents in the Undocumented Workers Survey reported that coyotes had treated them well. This is reflected in an account by Ana María. "It was eight o'clock at night when the coyote decided to cross me and my friend on a tube," he says. "When we were crossing the river, I could not see a thing. The coyote was holding on to my tube and my friend's at the same time so he could be aware if something happened to us. When we were getting closer to the other side of the river, I felt something catch my leg and so I screamed. The coyote immediately went under water and made sure to release me from the branches where I was stuck. When we were on the other side the coyote apologized for crossing us at night but explained it was so that the immigration officers would not see us. He even took us to one of his relatives' house that was near the town where we had crossed. They fed us and gave us shelter for the night."

Avoiding La Migra

Though undocumented immigrants face harsh treatment by border bandits and coyotes, they also know that being apprehended almost certainly means being sent back to their home country. In the border area, the Border Patrol is the agency they fear most. As they get farther north, immigration agents (who may or may not be Border Patrol officers) are the biggest threat. Benigno Portes, for example, says, "I was always afraid the immigration officers would come and discover me working without legal papers. Our foreman knew that a few of us were undocumented and he would warn us when he could. But I had to pay him almost half of what I earned each month to work there. When the officers came you could see people running and hiding everywhere. We hid under the machinery, under boxes, anywhere that would shield us from the officers. After the officers had left there would be a lot of joking, kidding, and laughing at the way we had run and hid like scared rabbits. I felt humiliated but I tried not to show it and usually joined in the jokes. My take-home pay was pretty low and after giving the foreman his bribe, very little was left to send to my family in Mexico." [24]

Some undocumented immigrants learn to fear not only the Border Patrol, but some overzealous U.S. citizens as well. Carmelo Rodriguez, a seventy-two-year-old Mexican, tells how he used to cross the U.S.-Mexico border in the Laredo area. "The gringo ranchers and Border Patrol agents," he says, "knew where the regular crossings were. They would wait by the crossing and catch the people as they went by. Since I was a good swimmer, I used to swim across the deep parts of the river where they did not expect anyone to cross. Sometimes they would see me but I would run into the brush. I was much faster than they were and I always got away. One day, I was resting after crossing the river. I saw three men with about four or five dogs running towards me. They belonged to the old gringo that owned the

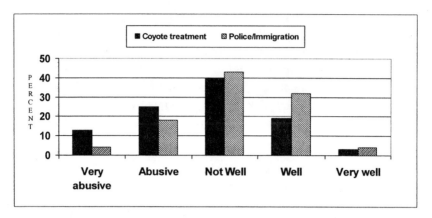

FIG. 5.1. Percent Undocumented Workers Survey respondents selecting each level of how abusive or well they were treated by coyotes and immigration officers/police

ranch. I knew right away why the dogs were there to hunt me down. I took off running. I could hear the dogs getting closer and closer so I made a big circle and returned to the river. The next time I crossed at that place I took a bag of powdered *chiles* [chili peppers] and sprinkled it on my tracks. After that, the dogs never even got close. I guess the old gringo didn't think I was smart enough to outsmart him or his dogs."[25]

Though accounts like those just described are not uncommon, the majority of undocumented immigrants seem to get by without harsh treatment by either smugglers or immigration officers. In the survey, we asked respondents to rate how they (or persons they knew) were treated by immigration officers and by smugglers. The results of this comparison are reported in Figure 5.1.

As Figure 5.1 indicates, less than 5 percent of respondents reported very abusive treatment by immigration agents. Arturo is one who harbors harsh feelings against INS officers. "The first time that I was caught," he says, "I was traveling on a bus and unexpectedly the immigration officers checked each of the passengers. They asked me for my papers and I told them that I was a U.S. citizen, and that I did not have any papers with me. I could not speak English and they did not believe me. They took me to jail where an immigration officer insulted me. I got angry and insulted him back. That was when he hit me. They took me to the border and made me go back to Mexico. The second time I came to the U.S. I was caught again. This time I wasn't going to let them hit me, so I told them that if they touched me I was going to report them to the police. They got angry and took me to court. I went through a trial and I was given five years of probation. The judge told me that if I were to get caught again in the U.S. as an undocumented, I was going to be sent to jail for six months."

Many undocumented immigrants are confused by what happens to them in their encounters with the Border Patrol. The law gives immigration officers such wide discretionary power that it is even difficult for some attorneys to understand what is happening. Immigration officers along the border have a lower burden of proof for showing cause when they stop someone for questioning than they do in other parts of the country. Once they stop someone, they can arrest them, or offer a "voluntary departure." [26] If they arrest someone, they may have the choice of charging them with an administrative law violation, a misdemeanor, or a felony. Immigration officers can conduct neighborhood or factory raids and they can arrest anyone they suspect of being illegal, holding them for up to twenty-four hours without filing any charges. They have the discretion, when someone is detained, to set bond, to serve papers in English or Spanish, and to determine what information they will give to apprehended individuals.

Because of such discretion, people like Arturo can be turned loose at the border or charged with a federal felony.[27] It should not be surprising, then, that a few agents will occasionally abuse their authority in dealing with undocumented immigrants. One Border Patrol officer explains. "In my own experience, I do not recall seeing any real physical harm done to undocumented workers. What I did witness were many Border Patrol officers who felt frustration every time they had to chase certain individuals during apprehension. After apprehending these individuals, they would call them something like *cabezas de tornillo* [screwheads], making them understand they had a hard head and no respect for authority. I would say there was more verbal abuse than any physical harm administered to those who were apprehended."

The presence of many people with Mexican origin living in South Texas presents a problem for immigration officers. They cannot always tell who is legal and who is not. María is a woman born in the United States but raised in Mexico. She had always crossed the border with no problems until one day when she was stopped by two Border Patrol officers. "I had my two-year-old child with me," she says, "and I wasn't worried because the Border Patrol had never given me any problems before. But the Hispanic officer insisted that I prove my U.S. citizenship. Because I didn't have my birth certificate with me, he started to really interrogate me. The questions he asked made me feel really bad. Then he decided to wake up my child to ask her if I was really her mom, though my child was too young to answer his questions. Finally, the other officer observed what was happening and decided to put an end to the interrogation. They let us go, but I never felt so embarrassed and humiliated in my life. From then on, I carry my birth-certificate with me all the time for fear of being detained again."

Though María carries her birth certificate with her, she is not required by law to prove her U.S. citizenship except on entry into the U.S. Federal law puts the burden of proof on immigration agents who must prove that a person has "entered without inspection." Of course, the only way to do so when illegal entry is not observed is through getting a confession. Because many Mexican origin people do not want the hassle of such interrogations, many carry a birth certificate.

The Border Patrol—A View from the Inside

One Border Patrol agent mentioned that many illegal aliens, as well as U.S. citizens, refer to Border Patrol agents as "La Migra" or "los Rinches" [Rangers]. "Some of them are afraid of us," he said. "When I apprehended a guy in El Paso he was shaking. I asked him if he was cold, and he said that he was shaking because he heard stories that the agents would beat illegal aliens until they were unconscious. I told him, 'As long as you respect me, I'll respect you.'"

Agent Martinez had a similar view on the way people perceive Border Patrol agents. "One of the illegal aliens I caught said that his father had warned him about Border Patrol agents. His father told him, 'No vayas allá porque te van a golpear' [Don't go over there because they are going to beat you]."

Most agents explain that the vast majority of aliens they deal with don't invite any rough treatment. Bob Cano explains a situation he had recently with some aliens who became very difficult. "About two weeks ago," he says, "my partner and I observed six men crossing the river at around midnight. We followed them until we caught them. Three men were very cooperative and followed our directions. The other three seemed to be under the influence of alcohol. They started calling us 'la pinche Migra" [the f——Border Patrol] and refused to get into our vehicle. They questioned how I, a Mexican American, could apprehend people of my own race. I answered that this was my job. Most aliens respect us except those who have had bad experiences with the Border Patrol."[28]

Situations like that just described illustrate the difficult job of the Border Patrol. They need to be careful not to unduly hassle people who are legally in the United States. At the same time, they are charged with keeping out those who don't belong. This is particularly difficult in a region like South Texas where almost 90 percent of the population is of Mexican or Latin American ancestry.

There are other frustrating aspects of the job. "The illegals are smart," says one agent. "They learn quickly how to work the system. The women learn quickly, for example, that if they are eight or nine months pregnant and we apprehend them, we will take them to Mexico immediately. So they wait until their water breaks and go into labor just before they cross the river. We cannot refuse them medical attention and we don't have the manpower to wait at the hospital for them to be released. We ask the hospital to notify us upon their release, but they usually get lost in the paperwork or the hospital doesn't care."

Border Patrol agents also face danger. One agent, who we'll call Abel Martinez, told of an incident when weapons were involved. "It was about 3:00 p.m. and a fellow agent and I stopped a vehicle close to the river," he says. "The driver was real nervous. After five minutes of talking to him we heard shots from across the river. One of the bullets went right over my head and severed some branches on the tree behind me. The person shooting at us was an accomplice to the person in the vehicle. He was trying to distract us so that his friend could get away."

Most work with undocumented aliens, however, is not dangerous. The greatest danger to Border Patrol officers comes in their work against drug trafficking. The Border Patrol apprehends more people with illegal drugs than any other law enforcement agency, including the Drug Enforcement Agency. Many times these apprehensions involve violent confrontations. These drug traffickers will at times resort to any means necessary to protect their investment, even if it means killing a federal officer. One agent says, "You have to remember that in their line of work, human life is not regarded with the same value as ours. Killing is no big thing to them. It's the normal way of doing business." (See Chapter 6.)

One former Hispanic agent tells us that the Border Patrol has the highest turnover rate of any federal law enforcement. "There are roughly 3,300 agents serving in the agency," he says. "Every year about 800 agents either transfer or quit to take other jobs. The hours are long and the pay is not great. If you're a college graduate, well, then it's low compared to other jobs where you can utilize that degree. You don't need a college degree to work for the Border Patrol. You only get paid a little extra. After a while you get burned out on this and you wonder if it's really worth it. I didn't like the way that I was becoming alienated from my family and relatives. It was hard to visit family and friends in Mexico and explain to them what I did and then having to justify it. When the costs started outweighing the benefits, I decided it was time to move on. I soon realized that I didn't want to spend the rest of my life conforming to things I really didn't believe in just to earn a living. If you're all 'gung-ho' and like the law enforcement aspect of the job, then the Border Patrol is for you. But when you have to go against your own moral values, then this job can cause you to question yourself." [29]

In the last several years, the Border Patrol has undergone some rather dramatic changes. Under the Bush administration, the number of agents has increased dramatically. In fact, the Border Patrol in 2003 did not fill many of the positions it had authorization for because those at the top felt the influx of new agents was just too rapid to accommodate more. The Border Patrol and the entire Immigration and Naturalization Service were incorporated into the new Department of Homeland Security. And for the past five or so years, the Border Patrol has emphasized a strategy of positing agents every several hundred yards in fixed positions in high traffic areas of the border to deter immigrants. This has resulted in more immigrants coming with the use of alien smugglers and more of them entering in remote desert locations where the number of deaths has increased dramatically. Finally, and in many ways more important, the agency has shifted from being mainly an organization used to prevent illegal immigration to one whose main function is drug interdiction. All of these changes have had a profound impact on the Border Patrol.

One of the agents interviewed five years ago commented on the level of changes at that time. "Many of these new recruits are Hispanics and women," he says. "Just a few years ago, let's say about nine or ten, what the Border Patrol used to do was enforce immigration laws, mainly by apprehending aliens along the border. That was a pretty safe job. Now since drug trafficking is mainly along the Rio Grande Border, we are finding ourselves doing the job that our police and FBI agents used to do."

Many agents, particularly those with Mexican ancestry, find that they have to deal with feelings of guilt. Carmen described this process when she started with the agency. "When I first started," she says, "I was timid. I felt every emotion towards the aliens—sympathy, guilt, compassion, et cetera. More so when they would tell me things like, "Please let me go. I just want to make it in this country like you," or "Please, you are Mexican. You should understand. Let us go!" Sometimes I would come home and cry, especially when women would beg me to let them go, to do it for their little children. It has gotten easier now. I see things in a whole new perspective. Everybody in this country has worked hard to be here. These people want to do it the easy way. They want the fast bucks, but no one wants to pay their dues! Most of these people can't get jobs anyway, so what do they do? Commit crimes! With that way of thinking it makes it easier to apprehend the criminal. And they are criminals as soon as they cross illegally."

As they undergo such change in thinking, Hispanic agents who still have family in Mexico seem to have the greatest difficulty. "When I started in McAllen," one says, "things seemed fine until it became known that my family was all from Mexico. McAllen was only three hours from Monterrey so I had the chance to visit relatives on weekends. When word of this reached my superiors at work, many displayed an 'us against them' attitude. I thought that this was kind of hypocritical since many of those displaying this attitude were Hispanics whose parents or relatives were also from Mexico. Even in cases that could be seen as a victimless crime, some of these agents enforce immigration laws to an extreme for first-time offenders. I remember one time where an illegal immigrant was arrested for working in a junkyard as a night watchman. This same immigrant had only recently been commended by the local police for helping break up a car theft ring. When I, being new to the job, suggested to other agents that we should find a way to help this man, they told me to not get involved because 'these people' were not worth it."

Those who don't change their thinking often end up leaving the agency. Beto, who has since left the Border Patrol, describes his feelings about illegals from Mexico. "I was born and raised on the border," he says, "so I knew about what these illegal aliens go through in trying to survive. Many of them just come to make some money and then return back. If I was driving around in a neighborhood and I knew that someone was illegal, but essentially not bothering anyone, like for example mowing a yard or gardening, well then I would tend to look the other way. Don't think I would do this all the time, but I was human and I felt sorry for them. After all, my parents were from Mexico. Some of the other agents would immediately arrest them. After a while, you come to realize that you're not there to help everyone; that you can't save everybody. That's why I got out of it. There were times when I really hated my job."

Many Mexican American officers, however, do not identify with people from Mexico. David Salinas, for example, says, "it's kind of funny that almost everybody thinks that because we're Hispanic we'll want to give Mexicans a break and let them go. If we did that, we would be out of job. Also every Border Patrol agent, I'm sure, has been approached time and time again by illegal aliens offering money to us to let them go. They do this because where they come from it's expected to give the police money. Down there they openly encourage it. When we catch them, a lot of them can't figure out why we won't take their money."

Though the influx of Hispanic officers into the Border Patrol in recent years has made it easier to be an Hispanic Border Patrol agent, some have run across prejudice from Anglo officers. Daniel says, "Yes, I had a problem with one of my Anglo supervisors who just didn't like Hispanics. I didn't have any problems with him personally. As agents in the Border Patrol, we get ranked twice a year. It's done on a form that our supervisor fills out to tell higher-ups how we're doing. It determines if we get a raise, a promotion, or get fired. Well, this supervisor gave me a bad ranking and I was looking forward to being promoted. When I saw my ranking, I went straight to him and demanded an explanation. I got nowhere and so l took it higher. It was known around the office how he felt about Hispanics, so it wasn't difficult for me to win this battle. In the end the supervisor had to change my ranking and I got my promotion."

Though outright prejudice is not as common as it once was, there is pressure among Hispanic agents to not be "too Mexican." "When I first got into the Border Patrol, says John Torres, "I had no idea how hard it was going to be. The training is extensive. You learn about U.S. immigration law, how to speak Spanish (if you don't already know it), and to become very physically fit. There are other areas that you cover, but those are the main three. I was really surprised that out of my class of fifty cadets, only seventeen were Hispanic. One of those was from Chile and another was from Puerto Rico. One of the cadets was a woman. There were no Blacks. Only two of the fifty had college degrees, I being one of them. From the outset, I felt like an outsider. Most Hispanics within the service, from observation, gave the appearance that it was socially unacceptable to be 'too Mexican' or Mexican American."

Conclusion

Immigration control along the South Texas border is not an easy job. As Mexico and the United States become more closely tied through NAFTA and other trade arrangements, the job gets even more difficult. With the tremendous pull of undocumented Mexicans begging for jobs, and jobs in the United States begging for undocumented workers, there seems to be little hope for stemming the flow. As a result, immigration agents must enforce laws that many people do not want enforced. This is especially true along the South Texas border, where the vast majority of the population is of Mexican ancestry.

Many border residents also oppose strict enforcement of immigration laws because they sense a bias of these laws against Mexico and Latin Americans. Canadians, for example, find it much easier to visit or even to work in the United States. In addition, many Americans who blame practically every problem on "illegal aliens" continue to hire them to tend their children, harvest and process their foods, and tend their gardens.

This leaves us with a strange situation. We can't do without inexpensive Mexican labor, but we don't want to change our laws to reflect the realities "on the ground." As a result, we have a system that promotes fraud and facilitates the exploitation of those who are providing a much needed service.

We could vastly improve this situation by allowing those who have worked for years at below poverty wages to legalize their status. Were it not for the fears of terrorism and the anti-immigrant bias, President Bush might have accomplished just that at the beginning of his presidency. Unless the issue of how to regulate the flow of undocumented workers can be examined in a more rational national discourse, however, we will continue to live with all the contradictions of a system that works only because it doesn't work.

Drug Smuggling

WITH LUPE TREVIÑO

Every weekend, Mom and Dad always picked up my sister and me after school. Whenever we would see them both in the car, we knew that we were going out of town on a trip. My parents packed clothes for us and when Dad stopped to gas up, we would run in the store and pick up some munchies and magazines. Before my sister and I knew it, we were at the checkpoint by Falfurrias. The Border Patrol agent would wave us on and my sister would wave back. Who would suspect that the trunk was full of contraband? Being as young as I was, I didn't see this as anything more than a long family weekend outing.

Like Ignacio, the young man relating this account, some South Texas children grow up with drug smuggling as a part of their lives.[1] One of the authors, Rosalva Resendiz, remembers her own childhood in Brownsville. "I grew up in the Valley," she says, "surrounded by the drug trafficking culture. Growing up along the border unavoidably exposed us to certain circles of criminality. Contact with drug smugglers and traffickers was unavoidable. It would happen through friends, classmates, relatives, legitimate businesses, and in social settings such as nightclubs. And although the drug business is looked down upon by greater society, on the border it is a social fact—one that is generally tolerated, if not embraced. It touches almost every aspect of life here. Sometimes it is conscious and deliberate, and sometimes you are not even aware that it is going on around you. This influence can be felt despite traditional family values, religion, and a good education."

Methodology

One indicator of the prevalence of a drug smuggling subculture along the South Texas border was the number of Borderlife Project students who chose to interview close friends, family members, or neighbors about drug smuggling.[2] Over the course of the Borderlife Project, seventy or more students interviewed individuals who were involved in either drug smuggling or in law enforcement. After we excluded those who did not authorize use of the interview information, a total of 211 interviews remained. We excluded another eleven interviews because we could not follow up to verify some data; this left a total of approximately 200 individuals whose accounts were at least tentatively accepted.

In addition, the Perceptions of Deviance Survey obtained fixed-response type data from 424 individuals regarding their feelings about how right or wrong certain actions or activities are. These items included three that specifically deal with drug smuggling. In each case, respondents were asked to indicate how right or how wrong it was for young adults in the Valley to (1) occasionally use illegal drugs at a party, (2) occasionally sell illegal drugs to finance their education, and (3) occasionally transport illegal drugs up north to support their family.

Drugs and the Border

The Rio Grande Valley of South Texas has the highest unemployment, poverty, and school dropout rates in the United States. These forms of dubious distinction are greatly compounded by the fact that the South Texas border area also has the highest rate of drug seizures in the nation.

According to Lupe Treviño, Hidalgo County, with the largest population in South Texas, has become the nation's number one crossing point for illegal drugs in recent years, followed by Laredo and El Paso.[3] In fact, seizures of marijuana and cocaine in Hidalgo County alone exceed the total seizures made along the entire Arizona border.[4] Over half of all drugs entering the United States are estimated to cross the Texas border, with the largest seizure rates in the McAllen sector of the border.[5]

The growing drug seizure rate is related to many aspects of the South Texas border. First, the rapid development of the maquiladora industry, coupled with the increased trade promoted by NAFTA (both closely related to globalization), has contributed to a rapid expansion of the flow of illegal drugs. In 2001, more than 20 million pedestrians, 51 million private vehicles, and nearly 3 million commercial trucks crossed into Texas from Mexico through border ports of entry.[6] This huge volume of cross-border traffic makes it increasingly difficult to detect and deter the flow of drugs into the United States.

According to law enforcement personnel,[7] the drug cartels prefer the McAllen area for a variety of other reasons as well. For one, there are many isolated crossing points. Another factor is a high unemployment rate and the enticement of quick money for unemployed and low-income individuals. People on both sides of the border with little education and no job skills are recruited as "mules" to cross the drugs. Many individuals carrying relatively small amounts present traffickers with fewer risks. These drugs are then generally loaded into tractor-trailers carrying agricultural products or manufactured goods for the trip further north. This trip requires another smuggling operation past the Border Patrol checkpoints sixty miles north of the border. Many families in Hidalgo and Starr Counties have smuggling networks that go back several generations. These networks can be relied upon to protect family members and are highly resistant to infiltration by drug agents.

O'Day has documented the development and continuity of drug trafficking in a nearby Mexican community in a study underscoring the centrality of strong family networks.[8] Utilizing methodology similar to our own, O'Day was introduced to this Mexican border town and its activities through a student from UT-PA who had grown up around the local mafiosos and had heard many stories of smuggling, betrayal, and murder.[9]

Money Laundering

Money laundering is a significant by-product of the drug trade. Though it is impossible to know the actual amount of money laundered each year, interagency estimates of the U.S. government suggest that between $100 billion and $300 billion in U.S. currency is laundered each year.[10] Currency seizure information reported by the Texas Department of Public Safety shows a 209 percent increase in money seizures from 1996 to 1999.[11] The money often travels south in the same vehicles used to transport the drugs north. Millions of dollars each year are hidden in luggage, gasoline tanks, transmissions, and even portable toilets. Smugglers have opened up a drug-cash pipeline from New York to Texas.[12] In FY 1998, $68.4 million was seized by U.S. Customs. Outbound seizures exceeded $11.9 million, with inbound seizures totaling a little more than $3 million in 1998.

Often, money is laundered through money exchange businesses [*casas de cambio*], small businesses, used car lots, and real estate purchases along the border. The U.S. government estimates that at least $50 billion—more than the entire budget of Texas—flows through Texas each year to Mexico.[13] Some of this money ends up in local banks and businesses. Indeed, the San Antonio Federal Reserve Bank has one of the largest cash surpluses in the nation. Texas officials report in excess of $560 million flowing annually through exchangers in the form of U.S. currency, checks, and wire transfers.[14]

In Mexico, the privatization of banks has allowed drug traffickers to buy stock in, and seek election to the boards of, Mexican banks, where they can ease the difficulty of laundering drug profits.[15] In addition, as the *New York Times* reported,[16] and as law enforcement intelligence confirms,[17] some maquiladoras have been purchased by Mexican drug lords. The drug lords are then able to procure special exemptions from duties on items shipped to the U.S. And, by establishing trucking subsidiaries, these smugglers are able to mix drugs with legitimate products.

All of these operations bring money to the border. Underground transactions are combined with the practice of some wealthy Mexicans using Texas banks to deposit legitimate profits. As a result, an area of extreme poverty ends up with high per capita bank deposits.[18]

Drug Usage along the Border

Illegal drugs have long been associated with the U.S.-Mexico border. South Texas has historically been used as a preferred route for smugglers of many items for generations. The smuggling of drugs first became an issue with the El Paso Ordinance of 1914. During and after the Mexican Revolution, when Mexican immigration was increasing, it was rumored among El Paso Anglos that immigrants' use of marijuana gave them superhuman strength. Fearful, El Pasoans outlawed its use. But the Drug War began in earnest in 1937, when marijuana was outlawed in the United States; in 1961, the United States convinced the members of the United Nations to do the same.

The problem of drug abuse is generally aggravated on the Texas-Mexico border in part because of the greater availability and lower price of drugs there. In the border region, for example, 20.5 percent of secondary students surveyed[19] reported that they had used powder cocaine, compared to

11 percent of non-border youths in the same school grades.[20] This finding is probably related to the price and availability of the drug: in 2003, a gram of powder cocaine cost $450 to $550 in McAllen, but $650 to $1,000 in Dallas.[21]

Certain other drugs are also more readily available along the border than in more northward cities. Rohypnol (often referred to as the rape drug) was reported to have been used at least once by about 11 percent of border high school students, as compared to only about 4 percent of high school youths in non-border areas.[22] Use of drugs which do not pass through the border (such as MDMA, the "rave" drug) is much less frequently reported by border students. In 2002, for example, only 6 percent of border high school students reported that they had ever used this drug, compared to 9 percent of high school students elsewhere in the state—even though MDMA is cheaper along the border.[23]

Surprisingly, however, the use of all illicit drugs may be lower in the South Texas border region than in any other part of Texas. The data from the Office of Applied Studies shows that the rates of any illicit drug use during the month prior to the survey were lower in the South Texas region (Region 11) than in any of the other ten regions, not only for twelve- to seventeen-year-olds, but also for those twenty-six years of age and older.[24] This finding is reflected by the Texas School Survey of Substance Use among Students: Grades 7–12, conducted in 2002, which found that 36.9 percent of Texas border seniors had ever used marijuana, compared with 47.8 percent of Texas seniors from non-border areas.[25] These results are especially surprising considering the cheaper price of marijuana along the border. In 2003, for example, the same commercial-grade marijuana cost $130 to $200 in McAllen, but $350 to $600 in Dallas.[26]

Clearly, then, it would be wrong to argue that high rates of drug abuse cause the high flow of drugs through South Texas. Yet it is also true that the flow of drugs across the border has increased dramatically. In 2002, for example, 555,324 kilograms of marijuana were seized in Texas—more than the 488,000 kilograms seized in all the other forty-nine states combined during that year. Of the amount seized in Texas, 83 percent was seized within 150 miles of the Mexican border.[27]

In recent years, the cocaine trade has also increased significantly in South Texas. For decades, South Florida was the thriving center for cocaine smuggling and distribution. The increase in federal law enforcement presence and specialized anti-narcotic programs there forced cocaine drug trafficking organizations to seek areas that were less heavily policed. It was at this time that Colombian and other South American cocaine suppliers began utilizing established Mexican smuggling families. In 2002, 17,008 kilograms of cocaine were seized in Texas, again, more than the amount seized in any other state.[28]

One rancher, a lifelong resident of one of the rural counties of the Valley, remembers the dramatic impact of the movement of drugs through South Texas. "Livestock was the main business prior to drugs," he says, "and now continues to be the main laundering business. Many of the best-known drug smugglers around this area are related to the men that received land grants from Spanish royalty. However, the arid environment had not been good for business for several years. As taxes increased over the years it seemed as if the government was the only one making a profit off useless land. This is why the drug business became an excellent fringe benefit to this area. With the help of drug money we were able to clear land, build small lakes, and plant grass for the cows to feed. Soon the cattle business started looking up. However, the drug money was much easier to get than ranching. So many people continued to traffic drugs and used the cattle to launder their money. Now we just hire Mexicans to look over our cows and land for a few hundred dollars a month. Drug smuggling I would say started picking up around this area around fifteen years ago and now is the biggest business. Many of the top city and county officials may not be trafficking themselves but they make lots of money by taking large payoffs to keep quiet. Those people that are not involved just don't say anything. This is mainly due to the fact that so many people are acquaintances or know each other through friends. A lot of us went to school together and many are now having their sons take over."

The Issues

The preceding discussion of the impact of drugs on the South Texas border raises a number of issues that have relevance far beyond the borderlands. These issues can be summarized as follows:

—Has the effort to stop the flow of drugs into the United States by interdicting the drugs at the border been successful, or has it increased lawlessness and deviance along the border and in the interior of both Mexico and the United States?

—Has the high rate of poverty along the Texas-Mexico border drawn the flow of drugs through this area, or are other factors more important?

—Is the flow of drugs through South Texas associated with an increased rate of drug dependency?

—Does the culture of the South Texas borderlands contribute to the flow of drugs through this area, or is the culture of the area being corrupted by this phenomenon?

—If the economic rewards for drug smuggling are so great, why aren't more poor people drawn into it?

The Drug Pipeline

In recent years, Mexico has greatly increased its efforts to seize drugs before they enter the United States. In 2001, for example, 29.2 metric tons of cocaine were seized in Mexico, representing a 60 percent increase over the previous year.[29] Approximately 70 percent of this amount was seized at or near the U.S.-Mexico border. Similarly, 2,007 metric tons of marijuana were seized by Mexico in 2001, with 53 percent of it being seized at or near the U.S. border.[30]

In many respects, the flow of drugs through Mexico to the United States represents a highly corrupting influence on Mexican society. Mexico faces not only the problem of increased drug availability, but the related challenges of drug transshipment, drug production, chemical processing, money laundering, organized crime, and the persistent influence of narcocorruption.[31]

This corrupting influence has reached virtually every segment of Mexican society, including the Mexican military, which for years was thought to be outside the web of corruption. Some U.S. law enforcement officials now recognize that the Mexican military has protected shipments of drugs as they are moved from point A to point B. There have even been a few reports of the Mexican military extending its operations into U.S. territory. O'Day, for example, reported an incident in which the Mexican military was sighted on the U.S. side by local Border Patrol agents.[32] Under further investigation, U.S. authorities refused to confirm this information. In another report, a Border Patrol official claimed that in 2001, there were twelve separate incursions across the border by the Mexican military.[33] When these units are caught with drugs, he reports, they simply claim that they have just confiscated them from drug smugglers.[34]

Getting illegal drugs across the U.S.-Mexico border and into U.S. cities is a highly complex operation. Many "specialists" are required to fund, package, transport, and sell the product. This process includes loaders, counter-surveillance operatives, local drivers, storage specialists, brokers, legitimate load (cover) providers, northbound drivers (tractor-trailer rigs), brokers outside the Valley, southbound money couriers, and money launderers.[35]

A few enterprising individuals handle much of the entire operation themselves, sneaking small loads of drugs across the bridge, making a second slip past the Border Patrol checkpoints, and then on to a final destination where they sell their product. Such lone operatives, however, are the exception. More often, a wide variety of "specialists" are involved in moving drugs into and out of the Valley. The individuals who actually smuggle drugs across the river are only a small part of the overall operation. Even this aspect, however, requires many operatives. Some drive drugs into the United States across the international bridges. Others fly it across, landing at clandestine airfields. Some actually swim or row it across the Rio Grande. Other smugglers land small fishing boats laden with contraband on South Padre Island after maneuvering around the mouth of the Rio Grande at the Gulf of Mexico.

Often, those who cross the drugs are small-time operatives called "mules." Most work for Mexican suppliers who help them avoid detection. Often, their work is very dangerous because they risk getting caught by the Mexican police, drowned in the river, caught by the Border Patrol, or robbed by underworld bandits and thieves. Most never rise much above this level because they don't have the capital to invest or the connections needed to buy, store, transport, or sell to points further north.

These small-time operatives related many accounts about the dangers of taking drugs across the Rio Grande at night. One, for example, said, "One night I had crossed the river with the package of drugs. When I got over here, I couldn't find my contact. I waited in the bushes for a long time. When I thought it was safe, I left the package hidden and went out to see if I could see someone. I found my contact tied up near a truck. He had been severely beaten. I quickly went back into hiding. Then, I heard someone behind me. There were two men. One asked me what I was doing. I told him that I had just crossed the river to look for work. When I also told them that some people behind me were crossing drugs and I didn't want to be near them, they told me to leave. Without them detecting me, I picked up the package and left. I traveled a little way down the riverbank and crossed back to Mexico. There, I was picked up and taken to return the package to the boss."

Other individuals take drugs across the river by car over the international bridge. One of them describes what this experience is like: "Our boss always brings three cars that are just alike. He has the bumper pads removed front and rear. This is where we keep the merchandise. Before we put it in the bumpers we have to compress the dope into rectangular size with a machine. When the blocks are done we wrap them up with cellophane and spray them with black under coating so that they won't show. After a brief inspection to make sure that the job is done right, we proceed to the bridge. The cars are licensed in different areas so that they won't be suspicious when crossing the bridge at Customs. We cross in fifteen- to twenty-minute intervals so that we won't get caught. Even though we feel excitement with the line of work, we run the chance of going to prison. Mostly, we don't think about it. We have been lucky."

One of the greatest fears for drivers who use the international bridge is having trained dogs inspect their cars. One relates an experience he had when the officer at "primary" inspection (the first contact) became suspicious and sent him to a "secondary" inspection (taken out of the flow of traffic and inspected much more carefully, often with dogs). "The officer there asked me to open the trunk and the hood of my car," he says, "and to please step aside as they searched the car. They also called out for a K-9 unit to inspect the car. The merchandise was wrapped with a powder dust used to coat the ground around slaughterhouses in Mexico to deter all kinds of animals. Luckily this idea worked and I was soon on my way. This was the closest I'd ever come to being arrested. The person that I worked for was experienced, and this has resulted in my long-term existence in this career."

The "mules" are often organized and paid by drug mafiosos in Mexico. These individuals must invest large sums of money to buy the drugs and get them to the border. Some of them trust their mules, but others go through the checkpoint a few minutes ahead to insure their product will make it across. Many also hire spotters to go ahead of the loaded cars to make sure dogs are not being used in their chosen lane at the checkpoint. If dogs are being used they call their mules by cellular phones. The mule will either turn back or keep on going, hoping to avoid looking suspicious. Often, the mule may drive a car loaded with a family to give the appearance that they are headed to the U.S. for shopping or for a vacation.

When smugglers first start, most have to either invest their own money or borrow it from dealers or loan sharks in order to purchase "the product." Those without cash to invest must choose the least favorable option—obtaining the merchandise on credit, or having it "fronted." Although this provides beginning smugglers with an opportunity, it also burdens them with a debt and tremendous pressure to not lose a load.

One independent dealer points out, "I'd rather invest with my own dough. If anything goes wrong the worst that can happen is that I lose my money and my freedom. However, if I borrow money or get the product fronted I can lose even more. The loan sharks charge a lot of interest, up to 10 percent per week. If anything happens, I still have to pay. If I can't, I stand the chance of losing something way more valuable—my life."

According to our respondents, the drug business has an intricate system of financing. There are those that invest in the smuggling operations, but are not involved in the transport of the drugs. Although the risk of arrest is lower, there is no risk-free involvement, since circumstantial evidence or witnesses can be used to prosecute. Many other participants aid the smuggling process via specialized tasks. Among these are those who package and load the drugs for shipment to the north. Often, this involves loading large produce trucks, as one interviewee explains. "After we receive the load of drugs from Mexico," he says, "we have our paid workers load the drugs into our truck. The loading process has to be very carefully done. The workers remove the crates of fruit in the truck until they reach the center. In the center they place the drugs, which are carefully wrapped. Then they reload all of the crates back in place. After that we drive the truck to the destination location, where it is again unloaded, and the drugs are exchanged with the buyer for a large amount of money."

Along the Texas-Mexico border, law enforcement officers are increasingly subjected to enticements to "look the other way." Many smugglers target small-town police departments, where salaries are notoriously low, as well as the ranks of federal law enforcement agencies. Periodic headlines in local newspapers highlight the arrest and indictments of local officials who have yielded to the huge sums offered. Some are accused of not only looking the other way, but also becoming more actively involved in actually protecting drug shipments and money laundering operations.[36]

According to many of those interviewed, the hardest part of the operation is crossing the Border Patrol checkpoints stationed at intervals along a line sixty miles parallel to the border. Although various methods are employed to get around this obstacle, the most common technique is to take large loads in hidden compartments of commercial vehicles.

Some individuals, however, prefer to hire drivers to carry smaller amounts by car. One man who uses this method tells his drivers to take the merchandise to Houston, using two cars at a time. He flies to Houston and waits for his drivers to arrive and make their connections. After they have made their connections he gets the money and returns home. When the drivers return, they place their cars in storage until the next job. After a few months, he will sell the cars and buy two different used cars—he can't afford to keep the same ones for very long because they might be recognized by law enforcement.

How It Starts

Student interviewers frequently ask their informants how they got started. One replied, "Well if you smoke pot you're going to hang out with people who smoke pot, then maybe you want to get a bag. So someone knows where to get something from someone. Eventually you meet that person, make friends, and other people start asking you to get bags for them from this person. So, I think if I get more I'll have to spend less. You start thinking of a 'volume discount.' Eventually you are saving money, then getting the stuff free, and finally, before you know it, you're dealing."

Valdez and Sifaneck found this same pattern among Mexican American gang members.[37] In order to maintain their habit, he found, many gang members become sellers. Among gang members interviewed in our research, some also reported using drugs to bolster their sense of courage in the face of the dangers confronting them in the trade. One member of a nationally known gang, for example, said, "At the age of fifteen, I got involved in one of the most popular gangs in town. I did a lot of drug dealing. My job within the gang was to set up when and where to deal the drugs and to warn the gang of danger. I'm what they call the point man. We use drugs to motivate ourselves to accomplish the crimes we intend to commit. I have committed many crimes in the past and continue to do so."

Obviously, many gangs also sell drugs for the money.[38] One of our interviewees, for example, said, "I didn't want to join a gang, but I felt had to. It was the only way I could help my mom pay the bills. When I joined the gang, they told me that all I had to do was tell how much of any kind of drugs I needed. When I sold the drugs, I gave them the money and they gave me a nice percentage of their profit. Whenever a customer refused to pay, all I had to do was tell my *clika* [gang] about it and they would find the offending customer and collect our money by any means necessary."

Another interviewee describes what life was like when he lived in Mexico. "We were very poor," he says. "I promised my family that we would be better off in the United States. When we got here, I could only find work as a migrant farmworker, so I didn't make much money. I got the courage to become a drug smuggler when I saw the easy money some men were making from dealing drugs. Now my heart always pounds with excitement when I see big smiles on my children's faces when I bring them food or toys. I don't like this kind of work, but I would do anything just so my children don't have to eat out of trash cans like I did when I was young."

Justifying one's association with the drug trade by the need to feed one's family is often more rationalization than reality, however. Few individuals enter the drug trade to put smiles on their children's faces or to keep them from eating out of trash cans. Many migrant farmworkers, for example, refuse to be lured into the drug trade despite rather severe economic challenges. Hidalgo County Sheriff Lupe Treviño, who for many years headed the Hidalgo County drug interagency task force, says, "From debriefing defendants and informants over several years, I have found that those who enter the drug business do so mainly for one reason—the lure of what they see as easy and quick money."

This desire for quick and easy money was evident in many of the interviews. One young man, for example, put it this way. "I got married young and had a low-paying job. After six months, we had a baby. There were more expenses with the baby. My wife also wanted things. She nagged me about not ever having enough money, how everyone dressed better, and owned their own homes, et cetera. I talked to some friends and they got me into the drug smuggling business."

In some of the smaller towns along the border, friends and family have a particularly significant impact on the decision to smuggle drugs. "It is very easy to become a drug smuggler in this area," stated a fifty-four-year-old man from Starr County. "This is a small town. A lot of us knew each other when we were young and most of us come from the old families of this area. Not too many new people come to live here and many of our young people can go to larger, more exciting cities. Most of the mafiosos around here got into the business because we got tired of picking crops and doing hard manual labor with little pay."

Thus, economic need, coupled with family connections, constitutes a common route into drug dealing. This is evident in the case of Arturo, who stated, "I started smuggling drugs at the age of fourteen. After my father died, my mother looked to me as the new head of the home. She started to work but she never made enough money to support us four children. One day, I got home from school and found her crying. After buying groceries and paying the bills, she didn't have any money left to buy the shoes we needed. From that moment on, I decided to go to work with my uncle, who smuggled drugs across the border."

All in the Family

Because a family traveling together is less likely to attract suspicion, some who transport drugs are tempted to involve their family. Some do not tell their spouse or children what they are doing. Others, however, involve them in many aspects of the operation. One Immigration officer at the Hidalgo Bridge remembers a sad situation involving a family. "About six years ago," he says, "a family of five came across the border in a gray van. I thought it was suspicious because the mom was driving and the father was in the backseat asleep. I asked the mother for the kids' ages and asked to see their documents. Everything matched, but the dad asleep in the back made me suspicious. I told the lady to get out of the van and open the back doors. I noticed that she started getting nervous. As she opened the door, I saw that the back of the middle seat looked as if it had been altered. As soon as I started to look closer, her husband jumped out and tried to run away but we caught him. Sure enough, 80 pounds of cocaine had been nicely fit inside that seat. We arrested the family, but it broke my heart to see the kids screaming and begging me not to take their daddy away. They said they were coming to celebrate Christmas. They could tell it got to me and started telling me all Immigration officers were mean. I told them that it was not my fault, that their daddy had done something bad and had to be taken away. The man tried to claim that someone had put the drugs in their van without them knowing, but we found out the van itself had been stolen. The guy was given twenty years in jail and I had to testify against him. I always remember it because it was Christmas. I couldn't believe the guy could actually involve his family and his kids in his mess."

Family is often involved in other ways as well. One man claimed that dealing and smuggling often turn into a family business. "The dad does it and his son starts to help. Before you know it, two or three sons and an uncle and a cousin are involved." Family unity can thus play a key role in the life of smugglers on the border. Indeed, sometimes having close family ties in Mexico allows family members to operate successfully on both sides of the border, keeping the operation within the family.[39]

For many, smuggling drugs has become a line of work passed on from father to son. Antonio remembers how he got his start in the drug business. "I got started when I finished school and saw that there were no jobs for me," he says. "After looking unsuccessfully for some time, I decided to do what my father had been doing. He was not what you really would call a smuggler. He always knew who had what and where, and for how much. He would help arrange deals, making a little profit each time, but never actually getting his hands dirty by seeing or touching the merchandise. He got started in this business when he was about my age. He came from a large family, never finished school, and married young. After one year of bad seasonal work, his friends helped him out the same way that he started me off. And like him, not being involved in the actual handling of the merchandise, I have never had any close calls."

Of course, dealing drugs poses great risks to a family. One man caught for dealing drugs comments, "Drug smuggling is a family affair, regardless of whether the family is involved or not. When the drug smuggler is arrested and sentenced, the family 'does time' together. When a husband is imprisoned, the wife becomes a single mother who must find some way to care for her children. The burden of the household rests on her, just like the burden of the pain rests on the father, who watches his children cry as he is taken away."

Many families live with such pain. One older man recalls, "Back in 1958, I was a migrant farmworker picking strawberries. I decided I needed to do something else if I was going to give my children what they needed. My friends told me that I was a fool not to because no one would suspect a migrant who always crossed the checkpoint migrating up north. Well, one time it got so bad for me that I decided I had no choice. I did it, but I got caught. My daughter had to pay for everything. I guess that's why she never got married. She had to support my wife, who couldn't read or write, and all my other eight children."

The danger to family members is much more than just getting caught, however. One man remembers a particularly scary incident a few years ago. "I remember the day I was busted by the Starr County task force," he says. "About twenty agents came to my house in the middle of the night. They broke down the doors and rushed in and demanded to know where the cocaine was stashed. They scared my wife and small children. I felt ashamed for causing so much pain to my family. The legal and moral aspect put a strain on my marriage and family."

The vulnerability of such families to police raids has created a new phenomenon along the South Texas border. Occasionally, bands of thugs disguised as police officers, or "pseudo-cops," conduct midnight raids on homes where they suspect drugs or drug money are kept. When they "confiscate" drugs or money, the unsuspecting victims are, of course, reluctant to report the raids to legitimate police agencies. Generally, they do not find out until after their attackers have beaten and left them that they have been victimized by pseudo-cops. Often, the pseudo-cops are drug dealers themselves seeking to make a quick buck or to weaken or frighten a competitor.

O'Day reports such a situation.[40] A local mafioso was being "ripped off" by his right-hand man, who arranged to have a large load of drugs confiscated by a group of pseudo-DEA (Drug Enforcement Agency) agents. These "agents" then took the drugs and fled into Mexico. According to O'Day, the subterfuge was discovered and resulted in the death of the right-hand man.

Sometimes, the family connection works through daughters and wives as well. Gina relates, "I have been involved in this business for a long time. My father started off with gambling and cockfights when we lived in Mexico. He had made sure that all of his children would be born in the U.S., and he only returned to Mexico when he needed to do business. My actual involvement in the smuggling business began when my husband of five years had to quit his job due to bad health. The responsibility of being the breadwinner then rested on my shoulders. There had been several friends that had offered their 'services.' At first I was rather reluctant, but as our money ran out, the prospect of making fast money had greater appeal. Being down to our last $20 was the final push. Reminiscing about how my father had conducted his business, I thought to myself, 'Why can't I do that?' I decided that I would rather take my chances with smuggling than deal with the embarrassment of standing in a welfare line for handouts. From that day on, with God by my side,[41] I was able to provide my family with the best of everything—food, shelter, clothing, money, transportation, jewelry, travel, and most importantly, an education. All I had ever wanted in life, for my children and myself, was made possible by this business. I have no regrets."

Risks and Dangers

"Got one!" said the Border Patrol agent, as he walked toward my truck. I felt my heart sink to my stomach. I had just pulled up to be inspected at the Falfurrias checkpoint. He went around to the front of my truck and bent down to look at the grill. Behind that grill there were several pounds of marijuana. Then he stood up holding a sparrow he had pulled off the front grill. With my heart in my throat, I tried to appear calm. I answered his questions and then drove off very slowly. After that close call I swore I would never do it again but here I am, a year later, still dealing.

Despite the risks and the close calls, the lure of big money keeps many individuals in the business. "Why should I have to break my back to earn minimum wage," said one man, "when I can make $10,000 in a week and not even break a sweat? My mom and dad both work and they can barely make it to provide for me and my five brothers and sisters. They are always careful to not let us know about how tight everything is, but I overhear their conversations. Mom is always worried about how the bills are going to be paid and Dad tells her not to worry. I don't have four years to wait to start to make some decent money. I know there's risk involved, but I don't want my parents having to struggle so much if I can help. I need things and so do my brothers and sisters. To me, the profits outweigh the risk."

Others disagree. One man from Starr County said, "It was the worst mistake I ever made. I'm living in danger all the time. I can't sleep at night just thinking of all the things that could go wrong. Maybe someone wants to kill me, or I might get caught. Someone in my family might be hurt. There are so many possibilities."

In addition to the risk of getting caught, there are many other pressures associated with trafficking. Sometimes lured by the idea of "easy money," drug traffickers quickly learn otherwise. A lot of time, labor, and resources must be invested in the business in the face of extremely high risks. Careful planning must be done at multiple stages—each with its own risks—from growing the product, exporting it, buying and selling it, maintaining the organization of the operation, and successfully reinvesting "dirty" money into the legitimate economy. "Being in this business is like having a thousand pounds on your back," stated one informant. "Freedom is the last thing I feel."

A man who has served a prison sentence for smuggling points out: "This is a serious game. Many people accuse us of earning easy money. The truth is, this business is more difficult than it seems. The majority of the people who start off in this business can't make a decent living. They might start off with a lucky deal or two but then go for long periods of time without being able to score money."

A smuggler who is now serving a five-year sentence for negotiating with a DEA informant had this to say: "Living this kind of life is stressful. You always live in fear of making a bad deal or the fear of being caught and arrested."

One drug-dealing middleman says that he rarely carries a gun, but that a gun is sometimes a necessity. "I almost never carry a gun, though I do keep one at home for security. When I do carry a gun, it's to conduct serious business. In those cases, I have to carry large amounts of cash or valuable merchandise. In this business there are a lot of bad apples who make a living by robbing smugglers. They know that if you get ripped off you can't bring the police into it. Carrying a gun provides me with at least some kind of security."

Sometimes deals go bad, but the suppliers still expect payment or the return of their merchandise. Says one, "The money has to be paid or the supply returned, no matter what! If you don't deliver, they'll find you, threaten you, or even kill you if you don't pay. In this business, you insure your word with your life."

One man who found himself unable to pay a debt found this true. "My family and I are always in danger," he says. "We live each day in terror. This year I owed money to another dealer, but I hadn't been able to come up with the money. So he sent someone to scare us. They fired gun shots all around the house. Thank God my family and I were not home when this happened."

One young man who had been involved in "enforcement" duties describes what this aspect of the business can be like. "The first time I went with a friend of mine and it wasn't so hard to do," he says. "But, the second time, the guy resisted and my friend and I were given orders to cut off one of his ears. We were told that if he still resisted, to cut off the other. Luckily as soon as we started he screamed that he would pay. I guess he thought we weren't serious, but we obviously were. I haven't gone through anything like that again, nor would I want to. Of course there have been some beatings but that's as far as it usually goes."

Sometimes, however, it doesn't end with a beating. Without the law to back them up, many dealers find their own ways to keep people "honest." One man relates a painful experience. "All I could do was stand there and watch," he says, "as my 'associates' beat up the guy that had stolen our storage of merchandise. While this was going on, I walked back to the car. I remember that I hadn't been sitting there for more than ten minutes when I heard two gunshots! It freaked me out because I hadn't even seen a gun. I guess I should have assumed there was one, but I hadn't. For a moment, I wasn't sure what to expect. Who had been shot? A few moments later, my friends returned to the car and proceeded to explain to me that they were not in the business of losing money, or getting ripped off without having someone pay for it. So now I was in really deep. I had started out as a dealer trying to collect a debt, and had become an accessory to a shooting. It was evident that there is a certain 'code of ethics' that has to be followed. Challenging that code could prove fatal."

Lupe Treviño comments that the "code of ethics" among drug dealers often has at its core the expectation that if you are caught, you will remain silent about others. "This was extremely important to the old-time Mexican drug traffickers," he says. "It used to be a very rare occasion to have a 'well-connected' Mexican informant giving us information. Mexican drug traffickers simply did not talk. That has all changed now, however. The severity of sentencing laws, arrest forfeiture procedures, and the inevitable effects on the family have forced more and more Mexican drug traffickers to talk. The conspiracy laws allow us to implicate parents, spouses, and other family members. Often, this forces them to talk. In exchange, they can get reduced charges and immunity for family members."

One of the older dealers agrees that times have changed. "It's different now," he says. "When I visit my sons, I don't go into town anymore. The gangs have taken over. I used to take *la mota* [marijuana] up to Chicago from the Valley and was never afraid of the guys I dealt with. I knew their families, and my word was good enough. Of course, we didn't smoke marijuana. Before I went to jail, my children didn't know I pushed drugs. I got caught after being in the business for a while. I had to deal with my friend's sons, who are *pen—s* [scum]. That's what I think. *La palabra* [your word] isn't good anymore. It's all guns and drugs now, and which *cab—n* [he-goat] has more of this or that. It's not good for *la familia* anymore. All these young pen—s don't know what they're getting into. We never smoked la mota. It was just that way. If you did, I wouldn't deal with you. A *loco* [drug user] is not good for business. I guess I'm glad I can talk about it now. I want to tell the young people that it isn't all glory and good times. You have to pay dues. It might be your life!"

Some, however, still hang on to the code of silence. One smuggler currently serving time says, "Sooner or later someone breaks down and you go. I ended up going to jail for something that occurred almost five years ago. I was arrested, not because of what I did, but because of what I knew. The government insisted that I tell them what I knew. Obviously, I didn't or I would be free. Well, I'm from the old school. I chose to be an outlaw and I lost. But at least I'm an 'honorable' outlaw."

In addition to having to worry about being cheated or killed by other dealers, smugglers also have to worry about being set up by undercover agents or even family members. A husband and wife discovered this at a time when they were in rather urgent need of selling some merchandise. "When my cousin told me he had a buyer," the man says, "we didn't even look too closely at many of the details of the deal. I talked to my cousin the day before, and he said that we had to go to Corpus to make the deal. It had been some time since we had gotten some real good money off the stuff, and I needed the money bad, so I didn't think twice about doing it. I should have been more careful. I totally forgot that my cousin had gotten busted just a few weeks before, and found it funny when he said that they had just let him go. My wife and I drove to Corpus, even taking our daughter Alicia with us. When we met there two hours later, we got busted. My cousin had helped set us up to get a lighter sentence for himself."

Sometimes, the danger is not so much what others can do to a dealer, but what dealing does to the individual. "I had barely begun dealing about a year ago," says one man. "My cousin had been caught and sent to prison. He told me to watch his house and take care of his wife and kids, so my wife and I moved in to his house. We were just getting started and we didn't have much money so his wife's brothers asked if I wanted to work for them. I agreed and really I wasn't doing anything except taking twenty or thirty pounds to Houston in my Blazer. I was making good money. Things were easy. Of course, crossing the checkpoint was my only worry, but once I passed it was an easy ride. But, as easy as it was to make money, it was even easier to spend it. I started dealing in bigger amounts and was making a lot of money. Then I got my own runners. They would take the stuff up to Houston for me. I didn't want to get my hands dirty anymore. By then I had bought a mobile phone, a beeper, and lots of real expensive clothes. I started having girlfriends and spending like crazy. I never saved any money, didn't invest in anything. I got to where I didn't care about my marriage anymore. I was having fun! But, I started feeling like everybody was watching me. I got real paranoid. It was too good to be true. I knew I had to go down. I just didn't think it would be this soon. I took off to Houston with seven other guys. I was going to bring back a little over $100,000. We kept waiting for the truck to get there. We must have used my mobile phone all night making calls to the Valley and all over. We ended up waiting a whole week. Finally we get news that the truck had unloaded and everything was OK. Then we got a call from Pete saying that all the pot had been stolen, probably by some kids. None of us believed him, but what could we do? We came back and I had no money and a $2,000 phone bill. I couldn't pay the bill so my phone was disconnected. I owed some money and couldn't pay so I had to give my truck as payment. Now I use my mother's car. I'm getting a divorce and just recently found a job. Don't laugh, but once I save some money after my divorce, I'm going to go to school to study to be a highway patrol officer. Is that funny or what?"

The Difficulty of Getting out of the Business

Because of the risks and dangers, many decide to get out of the business. Often, they find it's not so easy. "I wasn't born here in the United States," says one man. "I'm originally from Tampico, Mexico. I came here five years ago. First, I worked picking tomatoes and cucumbers but the pay was not enough and the foreman was terrible to work with. I have a family of five and did not want food stamps. I did not come to this country to be supported, like everybody thinks. I know a lot about mechanics but no one would give me a chance because I did not own my own tools or the money to start my own shop. One day, I met a friend in Reynosa and he asked me to cross a stuffed animal for him over to the states. I did not know what was in there. That same day he went to my house, picked up the stuffed animal and gave me $300. I had never seen so much money at one time. He continued to give me work and I continued to earn a lot of money; this was three years ago. I now have my own shop and send someone else to do that job [trafficking] for me. I want to stop but they won't let me since I am the only one with connections on this side of the border."

There are other factors that make it hard to quit. A smuggler in the Rio Grande City area mentions, "I was in college when my uncle asked me to help him out in a drug deal. The deal went sour and I ended up responsible for $80,000. I had no choice but to quit college and get into the business so I could make up the debt. After I made it up, I kept on dealing and made enough money so that I didn't have to deal anymore. I wanted to quit, but I had people trusting me. They depended on me. I was a leader. Now it's just a way of life. I have to stay with it. You see, when one runs an operation, there are a number of 'employees' that depend on you. Those that get caught depend on their 'boss' for attorney's fees. Or if it happens that they go to jail, the family needs money until he returns. So, you see, it is not easy to just abandon this way of life. I have been lucky to still be out of jail after so many years."

The experience for a wife whose husband is in prison can be very difficult. "Before my husband went to prison," says one woman, "my family and I never needed anything. He was bringing large amounts of money and never allowed me to work. Now he's in jail and we no longer have the money we used to. I am barely managing with the bills and I'm lucky to work for the school as an aide. If we had only saved money, or if he had gotten a decent job, maybe none of this would have ever happened."

Public Attitudes

To some, the life of individuals brought up around drug dealers may seem romantic. One young man in Rio Grande City, for example, said, "I think I will always favor the mafiosos because I was brought up with that type of an environment. Although sometimes I am afraid of some of them, I can't say I don't enjoy using their brand new Chevy trucks. And being with them certainly gives you a powerful image. Some people begin to look up to you. So, when I go places and people ask where I'm from I always say 'Starr County,' not only to feel respected, but you have no idea how much attention you get. I guess Starr County has been labeled as the 'Little Colombia' of Texas because of the drug smugglers. Once, for example, a store clerk accused me of stealing a bag of chips from the store. I got brave and told him, 'I don't need to steal because I'm from Starr County.' Sometimes, though, it has the opposite effect. Soon as some people find out where I'm from, right away they say, 'Hey, take out the weed!'"

In general, among the poor and working class, there is a fear and respect for mafiosos. They hold prestige and power, but they are still marginalized by the legitimate community, unless they invest in legitimate businesses. The respect they are given is based on the amount of wealth they have amassed by evading the law. That respect is mixed with fear and awe.

Many from Starr County, however, find that the mafioso image is exaggerated and unfair. "I'm a hard-working government employee from Roma," says one man. "I work hard to support my five children in school. I recently passed the checkpoint between Laredo and San Antonio. Eight cars in front of me went through without hardly slowing down. When I came up, they asked, 'Where are you from?' I replied, 'Starr County.' Forget it. Never again! They pulled me and my entire family out of the car to check out everything we had. They even checked my wife's and my little girls' purses. I felt so angry! I was definitely mistaken for a drug smuggler. But, hey, what can I do? I was born and brought up in Roma. I can't move out of there just because some people whose family came out of Mexico live crooked in my city."

Thus, the attitudes of lifelong residents of the Valley vary widely about the drug trafficking culture in the border. They see law enforcement waging a constant war against drug smugglers, with no signs that it will end soon. Though some local residents favor the use and selling of illegal drugs, they are in a distinct minority. This is reflected by responses to several items from our Perceptions of Deviance Survey. When asked about young adults using illegal drugs at a party, for example, the vast majority of respondents saw it as something bad (Fig. 6.1).

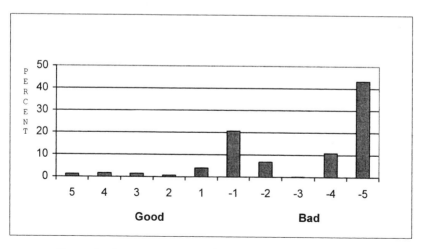

FIG. 6.1. Percent South Texas respondents selecting each level of how good or how bad it is for young adults to occasionally use illegal drugs at a party

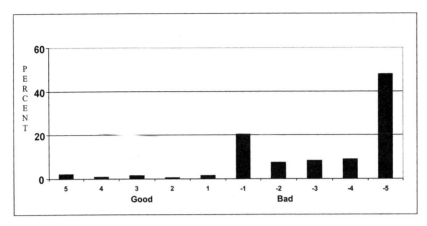

FIG. 6.2. Percent South Texas respondents selecting each level of how good or how bad it is for young adults to occasionally transport illegal drugs up north to support their family

Fully 91 percent of the respondents in our survey saw this form of behavior as something bad, with 45 percent labeling it as "very, very bad" (−5). We received similar responses to another item that asked how good or bad it was for juniors and seniors in high school to use marijuana. Ninety percent of our respondents said this was bad, with 45 percent again rating it as "very, very bad."

We used two additional items to assess how respondents felt about being involved in selling or transporting drugs. On both of these items, we intentionally introduced some of the justifications suggested by our in-depth interviews to see if more people would respond favorably. On the first of these two items, we asked how right or wrong it was for young adults in the Valley to occasionally transport drugs up north to support their family. The results for this item are presented in Figure 6.2.

As Figure 6.2 illustrates, again over 90 percent of respondents (93 percent) labeled this behavior as bad, with 48 percent labeling it as "very, very bad." On a similar question asking how right or wrong it was for young adults in the Valley to occasionally sell drugs to finance their education, 91 percent saw it as bad and 42 percent saw it as very, very bad.

When we examined the responses to these items by ethnicity, Anglos/Whites had lower disapproval averages than either Mexicans or Mexican Americans, though the results were not statistically significant. In addition, those who called themselves "Mexicans" had stronger disapproval averages than Mexican Americans, though again the results were not statistically significant.

The Image of Drug Smuggling in Popular Culture

People in the Valley are used to hearing outrageous stories about drug smuggling methods. There have been scandalous stories, in the press and across the back fence, about the methods they use—a couple with a dead baby filled with drugs, for example, or drugs hidden in a cage filled with rattlesnakes, cargo being transported by remote control airplanes, underground tunnels from Mexico to the U.S., and the numerous people that have died carrying drugs into the country. Sometimes, the stories of drug runners have even been documented in border *corridos*, or ballads, such as "La Banda del Carro Rojo" [The Red Car Gang]. Perhaps the first *narcocorrido* [drug ballad] was one called "El Contrabandista," which was recorded in San Antonio in 1934 by the duo Gaytán and Cantú. In the 1940s there was "La Carga Blanca" [The White Cargo], which became a popular border corrido.[42] Another famous corrido was that memorializing Mariano Reséndez, who smuggled textiles into Mexico.

Most such border corridos idealize smuggling, though some decry it. One interviewer compares lyrics from two border corridos—one that idolizes the get-rich-quick mentality and another that laments the long-term effects of drug smuggling on future generations. "La maldición de los jovenes son las drogas," it says. "Si el pueblo, se educaría, nuestra gente, no sufriría a manos de los poderosos." [The curse of the youth is drugs. If our people would get educated, they would not suffer at the hands of the powerful.]

The more romanticized view of drugs and smuggling can be traced to the old corridos that came out of the conquest of 1845–1848. When the border from the Nueces River to the Rio Grande was annexed by the United States in 1848, the law of the land was carried out by the Texas Rangers, who often abused the Mexican-origin inhabitants of the area. The racism and discrimination, which was often very harsh and overt, became documented in the oral history of the Rio Grande Valley, including corridos. One of the most famous *bandidos* [outlaws], for example, was Gregorio Cortez, who killed a law enforcement agent while defending himself and his brother. The official account and the written history of the time depict him as a bandido who evaded the law and killed innocent agents. In corridos and other forms of oral history of local Mexican Americans, however, such men are remembered as people who were abused at the hand of authorities.

The conflicted history of the region has shaped the way some people in South Texas view law enforcement and criminals in the Rio Grande

Valley. Those who remember the abuse tend to remember the so-called bandidos of that era as heroes, while the Texas Rangers who brutalized them are seen as villains. Those who remember and identify with the wrongly accused folk heroes of the past may see today's drug smugglers in a similar light. In corridos, a collective memory of hero worship remains. According to Américo Paredes, the border corrido has experienced considerable folklorization.[43] He cites the example of "The Ballad of José Mosqueda," a corrido about a train robber. Paredes notes that as the corrido evolved, criminals replaced political heroes as the protagonists in these songs.

Today, border corridos are no longer about famous battles. Rather, they speak of drug pushers who live and die. An element of this "Robin Hood mythology" is kept alive by a few individual drug smugglers who, according to several of our respondents, actually do help people in need. One respondent, for example, told about a man in his neighborhood, Manuel, who takes very good care of his immediate and extended family. He also makes efforts to occasionally help out other poor people that he knows. One neighbor, for example, had to go to the hospital for an operation. "When Manuel found out that her family had financial problems, he went to the hospital and paid all of her bills without telling anyone. The family found out later that he had paid the hospital bills. He never charged them a single penny."

Conclusion

In spite of major increases in law enforcement personnel along the border, the flow of drugs has only increased. This failure is reflected in statistics that show not only an ever-increasing volume, but a decline in drug prices as well. In 1987, for example, the DEA reported that a kilo of cocaine cost between $31,000 and $45,000. In 2003, the cost had fallen to somewhere between $14,000 and $24,000 per kilo, suggesting the drug has become even more easily available.

Several factors have been proposed to explain the increased flow of drugs through South Texas. Though the high rate of poverty along the Texas-Mexico border does draw some individuals into the trade, other factors are also very important. Primary among these is the government's emphasis on cutting supply, often at the expense of greater efforts to cut demand. The result of this policy seems to be greater lawlessness along the border, as well as increasing drug problems, not only in the interior of the United States, but in Mexico, as well.

The damage on the local population from the flow of drugs is everywhere present. One teacher at Rio Grande High School, for example, claims that she tries to get her students to earn better grades so they can go to a good college and earn a good education. "Everyday that I teach at the high school" she says, "I see students getting worse in their attitudes about school. Whenever I tell them to try harder, some will tell me, 'Why try harder? I'm just going to become a drug dealer like my dad.' Others tell me, 'I don't need to graduate because my parents are already rich, and they can support me!'"

Perhaps the most important question about the impact of the drug trade on South Texas is why more individuals, especially those in great poverty, are not drawn into it. Part of the answer, of course, is in the culture of the area, which places great importance on the family and on obedience to authority. South Texas parents teach their children to respect the law. In addition, as social control theory would suggest, most people in this area have a strong attachment to family and community. This attachment has been found to be very important in averting delinquency, even when economic circumstances might present a major temptation.

The culture of the area sometimes works in the opposite direction, however. The strong ties to family can work to the advantage of family drug operations. Indeed, the most successful smuggling operations in South Texas tend to be family operations. Trust, which is such an important part of running drugs, is often facilitated by family organizations where loyalty is high and involvement in the business follows family traditions.

This situation sometimes seems to throw certain sociological theories on their head. Social control theorists, for example, propose that strong ties associated with community, religion, and family help control criminal behavior. On the border, however, in some situations it can be the other way around. Although community, religion, and family may provide positive normative values, they can also support involvement in the drug trafficking underworld.[44]

7

Property Crime (Shoplifting and Auto Theft) along the Border

WITH JESSE GARCIA AND HECTOR GARCIA

> I really dislike the "river rats" that come over here from Mexico to steal from stores and houses. I've apprehended some of these guys ten to fifteen times only to have them sent back to Mexico because they are juveniles. I hate what they do. Most aliens that come here want to work and do not cause any problems, so I treat them with respect. Still, I have to do my job, so I send them back to Mexico.

The Border Patrol officer making this statement expresses the frustration of many law enforcement agents along the border. Juveniles on both sides of the border who become involved in criminal activities often use the border (and the different laws and legal systems on each side of it) to escape prosecution for their illegal activities. Law enforcement officers for the State of Texas refer Mexican juveniles to the Texas Youth Commission (T.Y.C.) only if they are accused of serious felony crimes or have confrontations with police that involve firearms. Since shoplifting and auto theft are property crimes, and since they often are charged as misdemeanors, almost no one wants to prosecute, especially if the perpetrators are juveniles.

As a result, most juvenile offenders from Mexico are simply turned over to the Border Patrol. The Border Patrol does not have facilities to house juveniles for any extended period. Neither do they have the authority to enforce state laws. And because the federal system along the border is so backlogged with drug and smuggling cases, juveniles arrested for property crimes or for misdemeanors are often simply taken to the border and told to return to Mexico. As a result, many juvenile offenders from Mexico simply "fall through the cracks."

This situation creates enormous gaps in law enforcement along the U.S.-Mexico border. One sixteen-year-old Mexican juvenile, whom we'll call Mario, was interviewed while serving the fourth month of a nine-month sentence for smuggling marijuana. Mario was born in the United States while his undocumented parents were working in the U.S. as farm-workers. He returned to Mexico with his parents when he was eight years old.

Though he was in the youth detention facility for his first drug-related offense, Mario proudly points to a well-defined tattoo of a marijuana leaf on his upper right arm. He was arrested, along with a female accomplice, by the Border Patrol after crossing the river in an attempt to deliver marijuana to a buyer. He had previously been arrested several times by the Border Patrol for crossing illegally. He also has a record with the local police for various shoplifting offenses. He says, "In Mexico, I was arrested for using drugs, shoplifting, and stealing cars. I often ended up in Mexican jails, but because I was a juvenile I was always kept isolated from other prisoners. They almost never kept me for more than twenty-four hours. Many times I went hungry in the Mexican jails because I had no family to bring me food."

Mario describes how he learned to manipulate the criminal justice system in the United States.

We lived for several years in Piedras Negras, Mexico. That's where I learned how to break into homes and to steal [shoplift] from Mexican stores. About the time I was fourteen years old, the police connected me to these crimes more than once. They got frustrated always picking me up. One day, one of them who knew that I was born in the United States asked me why I didn't change my methods. He suggested that I was crazy to be doing these crimes in Mexico because the legal system on the U.S. side would not prosecute me because I was a minor. They would think I was not a U.S. citizen and would just arrest me and return me to Mexico. At first, I didn't believe him, but I slipped across several times to shoplift at several stores. When they caught me, sure enough, they just kicked me back to Mexico. That's when I realized how easy it was and how right that Mexican police officer had been.

After that, I began to cross on a regular basis and I always returned to Mexico, whether I was caught or not. When they didn't catch me, I was able to sell in Mexico the items I stole in the U.S. Most of the time, I had customers who wanted to buy the items

I stole. It was easy. My customers in Mexico were usually people from the working class, and they would ask me to get such things as baby clothes or other clothing items. Sometimes, they would even give me a "shopping list" of what they wanted me to take.

If the American police did catch me, they would either send me back to Mexico or contact my aunt and grandmother who lived in the United States and just release me to their custody. Most of the time, though, I just told the police that I was a Mexican citizen. Then they would turn me over to the Border Patrol. They would hold me for processing for a few hours and then take me to the bridge, releasing me into the custody of the Mexican consulate at the bridge. They would call the Mexican police, who would then transport me to a house run by DIF [the Mexican child welfare office]. They would question me, but they were most interested in how the Border Patrol had treated me. After that, they would usually give me the choice of either staying there or going home. I would choose to go home.

By the time I was fifteen, I was pretty familiar with the riverbanks and knew the good spots to cross in either direction without being caught. I was able to cross anything that made money. Sometimes, it was undocumented aliens. By that time, I had a good reputation as a smuggler. My uncle told one of his friends about me. This man offered to have me smuggle drugs (mostly marijuana), but I still crossed whatever was profitable. My first job with drugs was ten kilos of marijuana, at $100 dollars per kilo. My uncle's friend explained how easy it was and that it was unlikely I would ever have to go to jail, even if I got caught, because I could say I was an undocumented immigrant and a minor. As my reputation grew, so did the loads and my profits. By the time I got caught, I was crossing about eighty kilos a trip [about 150 pounds] at least once, sometimes twice, a week. Each time, someone would drop me off at the river. After I crossed, someone else would pick me up and drive me to a stash house on the Texas side.

This time, I got caught on the way to the stash house. They sent me here to Evins [the T.Y.C. facility in Edinburg]. When I get out, I hope to go into construction with my uncle who lives here or to find some other vocation besides being an international smuggler and a thief. I don't think I will ever smuggle again.[1]

In 1998, the Texas Juvenile Probation Commission stated, "The challenge of what to do with juveniles who cross the border and break the law was great and had been around as long as anyone could remember ... the problem was endemic to border states and the situation was one to be endured ... Many attempts at remedying the problem were tried, but children kept breaking laws."[2]

As a result of this frustration, Texas initiated the Border Children Justice Project. This project was designed to return juvenile offenders from both sides of the border to the appropriate agency on the opposite side after processing them through their respective juvenile justice systems. Though the program was quite successful, most Texas border counties (including Hidalgo County in South Texas) were either not included or have since opted out. When the project was still functioning, Hidalgo County would turn some Mexican juveniles over to Cameron County to be adjudicated through the Border Children Justice Project. Many others, however, were simply returned to Mexico without being placed in the system.[3]

The absence of a system to adjudicate juveniles creates enormous problems. Some criminal elements, for example, have discovered that they can bring Mexican juveniles over to Valley cities to engage in shoplifting or auto theft. If the youths are apprehended, they simply abandon the stolen merchandise and are returned to Mexico, often without even being turned over to Mexican officials. Such treatment not only invites Mexican juveniles to break the law with virtual impunity but also invites criminals to exploit these youths by pressuring them to commit crimes.[4]

Property crimes along the border, particularly shoplifting and auto theft, present many challenges to local law enforcement agencies. In addition, these crimes are at the heart of many important questions, including the following:

—Do property thieves living along the border engage in shoplifting activities because of economic hardships, because of lax enforcement, or because of the ease with which they can escape prosecution in a border environment?

—Does the lack of cooperation by police agencies on both sides of the border contribute to the problems of shoplifting and auto theft, especially among juveniles?

—Does the failure to control other cross-border crimes, especially drug smuggling, contribute significantly to the high incidence of auto theft?

—Is cross-border auto theft limited to thefts in the United States, or are Mexicans also victimized?

Methodology

The research reported in this chapter comes from several distinct research projects. Most of the research on shoplifting was conducted by Hector Garcia for his master's degree in sociology at the University of Texas–Pan American.[5] Similarly, much of the research on auto theft reported herein was conducted by Jesse Garcia for his master's degree.[6] Though Jesse collected data for this project from a variety of sources, the majority of it was collected using in-depth interviews and observations on the border of South Texas and northeastern Mexico. Interviews were conducted with law enforcement officers on both sides of the border, community intervention specialists in the United States, and automobile thieves who were willing to share their experiences and observations. In addition, many UT-PA students who had participated in the Borderlife Project contributed interviews they had conducted with street-level and professional thieves.

Additional research on cross-border auto theft has been conducted by Rosalva Resendiz, the coauthor of this volume, who focused on exploring the organization of international professional auto theft on the Brownsville, Texas–Matamoros, Tamaulipas border.[7] Secondary sources of data were also consulted in public archives, including U.S. and Mexican periodicals. These data provide information on the international market for stolen cars on both sides of the border.

Finally, in 2004 Jesse Garcia and Chad Richardson conducted interviews with approximately twenty Mexican national juveniles in detention at a Texas Youth Commission facility in Hidalgo County to determine how these young people became involved in border crime and how they had been dealt with by law enforcement agencies on both sides of the border. The account of "Mario," given above, was obtained from this source.

Cross-Border Shoplifting

Yolanda, a middle-aged Hispanic female, was arrested for participating in a shoplifting ring. She says, "I know many people who shoplift for a living. The woman who got me and other women started was a Mexican national. She had a customer from Vera Cruz, Mexico, who hired her to steal clothes. She would organize us in groups to steal merchandise from different stores. Then she would cross it over to Mexico from Brownsville. She offered cash to people who would help her. Before we were arrested, she had already been shoplifting in the same store for five days in a row. She didn't seem to care. Everyone knew that she was stealing. Even some of the workers in that store were her clients."

Though shoplifting occurs with great frequency throughout the United States, its character in the border region is in many ways unique. It is estimated that the total retail loss to shoplifting in the U.S. is over $33 billion annually.[8] In Texas, of the 13 million committed thefts of property in the year 2002, 4.25 million property thefts were less than $50. Four and one-half million between $50 and $249 were reported, and 3.3 million were thefts of $200 or more.[9]

Hidalgo County has the largest population (590,285) of the four counties in South Texas. The principal city in Hidalgo County is McAllen, where there were 1,370 arrests for theft in 2002. Of this total, 285 (21 percent) were of people classified as Mexican nationals, while 1,006 were of people classified as Hispanic.[10]

There have been few studies of shoplifting along the U.S.-Mexico border.[11] Some researchers have focused on the costs of shoplifting in this region relative to other areas of the United States. Others, like Rushing, seek to determine the causes of shoplifting. Few researchers, however, seriously consider how the U.S.-Mexico border facilitates shoplifting.

In border communities and elsewhere, there are many hidden costs of shoplifting. One is the higher price that consumers have to pay for their goods. In order to recoup losses, retailers increase the sales price of their merchandise. A second cost is the added burdens that are placed on local law enforcement agencies and the courts, especially since most apprehensions do not result in actual convictions or punishments. Finally, shoplifting adds to the development of secondary or alternative markets, which impacts the profits of retailers when their merchandise is sold at a lower cost to prearranged clients or sold in local flea markets.

Mexican Shoplifters

> Most Mexican nationals stopped for shoplifting are customers with passports. They rarely get arrested. The ones that we do arrest more often are the Mexican illegals caught trying to steal. The illegals don't give us a hard time, but they do tend to run from us much more often than Americans. Documented Mexican nationals often have money or come from families with lots of money. Thus, I guess we don't perceive them as likely to shoplift in our store.

This respondent, a loss prevention officer at a large McAllen store, continues: "We have about a 20 percent rate of arrest when it comes to Mexican nationals. Before the devaluation of the Mexican peso in 1994, however, the arrest rate was something like 60 to 70 percent who were Mexican nationals. Now it has dropped." This officer speculates that the drop was caused by the poorer exchange rate for Mexicans, making it too expensive for many documented Mexican nationals to shop in the United States.

When asked if loss prevention officers treated documented Mexican nationals differently, the manager of one large store responded: "When we do catch them, we treat them the same as other shoplifters. Sometimes we'll arrest a Mexican national and they'll insist on buying the stolen merchandise. Some will get very angry if we don't let them pay for what they just stole. We tell them 'no' and that we arrest anybody that steals from our store. One time about ten years ago I was offered $199 by a Mexican national so I wouldn't arrest him. I just refused."

Many documented Mexican nationals who are detained or arrested for shoplifting ask to pay for the merchandise that was recovered. One loss prevention officer states, "Man, these documented Mexican nationals always insist on paying for stuff they steal. I know they have money, because they flash a stack of $100 bills and beg us to not send them to jail."

In some cases, those arrested are allowed to go free. Others are not. One security officer reported, "Most of time they tell me, 'Quiero pagar' [I want to pay]. I tell them that it does not work this way in the U.S. and then I take them in."

One police officer recalled an occasion when he arrived at a store and a documented Mexican national was being held for stealing a pocketknife. "This guy stole a cheap pocket knife and some other stuff valued at $60," he says. "He wanted to pay for it and pulled $500 from his pocket. I thought to myself, 'They have money . . . they're loaded . . . why do they steal?'"

Stories like this from many police officers and loss prevention officers indicate that some documented Mexican nationals detained for shoplifting have the resources to pay for merchandise. Because they believe they will be allowed to purchase the stolen item if caught in the act, they seem to shoplift as a calculated act. This may suggest that some shoplift not out of economic necessity, but for other reasons.

Many officers (store and police) were asked if they had ever been pressured to accept a bribe after arresting documented Mexican nationals. It is a common practice in Mexico and it is generally understood that, when one is stopped by the police, anything can be taken care of—for a price. The term *mordida* [bite, or bribe] is often used when a person has to pay a bribe in order to get out of legal difficulties there. One police officer reported, "It happens in about 3 percent of arrests when dealing with Mexican nationals. They usually ask me, '¿Cuánto me va a costar para arreglar el problema?' [How much is it going to cost me to correct this problem?]. I tell them, 'No se puede arreglar de esta manera' [It can't be fixed that way], and then I take them to the station, where they continue to ask to pay for the merchandise."

It was generally recognized by the officers interviewed that documented Mexican shoppers usually get more favorable treatment than those who are undocumented. One prosecutor, for example, states, "I remember when I was prosecuting misdemeanors. The cases that I enjoyed were those people from Mexico with money. I would read the offense report and would see that they had concealed over $200 worth of merchandise in their purse or bag. The report would also state that other merchandise worth over $1,000 had been recovered, but had been returned to the Mexican national because he or she had paid for it. We loved these cases because they were willing to pay a high fine and still pay for the merchandise that they had intended to steal. We collect $1,500 in cash for the fine and court costs. It's great because we get their money and they go back to Mexico."

Another prosecutor says, "The documented Mexican nationals show up in court with their lawyers. We usually gave them deferred adjudication and a fine. They were also ordered to report by mail. The deferment is given because a conviction would risk having their visas revoked or it could hurt them in the future if they applied to INS [Immigration and Naturalization Service] for a visa."

In most cases, wealthy documented Mexican nationals are offered plea bargains that include lighter sentences compared to U.S. residents and poor undocumented Mexican nationals. In Hidalgo County courtrooms, they are more likely to receive a deferred adjudication. That means the presiding judge does not hold a judgment against them. In other words, they are not found guilty of the shoplifting offense and will later have the charges against them dismissed if they complete a probation period without any violations. When these types of probation are granted, the documented Mexican national is often allowed to return to Mexico and to report by mail throughout their probation period. No direct supervision is ordered since they reside in Mexico. Some of these supervision periods are thirty to ninety days long. In addition, their visa status will not be affected due to the arrest since they have not been convicted.

Law enforcement treatment also varies when the arrested suspect is an undocumented Mexican national juvenile (under seventeen years of age). One police officer stated that he sometimes arrested some undocumented Mexican juveniles several times in only a day or two. Remembering one incident, he states: "We were called to this store and it turns out this illegal was a juvey [juvenile]. We took the report and then drove him down to get booked at the PD [police department]. Later on that day, he was released to BP [Border Patrol] and we thought that was the end of it. Two days later, I responded to another shoplifting call at the same mall, and guess who it was—the same juvey that I arrested the day before. Get this: I started to take his information down, then he gave us a different D.O.B. [date of birth] that showed him to be an adult. We processed him like any other shoplifter and then added another charge of tampering with a government document, since he signed the day before as being sixteen years old. This time he didn't just go to the border."

When an undocumented Mexican national juvenile is arrested for a theft offense of less than $50, police officers have the option of taking the juvenile to the border or calling Border Patrol to pick the juvenile up from the store where the arrest took place. If undocumented Mexican juveniles are being charged with stealing an amount greater than $50, they are usually taken to the police department and booked before being released to the Border Patrol.

Another trend that was revealed during the interviews was how some people used children to conceal merchandise or used them to shoplift. Several interviewees reported that they had seen people using children for shoplifting. One participant (a security camera operator) stated: "It's kinda sad when you see people using children to steal for them. I have seen many times where people have been sacking merchandise in bags and then giving the bags to children so they can walk outside without them being arrested themselves. We still file charges against them."

Types of Border Shoplifters

There are two basic types of shoplifters. The most common type is the amateur shoplifter. Amateur shoplifters routinely steal from retailers for their personal needs. Most are not highly skilled. They tend to be opportunistic when they steal, not setting out to make a living from it. Amateur shoplifters are estimated to account for nearly 85 percent of the total shopping losses, though it's difficult to determine whether these statistics are distorted because of the greater ease of apprehending amateur shoplifters.[12]

The second type of shoplifter is the "professional." Professionals steal for a living and use more sophisticated methods to steal merchandise. They are highly skilled in evading detection and in manipulating law enforcement systems. They tend to work in groups. One such shoplifter, a young Hispanic female, was interviewed shortly after pleading guilty to theft, having attempting to shoplift merchandise valued at over $1,200. She stated that shoplifting was her only alternative to poverty for her family. She says, "I just started shoplifting with this particular group of girls over the past three months. I knew that they stole for money, so I asked them if I could work with them. We would hit all the major brand stores like Guess, The Gap, and Abercrombie. Then we would divide all the clothes we'd taken. We'd do this about three times a week at different malls. We would steal about $3,600 in clothes every time we shopped, so I got about $1,200 in merchandise."

This young woman also reported that $400 to $600 in cash could be made from one organized shoplifting spree. It was estimated that her average share of the shoplifting crimes was about $1,200 to $1,800 a week.

Fencing the Merchandise

Along the border, organized shoplifting rings establish ready secondary markets for their stolen goods because many people from both sides of the border find it cost-effective to purchase stolen merchandise. These markets allow individuals to buy stolen name brand items at discounted prices with no sales tax. Stolen merchandise is easily accessible through personal contacts or local flea markets. These secondary markets attract large numbers of Mexican nationals because they are able to purchase stolen merchandise at drastically reduced prices. Many even hire professionals to shoplift for them. The stolen merchandise is then smuggled into Mexico, often to be resold at Mexican shops.

One participant claimed that she would resell most of the stolen merchandise to friends or clients at a discount of 50 percent of the tagged value of the item. Remaining items would be kept or would be bartered out for other goods, such as jewelry or other stolen merchandise.

Another respondent states, "You can find stolen clothes anywhere if you really want to. There are many people that sell stolen shoes, tops, watches— anything you want. Everyone knows it's stolen, but they still buy it."

This does not, however, indicate that Valley residents believe that shoplifting is OK. Indeed, when we asked respondents in the Perceptions of Deviance Survey to indicate how good or bad it was for young adults in the Valley to occasionally take items from a store without paying for them, 48 percent ranked it in the "very, very bad" category (-5). Only twenty-nine individuals (6.8 percent) ranked it as "acceptable" or "good" behavior. Figure 7.1 shows how responses to this item varied according to the demographic category of our respondents.

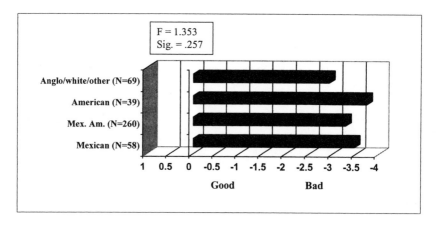

FIG. 7.1. Mean scores (from $+5$ to -5) of South Texas respondents in self-described racial/ethnic/national categories selecting each level of how good or how bad it is for Valley young adults to occasionally take items from a store without paying

As this figure illustrates, there were slight differences among the groups on this item (those calling themselves Americans[13] and Mexicans regarding it most negatively), though the differences were too minor to be considered statistically significant. These results do not support the idea that there is a culture of acceptance of shoplifting behavior among the Mexican-origin people of South Texas.

How Border Stores Deal with Shoplifting

Many of today's retail shoplifting policies are influenced largely by the cost of following an arrest through prosecution. Store personnel have also become extremely cautious about the civil liability consequences of detaining but not fully prosecuting a shoplifter. The rationale behind the policy at some retail stores in Hidalgo County is that simply stopping a thief, recovering merchandise, and questioning shoplifting suspects will deter shoplifters. Other retailers choose to take harsher steps, actively trying to apprehend shoplifters on the grounds of mere suspicion. This can, of course, become very expensive and embarrassing for the retailer. A South Texas jury, for example, found one of the largest retailers, Wal-Mart, guilty of wrongfully accusing a woman of being part of a shoplifting ring. The woman was arrested and then released thirty days later after her shoplifting case was dismissed by the local court. The South Texas jury ordered that Wal-Mart pay $13 million to the woman as compensation for her false arrest. As a result of such outcomes, some stores do not actively prosecute shoplifters.

Auto Theft

As I was driving in my patrol unit in Mission one day at 3:00 p.m., I observed a young male driving a new Suburban. I became suspicious when I saw that it was a brand new van with the windows rolled down on a hot, humid day. As I began to follow him, he drove faster. I figured he must be running from me because he didn't have a license. After a brief chase, he turned onto a dirt road and crashed into a light pole. He got out of the car and began to run. I caught him and cuffed him. When I looked over the Suburban, I saw that the window and steering column had been broken. I opened the van and found a Mexican license plate hidden under the seat. We ran the Texas plates through the computer and found that the van had been stolen. When we contacted the owners, they hadn't even noticed that their van had been stolen. The kid admitted that he had stolen the vehicle and was in the process of taking the car to Mexico. They were going to attach the Mexican plates and sell it in Mexico.

The case described by this police officer is not an unusual occurrence in communities along the South Texas border. Indeed, much of what he describes fits a general pattern. Professional car thieves often hire young men or women to steal vehicles. Often, they give the thief a "shopping list" of vehicles most desired in Mexico. Generally, these are U.S. cars that were manufactured or assembled in Mexico. Such vehicles can be easily sold in Mexico, allowing the thieves to avoid cars that are clearly imports. Other stolen cars are turned over to Mexican auto theft rings, which convert them into cars that are indistinguishable from Mexican-made vehicles. This process often involves exterior and interior changes, such as repainting the vehicle and grinding away engine and transmission vehicle identification numbers.[14]

According to Miller, cross-border auto theft is in some ways similar to and in other ways quite different from auto theft elsewhere in the United States.[15] As in other regions, vehicles that are taken to Mexico are stolen from streets and parking lots during business hours, when there is a high availability of targets. Furthermore, the vehicles targeted are selected from a shopping-list order. However, the delivery of the vehicle across the international boundary requires alternative methods. Once the vehicle is stolen, it is driven to Mexico via one of the international bridges. If problems are encountered with the Mexican authorities, mordidas of police and custom officers can facilitate the safe entry of the vehicle into Mexico.[16] In the following story, a Valley police officer illustrates how Mexican officials sometimes aid the auto thief to escape arrest.

One evening on patrol I got a call from dispatch of two men entering a vehicle at a local mall. While I was en route to the scene, the men managed to get the vehicle started and were heading south on the expressway. I chased the car to the gateway bridge and the vehicle ran the toll booths. The suspects stopped at just past the halfway point, which is now in Mexican jurisdiction, and got out of the vehicle and yelled, "F—you, gringo bastard," and drove on. It was obvious that I was in code-three pursuit, with lights and siren on. Well, the Mexican police just waved the suspects on through and were even joking as they passed. With police relations like that, how can you have any effect on auto theft?

Our policy disallows us to pursue a vehicle onto the bridge. As a matter of fact, one rookie was chasing a stolen car a few years ago and realized after it was too late that he was in Mexican territory. He was arrested in Mexico for possession of a gun, and the officials confiscated the vehicle and the officer's weapon and radio. Well, it took quite a bit of effort in negotiation in releasing the officer. The patrol unit was eventually returned six months later stripped of equipment.

Not all Mexican police, of course, are "on the take." Indeed, it is the lack of predictability of Mexican police that bothers many U.S. officers. In 1995, for example, two offenders, one seventeen and the other nineteen years of age, stole a new Isuzu cargo van. The officer involved in the chase describes the incident and its conclusion. "I chased the two suspects all the way to the Hidalgo Bridge," he says, "along with units from the Texas Highway Patrol and Hidalgo Police Department. We attempted to stop the stolen vehicle, but were unsuccessful. I had my dispatcher notify customs inspectors at the Hidalgo Bridge, who blocked off all southbound lanes. The two suspects then proceeded to break through the steel gates and made good their escape into Mexico. Customs inspectors at the bridge had managed to contact Mexican officers in Policía Federal de Caminos y Puentes [federal highway and bridge patrol]. When the stolen vehicle attempted entry into Mexico, five Mexican police officers were already waiting for them. The officers then started shooting at the vehicle with devastating results. One boy was killed, and the other was seriously injured. The truck was returned to the United States with a total of fifty-eight holes."

Indeed, some Mexican police officers feel frustrated that more is not done by police in the United States to stop stolen cars before they cross into Mexico. One Mexican officer, for example, expressed amazement that auto thieves manage to escape U.S. authorities for days. "Cars are stolen from all over the U.S.," he says, "even from New York. They drive all the way to Mexico, often traveling for two or three days in a stolen vehicle without being detected by the American police. Most of the time two guys do the job. If they do not commit any traffic violations, the police never stop them. They know this, so they are careful not to break any laws. Once in Mexico, they put Mexican plates on the stolen car. Often these plates are stolen from a Mexican. If we catch them using the wrong plates, they get a ticket, but it's only for 230 pesos [approx. US$23]. Traffic police hardly ever run a check with us [Policía Judicial del Estado, or state police] to see if the car is stolen because it takes too long to check with the American authorities. The only times we find out that the car is stolen is when it's involved in an accident. That's because the owner has to show proof of ownership in such cases. Most often, when someone driving a stolen car has a wreck, they simply abandon the car before they get arrested. It is a federal offense in Mexico to drive a stolen car."

Research on Border Auto Theft

Border auto theft has not been a widely studied subject.[17] The first research to call attention to auto theft as international organized crime was Miller's exploratory research.[18] Miller contended that the organization of auto theft varied from the Matamoros-Brownsville border to the Reynosa-McAllen border. Field, Clarke, and Harris found that the vehicles targeted in the border states were manufactured in both Mexico and the United States. The documented use of shopping lists provided concrete evidence for the existence of sophisticated organizations.[19] This finding was further supported by Resendiz,[20] who, like Miller,[21] also found that the level of sophistication varied, and that degree of organization was not uniform along the border. The present research also provides evidence of the diversity in the organization of auto theft.

The border itself, of course, is a major factor facilitating auto theft. Frequently, for example, it provides the gateway to a potential haven for criminals from either side. In addition, when border ports of entry and exit are understaffed, vehicle traffic cannot be adequately inspected on a consistent basis. At most crossing points, the sheer volume of vehicle traffic makes close inspection of all vehicles difficult, impractical, and even dangerous. Further, the border also provides an accessible market for selling stolen vehicles. Mexico's economic and population growth has created a ready market for used U.S. cars. According to Mexican informants, stolen U.S. cars are considerably cheaper than those legally available. Along the border in Mexico, stolen vehicles can be driven with U.S. plates. To go further into Mexico, the owners must acquire false papers of import or ownership. Sometimes this is accomplished by bribing underpaid Mexican civil servants. Attempts by the Mexican government to curtail such activities often result in mass demonstrations by affected citizens, who consider the price of legalizing their vehicles to be too high. As a result, Mexico tolerates such practices in spite of the loss of revenue to both the state and the auto-producing corporations.[22]

The Division of Labor in Border Auto Theft

Though auto theft along the border may involve individuals acting alone, it is often part of a larger enterprise. Auto thieves, like shoplifters, can be classified as professionals or amateurs. In general, much auto theft literature has characterized the amateur as a thrill-seeker or joyrider, but this type of classification is problematic because it limits economic motivation to professionals.[23] In previous research, as well as in the present data, we find that auto thieves along the border range in sophistication, their motivations are varied, and their status as professionals has more to do with their association with or role in an organization, however fleeting.[24] Despite the limitations of the usefulness of the categories, for the purpose of this research, the label "amateur" will be used to refer to the short-term unspecialized auto thief, and the label "professional" will be used to refer to those with specialized skills who are affiliated with an auto theft organization and who are involved in auto theft as a long-term career.

Amateurs

By our definition, amateurs lack experience; they may just be starting a criminal career. Often, the amateur auto thief may have fallen on hard times and is looking for a quick way to come up with some money. One South Texas police officer, for example, described a case where he observed a young man in his twenties driving a Cougar. When he looked more closely, he could see that the car did not have the required registration sticker. "I pulled the car over," he says, "and discovered that it was a stolen vehicle. When I made the arrest, I asked the driver to explain why he stole the car. He timidly confessed that he had been hired by a Mexican car dealer to steal cars and take them to his lot in Mexico. He told me it was the only way he could earn a living in Mexico."

As this case illustrates, amateurs are mainly single young men who are unattached to a highly organized criminal outfit. Many, however, have contacts with organized auto theft rings, which are willing to buy the stolen property from them. Amateurs tend to be opportunistic thieves; they drive around looking for cars that are not secured or in which keys have been left behind. These vehicles become targets because they do not require specialized skills. Such opportunistic theft results in a range of merchandise, such as radios, radar detectors, and other electronic gadgets.

Some amateurs are affiliated with gangs that use auto theft as a source of money. Their loyalties are to their gang, not to an auto theft organization. Often, these individuals are looking for a way to support a drug habit, and the use of drugs makes them dangerous and unpredictable. The irony is that chop shop owners dislike them for the above-mentioned reasons but occasionally must associate with them because they are an integral part of the business. Shop owners know that if caught, "gang" thieves are more likely than professionals to turn everyone in to the police in order to save themselves from prison.

Professionals

According to our contacts, the difference between amateur and professional thieves has a lot to do with their reasons for getting involved in auto theft. Although the primary motivation for professionals and amateurs is economic, the level of involvement is very different. For amateur thieves, auto theft is generally a short-term endeavor. One professional chop shop manager said that amateur thieves were mostly interested in securing funds for "partying." Professional thieves, in contrast, were invested in auto theft as a long-term career. Prosperous professionals invested in better lives for themselves and their families. When a shop manager sees a street thief with a "stable" head and no involvement with drugs, he becomes a candidate for recruitment into the organization. And full-time members of the organization get a larger share of the "take." The shop manager preferred these individuals because their judgment would be less likely to be clouded. In addition, they would be more dependable because their commitment to the organization would be stronger. They are preferred because they are less likely to divulge any information about the operation if caught and interrogated by the police.

One professional ringleader, for example, said, "We have been lucky that our crew has not turned to drugs as other groups have done. Not dealing with drugs is one of the rules that we really enforce here. In this shop we have all sorts of power tools, not to mention the welding equipment and gadgets that can really cause some damage when not used properly. If a dude comes in here wasted or high it can really slow down our operation if he gets hurt or hurts someone else. We care for each other and our families. Those *batos* [guys] who get involved in drugs really mess up their quotas. Instead of using their money to improve their lives, they use it to buy more drugs, which does no good for anyone."

Professional car thieves are very well organized. The organization is made up of two levels of "business": the branch, where the vehicle is brought initially after being stolen, and the central warehouse. In the branch there are usually ten to fifteen people. Their main task is to alter vehicle identification numbers, if the car is going to be sold on the black market, and to evaluate the car. Clients usually put in an order for a particular vehicle model. If the car is located and stolen, it is kept at the branch for about two weeks. Then it is transferred to the central warehouse. If demand for a particular car is low, it is stripped of its electronics and sold as scrap metal or for parts.

If the demand is high, the car is put through a chop shop operation in the central warehouse, where forty to fifty people work in an assembly-line manner. Their job is to alter the appearance of the vehicle, which is usually done by painting it and preparing the car to showroom standards in order to get the best price possible for it. Sometimes the client orders the vehicle to be painted a specific color or accessorized with custom parts. The majority of preordered cars are sold to Mexican businessmen.

Chop Shops

Chop shops,[25] where stolen vehicles are altered and even completely disassembled, are crucial to the goal of avoiding detection and prosecution. Located on both sides of the border, these operations generally require several individuals, often with different specialists performing particular operations. In most instances, persons wanting a specific vehicle or part contact the chop shop operator to place their order. Most vehicles are altered and sold into the interior of Mexico at cheaper than normal costs.

Or, the vehicle may be stripped for parts, which are often sold to buyers in the United States. U.S. clients consist of auto body shops, junkyards, and auto parts retailers who buy at a cheap price and resell at regular cost. Many times a customer will ask for a specific engine or chrome rims and other customizing accessories. For example, the regular cost of replacement air bags ranges from $800 to $1,200, whereas in the black market, the cost is about $200. A retailer who buys from the black market can thus buy an air bag for $200 and sell it for $800 or more. This pricing structure applies to all parts of a vehicle.

The Drug Trafficking Connection

Auto theft is also closely linked to drug trafficking. Stolen vehicles are frequently used to transport drugs since they cannot be traced to the drug traffickers. Sometimes this strategy backfires, though. In one case, an officer was tipped off by the suspicious behavior of a driver at a port-of-entry inspection station. As the man approached for inspection, the officer noticed that the car was a fairly new car compared to the clothing of the driver, who also wore a cap and avoided looking directly at the officer. "He wouldn't look at me, for he had his passport in front of his face."

Suspicious, the officer looked into the car. The first thing that caught his attention was that the driver only had the ignition and trunk keys on his key ring. "I immediately asked him to step out and open the trunk of the car," he says. "When he did so, I could see him getting nervous. All of a sudden, he threw down the keys and ran back across the bridge towards Mexico. I chased him for a few steps . . . what I am allowed. When I got back, I took a sniff and sure enough—not only had the car been stolen, but he was smuggling 350 pounds of cocaine."

Efforts to Prevent the Crossing of Stolen Vehicles

With the thousands of stolen vehicles taken across the border every year, many people have called for stepped-up inspection of vehicles crossing into Mexico. At most bridges in South Texas, however, the only stop most drivers experience is to pay a toll to use the bridge. When officers are assigned to spot stolen vehicles, either at the lanes leading to the bridges or in other parts of the Valley, they tend to look for a number of clues to help them spot potential thieves.

One law enforcement officer noted that most of the individuals arrested were between the ages of eighteen and twenty-five and most were males. "But there are many exceptions," he said. "We have arrested men in their forties and fifties. We've also arrested quite a few females. Mostly, though, the females have been caught with a male companion. The female juveniles that we've arrested tend to be part of a larger crew."

Because it's hard to find a good profile for drivers, however, many officers tend to look for other clues. Some officers, for example, said that the number of keys on a key chain can help you determine whether a car has been stolen. Many officers also look at the way the people are dressed. A poorly dressed person driving an expensive car is often seen as a sign that the car might be stolen.

"We can also tell by looking at a car that has family members," says one agent. "Sometimes they will just throw a bunch of kids in the car to make it seem like a normal family. What we do is that we start asking the kids' ages. When we ask them for their passports, if they don't match, then we will immediately pull the car over for inspection, and we find out if they have stolen the car [or] if they are smuggling drugs."

Another officer indicated that they are taught to look for behavioral clues as well. "We read body language," he says. "We look at what people are trying not to say, and how nervous they are, by how they are behaving. You can tell a lot from what people are trying *not* to show."

However, efforts to put officers in the lanes leading to the bridges to Mexico to detect stolen cars have met with mixed results. One McAllen police officer, for example, relates the following. "McAllen used to have a program called the leper operation," he says. "They had officers at the McAllen-Hidalgo [international] bridge. But then they did away with the program because it was very expensive to have an officer there twenty-four hours a day, or even during the day shift. It's just not in the budget, though. As it is, our agency is low in manpower right now. And for us to have an officer over there all the time is very hard."

Police officers all around South Texas recognize the magnitude of the auto theft problem. Many are always on the lookout for stolen cars, whether they are heading for Mexico or not. Some police officers believe they can spot auto thieves. "All we have to do is to observe the car and to observe the person driving it," says one officer. "We have to be checking for expensive cars driven by people that do not fit with that type of car. If I see a Hispanic or a Mexican guy driving a nice car with American plates, I stop him for revision. Not that I am prejudiced, but that is the way things work. When the insurance companies have losses, we end up paying for it. My job is to prevent these losses to the American people. I get paid to be like this."

Buyers of Stolen Automobiles

The concentration on stopping stolen cars from entering Mexico ignores the reality that cars are also stolen in Mexico and transported to the United States. "I remember several years ago while employed by the U.S. Customs in Brownsville," says one former agent. "We were conducting a special operation to identify stolen cars coming from Mexico and going to the Valley. We were seizing about ten stolen cars a day. The project did have positive results because the transferring of stolen automobiles was reduced. However, this is now only done once or twice a month because of limited funding from the government."

It is difficult to find much information on Mexican cars transported into the U.S. Most of what we found was anecdotal. One Mexican student attending a local university, for example, explained an incident that happened in 1995. "In April, I was buying a car and one of my friends referred me to a guy selling an '89 Nissan," he says. "I liked the car because it was Mexican. Since I'm an international student, I can legally drive a Mexican car while living in the U.S. When I asked the price, he told me it was $500 cash. I was confused because that price was too cheap for that car. Then he told me it was *caliente* [hot]. He told me that by avoiding traffic violations, nobody would find out it was stolen. I did not know what to say. I couldn't believe I was being offered a stolen car. I told him I needed a legal car because I travel very often to Monterrey and Missouri."

Occasionally, police agencies come across stolen car operations that extend beyond the U.S.-Mexico border area. Cars stolen in the U.S. or Mexico, for example, may be destined for shipment outside of either country. Sometimes, law enforcement agents come across car theft rings that transport expensive cars to places as far away as China or other parts of Asia. More common, however, are rings that steal cars in the U.S. and transship them over Mexico to Central America.

Relations between Police in Texas and Mexico

In 1937, a treaty for the return of stolen vehicles was ratified by the United States and Mexico. Difficulties continued, however, and the rate of returned stolen vehicles did not improve. A new convention was signed in 1981 aimed at eliminating the substantial documentation needed for the return of stolen vehicles, but difficulties still persisted.

Officers in the United States have had mixed results when dealing with the authorities in Mexico. Cooperation with the Mexican government has been inconsistent. There are officers that work as liaisons with the Mexican government. One of these agents works for the National Automobile Theft Bureau and provides expert assistance to federal, state, and local police agencies regarding vehicle theft, arson, and fraud. This officer also works extensively with Mexican officials in facilitating the return of stolen vehicles recovered by Mexican authorities.

According to U.S. agents, it has been difficult to recover stolen vehicles from Mexico due to practices by the Mexican authorities. When they confiscate stolen vehicles, they sometimes appropriate them for their official or personal use. Mexican agents driving stolen cars have been arrested by U.S. officers. One U.S. Customs agent, for example, related, "I remember this one time when I was working at the substation trying to locate and identify any stolen cars being driven through my lane. This one car fit the profile of a stolen car so I asked the driver to pull over underneath the canopy. The canopy is where we perform our inspection of any vehicle that appears stolen or fits the high profile of a stolen vehicle. This car in particular was a Ford T-Bird and was in very good condition. When I was able to confirm that the car was stolen, I placed the driver under arrest for possession of stolen property. What really surprised me was that the driver turned out to be a Mexican federal officer."

Another officer describes the personal effects of this situation. He was involved in the confiscation of stolen vehicles and arrested two officers from the Mexican state police. Then he heard that the Mexican officials had placed a "hit" on him. Although it was just a rumor, he is still cautious. "Nothing ever happened," he says, "but you'll never catch me going to Reynosa."

Many Mexican law enforcement officers, however, believe that Americans simply do not understand the situation in Mexico. "When crossing to Mexico," says one, "Mexican officials check the cars at random using a computerized system that chooses 1 out of 10 cars to be closely inspected for weapons and excessive merchandise being introduced into Mexico without paying taxes. We simply don't have the ability to detect all the stolen cars being crossed to Mexico from the U.S. If a car is highly noticeable, we might catch it. A very expensive car with American license plates, for example, driven by a Hispanic is one of the selected ones that might be checked. In such cases, we ask for identification and proof of ownership. If a Mexican is driving an American car, we confiscate the car. After that we check with a central office to see if the car is stolen, but that is usually not very effective. That is the only way we seize stolen cars, because most of the time we are just checking for merchandise being introduced into Mexico illegally or without paying the federal taxes. Sometimes they change the plates from American to Mexican plates before they cross the bridge, and that makes it even harder to detect them."

Although it is true that the Mexican government has not been very helpful in recovering and returning stolen vehicles to the United States, there are other problems that contribute to this problem. Most of the time, Mexican law enforcement does not have the personnel or the technology to check if vehicles are stolen. There are a few databases that can be used, but accessibility makes it difficult in identifying stolen vehicles.

People on both sides of the border resent the costs of auto theft. When we talked to respondents in the Perceptions of Deviance Survey, for example, we asked them to indicate how good or bad it was for people in Mexico to buy cars stolen in the United States. Half (49.9 percent) of all 424 respondents ranked it in the worst category (-5). Only 20 individuals (4.7 percent) ranked it as "acceptable" or "good" behavior. Figure 7.2 shows how responses to this item varied according to the self-described race/nationality of our respondents.

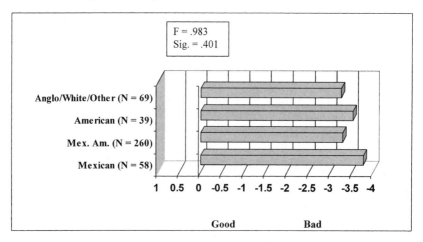

FIG. 7.2. Mean scores (from +5 to −5) of South Texas respondents in self-described racial/ethnic/national categories selecting each level of how good or how bad it is for people in Mexico to buy cars stolen in the United States

This figure not only shows a fairly strong negative reaction to selling stolen cars in Mexico, but also shows only slight differences among the different racial/ethnic/national groups on this item. Indeed, Mexicans and Americans regarded it most negatively, though the differences were too minor to be considered statistically significant.[26] Again, these results do not support the belief that people in South Texas, Mexican or American, condone selling stolen vehicles in Mexico.

Conclusion

The Texas-Mexico border region has a puzzling relation to such property crimes as shoplifting and auto theft. While the culture of the area still strongly supports obeying the law, there are simultaneous cultural undercurrents that promote a permissive acceptance of certain criminal activities.[27] Alongside a highly traditional culture that supports obedience to law, some aspects of corruption become not only allowed, but openly expected.

Likewise, the misalignment of political, economic, and law enforcement structures of Mexico and the United States creates an invitation to criminal activity, particularly shoplifting and auto theft by minors. The border also facilitates an underground economy that offers poverty-level residents goods such as vehicles, clothing, electronics, and prescription medicine that would otherwise be out of their reach.

Law enforcement officers also get caught in these crosscurrents. Even though there are strong efforts to maintain the integrity and honesty of law enforcement officials in both Mexico and the United States, corruption continues to be a major problem in the border cities of each country.[28] Personal correspondence with a convicted auto thief, for example, disclosed to one of the authors that vehicles stolen in the U.S. and transported into Mexico were given legitimate documents by Mexican officials.[29] Though the problem of corruption is not as serious with U.S. law enforcement officials, in recent years increasing numbers of agents have become involved in facilitating the drug trade, the crossing of undocumented workers, or other forms of corruption.[30]

There has been considerable debate about the reasons for the high rates of property crime on the border. One of the main issues is the question of whether criminal activity is caused by economic necessity, by increased opportunities for getting away with cross-border crimes, or such personal factors as greed and a criminal mentality. As we have seen, Mexican street kids can easily cross over to the United States to engage in shoplifting with relative impunity. Indeed, because of the facility with which it can be done, we need to ask not only why some do it, but, more importantly, why so many do not.

Americans experiencing economic hardship may also be drawn into criminal activities. Large segments of the Texas border population struggle just to move *up* to the poverty line. Nevertheless, most seem to be avoiding criminal involvement. Because of this, it is hard to believe that economic need or increased opportunities for crime can alone explain shoplifting and auto theft rates. Along the border, many other factors, such as the strength of family values and community bonds, are also very important. Peer associations are also factors that help explain the induction of some individuals into stealing cars or shoplifting.

Other structural factors are also important. The nationalism of each country promotes a lack of cooperation by police agencies on both sides of the border. In addition, Mexican police often not only fail to cooperate, but may sometimes be actively involved in these crimes. Further, one should not discount the impact of the huge underground cross-border drug trade. Its influence is felt in almost every other type of crime along the border.

Though the flow of money and goods resulting from these illegal activities, without doubt, helps the overall border economy, people on both sides of the border are more victims than beneficiaries. One indicator of this is the higher cost of auto insurance in South Texas. But there are many other costs, including a greater risk of being victimized. There is also an increased likelihood of having family members caught up in these crimes, with resulting insecurity and prison sentences. It is yet another instance where border residents are the most strongly affected by factors and decisions made in faraway centers of their respective states or nations.

American Lives, Mexican Justice

WITH JUAN JOSÉ BUSTAMANTE

Rocío, a young Mexican student, became involved in the Borderlife Project through a sociology class she took at the University of Texas–Pan American. She decided to conduct research on U.S. students in Mexican prisons. She chose to interview four Texas students who were in prison in Reynosa. At the conclusion of her research, she stated:

> Although there is corruption in the Mexican judicial and political systems, Americans who go into Mexico with the intention of committing a crime there deserve punishment for it. Though it is unfortunate that they have to go through so much for a petty offense, it is best not to mess with unfamiliar laws. If you plan to break Mexican laws, a surprise may be waiting.

In December 1991 these four young adults from Central Texas, a young woman twenty-three years old and three younger male companions, ages nineteen to twenty-two, crossed the border into the Mexican town of Reynosa. They wanted to purchase Valium and have some fun. Two of these young Americans had used Valium before for health problems; it seems that they may have hoped to possibly sell some of them. They found a doctor willing to give them two prescriptions totaling 270 pills. This is somewhat unusual, because doctors in Mexico can get in serious legal trouble by giving such large prescriptions for a psychotropic drug. The prescription, which cost $45 in Mexico, could be resold in Texas for around $800. Before going to a pharmacy to fill the prescription, the four young people stopped at several clubs. They then went to the pharmacy. They were arrested soon after they left, perhaps because of drunken behavior in public, or perhaps because someone tipped off the police. When the police found the Valium, the four were charged with drug trafficking. That began the worst nightmare of their lives.

First they were put in the local jail, but, because in Mexico defendants accused of drug trafficking are usually sent to a prison facility while their case is pending, they were soon transferred to the nearest Mexican prison.[1] These young people soon discovered that Mexico's legal system is more inclined to assume that people thus charged are guilty unless they can prove their innocence. The young woman, not wanting to be by herself in the women's portion of the prison, begged the authorities to let her stay with the three young men. Though such an arrangement is highly unusual, the Mexican authorities complied.

When they were finally able to get word to their families, the parents of one of the young men contacted a Mexican attorney, who tried unsuccessfully to locate and represent them before the Mexican courts. Another attorney was named under questionable circumstances to represent them, though it was later discovered that this particular lawyer was also representing the doctor who had illegally given them prescriptions. After two months, they were still in prison, awaiting trial. Each was facing a sentence of more than five years.

In February 1992, they managed to get another attorney. She sat on their case for four more months, repeatedly requesting money from the families under the pretense of trying to arrange a bribe to get them out of prison. Nothing came of this either.

When Rocío interviewed them in the prison, their situation seemed so desperate that she soon became deeply involved in trying to help them. She became a lifeline to the prisoners' families, who came to rely on her to help them work through the tangle of laws, Mexican police, judges, attorneys, and prison officials. She also got her professor (one of the authors) to make several visits to them in the Mexican prison. It became clear that the prison officials were treating these young people relatively well, considering the limited resources of Mexican prisons.

Then several key politicians and businesspeople on both sides of the border got involved, helping these families focus media and political attention on the case. With their help, two new lawyers were hired who managed to work with Mexican federal officials to get the young people released. This was ultimately accomplished when the federal attorney general's office in Mexico City ruled that the four Americans had been charged under the wrong section of the law. After nine and a half months of incarceration, the four walked away from the Mexican penitentiary and returned to the U.S. with their families.

Their situation then took one final tragic twist. Just hours after their release, the young woman suffered a heart attack brought on by a severe asthma attack (though possibly also compounded by their celebration on the night of their release). She died that night at the age of twenty-four.

No doubt, the criminal justice system in Mexico is flawed. Yet these young Americans committed a serious crime. In addition, they may have violated Mexican sensibilities by public drunkenness. Still, it is unfortunate that they had to pay such a high price for their mistakes.

Issues

In this chapter, we consider the impact of the Mexican criminal justice system on people from both sides of the border. We will address several key issues:

—Are teens from U.S. border communities who cross into Mexico to party and drink just having harmless fun, or does this practice represent a serious social problem?

—Are Mexican police corrupt and unethical, or are they simply representing a different set of customs and ethics?

—Does the Mexican system of jails and prisons serve to curtail crime, or is it mainly an instrument of exploitation and abuse by public officials?

Methodology

Most of the ethnographic accounts in this chapter were obtained by student interviewers from the Borderlife Project. We took their accounts from two main research topics. The first, "U.S. teens partying in Mexico," was based on accounts from approximately forty-five subjects. The second, "Valley residents who spent time in Mexican jails and prisons," was based on interviews with approximately sixty subjects. Much of the inside information about police and Mexican jails and prisons was obtained by the co-author of this chapter, Juan José Bustamante, a former Mexican police officer and now a Ph.D. student at Michigan State University.

Underage Drinking in Mexico

Many Americans find themselves in unfamiliar situations when they go to Mexico for drinking and fun. Though the laws in Mexico are quite different, and though police may wink at some forms of behavior that are prohibited in the United States, violating Mexican laws and customs can have severe consequences.[2]

Many young adults in the Rio Grande Valley freely admit to having engaged in underage drinking in Mexico during their teen years. James, a twenty-two-year-old resident of the Rio Grande Valley, is one of them. "When I was sixteen," he says, "we had nowhere to go for fun. It was just the movies or the skating rink. Every week, people would ask me what I did over the weekend and I'd say that I didn't do anything. But when I'd tell them I went to Mexico, they'd all be impressed. Like on *Cheers*, 'everybody would know your name!' and that would make me feel like someone special. When you're sixteen, anywhere in the United States, drinking is cool. If you drink, you'll have fun. But if you're not drinking, you feel like you're missing out. I had my first drink in Mexico. That was the first time I felt like an adult. I wouldn't give up the weekends that I spent in Mexico for anything."

As James indicates, drinking in Mexico is done not only for the physical enjoyment, but also to impress one's peers. Two other young men, Ben and Ricky, articulated a similar point of view. "There was a lot of peer pressure from friends," reports Ben. "We belonged to a high school group called 'The Brew Crew.' It was sort of like a gang, but was not centered on violence or vandalism. We were just a group of guys who got together to drink and hang out. After school, we'd go to Happy Hour at a bar called Cheers that is located in Mexico. Then on weekends we'd go to clubs—usually two a night."

Many of these young people develop serious problems with alcohol. Many have either been in accidents on the way home or know someone who was. Another young man, J.B., admits it's dangerous. "I've been pulled over drunk a few times," he says, "but I've never been taken to jail."

Though some parents of U.S. teens are unaware that their children go to Mexico to drink, others either tolerate or approve of such activities. "My parents don't know that I go to Mexico," says Eddie. "To this day, they still think I'm at a friend's house." Another teen, Araceli, says, "My mom doesn't like the idea. She used to take me and some friends to the mall thinking we would be there and that someone else would pick us up. Instead, we'd always go to Mexico. She would find out eventually, but by the time she did, it was a habit and she couldn't stop us. Finally, she just said to be careful."

In our Perceptions of Deviance Survey, we asked respondents to indicate how good or how bad it was for high school juniors and seniors to cross into Mexico to party (with drinking). We also asked related questions, such as how good or bad it is for underage minors to drink alcohol when they are with their family. Finally, we asked how good or bad it was for them to hang out with friends in public places late at night. The results are shown in Figure 8.1.

Several patterns are clear from the data presented in this figure. First, there is a pronounced "generation gap" in each of the three behaviors assessed. On the first question, partying in Mexico (including drinking), the thirty-two individuals in our sample who were eighteen or younger rated

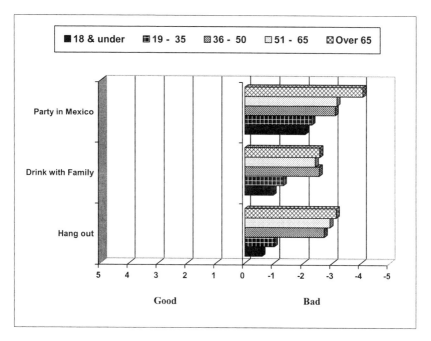

FIG. 8.1. Mean scores (from +5 to −5) of South Texas respondents in different age categories selecting each level of how good or bad it is for high school juniors and seniors to drink and party in Mexico, to drink with family, and to hang out with friends in public places late at night

this behavior much more moderately than did any of the older age categories (F = 3.527; Sig. = .008). The same age-related pattern was found in relation to how the respondents in our sample regarded these underage teens drinking with their families (F = 3.932; Sig. = .004), though respondents in all age categories saw this behavior less negatively than partying in Mexico. The greatest differences among age categories, however, was found on the third item, hanging out with friends in public places late at night (F = 10.176; Sig. = .000). While older adults tend to regard this as wrong, the youngest group either saw it as only slightly bad or even something good.

We need to emphasize, however, that the average score of even the youngest age category indicated disapproval of all three practices. Though some rated each item as a good thing, the majority regarded each item negatively. This is important since it supports the assertion that while some Valley teens may approve of these behaviors, most do not.[3]

Consequences

Many teens don't realize just how unprotected they are in a different country, with its different laws, customs, and societal systems. Mindy, who is eighteen, had a recent experience that made her more cautious. "My cousin and I were walking back across the bridge when one of those little boys came up trying to sell us some gum or get a handout. My cousin remarked at how cute he was and leaned down to hand him a quarter. Without warning, he reached up and ripped a $300 gold necklace from her neck and ran away. We were both in such a state of shock that we couldn't even run after him. We have never seen him again. We've learned to never wear expensive jewelry on the streets of Mexico."

Another young man, David, remembers an experience he had while living on the border in El Paso, Texas. "It's right across the border from Ciudad Juarez," he says. "Every weekend hundreds of teenagers, soldiers, and other people would fill the streets. I kept hearing what a good time my friends were having and I just got curious. I wanted to experience it for myself. So we went one Friday after school. As soon as we crossed the bridge I saw people everywhere and lots of beautiful women. Our first stop was a local bar which a lot of my friends frequented. My friends started me off with a 'bucket-o-beer,' which consisted of six beers in a bucket of ice for only $2. By the time I finished it, I was totally out of control. I ran around yelling and laughing and just being crazy. Most of it I can't even remember. They told me later that I drank seven shots of tequila and that I even swallowed the worm in the bottle. Around four in the morning, I found myself hugging the toilet like it was my mom. I felt like I was going to puke out my intestines. For the next three or four days I couldn't eat. To this day, I can't even stand the sight of a beer or alcohol, much less drink it. Although some people say 'never again,' they're back the next week. Not me. My trip to Mexico convinced me that drinking and Mexico were not for me."[4]

Some U.S. kids combine drinking in Mexico with drugs. "My friends and I decided to try a Mexican depressant," says Antonio. "It caused me to feel very mellow and gave me the sensation that I could drink forever. After drinking on this side of the border at an establishment that didn't enforce the drinking age, I was still feeling the effects of the drug. We decided to go across the border and continue partying. All I remember is walking back to the car and blacking out. I can't remember the drive, our conversation, or going across the border. I was in a state of total confusion. All of a sudden, I was back in the parking lot on the U.S. side getting into my car. As I was backing out, I hit a cable and blacked out again half a block away. Instantly there were three police cars. I remember not even trying to talk or argue, I simply turned around and put my hands on the car and assumed the position. I recall being very angry with myself. I felt humiliated with the handcuffs and then being put in a cage like an animal. I looked around the six-by eight-foot cell. I heard the conversations of the guys in there with me and I felt overwhelmed with degradation. I just didn't belong there. I knew how disappointing it would be to my parents when they found out their son was in jail. It was this thought that hurt me the most."

Often, these kids land in jail, not in Texas, but in Mexico. Another former high school student, Marco, remembers his graduation night. "My friends and I were ready to party," he says. "None of us were old enough to legally drink so we went to Mexico to have some fun. We spent all night in several different bars. On the way back, I ran a stop sign and we were stopped by a Mexican policeman. He was pretty nice until he found that we didn't have the money he asked for. He wanted $45 'para arreglarlo' [to take care of it]. A couple of the guys tried to persuade him to let us go, but he insisted that we pay the money. The situation got heated and the officer started pushing one of the guys. He took us to jail and locked us up for resisting arrest. In jail, they told us that our bail would be $150 each. We didn't have the money, so we spent the night in jail. The following morning our parents had to come with the money."

Mexican Police

It is difficult to understand the behavior of Mexican police officers unless one understands the structure of law enforcement in Mexico. Police forces in Mexico are divided into two main types: preventive and judicial. Preventive police agencies are generally uniformed and are charged with keeping order in towns and cities. Their main role is to prevent crime. The judicial police, on the other hand, conduct criminal investigations under the direction of a magistrate in the *ministerio público* [district attorney's office]. Municipal governments employ only preventive police, while states and the federal government have both preventive and investigative units. This means that city police departments do not have authority to investigate many crimes, such as drug trafficking, which profoundly affect life in the cities.[5]

In addition, the Mexican criminal justice system is dominated by the federal government in Mexico City. State and local governments are largely dependent upon the federal government for tax resources. States along the border have historically received proportionally fewer resources than those allocated for Central Mexico, for political reasons and because they are isolated from the centers of power. Though the border area is one of the fastest growing parts of Mexico, it gets far less back in resources than it generates in tax income. This leaves border police agencies vastly underfunded at a time when crime is growing dramatically along the border.

All levels of police in Mexico, however, do have authority to take people to a jail or before a magistrate. This gives Mexican police the opportunity to solicit a *mordida* [literally, a "bite," but translated as a bribe].[6] Though the governments of several recent Mexican presidents have made efforts to curtail this practice, it remains quite common. While Americans see la mordida as blatantly corrupt, Mexicans have a more mixed view. First, there is generally an understanding among Mexicans that bribes can be asked only when a true violation has taken place. It is relatively rare for police officers in Mexico to pull people over at random, for example, and demand a bribe. Second, the bribe is seen as a way of avoiding more serious or time-consuming entanglements. Most often, for example, the amount of the bribe will be less than one would have to pay by going through the official channels. It can also save time, many Mexicans reason, if a motorist can pay his or her fine directly to the police officer. Thus, many Mexicans see some benefits to the mordida system as long as the practice is not abused.

For those—like Marco and his friends in the preceding story—who are unfamiliar with the unspoken rules associated with la mordida, the process can be difficult or even dangerous. One unspoken rule, for example, is that the person paying la mordida should treat it as payment for a "service" that the officer is performing. Indeed, most police officers hope the person being detained will make an offer so they don't have to solicit it. In this respect, the unspoken assumption is that one is offering the officer a "tip" for saving him from greater inconvenience and higher costs. Another unspoken part of the exchange is an understanding of what is considered an "appropriate" amount. Usually, it should be an amount that would be considerably less than what would be required in the course of the official process. Thus, the appropriate amount depends on the nature of the offense and the trouble one would likely get into without the assistance of the officer. Most traffic violations, for example, can be handled for as little as a few dollars, with more serious offenses costing much more.

This is not to suggest that Mexicans like having their police officers solicit mordidas. Most recognize and have an aversion to the corruption associated with it. They also recognize that money from fines and fees that would otherwise be available for public projects ends up in someone's pocket. Indeed, when we asked respondents in our Perceptions of Deviance Survey to describe how good or bad they thought it was for Valley residents traveling in Mexico to try to bribe a police officer to keep from paying a fine, Mexican respondents rated it more negatively than any of the other respondents from the United States. This result is reflected in Figure 8.2.

As Figure 8.2 illustrates, respondents from all the racial/national categories rated this behavior as "bad." Still, those respondents who identified themselves as "Mexicans" were much more likely to rank it as "very bad" ($F = 4.637$; Sig. $=.001$). We found this surprising, especially given that the practice is so widespread in Mexico. Perhaps Mexicans living in the United States, who no longer have to put up with the practice, dislike this aspect of life in Mexico now that they have a different lifestyle.

It is also possible that Mexicans may be drawn into this practice on a societywide basis, while finding it personally offensive. The practice of la mordida seems to have become entrenched in Mexico, not because people like it, but because it has been institutionalized into both the culture and the structure of Mexican society.

It has become part of a *structure* of corruption because the money derived from mordidas flows through a network of connected officials. In-

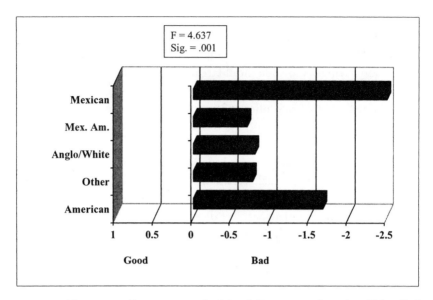

F = 4.637
Sig. = .001

Mexican

Mex. Am.

Anglo/White

Other

American

1   0.5   0   -0.5   -1   -1.5   -2   -2.5

Good   Bad

FIG. 8.2. Mean scores (from +5 to −5) of South Texas respondents in self-described racial/ethnic/national categories selecting each level of how good or how bad it is for Valley residents traveling in Mexico to pay a mordida to a police officer to keep from being fined

dividuals wanting to become police officers, for example, frequently have to "buy" their job (and to regularly pay a portion of what they take in to higher-ups). This not only corrupts otherwise good individuals who cannot get the job without under-the-table payments, but keeps them having to collect mordidas to pay off higher-ups who, in turn, may be paying to keep their jobs. Thus, police officers often find it very difficult to resist the structural pressures to demand bribes in order to keep their jobs.

Structural pressures for bribes among Mexican police officers have been documented by Arteaga Botello and López Rivera.[7] According to their research, bribing behavior among police officers is reinforced throughout the hierarchy and by means of social networks that include access to privileged positions by paying mordidas to higher-ups.[8] Novice police officers learn from veteran officers how to extort mordidas. In addition, as Arteaga Botello and López Rivera point out,[9] even when payoffs to higher-ups are not demanded directly, there is a subtle understanding that patrol officers have to collect money and then pay up to the next one in the chain of command.[10] It becomes understood among all ranks of police officers that the best neighborhoods (for the purpose of collecting bribes), patrol cars, and equipment are assigned according to the amount one is willing to pay his/her supervisor[11] for these advantages.

The mordida has also become profoundly entrenched in Mexican public *culture*. Once started, it is a very difficult practice to eliminate because virtually all members of society become accomplices. Once it becomes an acceptable way to get out of trouble, it is easy to use it to fix ever more serious offenses. Drug traffickers, for example, will find it easier to buy off police, judges, and even top political figures when la mordida is winked at for traffic offenses. Over time, the choice to not participate may be increasingly difficult. In some places along the border, for example, police who refuse to go along are given a stark choice by drug traffickers—"*plata o plomo*" [silver or lead]. In other words, if you cooperate, we will give you silver (money). If you refuse, you can expect lead (bullets).

So while many individuals on both sides of the border may dislike the practice of having to pay a mordida in Mexico, they go along, feeling they have little choice.[12] This is essentially what happened to Ricardo, a Mexican American visiting Mexico on his twentieth birthday. "I was driving around Reynosa at night," he says, "when suddenly a police car drives up behind me with his lights signaling to me to pull over. Two policemen got out of the car and told me that I was driving the wrong way on a one-way street. I explained that I had driven through there many times before with no problems from other policemen. They essentially ignored what I was saying and asked me to give them something 'for their troubles' and said that everything would be alright. While they were the ones causing me the inconvenience, I chose not to argue with them because I knew I could not win. I gave them $5 each and went on my way."

Some Americans, like Ricardo, believe that Mexican police "pick on" or profile them. And while this may sometimes be true, most Mexicans experience much the same treatment. Indeed, relatively few tourists driving in Mexico report problems with police demanding a mordida. Police in Mexico are much less involved in traffic enforcement, compared to police in the United States.

It is also the case that some accounts of corruption in Mexican law enforcement are exaggerated. The practice of la mordida is so well known in the U.S. and is so anathema to U.S. values that, not surprisingly, some folklore has developed around it. The following account, according to Juan José Bustamante, coauthor of this chapter and former Mexican police officer, contains several elements that render its veracity doubtful. We will relate the account and then comment on it.

A Hispanic man in one of the in-depth interviews described getting a call from his neighbor. He knew it had to be urgent because this neighbor seldom called him.

> I couldn't hear the voice very well, but I could tell it was Pepe, my neighbor. He sounded sick and asked me to please come to Miguel Alemán [across the border from Roma] to get him out of jail. When I got there, the officers denied having him in their jail. I insisted that he had just called me from there, so he finally went to check and brought Pepe back out with him. He was a mess. He had a broken arm and was bleeding from his nose and mouth. I paid $300 fine for him and we immediately left. As soon as we got to the car, I asked Pepe what had happened. He said that as he was driving on the main street, the light turned red and he stopped suddenly. He claimed a car hit him from behind. When he got out to investigate, he discovered that a police car had hit him. He told me they accused him of having backed into them and took him to the station. When he refused to admit guilt, they started to beat him up. After hearing that from him, I never go to Mexico anymore unless I really have to.

Juan José Bustamante notes several things about the preceding story that do not ring true. Though the police in Mexico are known to use torture on occasion to get confessions, such cases usually involve only more serious crimes. The offense described in this story does not sound like one for which police would require a confession. Even if they had used torture, however, they would know enough to leave no marks, much less a broken arm and cuts and bruises. If a victim were to claim his confession was induced through torture, judges would be inclined to believe the victim if there are physical signs of it. It's much more likely that Pepe was involved in something more serious and that he used the stereotype of corrupt officers to avoid telling his neighbor the whole story.

Police Torture

The issue of police torture is related to several important aspects of the relationship between Mexican police agencies and local jails. When the police detain someone, the *ministerio público* [district attorney's office] has seventy-two hours to process the charge. Then, he must ask the judge to either retain the prisoner or release him. No person should be retained more than seventy-two hours in a jail without an order from a state or federal judge. Municipal judges only have power to detain people for up to seventy-two hours, and then only for administrative violations. Needless to say, seventy-two hours is not enough time to complete many investigations. The difficulty of meeting this requirement invites some abuse by police officials. Because police officers need to have sound evidence for the district attorney to make a case, there is a temptation to hold some individuals for more than seventy-two hours without informing the district attorney.

In more serious cases, this time constraint also tempts police to use illegitimate means of obtaining evidence. Until the Salinas de Gortari administration, a forced confession was commonly accepted as evidence of guilt. By 1993, however, a signed confession, by itself, had technically become largely invalid in court.[13] Still, though police officers could not use torture (physical and psychological) as the primary basis of their case, they could use it to compel someone to give them additional evidence. This seems to be common in drug cases. A confession of transporting drugs, by itself, would not be sufficient. If the police get information that reveals where drugs are hidden or the names of higher-ups, however, even if induced by torture, such evidence could be considered valid. As a result, torture, though less common than before, is still used in some serious cases.

There are additional impediments to the use of police torture. The federal government, for example, oversees the prison systems through the Secretaría de Gobernación. This agency is supposed to prevent torture and other forms of abuse by police officers. In addition, a national ombudsmen's office, the Comisión Nacional de Derechos Humanos, seeks to prevent the violation of human rights. Finally, there are also several independent agencies funded by private foundations and organizations that attempt to curb police excesses.

One student who interviewed a former *comandante*, the equivalent of a police chief, asked him about the application of torture. "It was always effective in getting a criminal to confess his actions," he says, "especially when we knew he was guilty. We might start by refusing to let him use the bathroom facilities. If that didn't work, we would pour mineral water into his nose, with his head upside down. This is very painful, but leaves no marks. Sometimes, we would tie him up, lay him on his back on the floor, and place a wet towel over his face, making him unable to breathe."

Another official who was interviewed remembered another incident. "Two years ago," he says, "a drug dealer was arrested and we needed more information about where the drugs came from. The higher officials forced me to beat up the guy so he would talk. I felt bad about hitting the guy, but I had to or else I would have lost my job."

One former police officer also admitted using torture. "In some cases," he said, "we used electrical shock in a very painful manner, applying the shock to their tongues and genitals. Sometimes, a police officer will shake a club soda to pressure gas up their nose. This will cause them to lose their breath. These actions leave no marks, so there is no way they can prove any sort of police brutality."

Unfortunately, it seems that torture is still being practiced in some cities along the Texas-Mexico border. Human Rights Watch has documented torture practices extensively in border towns like Reynosa and Nuevo Laredo.[14] Their report demonstrates the impunity with which police forces often act, despite recent legal measures to prevent it. In Nuevo Laredo on January 4, 1997, for example, a young man detained for street fighting was transported to a municipal jail. Two hours later, he was found dead. The municipal police suggested that he committed suicide, but further investigation revealed that he had been tortured and murdered. Still, the state prosecutor failed to conduct a thorough investigation and no officials were ever arrested.[15]

Misunderstanding Mexican Laws and Customs

Americans who get in trouble in Mexico often do not understand the laws, public institutions, and the sensibilities of Mexicans. Arturo, for example, describes a recent experience with Mexican police. "I was drinking a little before I drove to a friend's house in Mexico," he says. "On my way, I stopped on the side of the road to urinate. I wasn't drunk, though. I was about through when a police car came up and parked close to my car. Two officers got out and began to ask me questions. They threatened to arrest me for public drunkenness. I showed them I was not drunk. Still, they asked for a mordida, but I refused to give them any money. We argued for a minute or so. Then they began hitting me. Next thing I knew, I was arrested for drunkenness, resisting arrest, and possession of drugs." Arturo spent ninety days in a prison awaiting a trial, learning the hard way that many of the rights and protections Americans take for granted are not so easily available in Mexico.

Indecent Public Behavior

Arturo's story illustrates how Americans who are insensitive to Mexican culture and law can get in trouble when they travel in Mexico. First, in most Mexican cities, urinating in a public place is considered a gross violation of Mexican sensibilities. Many Americans seem to have the impression that Mexicans don't care about such things. Second, if we understand that Mexicans have strong feelings about public drunkenness, we can understand why these police officers might have reacted as they did. Third, Arturo refused to give them a mordida, which police feel is equivalent to a fine. Finally, mouthing off to Mexican police is very unwise, especially when you have already given them good reason to arrest you.

Teenagers who go to Mexico to drink and party often get into difficulties when they misunderstand Mexican sensibilities. Tim and James learned this when they went to Mexico to buy liquor. "It was a Sunday afternoon and most of the stores were closed," says Tim. "So we went riding around town drinking beer. James decided to stop the car so he could go to the bathroom in some trees. While we were urinating, I felt a pistol against my ribs. James, being a little tipsy, dared the Mexican cop to shoot. He claimed the Mexican police didn't have any money to buy bullets. The officer got very angry and told us we would spend the night in jail. I was pretty scared and did not hesitate to get into the police car. James was reluctant at first because they told him to leave his brand new Ford in the middle of the road. After feeling the pistol barrel press against his ribs, though, he got in peacefully. The police were very rude and unprofessional. They took us to jail and put us in a large cell with eighteen other men. It was a pig pen. There was no bathroom and the odor was suffocating. Prisoners had to relieve themselves in a corner of the cell. There were flies everywhere. Three hours later, they finally let us out. They looked in my wallet and found $60. They told us that money would be the fine. An hour later James came back with the car and I was also released. They told us to get out of Mexico and go home. To this day, we have never gone back to Mexico."

In cases like this, it is amazing to hear Americans say the police are "very rude and unprofessional." These young men were drinking and urinating in public, mouthing off to police officers, refusing to do what they were told, and insulting Mexico and its police officers. They were fortunate indeed that something worse did not happen to them.

Because many teens can buy drinks in Mexican clubs, they often think that Mexico has no standards or laws about drinking. Most may not understand, for example, that drinking is permitted in bars and clubs, but not on the streets. Maricela describes what happened when she went "clubbing" with some friends in Reynosa. "It was a weekend," she says, "around two-thirty in the morning. After awhile, we wanted to get out and walk around a little. Since I hadn't finished my drink, I put it in a plastic cup and took it outside. As we were standing there talking, a policeman came up to me and asked me what I was drinking. I told him it was a coke, but he found out it wasn't, so I got arrested for drinking on the street. We argued with him, but he wouldn't listen. When he grabbed me to cuff me, he deliberately touched my chest. This got me furious so I pushed him away, but he just pushed me against a car and cuffed me very roughly. Fortunately, it didn't go any further than that, but I had never felt more humiliated and scared in my whole life."

Badmouthing Police

Many Americans take their rights in the United States for granted, assuming they are the same in Mexico. Mexican police, for example, are not required to read suspects their rights. Neither are they required to offer other rights contained in the standard "Miranda warning" that Americans are used to. They have no obligation to let someone they take to jail make a phone call. They also have little responsibility for providing food and blankets in jail. Those "amenities" are to be provided by family and friends (if one can get in touch with them). As a result, Americans who expect such "rights" often feel abused when they do not receive the treatment they would expect at home.

This tendency for U.S. youngsters to misunderstand their rights in Mexico is illustrated by an experience related by Joe Lopez. "A fight had broken out," he says, "and I was not even involved. The cops grabbed me and two of my friends and threw us into their car. Then they took us to jail. On the way to the jail, I leaned over to say something to my friend and the Mexican officer slapped me. In the jail, they wouldn't give us blankets or food and they wouldn't even let us use the phone. Because I knew Spanish, I was finally able to talk my way out. I was lucky because I only had $5 to my name." Clearly, this young man expected better treatment.

Some treatment by Mexican police officers is designed to teach respect for their laws. One Mexican officer, Atencio Ornelas, for example, says, "One night when I was working the streets of Reynosa, I saw two American boys loudly arguing with one another. I could see that they were both intoxicated. I went up to them and asked them a few questions. One of the boys became rude and obnoxious. I proceeded to arrest him and he tried to run. A fellow officer caught up to him and grabbed him from behind. I punched him a few times in the stomach. We then arrested both of them. While they were in the jail, all their money was taken from them. I admit they were treated harshly, but they needed to learn to respect Mexico and its laws."

Public Fighting

One type of behavior that brings strong police reaction in Mexico is public fighting. Nicolas ("Nick") and several of his teen friends discovered this one day when they went to lunch in Reynosa. After lunch they decided to go to a Mexican movie. Outside the theatre, when they were waiting to buy the tickets, some other guys standing close by began to make fun of them. "My friends got angry," he says, "and began to fight. I was not able to stop the fight, so I just stood aside and watched. The police arrived several minutes later and took my friends to jail. Several of us who had just been watching drove to the jail to wait for them. While we were parked outside, a cop came up to us and asked if we were in the fight too. When we said we were only watching it, he opened our car door and said, 'Sure you were. *Al bote* [To jail].' It was senseless to argue. When they put us inside, the whole place stank. Drunks were crying and yelling while sitting on their own vomit and litter. We didn't even know where to sit, so it was hard to get any rest. It was awful. We didn't know if we could make it through the night. During the night, a drunk came up to one of the guys and started making passes at him. The guy freaked out and began yelling at him. We joined in and pretty soon there was a lot of yelling. The guards came in and started beating up on the drunk. After they dragged him out, a guard turned to us and said, 'Do you want some too?' We said, 'No!' and they said, 'Then keep it quiet!' We were really scared and weren't about to argue. We didn't get any sleep at all. I'll never forget that night!"

Going to Jail

Several things about Mexican jails and attitudes are reflected in this story. First, public solicitations of homosexuality are often very severely sanctioned. Second, police and jail officers are more apt, relative to those in the U.S., to use violence. Third, municipal governments in Mexico, particularly those in border cities, have very little funding for jails, so such places can be extremely unsanitary. Finally, public fighting in Mexico is seen as disgraceful and can have rather severe consequences, as Nick and his friends discovered. When police are called in to break up a fight, it is fairly common for all participants to spend three days in a municipal jail. The time could be much longer if someone is injured and requires medical help.[16]

Municipal jails are both unique and complex. The guidelines and rules of each city must conform to its state constitution. As a result, prisons and jails in one city or state may vary greatly from those in another, depending upon each state's constitution. Jails, in general, are run by municipal, or city, governments. The majority of people confined in these city jails are accused of breaking city ordinances such as public intoxication, public fighting, and so on. People who commit federal and state crimes, however, may also be kept in a jail until their file is transferred to the respective judge. Often, those who have broken state and federal laws may be able to stay in a city jail if they manage to get an *amparo* (something like a writ of habeas corpus) from a federal judge. This prevents their transfer to a penitentiary. So, in municipal jails one may find people who just broke city ordinances interned with those accused of homicides, child abuse, burglary, and/or drug smuggling.

Jail Conditions

Many of the preceding stories describe the harsh conditions often found in Mexican jails along the border. Some jails, of course, have much better conditions than others. The condition depends in large part on the fiscal resources available to each municipality, which depends on such factors as party politics, favoritism, and the whims of federal authorities. The already limited resources in border cities are further diminished because of rapid growth, weak infrastructure, and such border problems as drug smuggling and the flight of Mexican workers to the United States. In addition, as has also been mentioned, Mexican jails are only supposed to incarcerate individuals for very short periods of time. As a result, almost no funds are available for food, blankets, or other personal needs of detainees. The Mexican system leaves it up to family and friends to meet such needs.

The result of such limited resources, coupled with occasionally overpopulated jails in border cities, leads to major sanitation problems in Mexican border jails. Ray Cavazos, for example, who spent a couple of days in a Mexican jail, says, "We were all crammed together in a small room. We also had cement beds with no sheets unless someone from our family provided them. Some prisoners complained that the sheet they received was not the one their family sent because it didn't look familiar. The jailers probably stole the good one and gave us this old dirty sheet in its place. The 'restroom' was a hole broken into a sewer pipe. If someone was there before you, he owned the restroom and might even charge you for using it."

Contrary to the preceding example, many of those who have spent time in a Mexican border jail describe how prisoners generally try to help each other out. "As I got acquainted with the other prisoners," comments Al, "I found they helped each other out a lot. Since the jail provided them with practically nothing, many shared the food brought in by their family. Since there were no beds, one coat that a prisoner had was shared by others. They also shared their *petates* [mats made of woven palm leaves], which they roll up when they're not being used. The worst part of all, though, was the total lack of toilet facilities or plumbing. If prisoners needed to have a bowel movement, they did it on a piece of newspaper, and then wrapped it up and put it into a garbage can."

Many American young people locked up in a Mexican border jail see things they may have never imagined. Gloria, an eighteen-year-old from McAllen, was very disturbed by her experience in a Reynosa jail. "I've never seen women kiss or touch other women," she says, "but I saw it there. Some of the women would look at me and my eyes would water for fear that they would come and touch me. I felt as though I was in hell. No one would want to be in my place that night. I felt like the worst was going to happen to me."

Going to Prison

Life in Mexican prisons can be even more difficult than spending time in the municipal jails of Mexico. Ignacio Ramirez, twenty-four, states: "I was only there for a year and a half, but that was the worst time of my entire life. The worst part was the danger. There was frequent violence, when people would end up dead or in critical condition. In the prison where I did my time, even the guards would kill a prisoner if someone from outside paid them to do it."

Ignacio also talked about how hard his prison time was on family members. "Since I was able to receive visits on Sundays only, my family would bring me little things from the store that I had asked them to bring. My wife had to go through a strict search of everything she brought. They looked in her purse and personal belongings. They even tasted the food that she made for me. When visiting time was over, the other inmates knew that I had received food from the U.S., so they would steal it from me. I didn't want more problems so I just gave them the gum, Fritos, and little things that my kids had sent me."

In large part, the conditions in Mexican jails and prisons are worse than in the U.S. because of the way the system is structured there. The federal government (which is much more powerful than state or local government) administers only high-profile penitentiaries in select Mexican states. The remainder of prisons, penitentiaries, and *ceresos* [social readaptation centers] are administered by the states, but funded by the federal government. These facilities hold both people who have violated state laws and those who have violated federal laws. People who smuggle illegal drugs, for example, are mixed in with those guilty of tax evasion, homicide, burglary, and pedophilia. Still, no one goes to a prison of any kind unless it is ordered by a federal or state judge. Only a judge can decide if an accused individual will go to prison or remain in a preventive (municipal) jail.

Recent research reveals a cumulative deterioration of the infrastructure in most prisons, due mainly to the lack of funding and apathy on the part of federal and state governments. As a result, many Mexican prisons suffer problems of overpopulation, corruption, understaffing, the ability of individuals with money to buy privileges, and promotions driven by political influence.[17]

In addition, though Mexican prisons hold prisoners accused or convicted of a wide range of offenses, they are increasingly being populated with individuals being held for drug offenses. Mario Granada, for example, lives in Reynosa. He ended up in prison on drug charges. "I have two kids and a wife," he says, "and I didn't make enough money to support them working in the maquiladoras. Consequently, I started selling drugs. I knew that dealing drugs was illegal, but I had to do something for money. It was either that or see my children starve. Necessity drove me towards the wrong path. Now, I regret it because I haven't seen my family for over three years."

Occasionally, innocent individuals may get swept up in the drug enforcement dragnet. Pablo Ozuna, a Mexican from Tampico, spent a year in prison before being found not guilty. "I was just visiting my *compadre*," he says, "when the police came and arrested both of us. We were accused of dealing drugs. They wouldn't let my compadre testify for me. They kept seeking more evidence against me until they finally decided that I really didn't know anything about his business. My family suffered a lot during that year. The police bothered them all the time for statements. They suffered a lot of humiliation. My wife had to work so our children could have something to eat. I thank God that now I am free and back with my family."

As in the U.S., accused or convicted police officers in Mexico sometimes end up in prison. Ricardo Lucio described his cell mate in a Nuevo Leon prison, Javier, as a forty-six-year-old police officer who had killed a child in a shoot-out. He was not subjected to any of the torment or abuse suffered by other inmates at the hands of guards. One of the main prison officers told Ricardo, "Javier is in this prison only until the commotion in his hometown dies down. He will then be relocated so he can perform his duties as a police officer again."

Prison Conditions

As Ricardo's account illustrates, Mexican prisons are much better for some prisoners than for others. Those from either side of the border with money and power can use these resources to create a comparatively comfortable existence. Antonio Pérez described how money talks in a Mexican prison. "I was able to buy almost anything I wanted," he says. "Private vendors were allowed into the prison to sell everything from toothpaste to toilet paper and coffee. Privacy for visits with wives or prostitutes was also available, sometimes for a price. In fact, even restaurant food could be purchased and brought into the prison for those with enough money to pay for it."

Mexican prisons generally have much more lenient restrictions than U.S. prisons on visits by family members.[18] Prisons in Mexico generally have separate facilities for conjugal visits. In addition, family members are often allowed to visit in the cells of inmates. Manolo Portales, who received frequent visits from his family while in prison, found such visits hard to take, however. "I felt ashamed and depressed all the time," he says, "but it was never as bad as the two Christmases my wife and kids spent with me in my prison cell. I was so ashamed that I became extremely depressed."

Perhaps those who suffer the most, though, are the prisoners who have no family members close enough to the prison to visit or to provide food, clothing, and other necessities. Gonzalo Campos, from El Salvador, ended up in a Mexican prison after he was arrested by Mexican police in Chiapas because he did not have any documents. No one from his family was able to make the long trip to visit him. "The guards treated us like animals," he says. "They never accepted that we were human beings who needed to be fed. When they did feed us, it was often not fit to eat. I remember the awful burn I felt in the pit of my stomach because I was so hungry. I had always complained to my mother if she took too long to cook dinner. While I was in prison in Mexico, I made a vow never to be ungrateful to anyone for making me a meal, no matter how long it takes."

Oscar Prieto described how money can improve one's situation. He was incarcerated in a large federal prison in Mexico City. "It was very overcrowded," he says. "I slept on the floor of a large room until I was moved to a smaller cell that was occupied by only five people. That arrangement cost me $10 a week, but it was worth it. I would have been willing to pay even more because I was scared all the time in the larger cell. Still, in the smaller cell I got bitten by insects while I slept. There were all kinds of cracks in the walls where the bugs could come in at night. After several nights of this, I got sick, but I could not get any medical attention. I thought I was going to die. After I got better, I made a mixture of toothpaste and sugar to fill in the cracks."

Overcrowding is a serious problem in many Mexican prisons. Guillermo Rosales was unable to pay for any special accommodations. "I slept in the patio of the prison for several days," he says. "In order for me to sleep in a cell, I had to buy one. Since I didn't have enough money at first, my family had to bring me a tent. Other relatives brought me blankets, electric skillet, money, gas lamp, and enough food for me to eat each day. Some of the inmates shared my tent, but they had to pay me a fee."

This situation of too few facilities for too many inmates often creates great strains that lead to fighting. Joel Diaz described how he was able to avoid many problems because he had money. "I believe the reason why I was excluded from the violence," he says, "was because I had money and I am an American. The officials at the prison knew that someone from the American Consulate would visit me once a month. Maybe that is why I was spared."

Though life in a Mexican prison can be harsh and inhumane, there are some ways in which Mexican prisons are more humane than prisons in the United States. First, as many of our stories have illustrated, Mexican prisons do not systematically seek to destroy individuality. Prisoners usually do not wear uniforms. If they have the money, they can decorate and equip their cells. Similarly, their lives during the day are not as thoroughly regimented.

Second, the Mexican criminal justice system recognizes the need for family and conjugal visits. Family members are allowed to visit prisoners in their cells, with fewer restrictions. Inmate rape, which is practically a way of life in U.S. prisons, seems to be much less common in prisons in Mexico, largely because of the provision for conjugal visits.

Ernesto, an American prisoner in his early twenties from Rio Grande City, has experienced life in several Mexican prisons. He served two years in a prison in Nuevo Laredo, two years in a prison at Las Islas Marías, and one month in a Reynosa prison. Mexican prison life had a sobering effect on him. "Prison scared me," he says. "I thought I was tough and that I could do anything I wanted. I thought I was on top of the world. I say this because my friends and I used to act this way before I landed in jail. During the time I spent in prison I realized how wrong I was and now I repent for my mistakes. But I still see young guys with the same attitude I used to have because they still don't see the reality of the world."

The Mexican Prison Guard's Perspective

Many of the conditions described by prisoners were confirmed in interviews with prison guards and officials. "We as officials have a lot of responsibility," says one guard. "When prisoners fight, we are at risk of getting injured. It's hard to control so many individuals. It's also hard to deal with people who are still smuggling drugs in prison. Some of them are powerful traffickers who feel untouchable."

Juan Treviño feels that his work as a guard is often dangerous. "The inmates get real frustrated when their cells are checked," he says, "or when we have to frisk them. I am currently in charge of taking inmates to their court hearings and I have to search them before they can go. This loss of privacy bothers most prisoners a great deal. I have a brother who's in prison in another state and every time I visit him they strip search me, so I know it's not a pleasant feeling. Some inmates get very angry and threaten me, saying some day they'll get out and find me."

Because of the danger and the poor working conditions, many guards find ways to improve their situation. Some do it by exchanging favors with other guards. Francisca Ortega, for example, says that she and other guards constantly exchange favors. "The other day," she says, "I was working at the entrance frisking females and a guard came up to me and asked me not to search a certain woman, apparently his sister. So I didn't search her. I know that some day I'm going to ask him for a favor. That's just how we work."

Many Mexican prison guards know they can be easily replaced. The requirements for working as a guard in a Mexican prison are not very high. Carlos Zamora, for example, admits that the educational requirements are quite low. "I dropped out of school when I was old enough to work," he says, "and I have been working as a guard for ten years. I was hired immediately, with no questions asked. I don't earn decent money, even though I work full-time. Sometimes, we have to work a lot of extra hours. I guess I prefer to be here than not have a job at all."

Generally, a high school diploma is not required for work as a prison guard and or municipal police officer. Municipal police agencies mainly hire poor and working-class people. They typically require no more than an elementary school background, though a few may require completion of middle or high school. Often their salary is no more than the equivalent of $300 a month. State police officers have higher standards and somewhat better salaries. They are required to have at least a high school diploma and a short period of training at a police academy. State police officers also enjoy such benefits as health care and pension plans. Still, the requirements for prison guards, as well as their salaries, vary considerably from state to state.

As a result of poor working conditions and low salaries, many guards look for other ways to supplement their income. One guard, for example, states, "I work as a prison guard during the day. During the night I work as a security guard in a club. All of this is very frustrating especially when you have a family to feed. Sometimes I have to take mordidas to make enough money." [19]

Prison guard Jesús Ontiveros explained the use of the mordida. "Prisoners are allowed visitors if they have been behaving well," he says. "One

Sunday morning a fight broke out between four prisoners. The three who were poor were placed in a dark room and lost their privileges of being able to see their family for awhile. The other prisoner didn't get punished, however, because he gave me a mordida to help me be more understanding. This is pretty common among us guards. We get mordidas so that we will treat some of them better than others. They might bribe me, for example, so that I won't work them so hard, punish them, or so that I'll allow visits even though they don't deserve them. I accept the money because I know other guards do and I need that extra money. Sometimes I reflect that it's immoral and I should stop accepting bribes. After awhile, though, I usually go back to doing it again."

Officers who work in Mexican prisons have considerable power. Juan Lara, who got a job as a prison guard, sought it for the opportunity of having a place to work. Soon, he found there were other temptations. "I felt different as soon as I began working," he said. "I was supposed to spy on the prisoners. My heart had to become as hard as a rock if I wanted to keep the job. I witnessed many cases where the prisoners were treated as if they were animals. It took me some time before I got used to the inhumane treatment given to some prisoners. After the first week of working there, I realized that wearing a uniform and carrying a gun made the guards feel superior. It happened to me also. I began to change when I saw how much power I had over the prisoners. I started to feel that the prison was my second home and my job was to teach them to do whatever we told them to."

One guard, José Torres, admitted that his work as a guard also changed him. "When I began working as a prison guard," he says, "my wife told me that I was changing. She saw me learning to be like the other guards, emotionally hard and not afraid to use my power. We were authorized to punish the prisoners if they broke the rules. Sometimes I felt I was being excessive, and I can see now that I became like the others, treating them more like animals than like humans."

De Tavira documented the practice whereby wealthy inmates and drug lords are able to attain special privileges because of their financial power.[20] The power of drug lords has also contributed to escapes by high-profile criminals. In addition, De Tavira found that much of this violence in Mexican prisons has been motivated by opposing groups fighting for the control of drugs, money, and privileges.

Perhaps the prisoners who receive the worst abuse are those who have been sent to prison for sexual offenses. Juan Dávila remembers one day when they brought in two young men who had been convicted of raping a twenty-seven-year-old woman. "These men had been beaten before they even arrived at the prison. Our cells were not locked so we were free to walk around during the day. When everyone found out what these men were in for, they were beaten some more. Almost everyone took their turn. I remember thinking I was glad I wasn't in for a sexual crime. I don't believe those men received any medical attention from the guards during the four or five days they experienced this beating. They were eventually moved to another cell for protection."

Julio Paredes described a similar experience. "Three days after they put me there," he says, "an older man was brought into the prison. One of the prison officials let it be known that this man was there for molesting his nine-year-old stepdaughter. At night I could hear his screams for mercy. I am not sure how many people did it, or even who it was, but someone beat the old man pretty bad. One afternoon some officials came for him. They pulled him through the sewage where it overflowed between two cells. They held his face in it for a while. It frightened me to hear the others cheering on the officials."

The Drug Connection in Mexican Prisons

The increasing flow of drugs across the Mexican border has had an enormous impact on what happens in Mexican prisons. On the one hand, the major drug traffickers use their considerable power and wealth to buy favorable treatment in prison. Those with less power, however, may find themselves the target of abuse or torture. These "mules," or lower-level drug runners, are often pressured to reveal where they have hidden their drugs or drug money. Manuel Robledo, who was arrested for transporting illegal drugs in Mexico, experienced such treatment. "The *judiciales* tortured me until I couldn't talk," he says. "I didn't have enough money to pay what they were asking for. They asked one large sum to avoid more torture and an even larger amount for my freedom. My wife heard about what they were doing and became concerned that the torturer would leave my body severely damaged. She was finally able to get a small amount of money from our friends. Then, at last, the judiciales stopped torturing me. I wasn't released until six months later when my wife somehow came up with the huge amount of money they required for my release."

Rolando Villa, a Mexican American, was caught by Mexican police in the process of transporting drugs across the border. Like many lower-level operatives in the drug trade, he experienced abuse and torture for the first week of his confinement. He finally managed to pay his way out of it by buying off his tormentors. He commented, "Two thousand dollars is a cheap price to pay for peace of mind and relaxation."

Not only has the flow of drugs increased the rates of incarceration for drug offenses, but the huge amounts of money behind the drug trade lead to corruption, bribery, and torture. In addition, drugs seem to be increasingly common in Mexican prisons. Many of the inmates who were interviewed explained that it is relatively easy to get drugs in Mexican prisons. One young man, José, said, "I never broke my drug habit while in prison because getting drugs was no problem as long as the guards were paid off."

Conclusion

Sometimes, people are "scared straight" by what happens to them in Mexico. Most often, however, they experience scars that last a lifetime. Teens from Texas often go to Mexico, for example, for "a little harmless fun." All too often, they experience harsh reality at the hands of Mexican police, in Mexican jails, or in tragic automobile accidents.

Some might argue that the "reality therapy" of the Mexican criminal justice system can have positive results. While there is little doubt that some individuals will learn from it, the harshness of life in Mexican jails and prisons seems to have, with most, the opposite effect. We witnessed this most clearly in the case, mentioned in the chapter opening, of the young woman who died the night she was released from prison in Mexico. The availability of drugs in prison and the corrupting influence of money seem to reinforce, rather than reform, deviance in many who go through the system.

Finally, it is obvious to us that the level of corruption among Mexican law enforcement agencies has reached epidemic proportions. Most Mexicans seem to have recognized this, though the cultural and structural aspects of corruption have become extremely resistant to reform. In recent years, the increased demand for drugs in the United States has seriously compounded this problem. It is hard for the United States to point a finger of blame at Mexico when our appetites and our dollars seem to be feeding the problem. And though the attendant problems are felt everywhere in both countries, those who live along the border are again the most seriously affected.

Dropping Out

WITH JOHN CAVAZOS

There were nine of us living in a small, two-bedroom house. My dad worked as a plumber, painter, or anything he could find work in. My two older brothers dropped out in the tenth grade to help our dad out. We didn't have enough money to buy new clothes, so we usually wore the same clothes two to three times a week. My oldest sister got pregnant, married, and then dropped out. I ended up dropping out in the eleventh grade to work in order to bring money to help the family out. Times got a little better so that my two younger brothers and my younger sister were able to graduate.

M any families in South Texas experience situations similar to that described here by Belinda, a twenty-two-year-old dropout. As she indicates, economic pressures and other problems contributed greatly to her having to drop out. Dropping out of school will also make it difficult for her own children to rise above her economic level.[1]

Though dropping out is a serious problem anywhere in the United States, it is particularly acute in South Texas. In the United States as a whole, 19.8 percent of the adult population (twenty-five years of age or older) has not completed high school, while in Texas, 24.3 percent of adults in this age category are noncompleters. In Hidalgo County, roughly half of the adult population (49.5 percent) has not completed high school.[2] In neighboring Starr County, the situation is even worse; 65.5 percent of adults have not completed high school.[3]

Though dropping out affects many low-income families, it seems to influence Hispanics disproportionately. Figure 9.1 indicates how the dropout rate of Hispanics over a thirty-year period compares with the rates for Anglos and Blacks.

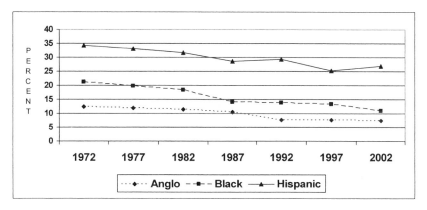

FIG. 9.1. Percent of U.S. high school dropouts (status dropouts) among persons sixteen to twenty-four years old, by race/ethnicity, 1972 to 2002 (status dropouts are sixteen to twenty-four years old, are not enrolled in school, and have not completed a school program, regardless of when they left school. Sources: U.S. Department of Commerce, Bureau of the Census, Current Population Survey, unpublished data; U.S. Department of Education, National Center for Education Statistics, Dropout Rates in the United States, October 2002)

Figure 9.1 reveals several important patterns. First, though Blacks also have a higher dropout rate than Whites (Anglos), their rate has declined considerably in the past thirty years and was only 5 percent higher than the White rate in 2002. Though the dropout rate has also declined somewhat for Hispanics, it is still almost four times greater than the rate for Anglos.

Family income, of course, significantly affects the dropout rate. Still, Blacks have approximately the same average family income as Hispanics. So income and poverty by themselves do not sufficiently explain why the Hispanic dropout rate is so high. In this chapter we will explore a variety of possible explanations for this situation, considering a number of questions:

— Can the vastly higher dropout rate for Hispanics, as compared to other ethnic groups, be explained better by personal, by cultural, or by structural factors?
— How does the proximity to the U.S.-Mexico border affect the dropout rate?
— Why are Mexican immigrant children so much more likely to drop out of school than other generations?

—Do bilingual education classes really help native Spanish speakers complete school, or do they contribute to a negative stigma and to lower expectations?

We will begin our examination of these issues by looking at some possible causes of the high Hispanic dropout rate. Later, we'll also look at the most important effects of dropping out. Let's start, however, by looking at how the dropout situation has changed for South Texas residents over time.

Then and Now

In our interviews with dropouts from earlier time periods, bigotry and exploitation played a much larger and more obvious role, especially in South Texas. One fifty-five-year-old woman, for example, recounted her school experience. "One morning during math class, the teacher called upon a boy from Mexico to answer a question. The boy, who was named Samuel, still couldn't speak English very well. After her question, he just sat there staring at the teacher with a blank expression. She repeated the question and he reacted the same way. Then, the teacher yelled, 'Samuel you stupid Mexican! Go to the corner.' I was totally shocked and afraid because I didn't speak English very well either. I knew that he knew the answer. He just didn't understand what the teacher was asking. As a result, Samuel never came back to school again."[4]

For many of these older adults who never finished school, cultural and economic factors also played a somewhat larger role than we find today. Maria, a sixty-six-year-old woman, for example, described why she never finished school. "We lived at a ranch," she says, "and had to walk a mile to get to the place where the bus would pick us up for school. My father didn't want me and my sisters to go to school because we had to pass a citrus orchard and he said that some men had caught women and raped them there. My mother couldn't leave the younger children alone to walk with us. When we later moved into town, my father still didn't want us to go to school. We didn't have shoes and he wouldn't buy us any because his brother-in-law told him it would be a waste of time and money and wouldn't accomplish anything. When we tried to go to school barefoot, my father got mad and said that women didn't need to go to school, that their husbands were supposed to support them. He said men had to go to school because they have to work and support their wife."

Though the reasons why Hispanics drop out of school may have changed over the years, their high dropout rate is still several times the rate of other low-income groups. For many observers, this remains something of a mystery.[5]

Methodology

Most of the ethnographic accounts contained in this chapter were obtained from approximately 180 in-depth interviews that were conducted in 2002–2003, as part of a special project using college student interviewers to determine why Hispanics in Valley schools drop out in such large numbers. In addition, we added four items to the Perceptions of Deviance Survey, also administered in 2002–2003 (N = 424), to determine whether there are any significant differences among different generations of Mexican-origin people in their attitudes about school and dropping out.

Causes of Dropping Out

PERSONAL AND STRUCTURAL FACTORS

Most of our ethnographic accounts of dropping out suggest that most individuals quit school for a combination of reasons. The factors most clearly visible, both to dropouts themselves and to outside observers, are personal choices and personal characteristics. Less visible are structural factors. Often, even dropouts themselves do not sense the importance of structural factors, such as economic conditions and the ways that schools can create problems. Thus, when young people say they quit school because of a family crisis, economic need, boredom, or poor grades, they may fail to see that a variety of structural factors helped create these personal problems. Miguel, for example, says, "In high school, I just started messing up, getting low grades and flunking classes. I started hating school, thinking it was a waste of time. I was skipping all the time and stopped doing any homework. I finally realized I didn't want to go to school anymore, so I stopped going."

Miguel would seem to be a classic case of a dropout who quit for purely personal reasons, including poor choices and just maybe even just plain laziness. If we stop to ask why he made such choices, and why he just gave up, we might discover a bad economic situation, a school system poorly suited to motivate Hispanic kids, and a system of weak support from family members, peers, and school personnel. Structural causes, which are less obvious than personal causes, often have the most profound impact.

As Hess indicates, researchers have historically looked for reasons for dropping out by examining deficiencies and problems among dropouts.[6] As a result, much of the research to date has focused primarily on demographic variables.[7] Although individual characteristics are certainly important factors, there are many structural and cultural factors that shape such decisions. Among these would be the structural characteristics of schools, the influence of peers, family environment, and other sociocultural influences. We will start by examining some of the factors related to individual characteristics and then relate these to structural and cultural factors.

ECONOMIC NEED   There is ample evidence that individuals from low-income families have a much higher dropout rate than students from middle- or upper-income families. In the year 2000, for example, 10 percent of fifteen- through twenty-four-year-olds from families in the bottom 20 percent of all families dropped out of school, compared to 1.6 percent of youths from families in the upper 20 percent of family incomes.[8]

Our interviews with Hispanic dropouts revealed that economic pressure has a major impact. Jose Zarate, for example, explains the economic pressures of trying to stay in school. "At the beginning of the school year," he says, "the teacher would pass out a list of all the materials we would need to buy. I would take this sheet home to show my mother and she would tell me that I would have to wait a few days because she was short of money. My father had been laid off from his job and we were trying to survive on food stamps and a monthly welfare check. Sometimes, weeks would go by before we had enough money to buy my materials. Then I was behind and felt there was no way I could catch up with the rest of the class. It really depressed me to think I would have to spend another year in the same grade. After years of going through that same ordeal, I just decided to quit. Then I would hang around with other dropouts from my neighborhood all day.

Sometimes, we would get together and would go to a rival neighborhood school and cause havoc."

Elia Garcia also felt severe economic pressure prior to dropping out of school. "There were many times," she remembers, "when I had to miss school because my younger siblings were sick and there was no way my parents' boss would let either one of them take time off. Their *jefe* would tell them if their kids made them miss work, then they should get another job. Their boss said that if either of them 'slacked off' or called in sick, they would both be in jeopardy of losing their jobs."

It would be easy to explain this harsh treatment as insensitivity on the part of their boss. While that is true, it ignores the impact of the structure of work in the United States. Parents in low-wage jobs generally have much less flexibility in meeting their children's needs than more affluent parents. As a result, they are frequently unable to stay home to help a sick child or otherwise meet the school-related needs of their children. As Beth Shulman points out in *The Betrayal of Work: How Low-Wage Jobs Fail 30 Million Americans*:

> Children of low-wage workers get less parental time and supervision than children of parents in higher-wage jobs. Their parents' jobs provide fewer vacation days and holidays, less family leave and sick leave, and many of their parents must work two jobs or overtime hours. The lack of time off and job flexibility deprive these workers' children of parental care when they are sick, have a problem at school, have an emergency, or just need the day-to-day attention that all children require.[9]

Though many Hispanic students leave school to help support their family, neither their culture nor their family is mainly responsible for their status as dropouts. Structural failure, rather than a lack of individual will, seems to be the major problem. This is supported by responses to an item on our Perceptions of Deviance Survey. In this survey, we asked respondents with family origins in Mexico how good or how bad it is for high school students to drop out to help their parents financially. The responses are reported in Figure 9.2.

As Figure 9.2 indicates, Mexican-origin people from each of the five generation-score categories uniformly regarded dropping out of school as bad even when it was done to help one's family financially. This similarity

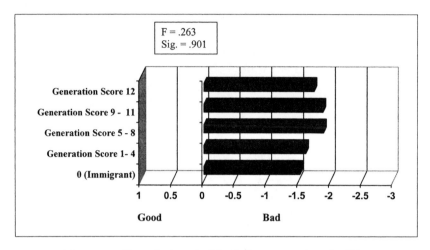

FIG. 9.2. Mean scores (from +5 to −5) of South Texas respondents in different generational categories selecting each level of how good or how bad it is for a high school student to drop out of school to help his or her parents financially

of responses among each generation category tends to refute the contention that Mexican culture does not value education or that Mexican immigrants and their children have ambivalent feelings about dropping out.

Responses to another item in the same survey further reinforce this finding. We asked respondents to indicate how good or how bad it is for high school students to drop out of school if they are failing many of their classes. The results, again organized by categories of generation scores, are presented in Figure 9.3.

Here also, respondents in each of the generation categories uniformly saw such behavior as bad. In fact, the responses on this item were even more negative than those related to dropping out to help one's family financially.

Responses on a third item showed a stronger relationship to generational status. We asked, "How good or how bad is it for high school students to miss school once or twice a year to have fun with friends?" These results are presented in Figure 9.4.

These results show a significant pattern among those interviewed toward increasing acceptance of "playing hooky" with each additional generation of Mexican-origin people in the United States. These results are reinforced by an examination of the same question in relation to the racial/ethnic/national status of respondents, as presented in Figure 9.5.

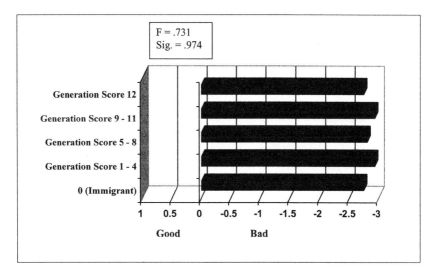

FIG. 9.3. Mean scores (from +5 to −5) of South Texas respondents in different generational categories selecting each level of how good or how bad it is for a high school student to drop out of school if he or she is failing many classes

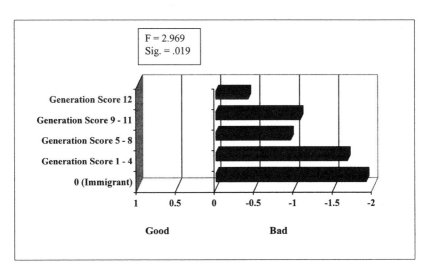

FIG. 9.4. Mean scores (from +5 to −5) of South Texas respondents in different generational categories selecting each level of how good or how bad it is for high school students to miss school once or twice a year to have fun with friends

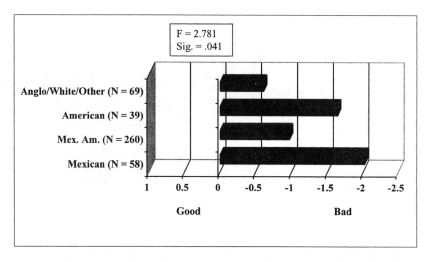

FIG. 9.5. Mean scores of South Texas respondents in self-described racial/ethnic/national categories selecting each level of how good or how bad it is for high school students to miss school once or twice a year to have fun with friends

Together, these findings support the idea that Mexican-origin people place considerable value on education (at least in terms of not missing school to have fun), though economic pressures may lead some individuals to quit school. As the final report of the Hispanic Dropout Project explains,

> Many Hispanic students often need to contribute materially to their families, and this need for a paycheck often causes even successful students to respond to daily crises rather than to maintain a future orientation. If students need jobs to meet their responsibilities, schools should help them get part-time job placements and work with businesses to develop effective schedules and learning opportunities that help students, their employers, and the schools.[10]

In some cases, the *stigma* associated with poverty, as much as poverty itself, promotes dropping out. Horacio, for example, explains, "One day I was on the bus going to school, and a friend of mine asked me why I wore the same clothes every day. All the other kids heard what he said and started laughing at me. I didn't say anything because I was mad and embarrassed. I just sat there. When I got home after school, I told my mom what had happened. She told me we didn't have enough money, but when we did she would buy me some new clothes. I didn't want to go to school anymore because I didn't want to have anybody make fun of me. After a while, I just quit going."

In addition to the stigma of poverty, the perceived financial benefits of finishing school must be weighed against its costs. Rumberger, for example, reports,

> Unemployment rates in October 1985 for White youths who dropped out of high school during the 1984–85 school year were almost twice as high as for high school graduates from the year before who were not enrolled in college. But for Hispanics, dropouts had an unemployment rate only slightly higher than high school graduates.[11]

An economic system that fails to reward Hispanic graduates with better jobs than dropouts may make dropping out seem like a rational choice.[12] The structure of opportunity in and out of school is a significant factor in decisions to stay in school or drop out.

MIGRANT FARMWORK   Hispanic migrant farmworkers in South Texas experience particularly strong economic pressures.[13] Frances Duarte comes from a migrant family. As the sixth of seven children, she was one of the few in her family to make it to high school. Although she didn't graduate, she at least finished the ninth grade, which was considered a real accomplishment in her family. "We were poor," she says, "and we all had to help during farming season. I was constantly falling behind at school." Often, each fall when she came back to start school, Frances was assigned to a different elementary school because there was no room in the one closest to her home. Frances had already attended three elementary schools in McAllen by the time she reached the sixth grade. Such structurally induced instability can prove detrimental to a child's learning.

Migrant students are forever trying to balance the demands of migrant life with those of school. Monica reports, "We had to work in the fields with our parents on weekends and then make sure we were catching up on all the missed schoolwork. It was really hard adjusting to new teachers and new faces while trying to catch up with what we had already missed."

Special programs designed to help migrant students overcome such difficulties may actually exacerbate the problem. Some migrant students found themselves placed in different classrooms, separated from "normal" students because they were migrants. Even when they were kept with other students, however, the perceived need to give them specialized treatment contributed to their status as "different." Julia remembers feeling apart from the other children in her classes. "I remember hearing the bell ring at four o'clock," she says, "and seeing all the other kids go home. Then we would have to stay an extra hour to get special help. It seemed so unfair. We always knew that somehow there was a difference between us and the non-migrants. As I look back on it now, I think that the school administrators thought they were not treating us any differently. In that last hour, we would have to do assignment after assignment. I always felt so dumb because they made us stay and do extra work."

There is some irony in the high dropout rate among migrant children, because many of them like school. Eriberto, for example, is a ten-year-old who likes the schools up north where his parents work. He says, "I like going to school because it's really nice in there and no bugs will be biting you. When you're in school, the sun doesn't make you too hot, and they have the water that's really cold and tastes good. They give you cookies and milk and it's a lot of fun sitting on your chair and talking with the other kids. One boy in my class wanted to know why I was going to leave soon. When I told him, he thought I was trying to fool him. I explained that I had to go because my daddy picks crops and we move along and have to attend school where he works. Sometimes it's embarrassing when you make friends in those schools because they would see us in the fields working and we know how some people feel about farmworkers."[14]

School is especially hard for undocumented migrant farmworkers from Mexico. Osvaldo, a Mexican seventeen-year-old struggling to stay in school, expressed surprise that his interviewer, a Mexican American, wanted to speak with him. "I'm just a poor Mexican," he says. "We don't want any problems. I came to the United States because my father was here. He wanted us to have a better life than we had in Matamoros. I live with my father, my mother, and my three brothers and a sister. My aunt and uncle live with us with their two sons. The house is small but at least I have a house. The kids at school make fun of me. They call me a poor wetback. All I want is for them to leave me alone. I just want to go to school and learn. In the summer I work in the fields or in packing sheds. I help my father so we can pay the bills and eat. All we want to do is work and better our lives for us and our families."

Osvaldo's interviewer did not believe that he would actually finish school. In addition to his economic problems, he is having problems with schoolwork and with English, and he has fallen behind other kids his age. Thus, though many of his problems have an economic base, they are also structural, related to issues of immigration, school, family, and culture. A brief examination of each of these structural elements will illustrate.

IMMIGRATION STATUS   The importance of one's immigration status is often misunderstood or understated by many researchers. In Osvaldo's case, dropping out is closely related to his language ability, his family's occupational status, his self-image, and his educational aspirations. But another, somewhat hidden, factor may outweigh all of these. If Osvaldo's parents move frequently in search of work, are apprehended by immigration agents, or go back to Mexico for some other reason, Osvaldo will likely drop out of school to accompany them, perhaps without even notifying his school.

In the year 2000, 44.2 percent of Hispanic young adults in the United States who were born outside of the country were school dropouts. In contrast, non-Hispanic immigrant children had a dropout rate of only 7.2 percent.[15] Clearly, immigrant status is a key factor here. Indeed, when *the* foreign born are excluded, the dropout rate for Hispanic youths (ages sixteen through twenty-four years of age) falls from the overall Hispanic rate of 27.8 percent to a rate of approximately only 15 percent.[16] This is only a few percentage points higher than the rate for Black youth. Thus, the "great puzzle" of the high Hispanic dropout rate may not be the great mystery that some researchers portray.[17]

So why do foreign-born Hispanics have a dropout rate of 44.2 percent when the rate for children in other immigrant groups is only 7.4 percent? Much of the problem, of course, is economic. Mexican immigrants tend to come from a much lower socioeconomic level than other immigrant groups. In addition, the proximity of the United States to Mexico brings in much larger numbers of undocumented immigrants.

Such factors show up in school-based data on dropouts in Texas. Data compiled in 2000 for the Texas Legislature, for example, reports reasons given for leaving a Texas school.[18] When high school completers and students who moved to another educational setting are excluded, reasons for dropping out can be calculated. These reasons, and the percentage of students who named each, are presented in Figure 9.6.

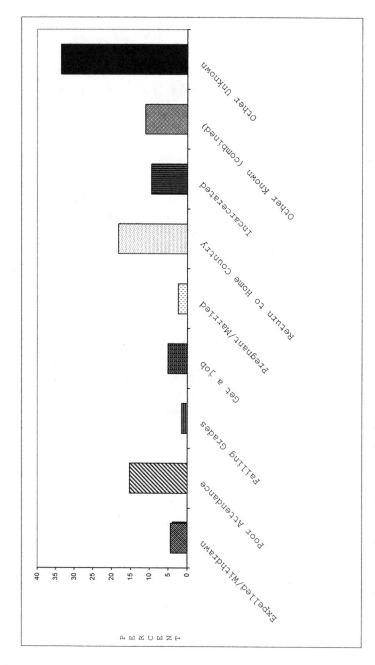

FIG. 9.6.   Percent students leaving Texas schools in 1997–1999 giving each category of reasons for leaving school

The data in Figure 9.6 show that approximately one-third of dropouts leave for unknown reasons. The highest *known* factor (18 percent), however, is "return to home country." This supports the suggestion that many foreign-born Hispanic students drop out of school because they return to their home in Mexico (or some other foreign country).

Their reasons for leaving the U.S., of course, vary. Some, like one of the young men we interviewed at the Evins Regional Juvenile Center (described at the beginning of Chapter 7), left school because his parents were deported. Another immigrant student, Judit, dropped out to return to Mexico for a few years. Though Judit finished school in Mexico, she would have been listed as a dropout.

Another family, the Garcías, took their children back to Mexico for different reasons. Mr. García, who had moved his family to Houston, Texas, in 1989, says, "When we got there things went well until our daughter started high school. Immediately, we started having problems with her. At first, my wife said that it was just her age and that we shouldn't worry about it. After a year, though, we found out that she was drinking and using drugs. When she also started getting bad grades in school, we really got worried. That's when we decided to return to Mexico. I think that's the best thing that we ever did."

Immigrants take their children back to Mexico for economic reasons as well. Julio brought his family to the Valley about three years ago, putting all of his children in school. He found work at a farm and then at a warehouse, but it wasn't enough to keep up with housing and other payments. "That is why I decided to go back to Mexico," he says. "If I'm going to suffer, I want to do it in my own country."

Regardless of why children with ties to Mexico return there, counting them as "dropouts" significantly inflates the Latino dropout rate. The preceding stories suggest that many are not really dropouts, since they continue school in Mexico.

PARENTAL SUPPORT—CULTURAL AND STRUCTURAL FACTORS

Much of the literature on the high Latino dropout rate blames low parental involvement for the failure of their children to finish high school.[19] This blaming of parents generally falls into two major categories. One is a "culture of poverty" approach that blames Hispanic parents for instilling negative values (e.g., low value on education, poor self-image, live-for-today attitudes, machismo, etc.). One study of school personnel revealed abundant evidence of such stereotyping among teachers and administrators.

> School personnel had many negative misconceptions about the motivations and values of parents. There was widespread belief that parents did not sufficiently value education and that they were unwilling to give sufficient time to rearing their children and participating in school activities . . . We found parents to be fearful and alienated from school authorities.[20]

The second approach to blaming parents examines the "structure of poverty," identifying conditions in other institutions of society that make it difficult for parents to fully help their children in school. Recall the situation of Elia Garcia, whose parents had a boss who threatened to fire them if they took time off to help their children. Such situations are not uncommon for low-income families because the structure of work in the United States is much less flexible for working-class parents than for middle-class parents.[21] Working-class parents are more likely to experience pressures for overtime, night shifts, layoffs, and temporary or seasonal work. They are also less likely to have adequate transportation, child care, insurance, or good health. Each of these structural factors limits their support for their child's education.

This is illustrated by Fabiana, a seventeen-year-old junior in high school. "It was the worst news I could have heard," she says. "I had one year to go in high school to graduate and I was real excited about going off to college. When my mother passed away, that was the end to all my hopes and dreams. I had five younger brothers and sisters and I had to accept the reality that I had to drop out of school to help my dad raise the younger children. I began working for a neighborhood store for minimum wage. I still hope that one day I can get my GED and fulfill those dreams I once had."

Although there are some elements of Mexican culture that might help explain why Fabiana dropped out of school (such as the expectation that she needed to help raise her brothers and sisters), the structural situation seems far more important. Not only was the family structured in a way that required her assistance in the home, but the structure of society on the South Texas border provides little assistance from any source except immediate family.

We did find a few cases where the lack of parental support might be related more to cultural factors. Evangelina, for example, says, "I come home from school and go straight to my room, where I stay long hours doing my homework and studying. My mother enters the room and starts nagging me that I need to help her in the kitchen and help clean the house. When

I explain to her that I am taking difficult courses she looks at me and says that won't help me find a husband and that I need to learn how to cook instead of wasting so much time on my schoolwork. I tell her that I won't be doing the cooking because I will be making enough money to have a maid. My mother laughs and tells me that he would be better off marrying the maid. She can get really annoying because she expects me to be like her but I don't want a life of servitude."

Parental culture might also be a factor in the case of Alberto, who also failed to finish school. "I was always getting into fistfights with guys from school," he says, "because they would always make fun of my family and me. They would make fun of everything from the clothes I wore to what I ate at lunchtime. After a fight, I would get sent home early and my mother would yell at me. Finally, she told me that instead of being useless I needed to get to work, so she had me do chores around the house. My behavior got so bad that my mother would depend on me getting dismissed from class early to help her around the house. My dad didn't think much about my fights. All he could say was, 'Si vas a pelear, vale más que ganes' [If you're going to fight, you'd better win]. He told me that if I didn't win I better not even disgrace him with my presence. The final straw was when my mother had sewn up a new shirt for me (for being such a great help around the house) to wear at school and some dumb kids pushed me into a mud puddle. I was so furious that I beat one guy up so bad he had to go to the hospital. The principal finally told me that I would no longer be able to come back into school until he had had a talk with both of my parents. My mother agreed to go but my father refused. He said all they wanted to do was criticize his son and make him feel like an uneducated fool. He also believed he would not be able to understand what the principal was saying since he couldn't speak English. That was the final word. From then on I became mama's permanent helper."

In Alberto's case, some observers might say that his father's insistence that he win fights, along with his refusal to talk to the principal, were caused by Mexican culture. Though culture certainly is a factor, asserting that culture as the cause of the problem would completely miss the point that schools often have a culture of their own that is unresponsive to language differences and that permits bullying.[22]

Some students who were interviewed did identify low educational aspirations of their parents as a primary problem. Carmen, one student who graduated and went to an Ivy League university, did so in spite of parental resistance. She states, "When I heard that I had gotten into Brown University, I was so excited! I immediately began thinking of what I was going to take with me up to Providence. Then I stopped dead in my tracks when I realized that I was going to have to tell my parents about this. My father had wanted me to stay close to home to work on our ranch full-time. He didn't even push me to attend the University of Texas–Pan American. It's like he didn't even want me to attend college at all. Most of my family didn't even graduate from high school and no one had ever attended college before. I wanted to be the first to go to college. I wanted to come back with a degree from Brown University. When I finally did tell my parents, they asked how I was planning to pay for college and how I would make it surrounded by a lot of rich, White kids. That just added to my worries about leaving home."

As appealing as it might be to say that Carmen's parents did not value education, other cultural factors might account for their lack of support. Many Mexican parents, for example, have strong beliefs that unmarried children (especially daughters) should live at home until they are married. This is illustrated by an interview with Jaquelín, a medical student from Monterrey, Mexico (visiting Texas). She was asked, for example, "What is the one thing from your culture that you would not change or give up, no matter what?" She answered, "I will never send my child to live on his own at eighteen. My parents would never do that to me. In fact I am not supposed to leave the house until I get married. This has never been said but I am sure that not even my brother is supposed to leave home until he gets married. From what I see here [in Texas], things are different. Parents don't seem to care for their children."

Thus, the American interpretation of parents' unwillingness to let a child go to college away from home as parental indifference to education might well be a form of cultural bias.[23] In Carmen's case, her parents opposed her leaving home to go to college not because they didn't value education, but because they felt that her going away to college would be irresponsible parenting. It seems that some educators and researchers misinterpret parental reluctance to support certain aspects of U.S. education.

A similar case of cultural bias may be involved in the different meaning that "dropping out" has for Mexican immigrants. Several second-generation dropouts indicated that their parents felt that ten or so years of school was probably enough. Antonio told his interviewer, "My parents never made it past the third grade. They told me, 'You have much more education than we did and you speak English. That should be enough to get a good job.'"

Though some may believe that Antonio's parents do not value education very highly, a closer look reveals that a more important factor is their idea of what makes a "good education." The cultural difference lies in how much education is enough. We don't claim that U.S. parents who fail to push their son or daughter to get a Ph.D. after graduating from college don't value education. In reality, a parent's idea of "enough education" is influenced by his or her culture and/or educational attainment.

Even so, we found many parents who themselves had low educational attainment who nevertheless held great aspirations for their children to get all the education they could. One migrant mother, Lydia, says, "I wanted all my kids to go to college. We used to migrate a lot. I did not want them to do that for the rest of their lives. I wanted them to do better. I made sure they always did their homework and made sure they did not fall behind. All except one of my children went to college. He joined the military. Education is important. People need to go to school. It may be hard but it is worth it."

In some cases, parents may be inappropriately blamed for their child's dropping out of school.[24] Lisa, a young woman who recently dropped out, attempts to blame her mother for her own failure to finish school. "I got pregnant," she says. "That's why I dropped out. It was either take care of my baby or go to school. Unfortunately, I was not blessed with a mother that was willing to take care of the baby, so I had to quit."

MARRIAGE/PREGNANCY Though several programs allow young women like Lisa to continue school, there are many reasons why they still drop out.[25] René is a fourteen-year-old who says, "My mom and dad told me that I couldn't live at home anymore because I was pregnant. They were very disappointed with me because my sister is doing so well and is attending UT-Austin and I guess they expected the same from me. I had to move into Bobby's house. I'm not going to school right now because I'm eight months pregnant and I don't want to go to the Teenage Parenting Program. There are girls there that don't like me. So I will just go to school next year. Bobby's mom helps me out a lot. Bobby and I are planning on getting married after he graduates from high school."

Sometimes teen pregnancy combined with having to raise a child alone spurs the young woman on to greater educational achievement. Pilar Gamboa, aged sixteen, described its effect on her. "When the test showed I was pregnant," she says, "I wanted to die because my boyfriend suddenly wanted nothing to do with me and I knew my parents would be very angry. They wanted to send me to Mexico with an aunt, but I said that I would not go. The birth of my son changed my life forever. I was not going to give up on my education and I was not about to give my baby up, so I had to make sure that I could take care of him. The high school has a day care center for teen mothers and that really helps a lot. I was never too good in school, but now I have someone who really loves me and depends on me. Now I have the initiative that I have always needed to do well in school."

Other personal factors going on in the individual lives of dropouts also contribute to their decision to quit school. Most of the following cases clearly show that not one, but many, factors are involved. In addition, it is clear that structural and cultural factors are frequently behind these seemingly personal choices.

DOING POORLY/BAD GRADES   Twenty-three-year-old Hugo dropped out of school several years ago. "To tell you the truth," he says, "I don't care anymore. As long as I have my barrio and my friends, I don't care about school. I have the women I want and besides, it's too late for me. Like I said before, I am a 'burro' [dummy]. I don't feel ashamed. Also, the teachers thought I was crazy. My mom was crazy, so I am too. This is my reason I can't finish school. I am crazy!" (He laughs.)

Most young people do care a great deal about what others think of them. Estela talked about how school was hard for her. "I never was good in math," she says. "I never could understand how some of the problems were solved. Still, I never asked questions because I didn't want people to think I was stupid. When it was time to take the tests, I ended up getting very low grades. My teacher would ask me if I needed help, but I would tell her that I didn't. I started hating school because of this. In high school, I was doing bad in my other classes so I just didn't want to go to school anymore."

Doing poorly in school is a major reason for dropping out. According to data from the National Center for Educational Statistics, 33 percent of sixteen- to twenty-four-year-olds who repeated a grade eventually dropped out of school.[26] Many dropouts themselves give this as the main reason for quitting school. When dropouts were asked why they had dropped out, 39 percent indicated that it was because they were "failing in school."[27]

Armando is a twenty-three-year-old who also dropped out because he was failing. "I've always been hardheaded," he says. Because of this, I did not like school. My parents always pushed my brothers and me to get an education. Even my teachers tried to push me very hard. They tried to help me learn the necessary skills to pass the TAAS exam. Every year from the fifth grade through the eighth grade, I failed it. Still they kept promoting me to the next grade. One teacher that really tried to help was Mr. Granados. Even with all the help he gave me, I still didn't pass it. One day I finally realized that I would never pass the exam, so I decided just to quit school before going to high school.

TROUBLEMAKING/GETTING EXPELLED   Other students report that they quit because they are always in trouble at school.[28] Ruben says, "At first, I was just late to class. Next, I stole hall passes from teachers' desks. I forged some teacher's or the principal's signatures. Then I started skipping classes. They started sending me to the A.E.P. [Alternative Education Program] Center. Sometimes it was for vandalism or drugs. Other times, it was because I got in fights. I have been expelled twice. The first time, two years ago, was because they caught me with marijuana. Last year it was because of a rumble. I hurt this guy pretty bad. Now they're talking about hitting me with a Penal Code violation that would get me expelled, so I just quit going."

Pedro is a twenty-nine-year-old male who finally dropped out when he was twenty-one years old. Pedro is an agreeable young man with many friends, but he is struggling without an education and has a drinking problem. Pedro was the youngest of five children and the one with the most problems in school. He failed the eighth grade and had to repeat it. "That's when everything started to go wrong," he says. "In high school I became a goofball in the hallways and in the classroom. It was nothing out of the ordinary, but I was disruptive. When I was sixteen I had a lot of trouble and got sent to the alternative school. When they let me back in, I set off a very big Mexican firecracker called a *paloma* in one of the hallways. That got me expelled for a year. While I was out, I started working and making money so I decided to stay out for another year. Later, my parents insisted that I go back. When I tried to go back, they told me I had to return to a different high school because of new boundaries. I was there for a few months until they told me that I was too old and that I would have to pay $600 per semester to continue. I only needed one semester and two credits to graduate but I didn't have the money and my parents refused to pay for something that I should have done for free in four years. So I quit school and never returned."

Pedro's interviewer was one of his older brothers. "When I asked him why he did all the things he did," he says, "he sheepishly said that he just wanted to be cool. Now, he seems to be more and more disappointed with life and it shows in his heavy drinking."

Felipe dropped out at age eighteen after four years of being a freshman. When Felipe entered high school, he began to use alcohol and drugs, sometimes getting high during school. He finally dropped out when he was caught smoking marijuana. He was sent to county jail and then to a youth village for thirty days. When he returned to school, he decided to drop out, thinking that he just wasn't smart enough to complete school. When his interviewer asked him what he thought about the future, he said, "I never think about the future. I just live for the moment. My mom does try to encourage me, but my dad's in jail. I'm looking for a job, but I'm still not too concerned about the future."

DRUGS   Many young Latinos who drop out of school mention drugs as a reason for dropping out, though few claim that it was the major factor that influenced them to quit school. Besides the relation to getting in trouble with school and police officials, drugs are also mentioned by some as a lead-in to the "wrong crowd." In addition, a few mentioned that marijuana has a tendency to lead its users to not care much about school or their future.[29]

Luis is a nineteen-year-old who associates drugs with getting expelled. "I had some marijuana for personal use in my locker," he says, and one day they brought some drug-sniffing dogs to school. I was busted for possession and was expelled from school and never went back. Boy, do I regret that day. Now I have three daughters and no job to support my wife and them. We do get food stamps and my parents help us with some of the bills. Everywhere I ask for a job, they say I need at least a high school diploma or a GED. I don't have either one."

Many of the dropouts we interviewed blame themselves for dropping out. Much of the research on Hispanic dropouts tends to "blame the victim," treating factors associated with the dropouts themselves as the primary cause of the high rate among Hispanics. Though such factors certainly do contribute to decisions to drop out, structural factors within the schools and the community also contribute heavily to high dropout rates. The structure of schools, for example, as well as the personnel in them, significantly affects these rates.[30] A brief examination of several structural school-related factors will illustrate how they might contribute to the high rate of school failure among Hispanic youths in South Texas.

THE STRUCTURE OF SCHOOLS AND COMMUNITY

The organization of U.S. schools on the basis of neighborhood residence is a structural feature that affects the dropout rate. Children are assigned to a school based on their residence, but these assignments change as enrollment patterns change. One young student, Frances, said that she had to attend a different school each year. At the beginning of the school year, they would tell her there was no room in her previous school. She had attended three separate elementary schools by the time she reached sixth grade. This instability can be detrimental to a child's learning and social adjustment.

NEIGHBORHOOD SCHOOLS AND SOCIAL CLASS   The structural feature of neighborhood schools is, in turn, related to social class. Because of the neighborhood concept of U.S. public education, schools from low-income neighborhoods often have disproportionate numbers of students with economic problems. Often, such schools concentrate on controlling behavior as opposed to fostering the natural curiosity of children. Schools in such neighborhoods can turn children off to learning. Summarizing several decades of research on teacher behavior in schools, Levine and Levine state, for example, "There is a tendency for schools with many lower-status students to place more stress on rote learning and discipline than do middle-class schools, which put relatively more emphasis on creative and independent learning."[31]

Lisa, who used to work for at a doctor's office in McAllen, was able to see the effects of such divergent teaching tactics. "Throughout the year," she says, "we invite schools from all around the community to bring students into the office. We give them a background on orthodontic work. It was interesting to see the difference in how teachers responded to their students. Teachers from the more affluent schools came into the office with enthusiasm. The children were allowed to 'Oo!' and 'Ah!' when they walked in. I clearly remember the difference when we had ___ Elementary [located in a poor South McAllen neighborhood]. The teachers all had this disturbed look on their faces, constantly apologizing for the children's excitement. They would snap at the children who dared let out a 'Look at that!' or a 'Wow!' Personally, I experienced fewer disciplinary problems with those students than from the other schools. These students seemed to appreciate the opportunity to learn something new. They all listened attentively and asked questions. The other students weren't too much of a problem, but their behavior was obnoxious at times. Ironically, the group that was least liked by our office staff were the students from a private school. How can we possibly expect students to excel when they are not being challenged to work to their fullest potential?"

TRACKING   Another important structural variable is tracking. Within most South Texas schools, tracking, or the sorting of students into ability groups, is very common.[32] Carmen recalls her years in the public schools. "All the kids were placed in one of three categories in the elementary years," she says. "There were the blue birds, red birds, and the yellow birds. The blue birds spoke English and had been to private kindergartens. The red birds were middle Hispanic kids. And the yellow birds couldn't speak English and had never been to school. It always seemed like a yellow bird was always in yellow-bird classes growing up. That's where they put me. One time, I stole a blue bird's assignment and answered all the questions correctly. I got in trouble for doing someone else's work. I just wanted to prove that I could do more work.

"In high school, there was also a ranking system. There was a first level, second level, and third level. The first level was the college prep courses. I was in the second level, which was a high school degree with an option of going to a junior college. The third level was vocational classes. We didn't associate much with students in the other levels."

This system of tracking creates many problems. "I was accepted to enroll in an advance track at school," says Paula. "That meant I would be taking honor courses. At my school, people in that track are mainly Anglos. When accepted, I was separated from my friends. That didn't go over too well with them. Within weeks they were calling me *prepa* [preppie] and *vendida* [sell-out]. From that point on high school was miserable and I couldn't wait to graduate. Yeah, it would have been easier to make friends with those in my honors classes, but you have to understand—they were not people from my neighborhood."

Perhaps much worse than the separation of children is the stigma attached to the lower tracks. Even when schools think up clever names to disguise the "slow" learners, the children all know which track has the slow children. Angela, for example, says, "I was placed in a class with other Mexican children who were not very good at speaking English. I did not feel so bad until I could see the smart kids were in the other classes."

The investigators from the Hispanic Dropout Project reported that in schools with high dropout rates, "tracking and other forms of ability grouping were used to write off whole segments of the student body."[33] In addition, they found that "low-track classrooms are overcrowded, have the least qualified teachers, have the fewest resources, and experience a low-level curriculum focused on remediation to the virtual exclusion of any new or interesting content."Grouping students by language ability is a form of tracking that strongly affects the dropout rate. Rolando, a fourteen-year-old, remembers his experience with language-based tracking. "I remember being told that I was going to be placed in a special class to help my English," he says. "At first I thought it would be a good idea, but then I saw how other people my age were at higher reading levels than I was. That made me feel stupid." A fifteen-year-old placed in a limited English proficiency (LEP) track made a similar discovery when a complete stranger told her that she was "just another dumb Mexican." Later, someone else who knew no more about her than the track she was in asked her if she was a member of a gang.

The ways schools react to children who don't speak English well may be even more important than the language problem itself. It is very common in South Texas (and elsewhere) for immigrants to be put into special English classes, often in a "bilingual education" program. The isolation and the grouping of these students, however, often results in a stigma of inferiority. Many of the dropouts (and others) we talked to related that in their schools, bilingual students were considered "slow." With older kids, like Victor, bilingual education also emphasizes their foreign origin, opening them up to the pejorative "*mojado*" label, which often gets applied even when they are legal residents or U.S. citizens.

Schools in South Texas that treat Spanish as a deficiency (which happens in many English immersion or bilingual education programs) contribute to this stigmatizing and discrimination. Schools with dual-language programs, in contrast, do not isolate these students. Dual-language programs start with the premise that all students need to be bilingual, teaching Spanish to native English speakers and English to those whose native language is Spanish. In such schools, students like Victor would be considered an asset because they can help someone else learn Spanish. They, in turn, can help him with his English. Unfortunately, few schools in the Rio Grande Valley have dual-language programs. The few that do tend to be in districts with a very low enrollment of Anglo students.

Because schools often get extra funding for each student needing to learn English, they often make decisions more favorable to their own interests than to the needs of the children. Cecilia, the mother of two girls, had enrolled them in a private school for their elementary school years. When they were old enough for middle school, she decided to let them attend the public schools. "After a few days," she says, "I was shocked to hear that the youngest of the two girls had been placed in an ESL [English as a Second Language] class. Because I had said during enrollment that Spanish was the primary language spoken at home, they decided she needed ESL. I was so upset. Both my girls are fluent in English and Spanish. And they speak the correct Spanish; not the Tex-Mex spoken around here. I was raised in Mexico. Spanish is a part of who we are. But that doesn't make us ignorant."

TEACHERS AND COUNSELORS   Problems with teachers and counselors also influence many students' decision to drop out. Many teachers, of course, genuinely try to help low-income students. However, there is a subtle form of both structural and cultural bias against Hispanic students in many schools and classrooms.[34] Teresa, for example, says, "I remember having fun and I did learn, but I always felt like an outsider. The first two years were very hard for me because nobody explained anything to me except in pictures. In high school I felt inferior to anyone who spoke English. The overall message I got in school was that I needed to leave my traditions and language in order to succeed in this country. They also emphasized in school that our parents needed to learn English. There was a time when I felt like everything my family did was wrong because we were Hispanic. For example, when a child has a birthday, aunts, uncles, and grandparents all come to the celebration. I wasn't proud of that, because I knew that in the Anglo culture, kids' parties were for kids only. They never taught us that it was good to be bilingual. They just wanted us to learn English. Now I know better and I embrace both cultures."

Counselors also may contribute to the dropout problem. Fabiana, who was born in Mexico, for example, says, "throughout my four years in high school, I noticed that the counselors never called in the Mexicans to talk about plans after graduation. One day I went to speak to my counselor about different universities. Before I could say much, she cut me off and told me, 'Before you can even think about college you need to take two tests. There is a sign-up sheet for those students wanting to take the test and the government will pick up the tab for *you people* who cannot afford things like this.' I was infuriated but did not want to risk getting into trouble so I let it go and found assistance elsewhere."

Fabiana continues, "Another thing was the scheduling process. Students would line up at tables to ask counselors for the classes they wanted. It never seemed to fail that whenever I went to the electives table, the first thing they offered me was sewing or homemaking. The Mexican boys got offered body shop or woodworking. Meanwhile, the Anglos were offered classes such as sign language, foreign languages, or opportunities to join clubs."

SOCIAL CLASS AND BULLYING   Social class and the ways schools react to class differences are additional structural factors that greatly impact the dropout rate. Often class differences result in class bias and bullying. One interviewer related the story of his brother, Ernesto, a young dropout. He says, "Ernesto is the smartest person that I've ever known! In Mexico, he had a scholarship that paid his full tuition. But when we came here, his teachers and counselors never gave my brother a chance to prove himself. They ended up putting him in special education classes! Other students would make fun of him because his clothes were too old or his shoes were out of style. I hated everyone that made fun of him. Some bullies in school beat him up several times. His teacher could see how he was treated and did nothing about it. Once, he even told the teacher that they were bothering him and the teacher sent *him* to detention for causing trouble. Then, when he got home, my dad hit him twice as hard for making him miss work to go to the school. He thought it was my brother's fault for not wanting to learn. He told him, 'Tú nunca quisiste aprender' [You never wanted to learn]. Can you possibly explain that to me? My brother was put down so many times, he was made fun of, he was humiliated, he was picked on, he was embarrassed, and then he was punished. My dad punished him even more by making him work in the fields before and after school each day. The only thing my brother learned from all this was that he would rather work in the fields than be made fun of at school. Today he is working in a dollar store as a janitor."

These accounts of discrimination by classmates involve more than Mexican students being poorly treated by Mexican American and Anglo students. In each of the preceding two cases, there were strong elements of class bias as well. This is a common experience for students from low-income homes. Maribel Salinas, for example, says, "I remember going to school with torn sandals while all the other little girls had pretty ones. My sisters and I would get one pair of shoes for the whole school year and about four to five dresses. We always wore the same dresses, and I remember always feeling embarrassed. Going to school was a dread for me. I didn't like going because I knew that I would be teased because of the way I was dressed."

The class-based discrimination by peers does not always occur in the form of taunting or bullying. Sometimes it is more subtle. Rosie, for example, says that students judge and rank each other according to where someone sits for lunch. "The elite groups," she says, "all sit in the new cafeteria. The poorer students end up sitting in the old cafeteria. Since the vending machines are in the new cafeteria, when someone poor goes there to buy something, the rich group will look at them as if saying, 'What are you doing here?' One day during lunch, I was looking for an empty seat and found one next to a group of the 'high society' students. I sat there, not thinking anything about it until they all stopped talking and were just looking at me. It was clear I didn't belong. I felt a big knot in my throat. I had to get up and move because they made me very uncomfortable. I ended up throwing my food away because I felt sick."

There seems to be a gender-based pattern in the responses of former students who felt isolated or picked on. Most of the young men, like Victor and Ernesto, would get in fights over derogatory comments, which in turn got them labeled as troublemakers. The young women, in contrast, seemed more likely to feel deeply hurt, but generally did not stand up for themselves as the young men did. Several of the young women indicated that their mothers would tell them to ignore what others had to say about them in order to avoid any disagreements or fights.

Though some observers might claim this is an individual or even a cultural problem, it seems clear that the way schools respond to bullying and name-calling significantly affects how students are treated. A few schools, for example, try to maintain a low tolerance of such behavior. Most, however, seem to ignore it. In some cases, even school officials themselves might contribute to it. One dropout, Eloy, for example, believes he was in such a school. He says "I don't know. Maybe it's the way I looked or dressed, but anytime I tried to talk to one of those chicks from the 'preps,' they would look at me as if I had a disease or something. It was the same way with my teachers, counselors, and even my principal. But, I don't care, man. They can all go to you know where."

Class-based peer pressure can contribute to high dropout rates in other ways, too. Many dropouts talked about pressure from "friends" to engage in behavior that kept them constantly in trouble with school and police officials. "When I was in the eighth grade," reports Isela, "I hated my English teacher. One day she caught me cheating on an exam. She gave me a zero and called my parents. They grounded me for a month. I told my friends what had happened. They told me I should slash her tires. At first

I was hesitant, but when my friends kept pressuring me, I couldn't say no. I slashed both her back tires, but I got caught. I was suspended for three days, and I ended up having to pay for new tires."

Virtually every study of dropouts makes some mention of the importance of one's peers on the decision to drop out.[35] This peer influence does not happen in a vacuum, however. It is not a matter of peers pulling one way and schools and parents another. Rather, when schools and parents fail to provide much of the support young people need, they often turn to peers to fill the gap. As the authors of the final report of the Hispanic Dropout Project state, "When respect, responsibility, membership, and opportunities for leadership are denied to students by their schools, then gangs and antisocial behaviors often fill the gap."[36]

This principle rests on a basic theoretical concept related to adolescent (and adult) behavior. Starting with Durkheim, sociologists have noted the importance of social solidarity as a prime motivator of human behavior.[37] In more recent years, many of the postulates related to the need for social bonds and social belonging have been put forth by advocates of control theory. Travis Hirschi, for example, proposed that the stronger the attachments to family and society are, the stronger our internal controls operate to prevent deviance.[38] This is what a 1989 study by Gary G. Wehlage and his coauthors concluded:

> The key finding from our research is that effective schools provide at-risk students with a community of support. School as a community of support is a broad concept in which school membership and educational engagement are central. *School membership is concerned with a sense of belonging and social bonding to the school and its members.* (emphasis added)[39]

ADOLESCENT GANGS   Gang membership is another key factor affecting the dropout rate. Janet Vela might be considered a classic dropout. She fits many of the media stereotypes. She is a seventeen-year-old female who had just dropped out of school a few weeks before her interview. She claimed that she doesn't like school and has better things to do with her time. She had just found out that she was two months pregnant. The father-to-be is also a teenager who just dropped out of school. They both belong to a gang. She sleeps during the day and drinks and gets high on drugs at night. Her mother was also a high school dropout and a teenage parent. Janet's interviewer was surprised at her apparent total lack of concern about the future.

Though Janet's decision to drop out of school would seem to have been entirely a personal decision, much of her case is a reflection of her social environment. That she is following in the footsteps of her mother reflects a strong negative influence from her family. Her involvement in a gang (and its influence on her) is likewise related to the social situation in her neighborhood, school, and community, as is the availability of alcohol and drugs.

Gangs affect dropping out in many ways, including negative peer pressure, getting in trouble with the law and with school officials, and school violence.[40] In addition, they also reflect the many negative community influences that foster gangs in the first place, all of which add to the pressures to quit school.

Not all gang members are dropouts, of course. One gang member whom we'll call Joe explained his feelings about school and gangs. "I know that I'm not taken very seriously," he says, "but I want a future that includes finishing high school and going to college. I hang out with a gang but I know where to draw the line. I'm clean and have no record with the law. No matter how far I get pushed, I won't do anything to mess up my future. I want to make something out of myself and pay back my parents for trying their best to take care of me."

The Effects of Dropping Out

As we have seen, there is considerable debate about the causes of the high Hispanic dropout rate. There is much greater agreement, however, on its effects. Marco, for example, is a twenty-four-year-old man who had a hard time talking about his status as a dropout. "This really hurts talking about it," he said to his interviewer. "I have a lot of regrets. An education can help someone go a long way in life. If I would have finished school, I would have a better chance for a good job to support my wife and our unborn child. It's pretty clear. No education—no money. If I'd stayed in school, I also wouldn't have been in gangs and I probably would have gone to college."[41]

Closely related to the economic and family-related effects of dropping out are the effects of the stigma that it carries. Marco had something to say about that also. "Some people," he says, "try to be encouraging, telling me it's never too late to go back and get an education to better myself. Ignorant people, though, treat me like a failure. Some of them tell me I've messed up my life and they make me feel pretty bad about myself. In other words, it's just a constant reminder every day. Every time I turn in an application, they notice that you did not graduate from high school. They pause and say it out loud and then just look at you. Then, if you get the job, you get to work all the hours nobody else wants to work."

Pamela also hates the stigma associated with being a dropout. "They talk to me slowly," she says, "and start explaining things as though I didn't understand them. One employer made me so furious that I told him, 'I dropped out because I had a baby, not because I'm stupid and can't understand what people are saying!' Of course, I didn't get the job but it is really frustrating. I would like to get more education but at the time it's really impossible."

Minerva, a twenty-one-year-old dropout, explains why it's so hard. "It's not good at all," she says, "being a dropout. There are not many places to look for a job. Yeah, there are the fast-food restaurants, being a waitress, or maybe even a cashier. Most places that would consider me just pay minimum wage.[42] That's not enough to raise two kids. Right now I'm on welfare and now they're not going to help anymore. I have to think of a way to go back to school. It's hard because I don't have a job, a car, or a babysitter, so I really don't know how I am going to do it."

Conclusion

The impact of the high Hispanic dropout rate is easy to observe in the Rio Grande Valley, where professional and high-skill jobs often remain unfilled and low-skill jobs seldom pay more than minimum wage. The reasons for this situation, however, are harder to detect. Most dropouts quit school for a variety of reasons, though cultural and structural factors are often interpreted as personal failure.

Mexican culture might indeed be a factor, but not in the sense often portrayed by those who propose a culture of poverty explanation. Hispanic students do not have a culture that gives low value to education, nor one that promotes a "live-for-today" casualness about schoolwork. Some Hispanic males may have fathers who teach them to fight when ridiculed, but that cultural element would cause problems only in a system where bullying and stereotyping are tolerated (or even subtly encouraged). Similarly, Hispanic kids do not come to school with a poor self-image. A negative self-image does often emerge, however, in a system that devalues their cultural heritage and shuffles them into an academic track that will stigmatize them as "losers" and "nobodies."

It seems likely that the greatest portion of the wide dropout gap between Hispanics and other ethnic groups has much more to do with structural factors, such as immigration, the socioeconomic status of Mexican immigrants, and the proximity of Mexico. Undocumented immigrants who have children living in the United States generally lead lives on the economic edge, creating great uncertainty. Moves are frequent and may occur without any notice to their children's schools. Many of these immigrants, or their children, will also leave school in the United States to return to Mexico, continuing their schooling there. They are often counted as "dropouts," thus inflating the figures. When these factors are fully considered, it is unlikely that the Hispanic dropout rate is much different from that of other minorities in their same socioeconomic situation.

It's not hard to find a lot of poor decisions in the lives of many Hispanic dropouts. If we search, we can also find some tendencies from Mexican culture that may contribute in small ways to the problem. The best solution, however, is not to fix Hispanic culture or to admonish Hispanic kids to make better decisions. Neither is the best solution more encouragement to make better choices (though we should certainly try). All of us make bad choices, but not all of us live so close to the edge that a bad choice sends us into the abyss. If we want to fix the problem, we would be better advised to put up better structural fences to keep these young people from falling off the cliff, as opposed to our present course of trying to maintain a worn-out "ambulance down in the Valley."[43]

Conclusion

Chrystell Flota, a business administration graduate student from Mexico enrolled in a sociology seminar on U.S.-Mexico border issues, commented in her seminar paper,

> Most of us Mexican nationals feel enormous loyalty to the Republic of Mexico. Our institutions and our national heroes gave us "patria, tierra, y libertad" (homeland, land, and liberty). When abroad, we cry at the sound of mariachi music—never mind that the marimba, a type of xylophone, is the more typical musical instrument of my home state. Since a very early age, we were made to memorize key historical dates, stories of our national heroes, and all the wonders of our country. Yet, in our wonderful country, over 40 percent of the population is classified as below the poverty level. Worse still, many people are driven to poverty by government edicts that push them from communal farms (*ejidos*), by overpopulation, and by natural disasters (mostly droughts). Because our institutions and political/economic system cannot guarantee the possibility of a decent living, every year large numbers of people from the interior of the country go north in search of a way to make a living. Yet we expect them to remain loyal to the country that denied them all opportunities—not only for advancement but for subsistence itself. In light of all this, what should be surprising is not that Mexican Americans ignore Mexico's historical and cultural heritage, but that they have managed to retain a few of those cultural celebrations in spite of all the discrimination they have endured from Mexicans and Anglos alike.

Chrystell, like many Mexican graduate students in South Texas, became acutely aware of the pressures Mexican immigrants and their children experience to drop their Mexican culture. She also knows well the counter-pressure from nationalistic Mexicans to maintain that culture while living in the United States. As a result of those pressures, Mexican-origin people in the U.S. attracted here by the forces of globalization face difficult choices and frequent dismay when they see their children abandon, or even ridicule, cherished cultural practices. Still, as we saw in Chapters 1 and 2, some of these practices remain much longer than others. Out of this process, a new form of culture emerges in the South Texas borderlands. Over time, this culture strongly supports U.S. national culture while still maintaining some strong border and Mexican influences.

Mexican immigrants who come from Mexico, either legally or illegally, have often been displaced by worldwide forces of globalization. As we saw in Chapter 3, some workers who were drawn from Mexico by migrant farmwork were able to get good assembly-line jobs, only to find themselves again displaced as globalization moved their jobs to Mexico and beyond. This process especially hurts displaced workers who have been unable to learn English. The case of displaced workers in the South Texas borderlands cries for remedies other than those designed elsewhere in the United States.

It is patently unfair for governmental and economic interests in the United States to push globalization on Mexico and then refuse to take responsibility for its unwanted effects, including the growing influx of Mexican workers streaming across our southern border. While globalization draws them in, our strong sense of nationalism and the desire to protect "American culture" keeps them in the status of "illegal aliens." This, of course, not only fails to prevent their entry, but also plays into the hands of employers seeking cheap labor and coyotes seeking to exploit them.

We create a great irrationality when we pursue globalization for economic advantage and then decry the flow of labor it creates because of our strong nationalistic sentiments. Many immigration agents sense this irrationality but find themselves unable to do much about it, as we saw in Chapters 4 and 5. So we end up with a policy that encourages Mexican workers to keep trying and, if successful, stay hidden. The result is an underground economy of cheap and exploitable labor, with the harshest effects experienced in the borderlands.

Another apparent irrationality created by the counterpressures of globalization and U.S. national culture is the increasing flow of illegal drugs across the South Texas border, described in Chapter 6. Globalization contributes to a culture that emphasizes the maximization of individual self-interest, including, for some, drug-induced pleasure. Along the U.S.-Mexico border, this conflict is greatly magnified at the point of entry of contraband into the U.S. This situation is compounded by the forces of globalization, which call for an open border responding to laws of supply and demand.[1]

The flow of illegal drugs into the U.S. is also related to the incidence of property crimes, such as auto theft and shoplifting, which we described in Chapter 7.[2] Auto thieves and shoplifting rings exploit the mismatch between the respective criminal justice systems of Mexico and the United States to steal property in one country and sell the stolen merchandise in the other. In addition, the disparities in how each nation treats juveniles, coupled with the U.S. tendency to dispose of juveniles by simply taking them back to Mexico, presents an enticement to crime that is difficult to resist by those with few family or community ties. As a result, the "free-trade" environment of the border presents an increased opportunity for property crimes, while decreasing the associated risks of punishment. As with the other social issues discussed, borderlands residents are most profoundly affected by these problems.

Juveniles from the U.S. side of the border also become involved in "free trade" as they take advantage of different laws in Mexico regarding drinking by adolescents. Nevertheless, as we saw in Chapter 8, some teens who turn to Mexico for unrestricted alcohol or drug consumption mistakenly assume that Mexicans will wink at drug use and public drunkenness. Many get a hard lesson to the contrary in Mexican jails and prisons. Though globalization should have produced greater uniformity of laws regarding imprisonment, U.S. residents who end up in Mexican jails and prisons soon discover that Mexican nationalism and national culture are clearly engrained in the Mexican criminal justice system.

Finally, in Chapter 9 we examined the high dropout rates of Hispanic adolescents, another "earthquake" or "volcano" resulting from pressures of globalization and nationalism. As globalization keeps pulling poorly educated Mexican workers into the borderlands, nationalism and efforts to impose our national culture in the schools contribute to an unusually high dropout rate among Mexican-origin people. Strong nationalism leads U.S. schools to Americanize Hispanic youngsters, distancing them from their parents and disadvantaging them both culturally and economically.

The Hispanic dropout problem is greatly compounded by the other "earthquakes and volcanoes" described in this volume. The conflict in South Texas schools between traditional Mexican culture and U.S. culture, for example, clearly contributes to the high dropout rate. So does the displacement of workers, which often requires youth to drop out of school to help parents who have been displaced from seemingly stable jobs. Similarly, drug smuggling and drug addiction compound the dropout problem, as does teen drinking in Mexico and the involvement of adolescents in border crime. The fluidity of the border and the need for undocumented immigrants to move back and forth across it (and from one place of hiding to another in the U.S.) also clearly impact school completion rates. Finally, even those programs developed to counter these pressures, such as bilingual education, end up stigmatizing participants as slow learners and leaving them unable to function on equal terms either with Anglos in Texas or more highly educated individuals in Mexico.

Choices: Where to from Here?

I am from Sinaloa and I decided to come to the United States to get a better paying job. My daughters know English because they have been in school here since kindergarten. There is more opportunity for a person to make a living in the United States than in Mexico. I want the best for them and that is why I have taken a job that takes me away from my family for long periods of time. I miss my family a lot when I am gone, but I can give them a better life now than what I could offer them in Mexico. I do miss Mexico. The way of living in the United States is very different than the way I was raised to live in Mexico. But even though I was very poor in Mexico, I was always together with my family. Here, I have to sacrifice the time I could spend with them for the money I need to support them. I would like to go back to Sinaloa with my family, but my kids are not willing to leave everything they have here behind.

Conflicts such as that expressed here by Felipe create pressures that must be resolved. Some individuals respond by abandoning Mexico and severing all ties to their family and friends there. Some even abandon Mexican culture and try to anglicize themselves, as the following case illustrates. Gloria says, "My husband is one of those people who really gets upset when he remembers his childhood. He believes that his Mexican culture kept the rest of his family from making something of themselves. He is very proud of the fact that he has made something of himself and credits his 'anglicized' self for that accomplishment.

"I too used to hate my culture and used to wish that I was someone else—someone with blond hair and green eyes. I was very fortunate, however, that my parents taught me to respect myself and to become what I wanted to be without pretending to be someone else. I guess these other people were not as lucky as I was."

Gloria's account of her struggle against giving up her culture reveals an unfortunate aspect of U.S. national culture—its tendency to regard Mexican culture and Mexican people as inferior. Indeed, our national "legacy" of racism continues to create pressures on people like Gloria to see black hair, a dark complexion, and brown eyes as inferior. And even though racism has clearly declined in U.S. national culture, we still maintain a strong ethnocentric tendency to see Anglo ways and culture as superior.

These two tendencies, a legacy of racism and an ethnocentric sense of superiority, are part of an underbelly of intolerance in U.S. national culture. The national cultures of Mexico and other countries are not without flaws either. The tendency of many Mexicans to resign themselves to political corruption and mordidas, for example, even while finding such practices offensive, contributes to the difficulties of modernizing Mexico's political system, as we described in Chapter 8. And Mexico, like the United States, tends to associate personal weakness with dark skin.

The underbelly of each nation's culture often finds its way into its national policy. One Canadian living illegally in South Texas, for example, talked about the degree to which U.S. immigration policy favors Canadians over Mexicans: "Our employers assured us they would take care of our papers, but because they didn't, we had to sneak our household stuff in at the border. When we crossed over here from Canada, I had to bluff my way through. The company never even got us our visas. Since we arrived, we've tried to obtain any type of legal residency. We asked for application forms from the INS, but they said, 'Oh you're Canadian. As long as you go to Mexico every six months, you'll be fine. We don't bother Canadians.' We have been here illegally for years, and everyone around us knows we are illegal, including the bank, and the INS."

Because our nationalistic culture tends to stigmatize much that is Mexican as inferior, Mexican Americans must often make difficult cultural and structural choices, as illustrated by the opening statement by Chrystell. Some choose to maintain their Mexican culture and their ties to Mexico but find themselves increasingly isolated from opportunities in their new country. Those who attempt to fully assimilate and cut all ties to Mexico find themselves losing an important part of their identity. Mexican Americans, those who attempt to find a middle ground, may find themselves ridiculed as *"pocho"* [too gringo] by nationalistic Mexicans and as "mojos" [pronounced "moe-joes" and short for *mojados*, or wetbacks] by Americans who insist on full assimilation. This creates some very strong pressures upon individuals of Mexican ancestry, as noted in the preceding chapters.

Transnationalism

One long-range option for those seeking to resolve the pressures of globalization and strong national cultures is transnationalism. Levitt and Waters use the term "transnationalism" to describe how ordinary individuals choose to orient their everyday lives across national borders, maintaining cultural practices and structural connections in both the sending and receiving countries. They state,

> At present, vocabularies of "diaspora" and "transnationalism" are both used to describe the ways in which globalization challenges social organization and identity construction. Scholars using these terms are interested in how heightened social, economic, and political interconnectedness across national borders and cultures enables individuals to sustain multiple identities and loyalties, create new cultural products using elements from a variety of settings, and exercise multiple political and civic memberships.[3]

These authors encourage us to look at situations where the size of the immigrant population is sufficient to produce *transnational social fields*, or sets of social expectations, cultural values, and patterns of human interaction that are shaped by the social, economic, and political systems of both countries. Accordingly, they propose that the thicker and more diverse a transnational social field is, the more it provides ways for migrants and their children to remain active in their homelands. They also propose that the more institutionalized these relationships become in the new country, the more likely it is that transnational membership will persist over time.

It is important to note that they propose that transnationalism can involve more than frequent trips across the border. Indeed, they suggest three types of transnationalists: (1) those who travel regularly between both countries; (2) those who remain primarily in either country, but are integrally connected with resources, contacts, and people from the other country; and (3) those who never cross the border, but are transnational because their lives are so permeated by social contacts and cultural influences of the migrant population. For the purposes of our own analysis, we will refer to three related forms of transnationalism, calling them *geographic* transnationalism (maintaining cross-border visiting patterns), *structural* transnationalism (maintaining cross-border relationships and contacts), and *cultural* transnationalism (maintaining the lifestyle and culture of the ancestral homeland).

In our Cultural Practices Survey, we asked three questions that are rough indicators of these three types of transnationalism. These questions were as follows: "How often do you visit family or friends in Mexico?" (as an indicator of geographic transnationalism); "How much contact do you maintain with family or friends in Mexico?" (an indicator of structural transnationalism); and "How much do you like the lifestyle of Mexico?" (an indicator of cultural transnationalism). Percent responses to these three questions are presented in Figure C.1.

The responses in this figure reveal that a majority of respondents either rarely or never visit family or friends in Mexico (32 percent and 25 percent, respectively) and that most either do not like, or like very little, the lifestyle of Mexico (24 percent and 29 percent, respectively). They were pretty evenly divided, however, on the question about whether they maintain contact with family or friends in Mexico. Nearly half (49.2 percent) indicated that they either have no family or friends in Mexico or have no contact with them.

We would expect, of course, that recent migrants from Mexico would be more likely than their children or grandchildren to have transnational contacts and to like the lifestyle of their native Mexico. Since Figure C.1 does not make this distinction, we need another way to assess the question about how long these forms of transnationalism persist over time. We can do this with an ANOVA assessment of how each response category on these three items is related to generational status (as we did in Chapters 1 and 2). Figure C.2 shows the mean generation score for each response category.

As this figure shows, there is a very strong difference in the mean generation score for each response category on each of these three measures of transnationalism. Individuals who have low generation scores (meaning fairly recent history of migration) are far more likely to visit family or friends in Mexico, maintain contact with these friends or family members,

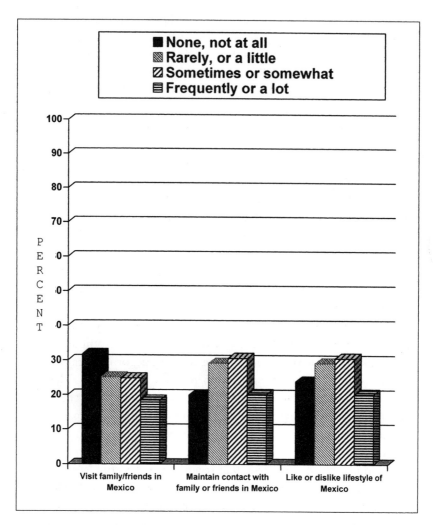

FIG. C.1. Percent South Texas Hispanics responding "none" to "frequently" on three measures of transnationalism among South Texas Hispanics

and to like the lifestyle of Mexico a lot. Indeed, the average generation score for individuals with this set of responses was near 3 (indicating those with a recent history of immigration). In contrast, those who indicated that they never visited family or friends in Mexico, had no contact with such individuals, or did not like the lifestyle of Mexico had mean generation scores of around 9 or 10 (out of 12). Clearly, the more generations one's family has been in the U.S., the lower their ratings on each form of transnationalism.

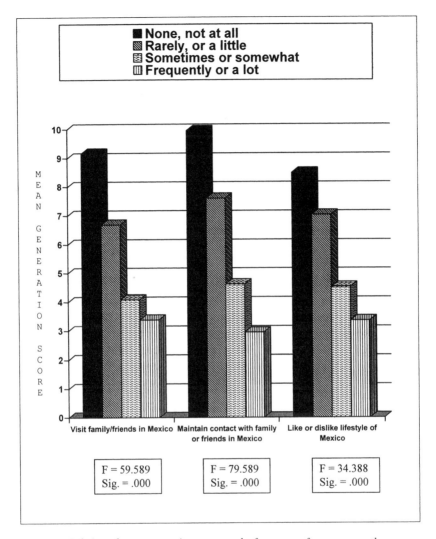

FIG. C.2. Relation of mean generation scores to the frequency of responses on three measures of transnationalism among South Texas Hispanics

This is also reflected in the F-scores, which show a very high level of association between each of these variables and mean generation scores.

These results further suggest that the forms of transnationalism that are most quickly lost with increasing time in the United States are the geographical and the structural, or those associated with maintaining contact with, and visiting, family and friends in Mexico (F-scores of 59.589 and 75.589, respectively). Expressing affinity for the lifestyle of Mexico, considered here a form of cultural transnationalism, also goes away rather quickly (in terms of generations in the United States), though apparently at a somewhat slower rate than the other two forms.[4] This is also supported by the analyses presented in Chapters 1 and 2 of the relationship of generational status to specific cultural practices. Most of these practices showed a statistically significant relation to generational status, though the F-scores were much lower than the F-scores shown in Figure C.2.

In several chapters of this volume, we have used generational status as a measure of how quickly certain aspects of one's immigrant roots fade away. Levitt and Schiller indicate that "we need methods that capture transnational connections over time."[5] For immigrants and their offspring, the element of time is not months or years, but the number of generations they remain in the host country. We suggest that this new way of measuring generational status offers a valuable methodological tool to accomplish this end.

Other Forms of Cultural Transnationalism

> Even though I may not know how to speak Spanish, have any relatives in Mexico, or ever visit Mexico, I still recognize many Mexican customs and traditions because I feel that my heritage and history are Mexican American. So there is no way that I can possibly consider myself Anglo and just be able to ignore what I feel is my culture.

The tendency to identify oneself with Mexico and/or certain aspects of Mexican culture, even when one has lost much of it, is illustrated by this statement by twenty-year-old Vicky. She maintains certain elements of identification with her roots, even though she may never set foot in Mexico or practice many of the customs of her immigrant ancestors. In the first two chapters of this volume, we examined the extent to which different forms of cultural transnationalism are maintained. In general, we found that most cultural practices are strongly related to generational status, though some are more stable and seem to remain in a somewhat modified form over succeeding generations. Even many Mexican Americans in South Texas who have lost their Spanish, for example, still tend to practice touching a child to prevent *ojo*.

The process by which some elements of Mexican culture are lost relatively quickly, while others remain in modified form for a much longer time, is further illustrated by preferences for musical styles. In the Cultural Practices Survey, for example, we asked respondents to rate how much they liked certain forms of music. We included forms of music from both sides of the border and one or two that had emerged in the South Texas borderlands. We then compared how strongly each of these response categories was related to mean generation score. The results are presented in Figure C.3.

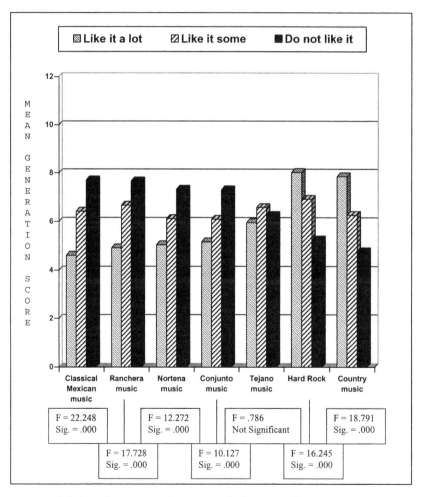

FIG. C.3. Relation of mean generation scores to the frequency of responses on seven measures of musical appreciation among South Texas Hispanics

As this figure illustrates, those forms of music that are strongly associated with the culture of Mexico or the United States show a high and positive statistical association with mean generation score. This would suggest that they disappear more quickly with each generation in the United States. In effect, the strong liking for traditional Mexican music (classical Mexican, Ranchera, and Norteña), as well as a more pronounced *dislike* of identifiably U.S. music (hard rock and country) have a strong association with generational status. As Mexican-origin people remain for increasing generations in the United States, their liking for traditional Mexican music, as indicated in this analysis, significantly declines, as does their dislike of identifiable forms of U.S. music. The relation between Tejano music, a new hybrid form that emerged primarily in the South Texas borderlands, and generational status, however, is not statistically significant, indicating that the preference for this type of music is resilient across generations among South Texas Mexican-origin people. Indeed, Tejano music had the highest percentage (43.7 percent) of "like it a lot" responses, followed by Ranchera (42.8 percent), Norteña (36.3 percent), Classical Mexican (36.1 percent), Conjunto (35.2 percent), Country (28.3 percent), and Hard Rock (19.8 percent).

A similar pattern emerges when we examine acculturation (the loss of one's ancestral homeland culture in a new country).[6] In an early study of cultural values (our Perceptions of Culture and Deviance Survey), we asked questions designed to assess both generational status and acculturation. For the acculturation items, we used six questions from a scale designed by Israel Cuellar. Figure C.4 shows the relation of mean generation scores and these six measures of acculturation.[7]

This figure rather clearly illustrates the difficulty of maintaining Spanish, even while living in a border environment. The two items dealing with Spanish (speaking it and enjoying it) show a very pronounced pattern of language loss with succeeding generations in the United States. The same pattern emerged in Chapter 2 in the very strong association of generational status with the item, "How often do you speak Spanish so children will learn it?" (F = 41.466).

Likewise, as Figure C.4 shows, the enjoyment of reading books in Spanish also seems to disappear rather quickly. This is probably because schools in Texas and elsewhere along the border do a very poor job of teaching Hispanic children to read and write in Spanish. The enjoyment of Spanish-language movies, however, appears to be virtually unrelated to genera-

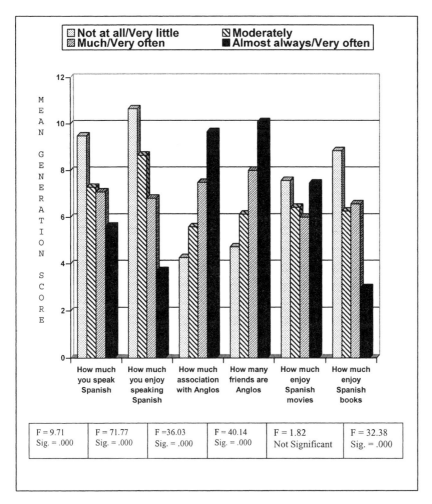

FIG. C.4. Relation of mean generation scores to the frequency of responses on six measures of acculturation among South Texas Hispanics

tional status in this border environment, probably because listening comprehension is one of the last language abilities to be lost.

Two of the items in Figure C.4 are more about structural (as opposed to cultural) transnationalism, dealing with developing relationships with Anglos. On both items, there is a pronounced pattern of avoiding (or not enjoying) association with Anglos for early generations, while both forms of association seem to increase rather dramatically among individuals with higher generation scores.[8]

Transnationalism and Deviance in a Border Environment

> From a parent's standpoint, the scariest part is when you learn
> that you are too close to the bridge for your kids. We thought we
> were protective of Mike [their son] and that he would never go
> across the bridge. Then we found out later he was in the entou-
> rage every Friday night going over there to drink. After a lot of ar-
> guing and fighting, we finally just decided to be honest with our-
> selves and accept that he was going.

As these parents discovered, living close to the border may promote a new
variety of transnationalism—one in which Anglos and Mexican-origin
people cross the border not to see family and friends, return to their cultural roots, or to conduct business, but to engage in behavior that is prohibited in their own country.[9] At the same time, people in Mexico come to
the U.S. to purchase items or to engage in activities that might be prohibited in Mexico. Because each country has different laws and different ways
of dealing with lawbreakers, the border promotes, for many individuals,
deviant forms of transnationalism. Geographic transnationalism, for example, is promoted among U.S. teens who can easily slip across the border to party and consume alcohol in Mexico, or among Mexican teens who
can slip across the border to shoplift in Texas with relative impunity. The
dropout problem is also exaggerated by the transnationalism of children of
immigrants who move back and forth across the border. Frequent moves
disrupt the child's education. At the same time, moving back and forth
across the border artificially raises the dropout rate for Hispanics; children
who are counted as dropouts in the U.S. may continue school in Mexico.

Structural transnationalism is also promoted by drug dealing, immigrant smuggling, auto theft, and money laundering, which bring together
individuals from both countries. As we have pointed out, much of this deviance is blamed on Mexico, on Mexican immigrants, or on the culture
that they bring with them. Indeed, advocates of U.S. nationalism such as
Samuel Huntington claim that the influx of immigrants is destroying U.S.
identity and our core culture. It is worth examining this contention one
more time to show how misguided it is, especially in relation to the idea
that Mexican culture will promote greater deviance and social problems.

We examined how several forms of transnational activities often considered deviant are related to generational status.[10] Figure C.5 presents

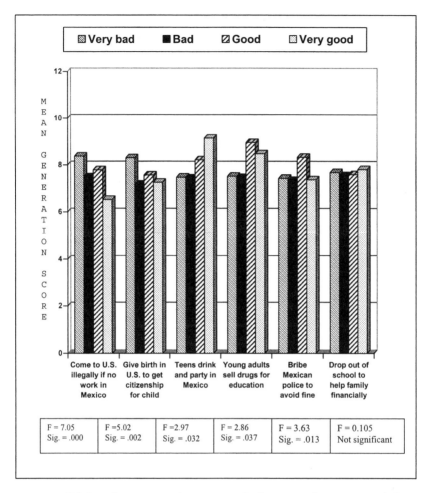

FIG. C.5. Relation of mean generation scores to the frequency of responses on six items measuring how good or how bad Mexican-origin people feel about different forms of deviance

this analysis for six forms of behavior discussed throughout this volume, five of which were significantly related to generational status and one that was not.

Two items in this figure ask how Hispanic respondents feel about "deviance" related to immigration (entering the U.S. illegally to work and coming to give birth so that the child can have U.S. citizenship).[11] On each of these items, recent immigrants were more likely than individuals with more time in the United States to regard these behaviors as acceptable.

In other words, the longer one's family has been in the United States, the more likely an individual is to consider these behaviors as deviant. For the items related to teens drinking and partying in Mexico, young adults selling drugs to finance their education, and bribing a Mexican police officer to avoid a fine, however, the reverse was found. Individuals with a recent immigration history in their family are more likely to regard these behaviors as deviant.

We included the final item, dropping out of school when one needs to help his or her family financially, even though it does not *directly* involve cross-border activity. As we indicated in Chapter 9, going back to Mexico can be a significant reason for dropping out. We also included it because some writers have proposed that many Hispanics might consider this a "legitimate" reason for dropping out. Those who take this view propose that since family comes first, furthering one's educational objectives may be seen as a legitimate reason to drop out. We found that 32 percent of our Mexican-origin respondents regarded this behavior as "very bad," while 43 percent regarded it as "bad." This means that a total of 75 percent did not approve of dropping out, even to help support one's family financially. The fact that there was no statistically significant difference between recent and long-term Hispanics on their perceptions of this behavior leads us to believe that neither Mexican nor Mexican American culture accepts dropping out, even when it is to help support one's family.

Throughout this volume, we have focused on many significant social issues and forms of deviance that are very pronounced in the South Texas border environment. We have examined the social landscape of the borderlands—its earthquakes and volcanoes, looking at how these issues affect the people who reside here. Though rates of crime are on the increase in this region (while declining elsewhere in the U.S.), South Texas still has a surprisingly low crime rate. Given the many opportunities to participate in crime on the border—where criminals from either side can take advantage of legal loopholes and where drug trafficking and property crime are well established—what begs explanation is why so few individuals become involved in crime. We attribute this phenomenon in large measure to the culture of the Mexican-origin people who live here. Most have a strong family orientation and a very positive ethic that supports law and authority.

As globalization pushed by U.S. economic nationalism pulls Mexican workers northward, U.S. cultural nationalists need not fear their influence on U.S. culture. Mexicans contribute to strong family values, the work ethic, and respect for authority—some of the very things that cultural nationalists believe are being weakened within the United States. Indeed, other aspects of the underbelly of U.S. culture, particularly the emphasis on individualism over community—with its concomitant emphases of pleasure over commitment and affluence over character—are cultural elements that Mexicans most fear might be carried southward by the forces of globalization and U.S. nationalism.

Borderlife Research Projects
Utilized in This Volume

Project Title	Type of Interviews	Year(s) Conducted*	Sample Size (N)
Cultural Practices In-Depth Interviews	Ethnographic and anecdotal	Mainly 1995–2001	250
Cultural Practices Survey	Survey	2001–2002	433
Displaced Workers Interviews	Survey and ethnographic	2002	82
Undocumented Workers In-Depth Interviews	Ethnographic and anecdotal	1982–2005	203
Undocumented Workers Survey	Survey	1994	150
Laser-Visa Holders Opinion Survey	Survey	2003, 2004	115
Drug Smugglers In-Depth Interviews	Ethnographic and anecdotal	1991–2004	200
Shoplifting and Auto Theft In-Depth Interviews	Ethnographic and anecdotal	2002–2004	92 (combined total)
Texas Teens Going to Mexico to Drink In-Depth Interviews	Ethnographic and anecdotal	1994–2002	45

Project Title	Type of Interviews	Year(s) Conducted*	Sample Size (N)
Americans in Mexican Prisons In-Depth Interviews	Ethnographic and anecdotal	1988–1997	60
Perceptions of Deviance Survey	Survey	2002–2003	424
Perceptions of Culture and Deviance Survey	(Pilot) Survey	1999–2001	303
School Dropouts In-Depth Interviews	Ethnographic and Anecdotal	2002–2003	180
Total no. interviews			2,548

*The dates for the ethnographic studies in this column reflect the main years such accounts were gathered. Other accounts and interviews are included, however, from related topics covered in other years.

Student Interviewers Whose Ethnographic Accounts Are Included in This Book

The following students at the University of Texas–Pan American contributed anecdotes that are included in this volume. Their names are listed alphabetically, with no designation of the chapter in which their stories appear, in order to better preserve the anonymity of the people interviewed. For those who provided more than one anecdote, the total number appears in parentheses after the student's name.

Acevedo, Lorena
Acevedo, Roxanna (4)
Aguilar, Monica J.
Alvarado, Leonel
Alvarez, Rocío
Amaya, Alma D.
Amiel, Edgar (3)
Arispe, Jaime
Ayala, Alma (4)
Badillo, Carrie
Baldillez, Yvette (2)
Ballardo, Melanie
Balli, Bobby
Barajas, Stephanie Ruiz
Barrientes, Hilda Ann (5)
Bautista, Aida
Bazan, Virginia (2)
Bernal, Tina T.
Borrego, Janoise L. (2)
Bracamontes, Claudia (2)
Briscoe, Adelaida
Canales, Deborah D. (2)
Cano, Anissa M.

Cantu, Ana Marie (3)
Cantu, Isaac (3)
Carrasco Ybarra, Christine (6)
Carrera, Richard E.
Carrera, Roberto
Carrillo, Saul (3)
Castellanos, Eva M.
Castillo, Maricela
Castro, Gloria C.
Castro, Joe (6)
Castro, Olga L.
Castro, Sabrina
Cavazos, Sonia
Cervantes, Patricia
Chapa, Elizabeth D. (4)
Chapa, Jose Luis (2)
Corpus, Dina (2)
Cruz, Arturo, Jr.
Cruz, Eric M. (3)
Cruz, Ismael (2)
Cruz, Sandy (4)
De Anda, Ricardo (2)
De La Cruz, Jesus

De la Fuente, Marcelino C. (2)
De la Garza, Maria
De la Rosa, Ebodio
De Leon, Alan
De Leon, Jacob Seth
Delgado, Elena
De Luna, Rosie (2)
Diaz, Jose R.
Dietz, Marilyn (6)
Espetia, Martin
Estrada, Joel (2)
Ezsitia, Martin
Fabela, Javier
Farias, A.
Flores, Diana (2)
Flores, Melissa (2)
Flores, Mercy (4)
Flores, Ruby
Galvan, Monica
Galvan, Norma (2)
Galvan, Zulema (3)
Garcia, Amelia
Garcia, Francisco, Jr.
Garcia, Jesse (10)
Garcia, Jessica
Garcia, Jesus V.
Garcia, Jose T., Jr.
Garcia, Lisa Margot
Garcia, Maria L.
Garcia, Monica
Garcia, Ralph
Garcia, Rosalinda G. (7)
Garcia, Tabita
Garcia, Vianey
Garcia, Victor H.
Garza, Carlos
Garza, Cecilia Denise
Garza, Diana Y.
Garza, Emily (2)

Garza, Guillermina
Garza, Jaime (2)
Garza, Jessica (3)
Garza, Juliana V. (5)
Garza, Lilia (2)
Garza, Maria M. (3)
Garza, Mary
Garza, Myra
Garza, Pamela (2)
Garza, Raul
Garza, Raychel
Gonzalez, Dina
Gonzalez, Hector, Jr. (2)
Gonzalez, Juana M. (2)
Gonzalez, Juanita
Gonzalez, Julissa (3)
Gonzalez, Lucia
Gonzalez, Maria Alba (2)
Gonzalez, Raul (3)
Gonzalez, Rebecca Ann
Gonzalez, Yadira (3)
Grimaldo, Veronica (2)
Guajardo, Mireya H.
Guerra, Andres (4)
Guerra, Leonel
Guerrero, Alicia (2)
Guillen, Rene
Gutierrez, Maribel
Hernandez, Carlos
Hernandez, Elena (2)
Hernandez, Florencio, Jr. (2)
Hernandez, Jose A.
Hernandez, Norma L.
Hernandez, Victoria A. (6)
Hernandez, Yvette
Herrera, Brenda
Herrera, Maricela
Herrera, Richard
Hinojosa, Iliana

Hinojosa, Jorge
Hinojosa, Raul, Jr.
Hood, Delma (2)
Jauregui, Blanca
Jimenez, Monica (2)
Jurado, Flavio (3)
Kerbow, Wanda B. (2)
Lara, Diana
Lara, Jesus (4)
Larsen, Dianira (2)
Laura, Diana
Leal, Rachel
Lopez, Bonnie (2)
Lopez, Jessica (2)
Lopez, Lemuel (2)
Lopez, Mavit A. (4)
Lopez, Monica
Lopez, Nora
Lopez, Roberto, Jr.
Lugo, Erika
Madrid, Benito, Jr. (3)
Martinez, Alex, Jr. (2)
Martinez, Armando (2)
Martinez, Cristina (2)
Martinez, Cristina M. (2)
Martinez, Delia A.
Martinez, Elizabeth
Martinez, Esperanza
Martinez, Juanita M. (2)
Martinez, Maria Luisa
Martinez, Marlene (2)
Martinez, Miriam
Martinez, Roberto
Medina, Erika
Melecia, Cathy (3)
Mercado, Carolina
Millan, Claudia
Miranda, Lucrecia
Montagne, Jennifer

Morales, Humberto Javier
Moreno, Milton
Munguia, Jesse (3)
Navarro, Mark Anthony
Negrete, Nadia
Ochoa, Jorge (2)
Olabarrienta, R.
Olague, Diego
Ornelas, Evangelina
Ortiz, Ana M.
Ortiz, Cristina (3)
Padilla, Joel
Partridge, Tracey
Peña, Martha Iliana (4)
Peña, Rene A. (3)
Pereda, Edmundo A. (2)
Perez, Angela Catlynn
Perez, Federico, Jr. (2)
Perez, Gerie (2)
Perez, Martina (4)
Perez, Yesenia A. (2)
Pineda, Deisy (2)
Porter, Lina M. (6)
Ramirez, Angela Y.
Ramirez, Jessica (2)
Ramirez, Lorena (4)
Ramirez, Rachel
Ramirez, Ramon
Ramirez, Sandra
Ramos, Ose L. (2)
Resendez, Flor
Retherford, Holly A. (3)
Reyes, Alejandra
Reyna, Christina M.
Reza, Ramiro
Riojas, Mark
Rivera, Jesus A.
Rodriguez, Alejandro (2)
Rodriguez, Ana L.(3)

Rodriguez, Carlos (6)
Rodriguez, Deanna M.
Rodriguez, Elizabeth
Rodriguez, Juan (5)
Rodriguez, Melinda
Rodriguez, Virginia (2)
Rosales, Margarita
Ruiz, Claudia (2)
Salaiz, David (7)
Salazar, Cindy (3)
Saldivar, Dolly L.
Saldivar, Ismael (7)
Salinas Jr., Amaro
Salinas, Juan
Salinas, Mario (2)
Salinas, Veronica V.
Sanchez, Cynthia L. (5)
Sanchez, Guadalupe
Sanchez, Romeo
Sanchez, Vanessa M. (2)
Saucedo, Esteban
Schulze, Joam
Schupp, Rocio
Segura, Michelle D.
Sepulveda, Agripin, Jr.
Sepulveda, Juanita Yvette
Sifuentes, Richard (2)
Smith, Brian
Solis, Victor H.
Spoor, Russell
Tabasco, Jose (3)

Tafolla, Andrea
Tijerina, Hector
Tijerina, Julio
Tijerina, Laura
Tijerina, Nicolas (2)
Torres, Angel (2)
Torres, Blanca E. (2)
Torres, Mike (3)
Treviño, Lupe (2)
Treviño, Roel Ben (4)
Trevino, Theresa
Trillayes, Maria (2)
Valdez, Nancy
Vallejo Jr., Rodolfo
Vasquez, Armando
Vasquez, Severa
Vasquez de Garcia, Amelia (3)
Vela, Myrna (2)
Velasquez, Armando
Velasquez, Rolando
Venecia, Ana M.
Villarreal, Estella (4)
Villarreal, Ignacio
Villarreal, Marcos (2)
West, Stephen (3)
Wrintle, Sean
Ybarra, Rafael (2)
Zapata, Sylvia
Zaryske, Gregory E. (3)
Zavala, Maria Isabel (4)
Zequeira, Cristina

Notes

PREFACE

1. Ken Bain, *What the Best College Teachers Do*, 60–63, 106, 175.

2. See R. M. Lee, *Doing Research on Sensitive Topics*. Also, Patrick Biernacki and Dan Waldorf, "Snowball Sampling: Problems, Techniques of Choice Referral Sampling," *Sociological Methods and Research* 10: 141–163.

3. Texas-Mexico Border Health Coordination Office, University of Texas System, *Texas-Mexico Border Counties, 1998*, 227.

4. Ibid., 201, 205, 217.

5. As a result, border municipalities are faced with difficulties when it comes to improving local infrastructure and coping with an increasing demand for government services. There has been some improvement in this area over the last decade through the adoption of fiscal decentralization measures by the Mexican government (known as fiscal federalism). Article 2 of Mexico's Ley de Coordinación Fiscal requires the federal government to return to the states only 20 percent of income and value-added taxes. As a result, most of the taxes collected remain with the federal government. Local governments in Mexico only manage to keep about 5 percent of total tax revenue collections, compared to over 30 percent in the U.S., Canada, and other industrialized countries. See José G. Tijerina and Antonio Medellín Ruiz, "La dependencia financiera de los gobiernos locales en México," *Ensayos* 19 (May 2000).

6. This is the conclusion of the U.S. Commission on Immigration Reform, a bipartisan commission charged in 1990 with examining the impact of immigration policy social, economic, and community relations in the United States. See T. Paul Schultz, *Immigrant Quality and Assimilation: A Review of the Literature*. He states: "The taxes immigrants pay flow primarily to the federal government, while the benefits are often funded at the local and state government levels, creating hardships that the federal system should explicitly address" (16).

7. Drug prosecutions in border courts more than doubled between 1994 and 2000. This led some Texas border district attorneys to refuse to take any additional cases from federal officers, because federal funding is so minimal and the costs are so great. Scott Balfauf, "Texas DAs Refuse Border Patrol Cases," *Christian Science Monitor*, October 24, 2000.

8. In the Cultural Practices Survey and the Perceptions of Deviance Survey, for example, students were instructed to interview at least one person born and raised in Mexico; one Mexican American born and raised in the Valley, but with at least one parent born and raised in Mexico; and one Mexican American with both parents born in the U.S., but with at least one grandparent born and raised in Mexico. This was done to insure that we would have an adequate representation of the entire range of generation scores.

INTRODUCTION

1. Ellwyn Stoddard, *U.S.-Mexico Borderlands Studies: Multidisciplinary Perspectives and Concepts*, 50.

2. Rupert Wilkinson states that scholars of American culture have found, as the most notable feature of American culture, the "preoccupation with individualism, either its fragility and contradictions or its excesses." See Wilkinson's *Pursuit of American Character*, 48. Wilkinson cites Samuel Huntington's "Globalization's Boosters and Critics (*National Interest* [Fall 1999], 70) as providing evidence from numerous worldwide studies.

3. David J. Keeling, "Latin American Development and the Globalization Imperative: New Directions, Familiar Crises," *Journal of Latin American Geography* 3 (2004). We are indebted to Keeling's insightful analysis of the effects of globalization on emerging countries, especially in Latin America.

4. Lester Thurow, *The Future of Capitalism: How Today's Economic Forces Shape Tomorrow's World*. Thurow identifies five "plates" that he believes are the primary forces of change in today's world. These are (1) the end of Communism, (2) the switch from industrial power to brainpower, (3) a massive demographic transition that includes massive migratory shifts and an aging population, (4) globalization and a global economy, and (5) the end of dominance by one or two economic, political, or military powers.

5. Arthur Schlesinger Jr., "Has Democracy a Future?" *Foreign Affairs*, September/October 1997.

6. Though globalization has been building for many years, it accelerated very rapidly during the 1980s, when many nations joined the General Agreement on Trade and Tariffs (GATT) and when the North American Free Trade Agreement (NAFTA) was signed. In addition, the development of the European Community and the fall of the Soviet Union during the 1980s contributed greatly to the acceleration of globalization.

7. Keeling, "Latin American Development and the Globalization Imperative," 4 (of draft copy).

8. Daniel Bell warns that if the implied promise that the rising tide of international capitalism will raise all boats is not fulfilled, it may well lead to strong nationalistic reactions. He states, "In almost every society, the distrust of the political order and of politicians is rising, often feeding reactionary forces that seek to channel the resentments of a population into religious fundamentalism or a rising nationalism." Daniel Bell, "Corruption in Democracies: The Old War," *New Republic*, August 23, 1993, 6.

9. Keeling, "Latin American Development and the Globalization Imperative."

10. For example, research in Argentina has suggested that for every new, internationally controlled Wal-Mart or Carrefour supermarket, 5,000 local mom-and-pop operations disappear. Margaret Hayes, "The Impact of Market Opening on Argentine Industry: A Survey of Corporate Impressions," in *Argentina: The Challenges of Modernization*, ed. J. S. Tulchin and A. M. Garland.

11. Richard Krooth, *Mexico, NAFTA, and the Hardships of Progress*.

12. Jeremy Brecher and Tim Costello, *Global Village or Global Pillage: Economic Reconstruction from the Bottom Up*.

13. John Tomlinson, *Globalization and Culture*.

14. Jacob Heilbrunn argues that this commercialization presents a distorted version of American culture, stating, "The essence of Western civilization is the Magna Carta, not the Magna Mac." Quoted in Huntington, "Globalization's Boosters and Critics," 118.

15. William Pfaff, *The Wrath of Nations: Civilization and the Furies of Nationalism*, 54.

16. Ibid., 55.

17. Anthony Smith, *Nations and Nationalism in a Global Era*, 55.

18. When everyone is a farmer or a hunter, for example, they have many common concerns and a common knowledge that provide a sense of group solidarity. When each person specializes in a different occupation, however, their dependence on each other for all the things they can no longer produce or do for themselves, rather than their commonality, becomes the bond that holds them together. Their "solidarity," then, has become much more structural (their web of relationships) than cultural (their set of common understandings).

19. Eric Hobsbawm, *Nations and Nationalism since 1780*.

20. Gi-Wook Shin, "The Paradox of Korean Globalization," January 2003; working paper at http://iis-db.stanford.edu/pubs/20125/Shin.pdf. Shin himself rejects this notion. Quoted with permission of the author.

21. Smith, *Nations and Nationalism*.

22. Ibid., 45.

23. See Shin, "The Paradox of Korean Globalization." M. D. R. Evans and Jonathan Kelley, for example, use cross-national studies to show that feelings of national pride and attachment to one's nation have not been eroded by rising globalization. M. D. R. Evans and Jonathan Kelley, "National Pride in the Developed World," *International Journal of Public Opinion Research* 14, no. 3 (2002): 303–338.

24. Benjamin R. Barber, "Jihad vs. McWorld," *Atlantic Monthly*, March 1992.

25. Samuel P. Huntington, *Who Are We? The Challenges to America's National Identity*.

26. We are using the term "Anglo" in this volume to refer to all non-Hispanic Whites.

1. TRADITIONAL HEALTH CARE PRACTICES

1. All names of respondents used in this and other chapters have been changed to protect their identity.

2. Jeiny Zapata and Raelene Shippee-Rice, "The Use of Folk Healing and Healers by Six Latinos Living in New England: A Preliminary Study," *Journal of Transcultural Nursing* 19, no. 2 (April 1999): 136–142.

3. For a discussion of the economic conditions of South Texas colonias, see chap. 2 of Chad Richardson, *Batos, Bolillos, Pochos, and Pelados: Class and Culture on the South Texas Border*.

4. Adela De la Torre, Robert Friis, Harold R. Hunter, and Lorena Garcia, "The Health Insurance Status of the US Latino Women: A Profile from the 1982–1984 HHANNES," *American Journal of Public Health* 86, no. 4 (April 1986): 533. Antonio L. Estrada, Fernando M. Trevino, and Laura A. Ray, "Health Care Utilization among Mexican-Americans: Evidence from HHANES 1982–1984," *American Journal of Public Health* 80, Supplement (December 1990): 31.

5. Joseph J. Wang, "Our Border Health at Risk: Poverty, Disease, and No Health Insurance," May 10, 2002, http://www.law.uh.edu/healthlawperspectives/MinorityHealth/020610border.html (accessed August 10, 2004).

6. James Pinkerton, "Health Care: Crisis at the Border; Poverty, Lack of Doctors Cloud Area's Future," *Houston Chronicle*, May 5, 2002.

7. Federico Gerardo De Cosio and Andrés Boadella, "Demographic Factors Affecting the US Mexico Border Health Status," in *Life and Death and In-Between on the US-Mexico Border—Así Es la Vida*, ed. Martha Oehmke Loustaunau and Mary Sanchez-Bane, 14.

8. Israel Cuellar, "Acculturation as a Moderator of Personality and Psychological Assessment," in *Handbook of Cross-cultural and Multicultural Personality Assessment,* ed. Richard H. Dana.

9. Susan E. Keefe and Amado M. Padilla, *Chicano Ethnicity.*

10. This last category was quite difficult for many of our interviewers to identify, not only because it is hard to tell from outward appearance where someone's grandparents are from, but also because fewer Mexican-origin residents of the Valley have lived here for several generations.

11. S. Dale McLemore, Harriet D. Romo, and Susan Gonzalez Baker, *Racial and Ethnic Relations in America,* 3–5.

12. Many researchers fail to take notice of the complexity and simply ask a respondent which generation they represent.

13. Israel Cuellar, Bill Arnold, and Genaro Gonzalez, "Cognitive Referents of Acculturation: Assessing Cultural Constructs in Mexican Americans," *Journal of Community Psychology* 23 (October 1995): 34.

14. Gilbert Granados, Jyoti Pavvula, Nancy Berman, and Patrick Dowling, "Health Care for Latino Children: Impact of Child and Parental Birthplace on the Insurance Status and Access to Health Services," *American Journal of Public Health* 91, no. 11 (November 2001): 1806–1807.

15. Though we anticipated giving one-half point for each great grandparent born in the United States, we found that most respondents were unaware of the place of birth of most of their great grandparents. As a result, we calculated a score that included only themselves, their parents, and their grandparents.

16. Texas Comptroller of Public Accounts, *Bordering the Future: Challenge and Opportunity in the Texas Border Region,* 105.

17. Fernando M. Trevino and Abigail J. Moss, *Health Indicators for Hispanic, Black, and White Americans,* 233–237.

18. Lack of standardized medical training and procedures when transferring of patients from the United States to Mexico adds to the pain of workers, family members, and patients overall. Kendall Moss and Marilyn Felker, "Patient Transfers along the US-Mexico Border," *LBJ Journal of Public Affairs* 40, no. 2 (1994): 4.

19. In addition to lack of health insurance, Mexican Americans encounter many other barriers that prevent them from obtaining the medical coverage. These barriers stem from cost, availability, long waits for appointments, inconvenient office hours, and lack of transportation. Three-fourths of the population felt that these barriers prevented them from obtaining medical attention. Estrada, 30; Isabel Ann Rodriguez, "Identifying Barriers to Healthcare Perceived by Hispanics in West Texas," 34.

20. Dave Carpenter, "Our Overburdened ERs," *Hospital and Health Networks* 75, no. 3 (March 2001): 45–47, http://www.hhnmag.com/ (accessed June 2004).

21. George, M. Walker, "Utilization of Health Care: The Laredo Migrant Experience," *American Journal of Public Health* 69, no. 7 (1991): 670; Stephanie Triantafillou, "North Carolina's Migrant and Seasonal Farmworkers," *North Carolina Medical Journal* 64, no. 3 (May/June 2003): 129; "Hispanic Health in the United States," *JAMA* 265, no. 2 (January 9, 1991): 252.

22. James J. Horn, "The Mexican Revolution and Health Care, or the Health of the Mexican Revolution," *Latin American Perspectives* 10, no. 4 (1983): 25.

23. De Cosio and Boadella, "Demographic Factors Affecting the US Mexico Border Health Status," 9; David C. Warner, "Health Issues at the US-Mexican Border," *JAMA* 265, no. 2 (January 9, 1991): 245.

24. Michael E. Fix and Jeffrey S. Passel, *Lessons of Welfare Reform for Immigrant Integration*, Washington, DC: Urban Institute, March 8, 2002, http://www.urban.org/url.cfm?ID=900497 (accessed August 2004).

25. Warner, "Health Issues at the US-Mexican Border," 245.

26. S. L. Applewhite, "Curanderismo: Demystifying the Health Beliefs and Practices of Elderly Mexican Americans," *Health and Social Work* 20, no. 4 (November 1995): 247–254.

27. Mary Jane Garza, "Healing Spirits," *Hispanic* 11, no. 6 (June 1998).

28. Robert T. Trotter II and Juan Antonio Chavira, *Curanderismo, Mexican American Folk Healing.* Applewhite, "Curanderismo," 247–254.

29. Trotter and Chavira, *Curanderismo.*

30. P. J. Guarnaccia, V. de la Cancela, and E. Carillo, "The Multiple Meanings of *Ataques de Nervios* in the Latino Community," *Medical Anthropology* 11, no. 1 (1989): 47–62.

31. Robert T. Trotter II, "Curanderismo: A Picture of Mexican-American Folk Healing," *Journal of Alternative and Complementary Medicine* 7, no. 2 (2001): 129–131, states that there are at least seven historical roots of modern curandismo. These include Greek humoral medicine, early Judeo-Christian healing traditions, Moorish influences, and Native American traditions from pre-Columbian times.

32. The first author as a child lived for several years in a small, predominantly Anglo farming village in southwestern New Mexico, where many Anglo residents believed that an older gentleman had a gift for healing that allowed him to diagnose medical problems by simply feeling the body of a sick person.

33. Garza, "Healing Spirits," 34–35.

34. Ibid., 34–35.

35. Don Pedro, originally from the state of Jalisco in Mexico, helped thousands of people while living at Los Olmos Ranch in Falfurrias. Water, either taken internally or given as a bath, was central to many of his cures. Though he died in 1907, he is still considered much like a saint, with an ability to cure from beyond the grave. He is the only known curandero in the United States to have a shrine built around his tomb and thousands of individuals, many from other parts of South Texas, visit his shrine seeking a miracle cure. Ibid., 30–32.

36. Sue Keri Hoppe and Peter L. Heller, "Alienation, Familism, and the Utilization of Health Services by Mexican Americans," *American Journal of Health and Social Behavior* 16, no. 3 (September 1975): 312.

37. Maria J. Gonzalez-Swafford and Mary Grace Tutierrez, "Ethno-Medical Beliefs and Practices of Mexican-Americans," *Nurse Practitioner* 8, no. 1 (November–December 1983): 29–34.

38. L. M. Pachter, "Culture and Clinical Care: Folk Illness Beliefs and Their Implications for Health Care Delivery," *JAMA* 271, no. 9 (1994): 690–694. In another national study of Mexicans and Mexican Americans in the United States, only 4 percent of the research sample admitted to the use of a curandero within the previous twelve months. J. C. Higginbotham, F. M. Treviño, and L. A. Ray, "Utilization of Curanderos by Mexican Americans: Prevalence and Predictor. Findings from HHANES 1982–84." *American Journal of Public Health Supplement* 80 (December 1990): 32–35.

39. Alejandro Murguía, Rolf A. Peterson, and Maria Cecilia Zea, "Use and Implications of Ethnomedical Health Care Approaches among Central American Immigrants," *Health and Social Work* 28, no. 1 (February 2003): 44.

40. Ardon Rolando Collado, Arthur J. Rubel, Carol W. O'Neill, and Raymond H. Murray, "A Folk Illness (Susto) as an Indicator of Real Illness," *The Lancet* 322, no. 8363 (December 10, 1983): 1362.

41. A. P. Chesney et al., "Mexican-American Folk Medicine: Implications for the Family Physician," *Journal of Family Practice* 11 (October 1980): 567–574.

42. I. F. Abril, "Mexican-American Folk Beliefs: How They Affect Health Care," *American Journal of Maternal Child Nursing* 2, no. 3 (May–June 1977): 168–173.

43. E. R. Krajewski-Jaime, "Folk-Healing among Mexican American Families as a Consideration in the Delivery of Child Welfare and Child Health Care Services," *Child Welfare* 70, no. 2 (March/April 1991): 1–8.

44. For a more complete description of the process used to cure a child of ojo, see J. Chavira, *Curanderismo: An Optional Health Care System.*

45. Some home remedies, for example, contain dangerous quantities of lead. Others may interact adversely with prescription medications or may mask symptoms that should be diagnosed. Applewhite, "Curanderismo."

46. June Macklin, "All the Good and Bad in This World," in Margarita B. Melville (ed.), *Twice a Minority: Mexican American Women*, 144.

47. Garza, "Healing Spirits," 34.

48. Krajewski-Jaime, "Folk-Healing," 5–6.

49. Higginbotham, Treviño, and Ray, "Utilization of Curanderos," 34.

50. Ibid., 33.

2. OTHER CULTURAL BELIEFS AND PRACTICES

1. In the final chapter of the preceding Borderlife Project book (*Batos, Bolillos, Pochos, and Pelados*, 1999), we talked about several nonbehavioral aspects of culture (which we called cultural orientations). This chapter is a continuation of that discussion, though our focus here will be on the behavioral aspect of culture; specifically, cultural practices.

2. Parillo defines ethnogenesis as the process by which an ethnic group selectively absorbs some elements of the host culture and modifies others, while at the same time modifying and dropping some of its native cultural heritage as it adapts to the new country. Vincent Parillo, *Understanding Race and Ethnic Relations*, 36. See also Andrew M. Greeley, *The American Catholic: A Social Portrait*, and Richard D. Alba, *Italian Americans: Into the Twilight of Ethnicity.*

3. For a review of these acculturation processes, see Cuellar, "Acculturation as a Moderator," 113–130.

4. P. J. Guarnaccia and O. Rodriguez, "Concepts of Culture and Their Role in the Development of Culturally Competent Mental Health Services," *Hispanic Journal of Behavioral Sciences* 18, no. 4 (1996): 419–443.

5. Few studies use cultural practices as a measure of culture. The few that do generally ask only about awareness or familiarity with the custom, rather than how frequently it is practiced. Keefe and Padilla's study (*Chicano Ethnicity*), for example, contained 137 items, but few addressed specific cultural customs and practices.

6. A coefficient alpha of $r = .91$ was obtained for the entire scale of 43 items, with item-total correlations ranging from = .20 to .60.

7. There have been many studies of the concept of machismo in Latin American societies. In many of these societies, there is general agreement that it means male virility, authority, and superiority, with much greater sexual freedom for males, regardless of marital status. See, for example, Lillian Comas-Diaz, "Mainland Puerto Rican Women: A Sociocultural Approach," *Journal of Community Psychology* 16 (1988): 21–31.

8. For a good discussion of machismo in a border context, see Andrew Rivera, "Remembrance and Forgetting: Chicano Masculinity on the Border," *Latino Studies Journal* 8, no. 2 (1997): 35–56.

9. Norma Williams, in a study of seventy-five Mexican American couples, found that the authority and power of Mexican American men has declined in recent decades. She attributes this, not to acculturation to Anglo society, but to the effects of modernization. Williams also contends that many of the portrayals of Mexican culture as male dominant are more a reflection of stereotypes in the dominant culture of the United States than actual cultural beliefs among this population. See Norma Williams, *The Mexican American Family: Tradition and Change.*

10. Norma Williams cites this practice as one that is widespread and gaining new support among Mexican Americans in the Rio Grande Valley. Ibid., 39.

11. According to the article "Quinceañera: A Celebration of Latina Womanhood," the word itself comes from the Spanish *quince*, "fifteen," and *años*, "years." The origins of the quinceañera are often attributed to the ancient customs of the Aztecs, but the ceremony and meaning behind it are similar to other ancient cultural initiation rites that occurred throughout the world. Mary Zwolinski, "Quinceañera: A Celebration of Latina Womanhood," *Voices* 28 (Fall–Winter 2002).

12. Norma Williams found in her study of South Texas couples that among Mexican Americans, particularly those of the working class, both men and women strongly supported the role of men as providers, generally considering it their primary role. She emphasizes, of course, that some changes are taking place in this traditional role and that individual couples often make adjustments in this role, behaving somewhat differently than the ways called for in the traditional version of it. Williams, *Mexican American Family*, 97–108.

13. Norma Williams found that this aspect of the male role is changing not only among Mexican Americans but among many couples. It was not uncommon among many of the couples she interviewed to find, for example, significant changes in the way power was shared over the years of their marriage. Ibid., 97–108.

14. Though some writers propose that Mexican culture allows—or even encourages—men to use force on their wives, our Perceptions of Deviance Survey revealed the strongest negative reaction among both women and men to the item "How right or wrong is it for a man to slap his wife if she talks back to him?" The mean negative response for women was -3.72 (out of -5 possible), while for men the score was -3.13. Though this difference between men and women was statistically significant (F = 7.428; sig. = .007), for both men and women no other item in our forty-eight-item scale was viewed more negatively. Even the mean negative scores for selling illegal drugs, shoplifting, and buying stolen cars were lower.

15. It may be recalled that we asked the 433 respondents in this survey to indicate how frequently they and those close to them practiced each custom, allowing them to choose "frequently," "occasionally," or "rarely or never." We also asked them to indicate how they felt about keeping each custom, allowing them to respond with "should be kept," "it doesn't matter," or "should be forgotten."

16. As we indicated earlier, this is essentially what Norma Williams has argued, though she is careful to explain the change, not as a form of Anglo-conformity, but a response to the pressures of modernization among Mexican Americans in the United States. Williams, *Mexican American Family.*

17. Though this practice is clearly associated with the Catholic religion, generally taking place at the time of a child's baptism, it is not uncommon among Mexican Americans who are Protestant.

18. Huntington argues that "the size, persistence, and concentration of Hispanic immigration tends to perpetuate the use of Spanish through successive generations." Huntington, "Hispanic Challenge," 6.

19. A *posada* is a nine-day search at Christmastime for an inn with a room to rent by a group singing and going door to door, usually in the evening, symbolic of the search by Mary and Joseph. Día de los Reyes is a gift-giving day twelve days after Christmas (January 6), and is symbolic of the arrival of the three kings in Bethlehem.

3. DISPLACED WORKERS

1. During the 2001 calendar year, almost 17,000 workers lost their jobs in the South Texas area. See José A. Pagan, introduction to *Worker Displacement in the US/Mexico Border Region: Issues and Challenges*.

2. Labor Council for Latin American Advancement, *Another America Is Possible: The Impact of NAFTA on the U.S. Latino Community and Lessons for Future Trade Agreements,* August 2004, 7–8. Data based on Bureau of Labor Statistics, "Current Employment Statistics," series ID CEU3231300001 (textile mills) and CEU3231500001 (apparel), www.bls.gov/PDQ/serv/et/surveyOutputServlet (accessed August 2005).

3. Pagan, *Worker Displacement*, 1.

4. The region's population has more than doubled, increasing from 535,000 in 1970 to 1.3 million in 2000. The growth has outpaced that of Texas and the United States. Growth is attributed to both a relatively young population and immigration. See Cynthia Brown, "Labor and Demographic Challenges of the US/Mexico Border Region," in *Worker Displacement in the US/Mexico Border Region*, ed. José A. Pagan, 7.

5. The unemployment rate in the counties directly on the border was at least twice the national average in the year 2000, and nearly three times the national average in the lower Rio Grande Valley. Brown, "Labor and Demographic Challenges," 14–15.

6. Adam Seitchik, "Who Are Displaced Workers?" in *Job Displacement: Consequences and Implications for Policy*, ed. John T. Addison.

7. Daniel S. Hamermesh, "What Do We Know about Worker Displacement in the United States?" *Industrial Relations* 28, no. 1 (Winter 1989): 51–59.

8. Paul Flaim and Ellen Sehgal, "Displaced Workers of 1979–1983: How Well Have They Fared?" Bulletin no. 240, U.S. Department of Labor.

9. Bruce Fallick, "A Review of Recent Empirical Literature on Displaced Workers," *Industrial and Labor Relations Review* 50, no. 1 (1996): 5–16.

10. Michael Podgursky, "The Industrial Structure of Job Displacement, 1979–89," *Monthly Labor Review* 115, no. 9 (September 1992): 17–25; Henry S. Farber, "The Incidence and Costs of Job Loss, 1982–91," *Brookings Papers: Microeconomics* (1993): 73–132; Fallick, "Literature on Displaced Workers."

11. Seitchik, "Who Are Displaced Workers?"

12. Farber, "Job Loss, 1982–91"; Paul Swaim and Michael Podgursky. "Do More-Educated Workers Fare Better Following Job Displacement?" *Monthly Labor Review* 112, no. 8 (August 1989): 43–46.

13. Daniel S. Hamermesh, "The Human Capital Losses of Displaced Workers," Discussion Paper no. 753-84, Institute for Research on Poverty, University of Wisconsin, 1984; Fallick, "Literature on Displaced Workers."

14. Louis Jacobson, Robert LaLonde, and Daniel Sullivan. "Earnings Losses of Displaced Workers," *American Economic Review* 83, no. 4 (September 1993): 685–709.

15. Fallick, "Literature on Displaced Workers."

16. Texas Comptroller of Public Accounts, *Bordering the Future.* According to data from the Current Population Survey of the 818,380 workers that were displaced in Texas, 15.4 percent (125,690) resided in the Texas/Mexican border. Of these, about 57 percent were employed at the time of the survey, compared to 75 percent in non-border regions (Brown, "Labor and Demographic Challenges," 2, 24).

17. The unemployment rates in Hidalgo County, Texas, stayed around 20 percent through the 1990s and fell to 14 percent in 2002. Brown, "Labor and Demographic Challenges," 7.

18. Ibid., 24. The per capita income ranges from 38 percent of the U.S. average to 60 percent (Ibid., 7).

19. In 2001, 16,881 jobs were lost on the Texas-Mexico border due to displacement. On average, for every three local jobs lost due to displacement, two additional local jobs were lost due to indirect/induced causes, or roughly two-fifths of jobs lost due to displacement. The hardest hit counties were Bexar, El Paso, Nueces, Hidalgo, and Cameron. Pagan, *Worker Displacement*, 3, 45.

20. Lori L. Taylor, "The Border: Is It Really a Low-Wage Area?" in Federal Reserve Bank of Dallas, *The Border Economy.*

21. This program provided up to fifty-two weeks of income support (after regular unemployment benefits had been exhausted) for workers enrolled in training at a program-qualified facility who had lost (or were threatened with losing) manufacturing jobs or substantial income as a direct result of Canadian or Mexican imports, or whose employer relocated production to one of those countries. As with the TAA program, only those groups of workers who filed for certification with the Department of Labor and who met all the criteria were eligible for benefits. According to data collected by Public Citizen, the DOL certified only 62 percent of NAFTA-TAA petitions that it received in the almost nine years of the program's existence.

22. General Accounting Office, *Trade Adjustment Assistance in Case Study Communities*, report no. GAO-01-838, August 2001.

23. This project was conducted by means of a research grant from the Levi-Strauss Foundation that enabled us to hire and train a single interviewer. The difficulty of tracking down displaced workers precluded the use of students from UT Pan American, although some of their interviews are also included in the study.

24. Hispanic workers have been among those hardest hit by worker displacement. In 1999, for example, 47 percent of the total number of workers who received federal assistance under a program for workers certified as having lost jobs as a direct result of NAFTA were Hispanic. See U.S. General Accounting Office, *Trade Adjustment Assistance: Trends, Outcomes and Management Issues in Dislocated Worker Programs*, report no. GAO-01-59, October 2000, Appendix 1.

25. We have chosen not to use the actual names of these companies and their plants to help preserve the anonymity of the workers we interviewed.

26. For more information about the effect of low levels of human capital on the U.S.-Mexico Border, see Brown, "Labor and Demographic Challenges," 8.

27. In 2002 manufacturing employment in Texas fell by 3.3 percent, with most of these losses concentrated in computers and electronics, primary and fabricated metals, transportation equipment, and apparel. Manufacturing employment at the end of 2002 dropped below

1 million for the first time since 1994, to a total of 991,000 (Texas Comptroller of Public Accounts, *Texas Economic Update*). During the 2001 calendar, almost 17,000 workers lost their job in South Texas. See Pagan, introduction to *Worker Displacement*. See also Carole Keeton Strayhorn, "Struggling Economy," *Texas Economic Update* (Spring 2003), www.window.state .tx.us/ecodata/teuspo3 (accessed August 18, 2004).

28. In the year 2000, nearly a third of the residents in the Lower Rio Grande Valley and a fifth of the residents along the Texas-Mexico border had less than a fifth-grade education, compared to 8 percent nationwide. Moreover only 20 percent had a high school diploma. Brown, "Labor and Demographic Challenges," 10.

29. In the year 2000, 39.2 percent of the residents in the Rio Grande Valley described themselves as not speaking English "very well." Ibid., 14.

30. In 2001 there were over 1,300 fewer manufacturing jobs than in 2000 in the five counties that comprise the Rio Grande Valley. Ibid., 15.

31. For more on the effects of advance knowledge of displacement on job search and joblessness, see Bruce Fallick, "The Endogenity of Advance Notice and Fear of Destructive Attrition," *Review of Economics and Statistics* 76, no. 2 (1994): 378–385; S. R. G. Jones and P. Kuhn, "Mandatory Notice and Unemployment," *Journal of Labor Economics* 13, no. 4 (1995): 599–622; and C. J. Ruhm, "Advance Notice, Job Search, and Postdisplacement Earnings," *Journal of Labor Economics* 12, no. 1 (1994): 1–32.

32. Fallick, "Literature on Displaced Workers," 13.

33. Alberto Davila and Andrés Rivas reported that of the 125,690 long-tenure workers who had been displaced between January 1997 and December 1999, 57 percent had been reemployed, 19.45 percent were still unemployed, and 23.54 percent were not in the labor force. Alberto Davila and Andrés Rivas, "Worker Displacement in the Texas/Mexico Border MSAs: Evidence from the Current Population Survey," in *Worker Displacement in the US/Mexico Border Region: Issues and Challenges*, ed. Jose A. Pagan, 23–33.

34. Fallick "Literature on Displaced Workers," 13.

35. Farber, "Job Loss, 1982–91," 73–132.

36. Fallick, "Literature on Displaced Workers," 10.

37. In the U.S., the earnings associated with education have increased during the past decade. Workers with a high school diploma earn 44 percent less than those with a college degree. Brown, "Labor and Demographic Challenges," 9.

38. Ibid., 12.

4. UNDOCUMENTED WORKERS

1. Academics like Samuel P. Huntington, chair of the Harvard Academy for International and Area Studies (and cofounder of the journal *Foreign Policy*), raises alarms about Hispanic immigrants being too different and unwilling to assimilate. In his book *Who Are We?* Huntington even proposes that Hispanics in the Southwest may attempt to break away from the United States in future years.

2. Inter-American Commission on Human Rights, *Annual Report of the Inter-American Commission on Human Rights 2001*, "Economic Consequences of Migration," http://www .cidh.org/migrantes/chap6a.2001.eng.htm#iv (accessed September 14, 2001).

3. Chirag Mehta, Nik Theodore, Iliana Mora, and Jennifer Wade, *Chicago's Undocumented Immigrants: An Analysis of Wages, Working Conditions, and Economic Contributions*, 35.

4. Inter-American Development Bank, "Latin American Immigrants in the United States to Send $30 Billion to Homelands in 2004," May 17, 2004, http://www.iadb.org/NEWS/DISPLAY/PRView.cfm?PR_Num=98_04&Language=English.

5. Thomas J. Espenshade, "Unauthorized Immigration to the United States," *Annual Review of Sociology* 21 (1995): 195.

6. According to the *New York Times*, an estimated 7 million illegal immigrant workers in the United States are providing the Social Security system with a subsidy of as much as $7 billion a year through the payroll taxes that are withheld from their wages. The Social Security Administration holds these contributions in an "earnings suspense file" that now totals $189 billion. Many of these workers, however, will not be eligible for any public pensions on retirement because they illegally purchased fake ID packages that include a Social Security card. The card provides a cover for their employers, who could be fined for knowingly hiring illegal immigrants under the IRCA reform law passed in 1986. See Eduardo Porter, "Illegal Immigrants Are Bolstering Social Security with Billions," *New York Times,* April 5, 2005, sec. A, p. 1.

7. Francisco L. Rivera-Batiz, "Underground on American Soil: Undocumented Workers and U.S. Immigration Policy," *Journal of International Affairs* 53, no. 2 (Spring 2000): 17.

8. Chirag Mehta et al., *Chicago's Undocumented Immigrants*, iv.

9. A study by Donald Huddle of Rice University is an exception, though it was never published in a peer-reviewed journal and was contested by some immigration experts.

10. Espenshade, "Unauthorized Immigration," 209.

11. Undocumented Workers Policy Research Project, *The Use of Public Services by Undocumented Aliens in Texas: A Study of State Costs and Revenues.*

12. Espenshade, "Unauthorized Immigration," 210.

13. Michael E. Fix and Jeffrey S. Passel, *Trends in Non-citizens' and Citizens' Use of Public Benefits Following Welfare Reform: 1994–1997,* http://www.urban.org/url.cfm?10=408086 (accessed March 1, 1999).

14. For an excellent discussion on how estimates of the number of undocumented Mexicans living in the U.S. are made, and the ways these statistical estimates are used and abused, see Ellwyn Stoddard, *U.S.-Mexico Borderlands Issues: The Bi-National Boundary, Immigration, and Economic Policies,* especially chap. 6.

15. Jeffrey S. Passel, Randolph Capps, Michael E. Fix, *Undocumented Immigrants: Facts and Figures,* Urban Institute Immigration Studies Program, January 12, 2004, http://www.urban.org/url.cfm?ID=1000587.

16. Ibid., 1.

17. Peter Brimelow, *Alien Nation: Common Sense about America's Immigration Disaster,* 182.

18. Rebecca L. Clark and Scott A. Anderson, *Illegal Aliens in Federal, State, and Local Criminal Justice Systems,* Urban Institute Report no. 410366, June 3, 2000, www.urban.org/url.cfm?=410366.

19. Clark and Anderson, *Illegal Aliens,* 6.

20. George Friedman, "Open Sources," *Stratfor Weekly,* January 5, 2004.

21. Ibid., 2.

22. Friedman further states, "The movement from Mexico is, from a legal standpoint . . . simply an internal migration within a territory whose boundaries were superimposed by history." Ibid.

23. Huntington, *Who Are We?* 253.

24. Linda Chavez, *Out of the Barrio: Toward a New Politics of Hispanic Assimilation.*

25. Ibid., 388.

26. Rodolfo Acuña, *Occupied America: A History of Chicanos,* 412.

27. Douglas S. Massey and Kristin E. Espinosa, "What's Driving Mexico-U.S. Migration? A Theoretical, Empirical, and Policy Analysis," *American Journal of Sociology* 102, no. 4 (January 1997): 987.

28. David Heer discusses the debate about the best type of sampling to use with undocumented individuals. He points out that some (like Wayne Cornelius) believe that the much higher response rate of snowball sampling (interviewing respondents that one knows and having them lead you to others) makes it superior to random sampling. Heer states his own preference for both types of sampling when interviewing undocumented individuals. David M. Heer, *Undocumented Mexicans in the United States.* Our own choice of snowball (or convenience) sampling was selected because of our use of student interviewers who chose individuals who already trusted them.

29. Douglas S. Massey, "The Settlement Process among Mexican Immigrants to the United States—New Methods and Findings," Appendix C in *Immigration and Statistics: A Story of Neglect,* 256.

30. According to their responses, 24 percent of those interviewed were U.S. citizens, 39 percent were legal residents, and 32 percent were undocumented. The survey was based on 3,802 interviews conducted between January and April of 2004. The states and the district covered in this survey represent more than 99 percent of the population of Latin American–born adults in the United States. It did not include Haitians or immigrants from the English-speaking Caribbean. Source: Inter-American Development Bank, State by State Survey of Remittance Senders: U.S. to Latin America, http.//idbdocs.iabg.org/wsdocs/getdocument.asp.?docnum=547238.

31. Banamex, *Review of the Economic Situation of Mexico* 80, no. 940 (April 2004): 150–152. The size of this cash inflow to Mexico can be better understood in relation to other sources of national income for Mexico. Only income from oil exports ($18.6 billion) topped income from remittances, www.banamex.com/esp/pdf_bin/esem/resemabni/09.pdf.

32. Massey and Espinosa, "What's Driving Mexico-U.S. Migration?"

33. Ibid., 998.

34. Michael B. Aguilera and Douglas S. Massey, "Social Capital and Wages of Mexican Migrants: New Hypotheses and Tests," *Social Forces* 82, no. 2 (December 2003): 671.

35. Wilson and Portes point to Miami and its population of Cubans enclaves as an example of the benefits and drawbacks they give undocumented workers. Kenneth L. Wilson and Alejandro Portes, "Immigrants' Enclaves: An Analysis of the Labor Market Experiences of Cubans in Miami," *American Journal of Sociology* 86, no. 2 (September 1980).

36. B. Lindsay Lowell and Roberto Suro, "How Many Undocumented: The Numbers behind the U.S.-Mexico Migration Talks," Pew Hispanic Center, March 21, 2002, 8, http://www.pewhispanic.org/reports/report.php?ReportID=6.

37. Massey, *The Settlement Process.*

38. According to Julie A. Phillips and Douglas S. Massey, in 1986 the Immigration Reform and Control Act (IRCA) granted amnesty to 3 million people. It gave citizenship to 1.7 million people who had been long-term residents in the United States; another 1.3 million workers were given citizenship as Special Agricultural Workers. Julie A. Phillips and Douglas S. Massey, "Consequences of Policy Shifts and Political Change—The New Labor Market: Immigrants and Wages after IRCA," *Demography* 36, no. 2 (1999).

39. George J. Borjas, *Friends or Strangers: The Impact of Immigrants on the U.S. Economy.*

40. Francisco L. Rivera-Batiz, "Underground on American Soil," 2000.

41. Francisco L. Rivera-Batiz, "Undocumented Workers in the Labor Market: An Analysis of the Earnings of Legal and Illegal Mexican Immigrants in the United States," *Journal of Population Economics* 12, no. 1 (1999): 91.

42. A study by Hood, Morris, and Shirkey proposes five hypotheses to explain why many Mexican Americans and other Hispanics do not favor undocumented workers and illegal immigration. First, some Hispanics may perceive limited cultural benefits from an expanding Hispanic population; second, Hispanics may not feel a strong sense of group identification with the undocumented; third, Hispanics may have become more acculturated; fourth, Hispanics may fear increased job competition from new immigrants; and fifth, more affluent and more highly educated Hispanics may be more likely to have a negative view of undocumented workers. M. V. Hood III, Irwin L. Morris, and Kurt A. Shirkey, "'¡Quédate o Vente!': Uncovering the Determinants of Hispanic Public Opinion toward Immigration," *Political Research Quarterly*, September 1997.

43. We obtained similar results when we compared categories based on their generation score. Those whose generation score was 0 (Mexican immigrants) had a mean score of +.54 on this item, compared to −.87 for those with Generation scores of 1–4; −.56 for those with Generation scores of 5–8; −.48 for those with Generation scores of 9–11; and −1.56 for those with the top Generation score of 12 (very American).

44. Chirag Mehta, Nik Theodore, Iliana Mora, and Jennifer Wade, *Chicago's Undocumented Immigrants: An Analysis of Wages, Working Conditions, and Economic Contributions,* 12–13, February 2002, http://www.uic.edu/cuppa/uicued/npublications/recent/undoc_full.pdf.

45. Tim Wise, "Defending the Unwelcome Stranger: The Truth about Immigration," LiPmagazine.org, September 26, 2003. http://www.lipmagazine.org/articles/featwise_immigrationexcerpt.shtml. Tax surplus has been $30 billion annually. Undocumented Workers Policy Research Project, "The Use of Public Services by Undocumented Aliens in Texas: A Study of State Costs and Revenues." Report, LBJ School of Public Affairs, University of Texas at Austin, 1984.

5. IMMIGRATION ENFORCEMENT ISSUES

1. Only ten years ago, 97 percent of all undocumented aliens apprehended were expelled by means of "voluntary departure." The percentage expelled by more punitive means has been steadily rising and now accounts for the forced removal of 15 percent of those detained. Based on INS 2001 Annual Report, Table 6.3.

2. Audrey Singer and Douglas S. Massey, "The Social Process of Undocumented Border Crossing among Mexican Migrants," *International Migration Review* 32, no. 3 (Autumn 1998): 574.

3. Apparently the number of times an undocumented person can be apprehended without formal charges varies from sector to sector within the Border Patrol, and from one director to another as administrators change.

4. The in-depth interview project was part of a larger project funded by the Center for Border Economic Studies at the University of Texas–Pan American to determine the probable impact of the US-VISIT program. For the results of this study, see Suad Ghaddar, Chad Richardson, and Cynthia Brown, "The Economic Impact of Mexican Visitors to the Lower Rio Grande Valley, 2003."

5. Keith Phillips and Carlos Manzanares, "Transportation Infrastructure and the Border Economy," in *The Border Economy*, 11.

6. *Border Business Briefs* (special issue), Center for Border Economic Studies, UT-PA, Edinburg, Texas, 2005, 10.

7. Ghaddar, Richardson, and Brown used survey evidence to estimate that 85 percent of visitors to the Rio Grande Valley were using the laser visa at the beginning of 2004. Ghaddar, Richardson, and Brown, "Economic Impact of Mexican Visitors."

8. The US-VISIT program was mandated by section 110 of the Illegal Immigration Reform and Immigrant Responsibility Act of 1996 (IIRIRA). It required the attorney general to develop an automated entry-exit system that would collect records on the arrival and departure of every foreign national entering and leaving the United States. After seven years, this system became operational at 115 airports and fourteen seaports in the United States. Congressional deadlines required the USCIS to expand this program to the top fifty high-traffic land border ports by December 2004 and to all remaining ports of entry by the end of 2005. Because the infrastructure to do so was not in place at the time, and because of strong opposition to the snarls it would create at border land ports, its implementation was delayed. Many residents of the U.S.-Mexico border expressed anger that the Department of Homeland Security exempted Canadian citizens from the US-VISIT requirements that were being imposed on Mexican visitors.

9. McAllen, Texas, leads the rest of Texas in "exported" retail sales—sales to Mexican nationals—largely as a result of its proximity to Monterrey, Mexico, home to nearly 4 million people (and some of the wealthiest families in Mexico). See Pia M. Orrenius and Anna L. Berman, "Growth on the Border or Bordering on Growth?" Maquila Portal, 3, http://www.maquilaportal.com/public/artic/artic183e.htm. McAllen's retail sales grew 138 percent during the 1990s to a current annual total of over 2 billion dollars and employing 27 percent of the workforce. See "McAllen Overview," http://www.mcallen.org/business/overview.

10. See Pia M. Orrenius and Anna L. Berman, "Growth on the Border."

11. In much of the Spanish-speaking world, it is a sign of disrespect to use the familiar form of speaking with an older person. Reese notes that Mexicans view themselves as coming from the "old tradition of the 'ranchos,' where respect is central to their cultural values." See Leslie Reese, "Morality and Identity in Mexican Immigrant Parents' Vision of the Future," *Journal of Ethnic and Migration Studies* 27, no. 3 (July 2001): 460.

12. Many of the people we interviewed who had crossed into the U.S. by land and by air said they are treated much better by immigration officers at U.S. airports. The official attitude at border ports of entry seems to be that their function is mainly law enforcement. The official attitude at airports, in contrast, appears to be closer to the idea of providing a service.

13. The tight limits that the Mexican government puts on cross-border shoppers, with the attendant risks of having some purchases confiscated, was a commonly expressed concern.

14. Ghaddar, Richardson, and Brown calculated that the average traveler by auto spent almost $5,000 a year. Ghaddar, Richardson, and Brown, "Economic Impact of Mexican Visitors," i.

15. Over 74 percent of undocumented workers are estimated to be employed in service jobs, mostly housecleaning, farmwork, janitorial work, food service, and child care. Most of the remaining are employed in low-paying clerical or technical jobs as, for example, dressmakers and machine operators, while a small percentage of them work in sales. Ibid., 101–102.

16. Agriculture has been defined as the second-most hazardous industry in the United States. Farmworkers have the highest mortality and morbidity rate of all occupational catego-

ries, mainly due to their high level of poverty, mobility, and employment in dangerous work. In addition, as a group, they lack access to health care. See Triantafillou, "North Carolina's Migrant and Seasonal Farm Workers," 129.

17. Despite the abuse that many illegals are subject to while living in the United States, 84 percent describe their lives in the U.S. as better than in Mexico. Rodolfo O. De la Garza and Louis DeSipio, "Interest Not Passions: Mexican American Attitudes toward Mexico, Immigration from Mexico, and Other Issues Shaping U.S.-Mexico Relations," *International Migration Review* 32, no. 2 (Summer 1998): 404; Chavez, *Out of the Barrio*, 103.

18. For a discussion of this process and the many hazards it presents, see Chad Richardson and Joe Feagin, "The Dynamics of Legalization: Undocumented Mexican Immigrants in the United States," *Research in Political Sociology* 3 (1987): 179–201.

19. Currently, the income level required is 125 percent of the official poverty line.

20. According to the INS, there is a greater demand for counterfeit documents because the levels of enforcement along the border have increased. In May 1998 the INS office in Los Angeles seized more than 24,000 counterfeit documents such as Social Security cards, alien cards, and driver's licenses.

21. "Immigration Information: Investigations," 2002, http://uscis.gov/graphics/shared/aboutus/statistics/msrmar03/IVST.HTM (accessed August 23, 2004).

22. Jennifer Muir and Angeles Negrete, "Trafficker Has History of Smuggling Immigrants," *Brownsville (TX) Herald*, May 20, 2003.

23. Beto's comments once more confirm the finding reported by Rivera-Batiz in reference to the higher economic status of OTMs. Rivera-Batiz, "Underground on American Soil," 496.

24. Rivera-Batiz found in his wage analysis of undocumented workers vis-à-vis legal Mexican American workers that on average the first earn 41.8 percent less than those with work permits. Rivera-Batiz, "Undocumented Workers in the Labor Market," 100.

25. In addition to an increase in the number of private citizens "deputizing" themselves to protect their territory and the border region, as Carmelo experienced, laws have also become more restrictive (Michael Fix and Karen Tumlin, *Welfare Reform and the Devolution of Immigrant Policy*; Steven P. Wallace, Vilma Enriquez-Haass, and Kyriakos S. Markides, "The Consequences of Color-Blind Health Policy for Older Racial and Ethnic Minorities," *Stanford Law and Policy Review* 9 [Spring 1998]: 329–346; Jacqueline L. Angel, "Late-Life Immigration, Changes in Living Arrangements and Headship Status among Older Mexican-Origin Individuals," *Social Science Quarterly* 81, no. 1 [March 2000]: 390). Americans fear that illegal aliens become dependent on public welfare programs, therefore immigrants that arrived in the U.S. after August 22, 1996, cannot apply for SSI (Anne Durkelberg, *Impact on Immigrants*).

26. Technically, each person arrested while entering the United States has the right to a hearing before an immigration judge, but neither the migrant nor the Border Patrol agent has interest in pursuing this course of action. On the contrary, it is in their self-interest that the migrant be "voluntarily returned" to Mexico as soon as possible. Singer and Massey, "Social Process of Undocumented Border Crossing," 564.

27. For a discussion of the effects of such discretionary authority, see Richardson, *Batos, Bolillos, Pochos, and Pelados*, 179–201.

28. Cano's experience and response are very common among Mexican American INS officers. Josiah Heyman charted the attitudes of INS officers and found that a greater majority (85 percent) of Mexican American officers favor immigration restrictions than Whites (Ang-

los) (79 percent). He suggests that this is due to the importance that a "good government job" signifies for the Mexican American officers. Josiah McC. Heyman, "U.S. Immigration Officers of Mexican Ancestry as Mexican Americans, Citizens, and Immigration Police," *Current Anthropology* 43, no. 3 (June 2002): 485–486.

29. Many Mexican American agents find themselves in this dilemma. However, some justify their behavior by accepting the common stigma associated with illegal immigrants, which is that they are criminals because they have entered the country illegally. Therefore, it is easier for agents to arrest them when they feel they are enforcing the law. Robert Short and Lisa Magaña, "Political Rhetoric, Immigration Attitudes, and Contemporary Prejudice: A Mexican American Dilemma," *Journal of Social Psychology*, 142, no. 6 (2002): 703.

6. DRUG SMUGGLING

1. Tom Barry, Harry Browne, and Beth Sims, *Crossing the Line: Immigrants, Economic Integration, and Drug Enforcement on the U.S.-Mexico Border.*

2. From the inception of the Borderlife Project in 1979, students were free to choose a topic for a course paper without getting prior approval. We constantly stressed to students who *might* choose to interview people violating the law that they had to be extremely careful to avoid dangerous situations, to interview only people they could trust, and to be scrupulously careful in protecting the identity of those interviewed.

3. Lupe Treviño, at that time director/commander, McAllen Office, Hidalgo County South Texas High Intensity Drug Trafficking Area, was interviewed by Chad Richardson, October 2000. He is now the sheriff of Hidalgo County.

4. Ibid.

5. *South Texas HIDTA FY 2000 Strategy.*

6. National Drug Intelligence Center, *National Drug Threat Assessment 2003: Money Laundering,* http://www.usdoj.gov/ndic/pubs3/3300/money.htm#Top:3 (accessed August 28, 2004). In 2004, there were 17,444,585 private vehicle crossings into the U.S. over bridges into the Lower Rio Grande Valley and 6,705,335 pedestrian crossings. *Border Business Briefs,* 10.

7. Lupe Treviño, interviewed by authors, October 2000.

8. Patrick O'Day and Rex Venecia, "Cazuelas: An Ethnographic Study of Drug Trafficking in a Small Mexican Border Town," *Journal of Contemporary Criminal Justice* 15, no. 4 (1999): 412.

9. Ibid.

10. National Drug Intelligence Center, *National Drug Threat Assessment 2003.*

11. Lupe Treviño, interviewed by authors, October 2000.

12. National Drug Intelligence Center, *Texas Drug Threat Assessment,* 13–14.

13. The magnitude of this amount can be understood if one knows that the economy of Texas would make it the world's tenth-largest economy if it were an independent nation. See Texas Comptroller of Public Accounts, *Bordering the Future,* 146.

14. Lupe Treviño, interviewed by authors, October 2000.

15. Lynn Duke, "Key Mexican in Corruption Case Kills Self; Ex-Narcotics Prosecutor Faced Charges in U.S." *Washington Post,* September 16, 1999, sec. A-17.

16. Tim Weiner and Tim Golden, "Free-Trade Treaty May Widen Traffic in Drugs, U.S. Says." *New York Times,* May 24, 1993.

17. Lupe Treviño, interviewed by authors, October 2000.

18. Bank deposits in Hidalgo County rose from $2.7 billion in 1994 to $6.6 billion in 2004, an increase of almost 250 percent in only ten years. *Border Business Briefs*, 18.

19. From Jane Carlisle Maxwell, *Substance Abuse Trends in Texas, June 2004*, http://www .utexas.edu/research/cswr/gcattc/Trends/trends704.pdf (accessed August 28, 2004).

20. Ibid., 3.

21. Ibid., 7.

22. Rohypnol, also known as roofies, rophies, roche, and the forget-me pill, is odorless and tasteless and dissolves completely in liquid. It produces sedative-hypnotic effects, including muscle relaxation and amnesia, and can cause psychological and physiological dependence. Because of its sedative properties, it is often used in the commission of drug-facilitated rape. Though Roche, the manufacturer of the drug, makes it with a blue dye, this warning is often ineffective when it is served in blue tropical drinks and punches. Generic versions do not even contain the dye.

23. Office of Applied Studies, *Substate Estimates from the 1999–2001 National Surveys of Drug Use and Health* (Rockville, MD: Substance Abuse and Mental Health Services Administration, 2005), http:www/drugabusestatistics.samhsa.gov/substate2k5/secA.htm (accessed October 2005).

24. Liang Y. Liu, *Texas School Survey of Substance Use among Students: Grades 7–12, 2002*, http://www.tcada.state.tx.us/research/survey/grades7-12/SchoolSurvey2002.pdf (accessed 28 August 2004).

25. "Results from the 2003 Monitoring the Future Study," ONDCP fact sheet, National Institute on Drug Abuse, March 2003, http://www.nida.nih.gov/Newsroom/03/2003MTFFactSheet.pdf (accessed August 28, 2004).

26. Jane Carlisle Maxwell, *Substance Abuse Trends in Texas, December 2003*, 19, http://www.utexas.edu/research/cswr/gcattc/Trends/trends1203.pdf (accessed 28 August 2004).

27. National Drug Intelligence Center, *Texas Drug Threat Assessment*, 27–29.

28. National Drug Intelligence Center, *National Drug Threat Assessment 2003*, 3.

29. A metric ton is equal to 1,000 kilograms.

30. *Drug Intelligence Brief: Mexico: Country Brief, July 2002*, prepared by the DEA Intelligence Division, International Strategic Support Section, Mexico/C. America Unit, http://www.usdoj.gov/dea/pubs/intel/02035/02035p.html.

31. U.S. House Committee on Banking and Financial Services Subcommittee on General Oversight and Investigations, "Money Laundering Activity Associated with the Mexican Narco-Crime Syndicate."

32. Patrick O'Day, "The Mexican Army as Cartel," *Journal of Contemporary Criminal Justice* 17, no. 3 (2001): 278–295.

33. Terence P. Jeffrey, "Do Mexican Troops Bring Drugs to U.S.?" Human Events, July 1, 2002, www.freerepublic.com/focus/news/707827/posts.

34. Ibid., 2.

35. Lupe Treviño, interviewed by authors, October 2000.

36. Ibid.

37. Avelardo Valdez and Stephen J. Sifaneck, "Getting High and Getting By: Dimensions of Drug Selling Behaviors among U.S. Mexican Gang Members in South Texas," *Journal of Research in Crime and Delinquency* 41, no. 1 (2004).

38. National Drug Intelligence Center, *National Drug Threat Assessment 2003*, 8.

39. O'Day and Venecia, "Cazuelas"; Valdez and Sifaneck, "Getting High and Getting By."

40. O'Day and Venecia, "Cazuelas."

41. While this reference to God aiding her in smuggling drugs may seem unusual, we found that many of our respondents believed God sided with them in their efforts. Indeed, some make it a practice to pray to "San Malverde" each time they make a run, to request help in avoiding capture.

42. Elijah Wald, *Narcocorrido: A Journey into the Music of Drugs, Guns, and Guerillas.*

43. Américo Paredes, *A Texas-Mexican Cancionero: Folksongs of the Lower Border;* Américo Paredes, *With His Pistol in His Hand: A Border Ballad and Its Hero.*

44. Sebastian Rotella, *Twilight on the Line: Underworlds and Politics at the U.S.-Mexico Border.*

7. PROPERTY CRIME

1. Though Mario, like many incarcerated youth, is probably serious about his resolve to stop smuggling, the lure of quick profits, old friends, and "criminal embeddedness" will make it very difficult for him to keep his resolve. See Joan McCord, Cathy Spatz Wisdom, and Nancy A. Crowell, eds., *Juvenile Crime, Juvenile Justice,* 194–203.

2. Susan Dow, *Border Children Justice Projects,* 1, October 1998, http://www.tjpc.state.tx .us/publications/reports/border%5Fchildren.htm (accessed 31 August 2004).

3. Ibid., 6.

4. One Border Patrol officer, interviewed in June 2004 by one of the authors, indicated that Mexican juveniles have a virtual license to steal in the U.S. because of the lack of cross-border cooperation on this issue.

5. Data were collected via numerous interviews designed to elicit information related to shoplifting and those arrested for shoplifting. People interviewed had experience in apprehending and prosecuting shoplifters and included local law enforcement officers and prosecutors. Also interviewed were individuals who bought stolen merchandise, as well as shoplifting offenders who were in custody at the Hidalgo County Detention Center and those on probation at the Hidalgo County Courthouse. Additional data were collected through direct observation and unobtrusive observational recording of individuals engaging in shoplifting.

6. Both of these students worked under the direction of Chad Richardson and had access to material from the Borderlife Archive.

7. Rosalva Resendiz, "International Auto Theft: An Exploratory Research of Organization and Organized Crime on the U.S./Mexico Border," *Criminal Organizations* 12 (1998); Rosalva Resendiz and David M. Neal, "International Auto Theft: The Illegal Export of American Vehicles to Mexico," in *International Criminal Justice: Issues in Global Perspective,* ed. D. Rounds; Rosalva Resendiz, "Taking Risks within the Constraints of Gender: Mexican American Women as Professional Auto Thieves," *Social Science Journal* 38, no. 3 (2001).

8. "Theft Surveys," Hayes International, 2001, http://www.hayesinternational.com/thft_ srvys.html.

9. "Crime Characteristics 2002," Bureau of Justice Statistics, http://www.ojp.usdoj.gov/ bjs/cvict_c.htm (accessed August 31, 2004).

10. "Crime in McAllen, 2002: City of McAllen Crime Report," McAllen Police Department, http://www.mcallen.net/police/docs/2002crimeinmcallen.pdf (accessed August 31, 2004).

11. Rushing's "Class, Culture, Social Structure, and Anomie" is an important exception. Rushing studied the goals and aspirations of lower-class Hispanic farmworkers and upper-

middle-class Anglo farmers. He examined whether shoplifting among low-income people was related more to normlessness or to economic need. He concluded that culture does not play a major role in shoplifting, either in the level of aspiration and goals of individuals or in the level of their "normlessness." William A. Rushing, "Class, Culture, Social Structure, and Anomie," *American Journal of Sociology* 76, no. 5 (1971).

12. "Facts about Shoplifting," Shoplifters Alternative, 2003, http://www .shopliftersalternative.org (accessed September 1, 2004).

13. People in this category refused to identify themselves in a standard ethnic category and preferred to use the term "American." Other data on these individuals showed that many were of Hispanic origin, but did not accept being so classified.

14. For a description of this process, see Michael V. Miller, "Vehicle Theft along the Texas-Mexico Border," *Journal of Borderlands Studies* 2, no. 2 (1987).

15. Ibid.

16. Ibid.

17. For a comprehensive list of references of auto theft studies, see Rosalva Resendiz, "International Auto Theft: An Exploratory Research of the Property Offender and the Organizational Crime Process in the U.S./Mexico Border."

18. Miller, "Vehicle Theft along the Texas-Mexico Border."

19. A study on theft recovery rates from insurance companies was done by S. Field, Ronald V. Clarke, and P. M. Harris. Reports made in 1985 were used for models dating from 1983 to 1985. The study found that particular models were targeted: "Buick Century, Chevrolet Malibu, Chevrolet Citation, Chevrolet Celebrity, Chevrolet Caprice/Impala, Chevrolet Monte Carlo, Chrysler E Class/New Yorker, Chrysler Le Baron, Ford Mustang, Ford Thunderbird, Mercury Topaz, Mercury Cougar, Nissan Sentra, Renault Alliance, Renault 181, Volkswagen Jetta, Volkswagen Golf, Volkswagen Rabbit," 2. See S. Field, Ronald V. Clarke, and P. M. Harris, "The Mexican Vehicle Market and Auto Theft in Border Areas of the United States," *Security Journal* 2, no. 4 (1991): 205–210.

20. Resendiz, "International Auto Theft: An Exploratory Research of Organization and Organized Crime on the U.S./Mexico Border"; Resendiz and Neal, "International Auto Theft"; Resendiz, "Taking Risks within the Constraints of Gender."

21. Miller, "Vehicle Theft along the Texas-Mexico Border."

22. *Noticias Paragon* (Mexico) news release, March 12, 2001, http://www.paragon.com.mx.

23. C. H. McCaghy, P. C. Giordano, and T. K. Henson, "Auto Theft: Offender and Offense Characteristics," *Criminology* 15, no. 3 (1977): 367–385.

24. Ronald V. Clarke and P. M. Harris, "Auto Theft and Its Prevention," in *Crime and Justice: A Review of Research,* vol. 16, ed. M. Tonry; A. Karmen, "Auto Theft: Beyond Victim Blaming," *Victimology* 5 (1980); McCaghy, Giodano, and Henson, "Auto Theft"; P. Tremblay, Y. Clermont, and M. Cusson, "Jockeys and Joyriders: Changing Patterns in Car Theft Opportunity Structures," *British Journal of Criminology* 34 no. 3 (1994); Resendiz, "International Auto Theft: An Exploratory Research of the Property Offender and the Organizational Crime Process in the U.S./Mexico Border."

25. The data presented on chop shops are from 1991 to 1996. Informants were chop shop operators, auto thieves, and law enforcement officers.

26. As indicated previously, the category of "American" was chosen by some who preferred not to distinguish their ethnicity.

27. Peter A. Lupsha, "The Border Underworld," in *Borders and Frontiers: Teaching about International Boundaries,* ed. G. M. Hansen, 1.

28. Previous research on auto theft indicates that federal agents from Mexico have been involved in or associated with auto theft rings. See, for example, Miller, "Vehicle Theft along the Texas-Mexico Border."

29. Convicted auto thief, personal correspondence with Rosalva Resendiz, 2002.

30. Al Giordano, "Narco-Corruption at U.S. Customs Service," Free Republic, August 3, 2001, http://www.freerepublic.com/forum/a3b6ab3454de7.htm (accessed August 31, 2004); Texas Commission of Law Enforcement Officer Standards Education (TCLEOSE), newsletters, http://www.tcleose.state.tx.us (accessed August 31, 2004).

8. AMERICAN LIVES, MEXICAN JUSTICE

1. According to a letter from Gustavo Petricioli, ambassador of Mexico to the United States, to Congressman Kika de la Garza, May 27, 1992, they were not eligible for bail because Mexican law requires preventive imprisonment in cases where people have been charged with crimes associated with longer sentences, such as drug trafficking.

2. Recent research by James E. Lange and Robert B. Voas, "Youth Escaping Limits on Drinking: Binging in Mexico," *Addiction* 95 (2000), and James E. Lange, Robert B. Voas, and Mark B. Johnson, "South of the Border: A Legal Haven for Underage Drinking," *Addiction* 97 (2002), has found that even though underage drinking tends to be more associated with males, there is a recent tendency among females to cross the Mexican border to engage in underage and binge drinking. In our own Perceptions of Deviance Survey, females were significantly more negative about drinking in Mexico than males, with mean scores of -2.86 and 2.19, respectively ($F = 6.878$; Sig. $= .009$). Two predominant themes among underage drinkers who cross the Mexican border are that (1) it is a rite of passage, in which adolescents who turn eighteen go to Mexico to drink alcohol out of reach of U.S. authorities and away from parental hassles; and (2) drinking regulations are not enforced on the Mexican side. Lange, Voas, and Johnson, "South of the Border," found that drinking in Mexico was associated with the low price of alcohol and the significantly less serious consequences resulting from getting drunk.

3. In the youngest age category, twenty-five individuals ranked hanging out with friends late at night in one of the negative categories (-1 through -5), while only seven ranked it in one of the positive categories ($+1$ through $+5$).

4. Two studies found that minors living in border towns, where access to alcohol is relatively unimpeded, are at high risk of alcohol abuse, including driving while intoxicated. See Lange, Voas, and Johnson, "South of the Border," and Sarah McKinnon, Kathleen M. O'Rourke, Sharon E. Thompson, and Jessica H. Berumen, "Alcohol Use and Abuse by Adolescents: The Impact of Living in a Border Community," *Journal of Adolescent Health* 34 (2004).

5. José María Ramos and David A. Shirk, "Binational Collaboration in Law Enforcement and Public Security Issues on the U.S.-Mexican Border," presented at the conference "Reforming the Administration of Justice in Mexico," Center for U.S.-Mexican Studies, University of California, San Diego, 2003.

6. Arteaga Botello and López Rivera have documented how corruption works inside Mexican police organizations. Corruption, as these researchers point out, is institutionalized in police departments at all levels (local, state, and federal). They found that corruption is the rule, while honesty tends to be considered deviant. See Nelson Arteaga Botello and Adrián

López Rivera, "Everything in This Job Is Money: Inside the Mexican Police," *World Policy Journal* 17, no. 3 (2000). Stephen D. Morris has made the same point in "La política acostumbrada o política insólita? El problema de la corrupción en México," in *Vicios públicos, virtudes privadas: La corrupción en México,* ed. Claudio Lomnitz.

7. Arteaga Botello and López Rivera, "Everything in This Job is Money."

8. Ibid., 63.

9. Ibid.

10. Ibid., 65.

11. Ibid., 67.

12. There has been some effective resistance to the practice through united action. Some maquiladora associations along the border, for example, have an official agreement to refuse paying any mordidas to customs officers, recognizing that once some start, the pressure for others to follow will be great.

13. In 1993 a constitutional amendment transformed torture practices among all levels of police in Mexico. This law stipulated that a signed confession gained by police interrogation would become largely invalid in court. Further, for a confession to be valid, it must be signed in front of the district attorney [fiscal], the judge, and the defendant's attorney. See Luis De la Barreda Solórzano, *La lid contra la tortura.*

14. Human Rights Watch, *Human Rights in Mexico: A Policy of Impunity.*

15. Human Rights Watch, *Systemic Injustice: Torture, "Disappearance," and Extrajudicial Execution in Mexico,* 73.

16. Jail time may also be required if a person is involved in an automobile accident in which someone is injured, regardless of who is at fault. For this reason, many Mexicans involved in an accident in which there has been an injury will leave their vehicle and flee the scene to avoid being taken to jail when the police arrive. Those who flee can get an *amparo* [protection] from a judge that keeps them out of jail until a trial or investigation takes place. This practice occasionally spills across the border into Texas, where some Mexican drivers flee the scene of an accident, even one in which they are not at fault, to avoid being taken to jail. They discover, of course, that even more serious charges, such as failure to render aid or leaving the scene of an accident, may result.

17. Juan Pablo De Tavira, *¿Por qué Almoloya? Análisis de un proyecto penitenciario;* José María Rico, *Justicia penal y transición democrática en América Latina.*

18. As De Tavira points out, Mexican prisons, in principle, are based on a humanistic approach. The basic assumption behind this approach is that inmates should be enabled to socially reform themselves in order to be reinstated in society. As a result, and contrary to U.S. prison policy, Mexico allows inmates to have sexual contact with their partners and direct interaction with their families. De Tavira, *¿Por qué Almoloya?*

19. Juan Bustamante says, "I was in the Policía Judicial [State Judicial Police] of Nuevo Leon for almost two years. The director was trying to reform the agency structurally and culturally. It was a tough job for him. Because of his protection, when I worked in the streets nobody asked me to collect bribes or do anything beyond the law. I openly disclosed that I would not promote, witness, or support any kind of torture or bribing, so I did not personally witness such abuses. Still, I knew it was going on because everyone would hear about it. I finally resigned because I was transferred to a new narcotics unit that worked with the Policía Judicial Federal [Federal Judicial Police]. I didn't like the pressures for extortion, bribery, and the danger, all of which were much higher there. I was also alienated from the other officers and

labeled as unfriendly and "too honest." My wife and family wanted me to quit and I eventually agreed, in part because of the paltry salary I received. Since I was not committed to taking bribes or extorting people, I had to rely only on my monthly check. I already had two children, so it was very hard financially. I remember that I supplemented my income with an allowance my mother gave me. Those were tough times!"

20. De Tavira, *¿Por qué Almoloya?*, 101.

9. DROPPING OUT

1. The final report of the Hispanic Dropout Project, which details many of the causes and consequences of dropping out for Hispanics, states: "For students, dropping out forecloses a lifetime of opportunities—and in turn makes it far more likely that their own children will grow up in poverty and be placed at risk." Walter G. Secada et al., *No More Excuses: The Final Report of the Hispanic Dropout Project*, 6.

2. Dropout rates are difficult to come by in Texas. Texas is not eligible for federal money for dropout prevention because of the way it determines dropout rates. The Intercultural Development Research Association (IDRA), however, has used an attrition formula developed with five years of data to calculate the dropout rate, making it available by county. According to the data, the dropout rate for Hidalgo County is 50 percent, while the rate in neighboring Cameron County is 47 percent. IDRA, http://www.idra.org/Research/dout2001.htm.

3. U.S. Census Bureau, Census 2000 Summary File 4, Matrices PCT38, PCT61, PCT63, PCT64, PCT65, and PCT66.

4. Though ethnic bias has declined over the past forty years as a cause of dropping out, it still has a major impact on many Hispanic students. See Jeffrey C. Wayman, "Student Perceptions of Teacher Ethnic Bias: A Comparison of Mexican American and Non-Latino White Dropouts and Students," *High School Journal* 85, no. 3 (2000).

5. National Center for Educational Statistics, *The Educational Progress of Hispanic Students*.

6. Robyn S. Hess, "Dropping Out among Mexican American Youth: Reviewing the Local Literature through an Ecological Perspective," *Journal of Education for Students Placed at Risk* 5, no. 3 (2000).

7. Ibid., 269.

8. Phillip Kaufman, Martha Naomi Alt, and Christopher Chapman, *Dropout Rates in the United States: 2000*, 4, National Center for Education Statistics report.

9. Beth Shulman, *The Betrayal of Work*, 87.

10. Secada et al., *No More Excuses*, 15.

11. Russell Rumberger, "Chicano Dropouts: A Review of Research and Policy Issues," in *Chicano School Failure and Success: Research and Policy Agendas for the 1990s*, ed. Richard R. Valencia, 77.

12. One speaker at hearings regarding Hispanic dropouts in San Antonio echoed this idea, commenting, "Dropping out is sometimes a healthy response to an intolerable situation." Reported in Secada et al., *No More Excuses*, 11.

13. Among all Hispanics, the children of migrant farmworkers have the highest dropout rates, ranging from 45 percent to as high as 65 percent. See Yolanda G. Martinez and Ann Cranston-Gingras, "Migrant Farmworker Students and the Educational Process: Barriers to High School Completion," *High School Journal* 80, no. 1 (October/November 1996).

14. For a more complete discussion of how farmworkers are treated, see chap. 1 of *Batos, Bolillos, Pochos, and Pelados.*

15. National Center for Educational Statistics, "Dropout Rates in the United States," 4.

16. Ibid., 13.

17. Robyn S. Hess, citing a 1996 NCES study, for example, states, "The factors that contribute to school dropout are well known by researchers and educators alike . . . What is not known is why the dropout rate among Latinos is almost twice as high as for other low-income students." Hess, "Dropping Out among Mexican American Youth," 268.

18. Legislative Budget Board, State Auditor's Office, and Texas Education Agency, *Dropout Study: A Report to the 77th Texas Legislature,* December 2000.

19. Joyce L. Epstein, "School and Family Partnerships," in *Encyclopedia of Educational Research,* ed. M. Alkin, 1141.

20. K. Larson and R. Rumberger, "Doubling school success in highest-risk Latino youth: Results from a middle school intervention study." In *Changing Schools for Changing Students,* ed. R. F. Macias and R. Ramos, 157–179.

21. Shulman, *The Betrayal of Work.*

22. According to a study by the National Center for Educational Statistics, the percentage of students who reported that they had been bullied at school increased from 5 percent in 1999 to 8 percent in 2001. Among Hispanics, the increase was from 4 percent in 1999 to 8 percent in 2001. See Jill F. DeVoe et al., *Indicators of School Crime and Safety: 2003,* 16.

23. See Richardson, *Batos, Bolillos, Pochos, and Pelados,* 15, for a discussion of cultural bias.

24. The Hispanic Dropout Project found that "Hispanic parents and families are frequently perceived as indifferent to their children's education . . . Parents are said to be ignorant, poor, products of bad schools, in conflict with their children, and in general, culturally deprived." Further, the HDP cites research indicating that there was a widespread belief among educators that Hispanic parents did not sufficiently value education and were unwilling to give sufficient time to rearing their children and participating in school activities. In HDP interviews with parents, however, interviewers found that "in order to become involved, [parents] must often overcome school resistance and hostility to that involvement." See Secada et al., *No More Excuses,* 21, 22.

25. According to data from the National Center for Educational Statistics, the Hispanic Dropout Project calculated that 31 percent of Hispanic females listed pregnancy as their main reason for dropping out. The percent of Black females listing this reason was 35 percent, while the percentage for Whites was 26 percent. Hispanic Dropout Project Data Book, 27, http://bingaman.senate.gov/databook.pdf.

26. Ibid., 25.

27. M. M. McMillen, P. Kaufman, and S. D. Whitener, *Dropout Rates in the United States: 1993,* National Center for Education Statistics report. It should also be noted that when dropouts are asked to give the reason for dropping out, 41 percent of Hispanic students, 40 percent of Black students, and 37 percent of Whites listed "I was failing school" as a primary reason. See Bingaman, Hispanic Dropout Project Data Book, 27, http://bingaman.senate.gov/databook.pdf.

28. The importance of this factor is documented by W. Velez, "High School Attrition among Hispanic and Non-Hispanic White Youths," *Sociology of Education* 62 (1989).

29. The 2004 National Household Survey on Drug Abuse showed that high school dropouts are more likely to use drugs than high school graduates. Current marijuana use among

dropouts was 14.1 percent, compared to 7.9 percent for graduates. U.S. Department of Health and Human Services, September 2005, Office of Applied Studies, Results from the 2004 National Survey on Drug Use and Health: National Findings, www.oas/samha.gov/nsduh/2knsduh/sk4Results/2k4Results.htm#2.8.

30. Eitzen and Smith state, for example, that "the structure of education results in a disproportionate number of poor children failing in school" (146). Further, they state, "The structural explanation for poverty, then, rests on the assumption that the way society is organized perpetuates poverty, not the characteristics of poor people" (18). D. Stanley Eitzen and Kelly Eitzen Smith, *Experiencing Poverty: Voices from the Bottom.*

31. Daniel U. Levine and Rayna F. Levine, *Society and Education,* 91.

32. Trueba, Spindler, and Spindler state: "A persistent theme . . . is the observation that our educational system requires failure of some in order to assure success for others . . . We spend enormous amounts of money and time locating children that we perceive as predestined for failure, often because they do not meet the expectations of the cultural patterns of the mainstream" (2–3). H. T. Trueba, G. Spindler, and L. Spindler, eds., *What Do Anthropologists Have to Say about Dropouts?*

33. Secada et al., *No More Excuses,* 32, 37.

34. "Teacher ability, measured with both verbal and written proficiency scores, decreases with campus percentage black and Hispanic and increases with the campus percentage of higher income students . . . Texas teachers employed in schools with high fractions of disadvantaged minority students have fewer years of education and less experience and have more students in their classes." J. F. Kain and K. Singleton, "Equality of Educational Opportunity Revisited," Paper presented at the Federal Reserve Bank of Boston Symposium, 1996. Cited in Secada et al., *No More Excuses,* 48.

35. Russell Rumberger states, "Recent research reveals that peers exert a powerful influence on children, especially teenagers." Although the influence of peers on dropout behavior has not been the subject of much study, ethnographic studies report that dropouts of all ethnic backgrounds are more likely to associate with other youth who drop out or have low educational aspirations." Rumberger, "Chicano Dropouts," 76.

36. Secada et al., *No More Excuses,* 18.

37. Emile Durkheim, *The Division of Labor in Society.*

38. Travis Hirschi, *Causes of Delinquency.*

39. Gary G. Wehlage et al., *Reducing the Risk: Schools as Communities of Support,* 223.

40. For an excellent review of the literature on the relationship between gang membership and dropping out, see James R. Lasley, "Age, Social Context, and Street Gang Membership: Are Youth Gangs Becoming Adult Gangs?" *Youth and Society* 23, no. 4 (June 1992). Also, I. Spergel, "Youth Gangs: Problem and Response: A Review of the Literature. Assessment Part I."

41. According to data from the National Center for Education Statistics, annual earnings for Hispanic high school graduates (or those with a GED) were $6,744 higher than earnings for Hispanics who did not graduate from high school. See John Wirt et al., *The Condition of Education 2004,* 133.

42. In 2002, both men and women who had previously dropped out of school earned, on average, only 75 percent of the median annual earnings of all full-time, full-year wage and salary workers. Ibid., 54.

43. Based on the poem "A Fence or an Ambulance," attributed to Joseph Malins, 1895. *CentrePiece* 7 (Fall 1998), http://www.umanitoba.ca/centres/mchp/cprkives/cprkiv10.htm.

CONCLUSION

1. James H. Mittleman, "How Does Globalization Really Work?" in *Globalization: Critical Reflections*, ed. James H. Mittleman.

2. Mittleman states, "A major aspect of globalization is drug trafficking, which accounts for about one-half of the revenue from international organized crime. But transnational criminal groups are also heavily involved in car theft, trade in nuclear materials, smuggling of migrants, arms deals, money laundering, and sales of human organs. The UN estimates that major crime syndicates have combined annual sales of $750 billion, aided by the use of modern management, strategic transnational alliances, computer technology, and investment in research and technology." Ibid., 237.

3. Peggy Levitt and Mary C. Waters, eds., *The Changing Face of Home: The Transnational Lives of the Second Generation*, 6.

4. As the results from these three analyses suggest, we can use F-scores, which measure the strength of association between generation score and each variable, to assess how quickly (in terms of generations) any variable tends to disappear among Mexican-origin people living in the United States. Variables with a high F-score in relation to generational status would disappear rather quickly. In contrast, when the F-score on an association between any variable and generational status is low (and there is no statistical significance), such results would be evidence that the variable in question is less related to the number of generations respondents have been in the United States.

5. Peggy Levitt and Nina Glick Schiller, "Transnational Perspectives on Migration: Conceptualizing Simultaneity," *International Migration Review* 38 (Fall 2004).

6. See Israel Cuellar, "Acculturation and Mental Health: Ecological Transactional Relations of Adjustment," in *Handbook of Multicultural Mental Health*, ed. Israel Cuellar and F. A. Paniagua.

7. Ibid.

8. Because the ethnographic and survey data presented throughout the book are based on purposive sampling techniques, we must be cautious in claiming that they statistically represent local populations. As we stated in the preface, we were unable to utilize randomized sampling techniques for a variety of reasons—chief among them the illegal nature of many of the activities we investigated. Nevertheless, we believe that our samples do approximate the wider population of the region. When we compared them to census data, for example, most survey samples conformed rather well to the known characteristics of the groups we described. Still, we intend to follow up on these exploratory studies, to the extent possible, with future surveys utilizing randomized sampling techniques.

9. Some scholars choose to distinguish between cross-border activities and more transnational forms of contact, proposing that cross-border transactions occur specifically at the border and require direct proximity to it. See, for example, Oscar Martinez, *Border People: Life and Society in the U.S.-Mexico Borderlands*. While we appreciate that many cross-border activities are limited specifically to the border, there are so many activities that could fit either category that we choose not to try to distinguish transnationalism from cross-border activities.

10. An ANOVA conducted on most of the items in the Perceptions of Deviance Survey in relation to generational status revealed few statistically significant relationships.

11. Though a child born in the United States is entitled to U.S. citizenship, the parents will receive no immigration benefit until the child turns eighteen and is able to solicit residency for the parents.

Glossary

AMPARO: similar to a writ of habeas corpus.

BANDIDO/A: bandit, outlaw.

BARRIDA: the custom of sweeping a person who is lying down, usually with herbs, to cure an illness.

BATO: guy; "dude."

BOLILLA/O: Anglo (from "bolillo," a white bread roll).

BUÑUELO: fried pastry.

BURRO: dummy.

CABEZA DE TORNILLO: screwhead.

CALIENTE: hot (temperature).

CASA DE CAMBIO: money exchange office.

CERESO: social readaptation center.

CHICOTE: whip; braided leather club.

CHILE: chili pepper.

CLIKA: gang.

COLONIA: low-income rural housing enclave.

COMANDANTE: police chief equivalent.

COMPADRE: co-parent.

CORRIDO: ballad.

COYOTE: smuggler.

CURANDERISMO: system of folk healing.

CURANDERO/A: folk healer.

EJIDO: cooperative farm.

ESTILO GRINGO: Anglo style.

EMPACHADA/O: bloated.

FEDERAL: federal police officer.

HIERBA: herb.

HIERBERA/O: one who dispenses healing herbs.

HIERBERÍA: store selling folk medicines.

JUDICIAL: judicial police officer.

LA MIGRA: see "Migra."

LOCO/A: drug user; crazy person.

MAL DE OJO: see "ojo."

MAL PUESTO: hex put on someone.

MANZANILLA: chamomile.

MARIQUILLA: goldenrod.

MASA: dough.

MIGRA/LA MIGRA: Border Patrol.

MINISTERIO PÚBLICO: district attorney's office.

MOJADO: "wetback"; wet, drenched.

MOLCAJETE: stone grinding bowl for spices.

MORDIDA: bribe; bite.

MOTA: marijuana.

OJO/MAL DE OJO: illness from being looked at with a powerful gaze and not being touched afterward.

PADRINO/A: godparent.

PADRINO DEL QUEQUE: godfather of the cake.

PARTERA: midwife.

PATRÓN/PATRONA: boss.

PENDEJO: scum; low-life.

PETATE: mat made of woven palm leaves.

POCHO: a derogatory term used to denigrate Mexican Americans who have become too gringo.

POLLO: chicken.

PROMESA: promise.

PULGA: flea market.

QUINCEAÑERA: celebration of a girl's fifteenth birthday.

RAZA/LA RAZA: the (Mexican) race.

REMEDIOS CASEROS: home remedies.

RUDA: rue (herb).

SUSTO: illness in which a person or animal suffers from fright.

TARJETA DE RESIDENCIA: resident alien visa.

Bibliography

Abcock, Linda, Mary Ellen Benedict, and John Engberg. "Structural Change and Labor Market Outcomes: How Are the Gains and Losses Distributed?" Unpublished paper, Carnegie Mellon University, 1994.

Abril, I. F. "Mexican-American Folk Beliefs: How They Affect Health Care." *American Journal of Maternal Child Nursing* 2, no. 3 (May–June 1977): 168–173.

Acuña, Rodolfo. *Occupied America: A History of Chicanos.* New York: Longman, 2000.

Addison, John, and Pedro Portugal. "Job Displacement, the Age-Earnings Profile, and Relative Earnings Losses." Mimeographed paper, University of South Carolina, 1986.

Aguilera, Michael B., and Douglas S. Massey. "Social Capital and Wages of Mexican Migrants: New Hypotheses and Tests." *Social Forces* 82, no. 2 (December 2003): 671–701.

Alba, Richard D. *Italian Americans: Into the Twilight of Ethnicity.* Englewood Cliffs: Prentice-Hall, 1985.

Angel, Jacqueline L. "Late-Life Immigration, Changes in Living Arrangements, and Headship Status among Older Mexican-Origin Individuals." *Social Science Quarterly* 81, no. 1 (March 2000): 389–403.

Applewhite, S. L. "Curanderismo: Demystifying the Health Beliefs and Practices of Elderly Mexican Americans." *Health and Social Work* 20, no. 4 (November 1995): 247–254.

Arteaga Botello, Nelson, and Adrián López Rivera. "Everything in This Job Is Money: Inside the Mexican Police." *World Policy Journal* 17, no. 3 (2000): 61–70.

Bain, Ken. *What the Best College Teachers Do.* Cambridge, MA: Harvard University Press, 2004.

Banamex. *Review of the Economic Situation of Mexico* 80, no. 940 (April 2004): 150–152. http://www.bancanet-empresarial.com/esp/pdf_bin/esem/resemabril04.pdf.

Barber, Benjamin R. "Jihad vs. McWorld." *Atlantic Monthly,* March 1992.

Barry, Tom, Harry Browne, and Beth Sims. *Crossing the Line: Immigrants, Economic Integration, and Drug Enforcement on the U.S.-Mexico Border.* Albuquerque: Resource Center Press, 1994.

Bell, Daniel. "Corruption in Democracies: The Old War." *New Republic,* August 23, 1993.

Biernacki, Patrick, and Dan Waldorf. "Snowball Sampling: Problems, Techniques of Choice Referral Sampling." *Sociological Methods and Research* 10: 141–163.

Bingaman, Jeff. *Hispanic Dropout Project Data Book.* n.d. http://bingaman .senate.gov/databook.pdf.

Blau, Francine, and Lawrence Kahn. "Causes and Consequences of Layoffs." *Economic Inquiry* 19 (1981): 417–469.

Border Business Briefs. Center for Economic Studies, Edinburg, TX, 2005.

Borjas, George J. *Friends or Strangers: The Impact of Immigrants on the U.S. Economy.* New York: Basic Books, 1990.

Brecher, Jeremy, and Tim Costello. *Global Village or Global Pillage: Economic Reconstruction from the Bottom Up.* Boston: South End Press, 1994.

Brimelow, Peter. *Alien Nation: Common Sense about America's Immigration Disaster.* New York: Harper Perennial, 1995.

Brown, Cynthia. "Labor and Demographic Challenges of the US/Mexico Border Region." In *Worker Displacement in the US/Mexico Border Region: Issues and Challenges,* ed. by José A. Pagan. Northampton, MA: Edward Elgar, 2004.

Carpenter, Dave. "Our Overburdened ERs." *Hospital and Health Networks* 75, no. 3 (March 2001): 45–47. http://www.hhnmag.com/ (accessed June 2004).

Carrington, William. "Wage Losses for Displaced Workers: Is It Really the Firm That Matters?" *Journal of Human Resources* 28, no. 3 (Summer 1993): 435–462.

Carrington, William, and Asad Zaman. "Inter-industry Variation in the Costs of Job Displacement." *Journal of Labor Economics* 12, no. 2 (April 1994): 243–276.

Chavez, Linda. *Out of the Barrio: Toward a New Politics of Hispanic Assimilation.* New York: Basic Books, 1991.

Chavira, J. *Curandismo: An Optimal Health Care System.* Edinburg: University of Texas–Pan American, 1984. Looseleaf.

Chesney, A. P., B. L. Thompson, A. Guevara, A. Vela, and M. F. Schott-staedt. "Mexican-American Folk Medicine: Implications for the Family Physician." *Journal of Family Practice* 11 (October 1980): 567–574.

Clark, Chavira J. *Curanderismo: An Optional Health Care System.* Edin-burg: University of Texas–Pan American, 1975.

Clark, Rebecca L., and Scott A. Anderson. *Illegal Aliens in Federal, State, and Local Criminal Justice Systems.* Urban Institute Report no. 410366, June 2000. www.urban.org/url.cfm?=410366.

Clarke, Ronald V., and P. M. Harris. "Auto Theft and Its Prevention." In *Crime and Justice: A Review of Research,* vol. 16, ed. M. Tonry, 1–54. Chi-cago: University of Chicago Press, 1992.

Collado, Ardon Rolando, Arthur J. Rubel, Carl W. O'Neill, and Raymond H. Murray. "A Folk Illness (Susto) as an Indicator of Real Illness." *The Lancet* 322, no. 8363 (December 10, 1983).

Comas-Diaz, Lillian. "Mainland Puerto Rican Women: A Sociocultural Approach." *Journal of Community Psychology* 16 (1988): 21–31.

"Crime Characteristics 2002." Bureau of Justice Statistics. U.S. Depart-ment of Justice, Office of Justice Programs. http://www.ojp.usdoj.gov/bjs/cvict_c.htm (accessed August 31, 2004).

"Crime in McAllen, 2002: City of McAllen Crime Report." McAllen, TX: McAllen Police Department, Crime Records Bureau, 2002. http://www.mcallen.net/police/docs/2002crimeinmcallen.pdf (accessed Au-gust 31, 2004).

Cuellar, Israel. "Acculturation and Mental Health: Ecological Transac-tional Relations of Adjustment." In *Handbook of Multicultural Mental Health,* ed. Israel Cuellar and F. A. Paniagua, 45–62. San Diego: Aca-demic Press, 2000.

———. "Acculturation as a Moderator of Personality and Psychological Assessment." In *Handbook of Cross-cultural and Multicultural Personal-ity Assessment,* ed. Richard H. Dana. Mahwah, NJ: Lawrence Erlbaum Associates, 2000.

Cuellar, Israel, Bill Arnold, and Genaro Gonzalez. "Cognitive Referents of Acculturation: Assessing Cultural Constructs in Mexican Americans." *Journal of Community Psychology* 23 (October 1995): 339–356.

Davila, Alberto, and Andrés Rivas. "Worker Displacement in the Texas/Mexico Border MSAs: Evidence from the Current Population Survey." In *Worker Displacement in the US/Mexico Border Region: Issues and Challenges,* ed. Jose A. Pagan. Northampton, MA: Edward Elgar, 2004.

De Cosio, Federico Gerardo, and Andrés Boadella. "Demographic Factors Affecting the US-Mexico Border Health Status." In *Life, Death, and In-Between on the US-Mexico Border: Así es la Vida,* ed. Martha Oehmke Loustaunau and Mary Sanchez-Bane. Westport: Bergin and Garvey, 1999.

De la Barreda Solórzano, Luis. *La lid contra la tortura.* Mexico City: Cal y Arena, 1995.

De la Garza, Rodolfo O., and Louis DeSipio. "Interest Not Passions: Mexican-American Attitudes toward Mexico, Immigration from Mexico, and Other Issues Shaping U.S.-Mexico Relations." *International Migration Review* 32, no. 2 (Summer 1998): 401–422.

De la Torre, Adela, Robert Friis, Harold R. Hunter, and Lorena Garcia. "The Health Insurance Status of US Latino Women: A Profile from the 1982–1984 HHANNES." *American Journal of Public Health* 86, no. 4 (April 1986): 533–537.

De Tavira, Juan Pablo. *¿Por qué Almoloya? Análisis de un proyecto penitenciario.* México City: Editorial Diana, 1995.

DeVoe, Jill F., et al. *Indicators of School Crime and Safety: 2003.* NCES 2004-004/NCJ 201 257. Washington, DC: U.S. Departments of Education and Justice, 2003.

Dow, Susan. *Border Children Justice Projects.* Austin: Texas Juvenile Probation Commission, October 1998. http://www.tjpc.state.tx.us/publications/reports/border%5Fchildren.htm (accessed August 31, 2004).

Drug Intelligence Brief: Mexico: Country Brief, July 2002. Prepared by the DEA Intelligence Division, International Strategic Support Section, Mexico/C. America Unit with information received prior to March 2002. Washington, DC: Intelligence Production Unit, Intelligence Division, DEA Headquarters. http://www.usdoj.gov/dea/pubs/intel/02035/02035p.html (accessed 28 August 2004).

Durkelberg, Anne. *Impact on Immigrants.* White Paper issued by the Center for Public Policy Priorities, 900 Lydia Street, Austin, TX, 1997.

Durkheim, Emile. *The Division of Labor in Society.* 1893. Reprint, New York: Macmillan, 1960.

Eitzen, D. Stanley, and Kelly Eitzen Smith. *Experiencing Poverty: Voices from the Bottom.* Belmont: Thompson, Wadsworth, 2003.

Epstein, Joyce L. "School and Family Partnerships." In *Encyclopedia of Educational Research,* 6th ed., ed. M. Alkin, 11–41. New York: Macmillan, 1992.

Espenshade, Thomas J. "Unauthorized Immigration to the United States." *Annual Review of Sociology* 21 (1995): 195–216.

Estrada, Antonio L., Fernando M. Trevino, and Laura A Ray. "Health Care Utilization among Mexican-Americans: Evidence from HHANES 1982–1984." *American Journal of Public Health* 80, Supplement (December 1990): 27–31.

Evans, M. D. R., and Jonathan Kelley. "National Pride in the Developed World." *International Journal of Public Opinion Research* 14, no. 3 (2002): 303–338.

"Facts about Shoplifting." Shoplifters Alternative, 2003. http://www.shopliftersalternative.org/ (accessed September 1, 2004; site owner now named National Association for Shoplifting Prevention).

Fallick, Bruce. "The Endogenity of Advance Notice and Fear of Destructive Attrition, *Review of Economics and Statistics* 76, no. 2 (1994): 378–385.

———. "A Review of Recent Empirical Literature on Displaced Workers." *Industrial and Labor Relations Review* 50, no. 1 (1996): 5–16.

Farber, Henry S. "The Incidence and Costs of Job Loss, 1982–91." In *Brookings Papers: Microeconomics, 1993*, ed. Martin N. Bailey, Peter C. Reiss, and Clifford Wilson, 73–132. Washington, DC: Brookings Institution, 1993.

Field, A. S., Ronald V. Clarke, and P. M. Harris. "The Mexican Vehicle Market and Auto Theft in Border Areas of the United States." *Security Journal* 2, no. 4 (1991): 205–210.

Fix, Michael E., and Jeffrey S. Passel. *Lessons of Welfare Reform for Immigrant Integration*. Washington, DC: Urban Institute, March 8, 2002. http://www.urban.org/url.cfm?=408086 (accessed March 1, 1999).

Fix, Michael E., and Jeffrey S. Passel. *Trends in Non-citizens' and Citizens' Use of Public Benefits Following Welfare Reform: 1994–1997*. Washington, DC: Urban Institute, March 1999. http://www.urban.org/url.cfm?ID=408086 (accessed March 1, 1999).

Fix, Michael E., and Karen Tumlin. *Welfare Reform and the Devolution of Immigrant Policy*. Series A, no. A-15. Washington, DC: Urban Institute, 1998.

Flaim, Paul, and Ellen Sehgal. "Displaced Workers of 1979–1983: How Well Have They Fared?" Bulletin no. 240. Washington, DC: U.S. Department of Labor, Bureau of Labor Statistics, 1985.

Friedman, George. "Open Sources." *Stratfor Weekly*, January 5, 2004.

Garza, Mary Jane. "Healing Spirits." *Hispanic* 11, no. 6 (June 1998): 30–35.

General Accounting Office. *Trade Adjustment Assistance in Case Study Communities*. Report no. GAO-01-838. August 2001.

————. *Trade Adjustment Assistance: Trends, Outcomes and Management Issues in Dislocated Worker Programs*. Report no. GAO-01-59. October 2000.

Ghaddar, Suad, Chad Richardson, and Cynthia Brown. "The Economic Impact of Mexican Visitors to the Lower Rio Grande Valley, 2003." Edinburg, Texas: Center for Border Economic Studies, May 2004.

Giordano, Al. "Narco-Corruption at U.S. Customs Service." Fresno, CA: Free Republic, August 3, 2001. http://www.freerepublic.com/forum/a3b6ab3454de7.htm (accessed 31 August, 2004).

Gonzlez-Swafford, Maria J., and Maria Grace Gutierrez. "Ethno-Medical Beliefs and Practices of Mexican-Americans." *Nurse Practitioner* 8, no. 1 (November–December 1983).

Granados, Gilbert, Jyoti Pavvula, Nancy Berman, and Patrick Dowling. "Health Care for Latino Children: Impact of Child and Parental Birthplace on the Insurance Status and Access to Health Services." *American Journal Public Health* 91, no. 11 (November 2001): 1806–1807.

Greeley, Andrew M. *The American Catholic: A Social Portrait*. New York: Basic Books, 1977.

Guarnaccia, P. J., V. de la Cancela, and E. Carillo. "The Multiple Meanings of *Ataques de Nervios* in the Latino Community." *Medical Anthropology* 11, no. 1 (1989): 47–62.

Guarnaccia, P. J., and O. Rodríguez. "Concepts of Culture and Their Role in the Development of Culturally Competent Mental Health Services." *Hispanic Journal of Behavioral Sciences* 18, no. 4 (1996): 419–443.

Hamermesh, Daniel S. "The Human Capital Losses of Displaced Workers." Discussion paper no. 753–784, Institute for Research on Poverty, University of Wisconsin, 1984.

————. "What Do We Know about Worker Displacement in the United States?" *Industrial Relations* 28, no. 1 (Winter 1989): 51–59.

Hayes, Margaret. "The Impact of Market Opening on Argentine Industry: A Survey of Corporate Impressions." In *Argentina: The Challenges of Modernization*, ed. J. S. Tulchin and A. M. Garland. Wilmington, DE: Scholarly Resources, 1998.

Heer, David M. *Undocumented Mexicans in the United States*. New York: Cambridge University Press, 1990.

Hess, Robyn S. "Dropping Out among Mexican American Youth: Reviewing the Local Literature through an Ecological Perspective." *Journal of Education for Students Placed at Risk* 5, no. 3 (2000).

Heyman, Josiah McC. "U.S. Immigration Officers of Mexican Ancestry as Mexican Americans, Citizens, and Immigration Police." *Current Anthropology* 43, no. 3 (June 2002): 479–507.

Higginbotham, J. C., F. M. Treviño, and L. A. Ray. "Utilization of Curanderos by Mexican Americans: Prevalence and Predictors. Findings from HHANES, 1982–84." *American Journal of Public Health Supplement* 80 (December 1990): 32–35.

Hirschi, Travis. *Causes of Delinquency.* Berkeley: University of California Press, 1969.

"Hispanic Health in the United States." *JAMA* 265, no. 2 (January 9, 1991): 248–252.

Hobsbawm, Eric. *Nations and Nationalism since 1780.* Cambridge: Cambridge University Press, 1990.

Hood, M. V., III, Irwin L. Morris, and Kurt A. Shirkey. "'¡Quédate o Vente!': Uncovering the Determinants of Hispanic Public Opinion toward Immigration." *Political Research Quarterly* (September 1997): 627–649.

Hoppe, Sue Keri, and Peter L. Heller. "Alienation, Familism, and the Utilization of Health Services by Mexican Americans." *American Journal of Health and Social Behavior* 16, no. 3 (September 1975): 304–314.

Horn, James J. "The Mexican Revolution and Health Care, or the Health of the Mexican Revolution." *Latin American Perspectives* 10, no. 4 (1983): 24–39.

Human Rights Watch. *Human Rights in Mexico: A Policy of Impunity.* New York: Human Rights Watch, 1990.

———. *Systemic Injustice: Torture, "Disappearance," and Extrajudicial Execution in Mexico.* New York: Human Rights Watch, 1999.

Huntington, Samuel P. "Globalization's Boosters and Critics." *National Interest* (Fall 1999).

———. "The Hispanic Challenge." *Foreign Policy* (March/April 2004). http://www.foreignpolicy.com/.

———. *Who Are We? The Challenges to America's National Identity.* New York: Simon and Schuster, 2004.

"Immigration Information: Investigations, 2002." Washington, DC: U.S. Citizenship and Immigration Services, 2003. http://uscis.gov/graphics/shared/aboutus/statistics/msrmar03/IVST.HTM (accessed August 23, 2004).

INS (U.S. Immigration and Naturalization Service). 2001 Annual Report, Table 6.3. http://www.ins.usdoj.gov/.

Inter-American Commission on Human Rights. Annual Report of the Inter-American Commission on Human Rights 2001. *Economic Consequences of Migration.* http://www.cidh.org/Migrantes/chap.61.2001. eng.htm#IV (accessed September 14, 2005).

Inter-American Development Bank. "Latin American Immigrants in the United States to Send $30 Billion to Homelands in 2004." May 17, 2004. http://www.iadb.org/NEWS/DISPLAY/PRView.cfm?PR_Num=98_ 04&Language=Engligh.

———. "State by State Survey of Remittance Senders: US to Latin America, January–April 2005." http://idbdocs.iabg.org/wsdocs/getdocument.asp?docnum=547238.

Intercultural Development Research Association (IDRA). "Attrition and Dropout Rates in Texas." http://www.idra.org/Research/dout2001.htm.

Jacobson, Louis, Robert LaLonde, and Daniel Sullivan. "Earnings Losses of Displaced Workers." *American Economic Review* 83, no. 4 (September 1993): 685–709.

Jeffrey, Terence P. "Do Mexican Troops Bring Drugs to U.S.?" *Human Events,* July 1, 2002. www.freerepublic.com/focus/news/707827/posts.

Jones, S. R. G., and P. Kuhn. "Mandatory Notice and Unemployment." *Journal of Labor Economics* 13, no. 4 (1995): 599–622.

Karmen, A. "Auto Theft: Beyond Victim Blaming." *Victimology* 5 (1980): 161–174.

Keefe, Susan E., and Amado M. Padilla. *Chicano Ethnicity.* Albuquerque: University of New Mexico Press, 1987.

Keeling, David J. "Latin American Development and the Globalization Imperative: New Directions, Familiar Crises." *Journal of Latin American Geography* 3 (forthcoming, 2005).

Krajewski-Jaime, E. R. "Folk-Healing among Mexican-American Families as a Consideration in the Delivery of Child Welfare and Child Health Care Services." *Child Welfare* 70, no. 2 (March/April 1991): 1–8.

Krooth, Richard. *Mexico, NAFTA, and the Hardships of Progress.* London: McFarland, 1995.

Labor Council for Latin American Advancement. *Another America Is Possible: The Impact of NAFTA on the U.S. Latino Community and Lessons for Future Trade Agreements.* Washington, DC: Labor Council for Latin American Advancement, August 2004. www.LCLAA.org/Latinosreport.pdf.

Lange, James E., and Robert B. Voas. "Youth Escaping Limits on Drinking: Binging in Mexico." *Addiction* 95 (2000): 521–528.

Lange, James E., Robert B. Voas, and Mark B. Johnson. "South of the Border: A Legal Haven for Underage Drinking." *Addiction* 97 (2002): 1195–1203.

Larson, K., and R. Rumberger. "Doubling School Success in Highest-Risk Latino Youth: Results from a Middle School Intervention Study." In *Changing Schools for Changing Students*, ed. R. F. Macias and R. Ramos, 157–179. Santa Barbara: University of California Linguistic Minority Research Institute, 1995.

Lasley, James R. "Age, Social Context, and Street Gang Membership: Are Youth Gangs Becoming Adult Gangs?" *Youth and Society* 23, no. 4 (June 1992): 443–451.

"Latin American Immigrants in the United States to Send $30 Billion to Homelands in 2004." News release. Inter-American Development Bank, May 17, 2004. http://www.iadb.org/NEWS/Display/PRView.cfm?PR_Num=98_04&Language=English.

Lee, R. H. *Doing Research on Sensitive Topics*. Newbury Park, CA: Sage.

Legislative Budget Board, State Auditor's Office, and Texas Education Agency. *Dropout Study: A Report to the 77th Texas Legislature*. Austin: Texas Education Agency, December 2000. http://www.tea.state.tx.us/research/pdfs/rider71.pdf .

Levine, Daniel U., and Rayna F. Levine. *Society and Education*. Boston: Allyn and Bacon, 1996.

Levitt, Peggy, and Nina Glick Schiller. "Transnational Perspectives in Migration: Conceptualizing Simultaneity." *International Migration Review* 38 (Fall 2004): 926–949.

Levitt, Peggy, and Mary C. Waters. Introduction to *The Changing Face of Home: The Transnational Lives of the Second Generation*, ed. Peggy Levitt and Mary C. Waters. New York: Russell Sage Foundation, 2002.

———, eds. *The Changing Face of Home: The Transnational Lives of the Second Generation*. New York: Russell Sage Foundation, 2002.

Liu, Liang Y. *Texas School Survey of Substance Use among Students: Grades 7–12, 2002*. Austin: Texas Commission on Alcohol and Drug Abuse, 2002. http://www.tcada.state.tx.us/research/survey/grades7-12/SchoolSurvey2002.pdf (accessed August 28, 2004).

Loker, William M. *Globalization and the Rural Poor in Latin America*. Boulder: Lynne Rienner Publishers, 1999.

Lowell, B. Lindsay, and Roberto Suro. "How Many Undocumented: The Numbers behind the U.S.-Mexico Migration Talks." Pew Hispanic Center, March 21, 2002. http://www.pewhispanic.org/reports/report.php?ReportID=6

ON THE EDGE OF THE LAW

Lupsha, Peter A. "The Border Underworld." In *Borders and Frontiers 1: Teaching about International Boundaries,* ed. G. M. Hansen. Las Cruces: Joint Border Research Institute, New Mexico State University, 1985.

Macklin, June. "All the Good and Bad in This World." In *Twice a Minority: Mexican American Women in St. Louis,* ed. Margarita B. Melville, 127–148. St. Louis: Mosby, 1980.

Malins, Joseph. "A Fence or an Ambulance." *CentrePiece* 7 (Fall 1998). http://www.umanitoba.ca/centres/mchp/cprkives/cprkiv10.htm.

Martinez, Oscar. *Border People: Life and Society in the U.S.- Mexico Borderlands.* Tucson: University of Arizona Press, 1994.

Martinez, Yolanda G., and Ann Cranston-Gingras. "Migrant Farmworker Students and the Educational Process: Barriers to High School Completion." *High School Journal* 80, no. 1 (October/November 1996): 28–38.

Massey, Douglas S. "The Settlement Process among Mexican Immigrants to the United States—New Methods and Findings." Appendix C in *Immigration Statistics: A Story of Neglect,* ed. Daniel B. Levine, Kenneth Hill, and Robert Warren. Washington, DC: National Academy Press, 1985.

Massey, Douglas S., and Kristin E. Espinosa. "What's Driving Mexico-U.S. Migration? A Theoretical, Empirical, and Policy Analysis." *American Journal of Sociology* 102, no. 4 (January 1997).

Maxwell, Jane Carlisle. *Substance Abuse Trends in Texas, December 2003.* Austin: Center for Excellence in Drug Epidemiology, Gulf Coast Addiction Technology Transfer Center, School of Social Work, Center for Social Work Research, University of Texas at Austin. http://www.utexas.edu/research/cswr/gcattc/Trends/trends1203.pdf (accessed 28 August 2004).

———. "Texas School Survey of Substance Abuse: Grades 7–12." In *Substance Abuse Trends in Texas, June 2004.* Austin: Center for Excellence in Drug Epidemiology, Gulf Coast Addiction Technology Transfer Center (accessed August 28, 2004). http://www.utexas.edu/research/cswr/gcattc/Trends/trends704.pdf; Internet.

"McAllen Overview." McAllen Chamber of Commerce, 2004. http://www.mcallen.org/business/overview.

McCaghy, C. H., P. C. Giordano, and T. K. Henson. "Auto Theft: Offender and Offense Characteristics." *Criminology* 15, no. 3 (1977): 367–385.

McCord, Joan, Cathy Spatz Wisdom, and Nancy A. Crowell, eds. *Juvenile Crime, Juvenile Justice.* Washington, DC: National Academy Press, 2001.

McKinnon, Sarah, Kathleen M. O'Rourke, Sharon E. Thompson, and Jessica H. Berumen. "Alcohol Use and Abuse by Adolescents: The Impact of Living in a Border Community." *Journal of Adolescent Health* 34 (2004): 88–93.

McLemore, S. Dale, Harriet D. Romo, and Susan Gonzalez Baker. *Racial and Ethnic Relations in America.* Boston: Allyn and Bacon, 2001.

McMillen, M. M., P. Kaufman, and S. D. Whitener. *Dropout Rates in the United States: 1993.* National Center for Education Statistics report. Washington, DC: U.S. Department of Education, Office of Educational Research and Improvement, 1993.

Mehta, Chirag, Nik Theodore, Iliana Mora, and Jennifer Wade. *Chicago's Undocumented Immigrants: An Analysis of Wages, Working Conditions, and Economic Contributions.* Chicago: Center for Urban Economic Development, University of Illinois at Chicago, February 2002. http://www.uic.edu/cuppa/uicued/npublications/recent/undoc_full.pdf.

Miller, Michael V. "Vehicle Theft along the Texas-Mexico Border." *Journal of Borderlands Studies* 2, no. 2 (1987): 12–32.

Mittleman, James H. "How Does Globalization Really Work?" In *Globalization: Critical Reflections,* ed. James H. Mittleman. Boulder: Lynne Rienner Publishers, 1996.

Morris, Stephen D. "La política acostumbrada o política insólita? El problema de la corrupción en México." In *Vicios públicos, virtudes privadas: La corrupción en México,* ed. Claudio Lomnitz. Mexico City: Centro de Investigaciones y Estudios Superiores en Antropología Social, 2000.

Moss, Kendall, and Marilyn Felker. "Patient Transfers along the US-Mexico Border." *LBJ Journal of Public Affairs* 40, no. 2 (1994): 1–6.

Muir, Jennifer, and Angeles Negrete. "Trafficker Has History of Smuggling Immigrants." *Brownsville (TX) Herald,* May 20, 2003.

Murgia, Alejandro, Rolf A. Peterson, and Maria Cecilia Zea. "Use and Implications of Ethnomedical Health Care Approaches among Central American Immigrants." *Health and Social Work* 28, no. 1 (February 2003): 43–51.

National Center for Education Statistics. *Dropout Rates in the United States: 2000.* Washington, DC: U.S. Department of Education, Office of Educational Research and Improvement, 2002. http://nces.ed.gov/pubsearch/pubsinfo.asp?pubid=2002114.

———. *The Educational Progress of Hispanic Students.* Washington, DC: U.S. Department of Education, Office of Educational Research and Improvement, 1995.

National Drug Intelligence Center. *National Drug Threat Assessment 2003: Money Laundering.* U.S. Department of Justice, January 2003. http://www.usdoj.gov/ndic/pubs3/3300/money.htm#Top: 3 (accessed August 28, 2004).

———. *Texas Drug Threat Assessment.* Document 2003-S0387TX-001. Washington, DC: U.S. Department of Justice, October 2003. http://www.usdoj.gov/ndic/pubs5/5624/.

Noticias Paragon (Mexico). News release, March 12, 2001. http://www.paragon.com.mx/.

O'Day, Patrick. "The Mexican Army as Cartel." *Journal of Contemporary Criminal Justice* 17, no. 3 (2001): 278–295.

O'Day, Patrick, and Rex Venecia. "Cazuelas: An Ethnographic Study of Drug Trafficking in a Small Mexican Border Town." *Journal of Contemporary Criminal Justice* 15, no. 4 (1999): 421–444.

Orrenius, Pia M., and Anna L. Berman. "Growth on the Border or Bordering on Growth?" El Paso: Maquila Portal, 2002. http://www.maquilaportal.com/public/artic/artic183e.htm.

Pachter, L. M. "Culture and Clinical Care: Folk Illness Beliefs and Their Implications for Health Care Delivery." *JAMA* 271, no. 9 (1994): 690–694.

Pagan, José A., ed. *Worker Displacement in the US/Mexico Border Region: Issues and Challenges.* Northampton, MA: Edward Elgar, 2004.

Paredes, Américo. *A Texas-Mexican Cancionero: Folksongs of the Lower Border.* Urbana: University of Illinois Press, 1976.

———. *With His Pistol in His Hand: A Border Ballad and Its Hero.* Austin: University of Texas Press, 1958.

Parillo, Vincent. *Understanding Race and Ethnic Relations.* Boston: Allyn and Bacon, 2002.

Passel, Jeffrey S., Randolph Capps, and Michael E. Fix. "Undocumented Immigrants: Facts and Figures." Urban Institute Immigration Studies Program, January 12, 2004. http://www.urban.org/url.cfm?ID=1000587.

Pfaff, William. *The Wrath of Nations: Civilization and the Furies of Nationalism.* New York: Simon and Schuster, 1993.

Phillips, Julie A., and Douglas S. Massey. "Consequences of Policy Shifts and Political Change—The New Labor Market: Immigrants and Wages after IRCA." *Demography* 36, no. 2 (1999).

Phillips, Keith, and Carlos Manzanares. "Transportation Infrastructure and the Border Economy." In *The Border Economy.* Dallas, TX: Federal Reserve Bank of Dallas, 2001. http://www.dallasfed.org/research/border/tbe_phillips.html.

Pinkerton, James. "Health Care: Crisis at the Border; Poverty, Lack of Doctors Cloud Area's Future." *Houston Chronicle,* May 5, 2002.

Podgursky, Michael. "The Industrial Structure of Job Displacement, 1979–89." *Monthly Labor Review* 115, no. 9 (September 1992): 17–25.

Porter, Eduardo. "Illegal Immigrants Are Bolstering Social Security with Billions." *New York Times,* April 5, 2005, sec. A, p. 1.

Ramos, José María, and David A. Shirk. "Binational Collaboration in Law Enforcement and Public Security Issues on the U.S.-Mexican Border." Paper presented at the conference "Reforming the Administration of Justice in Mexico," Center for U.S.-Mexican Studies, University of California, San Diego, May 15–17, 2003.

Reese, Leslie. "Morality and Identity in Mexican Immigrant Parents' Vision of the Future." *Journal of Ethnic and Migration Studies* 27, no. 3 (July 2001): 455–473.

Resendiz, Rosalva. "International Auto Theft: An Exploratory Research of Organization and Organized Crime on the U.S./Mexico Border." *Criminal Organizations* 12 (1998). Published by the International Association for the Study of Organized Crime.

Resendiz, Rosalva. "International Auto Theft: An Exploratory Research of the Property Offender and the Organizational Crime Process in the U.S./Mexico Border." Master thesis, University of North Texas, 1996.

———. "Taking Risks within the Constraints of Gender: Mexican American Women as Professional Auto Thieves." *Social Science Journal* 38, no. 3 (2001).

Resendiz, Rosalva, and David M. Neal. "International Auto Theft: The Illegal Export of American Vehicles to Mexico." In *International Criminal Justice: Issues in Global Perspective,* ed. D. Rounds, Jr. Boston: Allyn and Bacon, 1999.

"Results from the 2003 Monitoring the Future Study." ONDCP fact sheet. Washington, DC: National Institute on Drug Abuse, March 2003. http://monitoringthefuture.org/data/03data.html#2003data-drugs (accessed 28 August 2004).

Richardson, Chad. *Batos, Bolillos, Pochos, and Pelados: Class and Culture on the South Texas Border.* Austin: University of Texas Press, 1999.

Richardson, Chad, and Joe Feagin. "The Dynamics of Legalization: Undocumented Mexican Immigrants in the United States." *Research in Political Sociology* 3 (1987): 179–201.

Rico, José María. *Justicia penal y transición democrática en América Latina.* Mexico City: Siglo XXI Editores, 1997.

Rivera, Andrew. "Remembrance and Forgetting: Chicano Masculinity on the Border." *Latino Studies Journal* 8, no. 2 (1997): 35–56.

Rivera-Batiz, Francisco L. "Underground on American Soil: Undocumented Workers and U.S. Immigration Policy." *Journal of International Affairs* 53, no. 2 (Spring 2000): 485–501.

———. "Undocumented Workers in the Labor Market: An Analysis of the Earnings of Legal and Illegal Mexican Immigrants in the United States." *Journal of Population Economics* 12, no. 1 (1999): 91–96.

Rodriguez, Isabel Ann. "Identifying Barriers to Healthcare Perceived by Hispanics in West Texas." Master's thesis, Texas Tech University Health Science Services, August 1996.

Rotella, Sebastian. *Twilight on the Line: Underworlds and Politics at the U.S.-Mexico Border.* New York: W. W. Norton, 1998.

Ruhm, Christopher J. "Advance Notice, Job Search, and Postdisplacement Earnings." *Journal of Labor Economics* 12, no. 1 (1994): 1–32.

———. "Are Workers Permanently Scarred by Job Displacements?" *American Economic Review* 81, no. 1 (March 1991): 319–324.

Rumberger, Russell. "Chicano Dropouts: A Review of Research and Policy Issues." In *Chicano School Failure and Success: Research and Policy Agendas for the 1990s,* ed. Richard R. Valencia. New York: Falmer Press, 1991.

Rushing, William A. "Class, Culture, Social Structure, and Anomie." *American Journal of Sociology* 76, no. 5 (1971).

Schlesinger, Arthur, Jr. "Has Democracy a Future?" *Foreign Affairs,* September/October 1997. http://www.foreignaffairs.org/19970901faessay3792/arthur-m-schlesinger-jr/has-democracy-a-future.html.

Schultz, T. Paul. *Immigrant Quality and Assimilation: A Review of the Literature.* Washington, DC: U.S. Commission on Immigration Reform, 1995.

Secada, Walter G., et al. *No More Excuses: The Final Report of the Hispanic Dropout Project.* Washington, DC: U.S. Department of Education, 1998. http://www.idra.org/Research/dout2001.htm.

Seitchik, Adam. "Who Are Displaced Workers?" In *Job Displacement: Consequences and Implications for Policy,* ed. John T. Addison. Detroit: Wayne State University Press, 1991.

Shin, Gi-Wook. "The Paradox of Korean Globalization." Manuscript under review.

Short, Robert, and Lisa Magaña. "Political Rhetoric, Immigration Attitudes, and Contemporary Prejudice: A Mexican American Dilemma." *Journal of Social Psychology* 142, no. 6 (2002): 703.

Shulman, Beth. *The Betrayal of Work: How Low-Wage Jobs Fail 30 Million Americans and Their Families.* New York: New Press, 2003.

Singer, Audrey, and Douglas S. Massey. "The Social Process of Undocumented Border Crossing among Mexican Migrants." *International Migration Review* 32, no. 3 (Autumn 1998): 561–592.

Smith, Anthony. *Nations and Nationalism in a Global Era.* Cambridge: Polity Press, 1995.

South Texas HIDTA FY 2000 Strategy. San Antonio: South Texas HIDTA Printing, 1999.

Spergel, I. "Youth Gangs: Problem and Response: A Review of the Literature. Assessment Part I." National Youth Gang Suppression and Intervention Project, with the Office of Juvenile Justice and Delinquency Planning, U.S. Department of Justice, Washington, DC.

Stoddard, Ellwyn. *U.S.-Mexico Borderlands Issues: The Bi-National Boundary, Immigration, and Economic Policies.* El Paso: Promontory, 1999.

———. *U.S.-Mexico Borderlands Studies: Multidisciplinary Perspectives and Concepts.* El Paso: Promontory, 2000.

Swaim, Paul, and Michael Podgursky. "Do More-Educated Workers Fare Better Following Job Displacement?" *Monthly Labor Review* 112, no. 8 (August 1989): 43–46.

Taylor, Lori L. "The Border: Is It Really a Low-Wage Area?" In *The Border Economy.* Dallas, ed. Federal Reserve Bank of Dallas. Dallas, TX: Federal Reserve Bank of Dallas, 2001.

Texas Commission of Law Enforcement Officer Standards Education (TCLEOSE). Newsletters, April 2001–June 2003. http://www.tcleose.state.tx.us/(accessed August 31, 2004).

Texas Comptroller of Public Accounts (TCPA). *Bordering the Future: Challenge and Opportunity in the Texas Border Region.* Austin: TCPA, 1998.

———. *Texas Economic Update.* Austin, TX: Texas Comptroller of Public Accounts, 2003. Update for 2002.

Texas-Mexico Border Health Coordination Office, University of Texas System. *Texas-Mexico Border Counties, 1998.* TMBHCO series report 98–99, no. 1. Edinburg: University of Texas System, 1998.

"Theft Surveys." Fruitland, FL: Hayes International, 2001. http://www.hayesinternational.com/thft_srvys.html.

Thurow, Lester. *The Future of Capitalism: How Today's Economic Forces Shape Tomorrow's World.* New York: Penguin Books, 1996.

Tijerina, José G., and Antonio Medellín Ruiz. "La dependencia financiera de los gobiernos locales en México." *Ensayos: Revista de Economía* 19, no. 1 (May 2000).

Tomlinson, John. *Globalization and Culture.* Chicago: University of Chicago Press, 1999.

Tremblay, P., Y. Clermont, and M. Cusson. "Jockeys and Joyriders: Changing Patterns in Car Theft Opportunity Structures." *British Journal of Criminology* 34, no. 3 (1994): 307–321.

Trevino, Fernando M., and Abigail J. Moss. *Health Indicators for Hispanic, Black, and White Americans.* Hyattsville, MD: U.S. Department of Health and Human Services, Public Health Service, National Center for Health Statistics, 1984: 233–237.

Triantafillou, Stephanie. "North Carolina's Migrant and Seasonal Farmworkers." *North Carolina Medical Journal* 64, no. 3 (May/June 2003): 129–132.

Trotter, Robert T., II. "Curanderismo: A Picture of Mexican-American Folk Healing." *Journal of Alternative and Complementary Medicine* 7, no. 2 (2001): 129–131.

Trotter, Robert T., II, and Juan Antonio Chavira. *Curanderismo, Mexican American Folk Healing.* Athens: University of Georgia Press, 1981.

Trueba, H. T., G. Spindler, and L. Spindler, eds. *What Do Anthropologists Have to Say about Dropouts?* New York: Falmer Press, 1989.

Undocumented Workers Policy Research Project, *The Use of Public Services by Undocumented Aliens in Texas: A Study of State Costs and Revenues.* Austin: University of Texas, Lyndon B. Johnson School of Public Affairs, 1984.

U.S. Census Bureau. Census 2000 Summary File 4, Matrices PCT38, PCT61, PCT63, PCT64, PCT65, and PCT66. http://factfinder.census.gov/servlet/ProductBrowserServlet?id=102067&product=Census% (accessed September 29, 2005).

U.S. Department of Labor, Bureau of Labor Statistics. Employment, Hours, and Earnings from the Current Employment Statistics Survey. http://data.bls.gov.PDQ/servlet/survey/outputservlet (accessed September 2005).

U.S. Department of Health and Human Services. "Substate Estimates from the 1999–2001 National Surveys on Drug Use and Health." http://drugabusestatistics.samhsa.gov/substate2KS/secA.htm (accessed October 2005).

U.S. House Committee on Banking and Financial Services, Subcommittee on General Oversight and Investigations. "Money Laundering Activity Associated with the Mexican Narco-Crime Syndicate." Washington, DC: U.S. Printing Office, 1996.

Valdez, Avelardo, and Stephen J. Sifaneck. "Getting High and Getting By: Dimensions of Drug Selling Behaviors among American Mexican Gang Members in South Texas." *Journal of Research in Crime and Delinquency* 41, no. 1 (2004): 82–105.

Velez, W. "High School Attrition among Hispanic and Non-Hispanic White Youths." *Sociology of Education* 62 (1989): 119–133.

Wald, Elijah. *Narcocorrido: A Journey into the Music of Drugs, Guns, and Guerillas.* New York: Rayo/HarperCollins, 2002.

Walker, George M. "Utilization of Health Care: The Laredo Migrant Experience." *American Journal of Public Health* 69, no. 7 (1991): 667–672.

Wallace, Steven P., Vilma Enriquez-Haass, and Kyriakos S. Markides. "The Consequences of Color-Blind Health Policy for Older Racial and Ethnic Minorities." *Stanford Law and Policy Review* 9 (Spring 1998): 329–346.

Wang, Joseph J. "Our Border Health at Risk: Poverty, Disease, and No Health Insurance." May 10, 2002. http://www.law.uh.edu/healthlawperspectives/MinorityHealth/020610border.html (accessed August 17, 2005).

Warner, David C. "Health Issues at the US-Mexican Border." *JAMA* 265, no. 2 (January 9, 1991): 242–247.

Warner, R. Stephen. "Coming to America: Immigrants and the Faith They Bring." *Christian Century* 121, no. 3 (February 10, 2004): 20–23.

Wayman, Jeffrey C. "Student Perceptions of Teacher Ethnic Bias: A Comparison of Mexican American and Non-Latino White Dropouts and Students." *High School Journal* 85, no. 3 (2000): 27–38.

Wehlage, Gary G., R. A. Smith, N. Lesko, and R. R. Fernandez. *Reducing the Risk: Schools as Communities of Support.* London: Falmer Press, 1989.

Weiner, Tim, and Tim Golden. "Free-trade Treaty May Widen Traffic in Drugs, U.S. Says." *New York Times,* May 24, 1993.

Wilkinson, Rupert. *The Pursuit of American Character.* New York: Harper and Row, 1988.

Williams, Norma. *The Mexican American Family: Tradition and Change.* Dix Hills, NY: General Hall, 1990.

Wilson, Kenneth L., and Alejandro Portes. "Immigrants' Enclaves: An Analysis of the Labor Market Experiences of Cubans in Miami." *American Journal of Sociology* 86, no. 2 (September 1980): 295–319.

Wirt, John, et al. *The Condition of Education 2004.* Washington, DC: U.S. Department of Education, National Center for Education Statistics, 2004.

Wise, Tim. "Defending the Unwelcome Stranger: The Truth about Immigration." LiPmagazine.org, September 26, 2003. http://www.lipmagazine.org/articles/featwise_immigrationexcerpt.shtml.

Zapata, Jeiny, and Raelene Shippee-Rice. "The Use of Folk Healing and Healers by Six Latinos Living in New England: A Preliminary Study." *Journal of Transcultural Nursing* 19, no. 2 (April 1999): 136–142.

Zwolinski, Mary. "Quinceañera: A Celebration of Latina Womanhood." *Voices* 28 (Fall–Winter 2002).